Prisoners' Letters to the Bank of England 1781–1827

edited by Deirdre Palk

LONDON RECORD SOCIETY PUBLICATIONS

VOLUME XLII

This volume has been published with the help of a grant generously provided by Freshfields Bruckhaus Deringer.

PRISONERS' LETTERS TO THE BANK OF ENGLAND 1781–1827

EDITED BY

DEIRDRE PALK

LONDON RECORD SOCIETY
VOLUME XLII

ISBN 978–0-900952–42–5

Printed and bound by Q3 Print Project Management Ltd, Loughborough

CONTENTS

Abbreviations

ass.	assizes
Bank	Bank of England
BECLS	Bank of England Committee for Law Suits
cap. ch.	capital charge
cap. conv.	capitally sentenced
d.	pence
HO	home office records
M	Minutes of Bank of England Committee for Law Suits
NBB	New Bank Buildings (offices of Freshfields)
NSW	New South Wales
OB	Old Bailey
OBSP	Old Bailey session papers
PB	plea-bargain offered or accepted (to plead guilty to non-capital charge, with capital charge not put in court)
resp.	sentence respited
s.	shilling(s)
sec./state	secretary of state at home office/home department
TNA	The National Archives, Kew
trspn	transportation
yrs	years

Counties abbreviated as follows:

Beds.	Bedfordshire
Berks.	Berkshire
Bucks.	Buckinghamshire
Cumb.	Cumberland
Denb.	Denbighshire
Derbys.	Derbyshire
Devon	Devonshire
Glos.	Gloucestershire
Hants	Hampshire
Herts.	Hertfordshire
Lancs.	Lancashire
Leics.	Leicestershire
Lincs.	Lincolnshire
Mdx	Middlesex
Mon.	Monmouthshire
Norf.	Norfolk
Northants.	Northamptonshire
Notts.	Nottinghamshire
Salop	Shropshire
Som.	Somersetshire
Staffs.	Staffordshire
Suff.	Suffolk
Warws.	Warwickshire
Worcs.	Worcestershire

INTRODUCTION

Mary England, and her husband James, were arrested in London in January 1814 when uttering (circulating) forged Bank of England notes. This was an offence which carried the death penalty. The Bank decided not to prosecute James, who promptly abandoned Mary and their four children and went to sea. Mary accepted an arrangement offered by the Bank; to avoid the possibility of being executed if found guilty, she would plead guilty to possessing the notes rather than uttering them and be transported for fourteen years. Her trial took place at the Old Bailey in February 1814. She was then taken to the grim and insalubrious prison of Newgate, her four young children in tow, there to wait for a ship to be made ready to convey convicts to New South Wales. She was destitute. By April, she had pawned her clothes, her children's clothes and any small belongings she had. This little family was attempting to exist on the gaol allowance of bread and water, supplemented by what could be bought with the money from the pledged items. They were to remain in Newgate for nine dreadful months. At the end of November, they all boarded the *Northampton* at Deptford, sailing in January 1815. Behind this tale of misery lies another story of extraordinary benevolence. The benevolent party was none other than the Bank of England, the institution which had ensured their distress. On receiving a letter from Mary in April 1814, pleading her destitution, the Bank's solicitors arranged to pay her the considerable sum of 10*s*. 6*d*. a week until she left Newgate for Deptford. On receipt of a further letter from her on board the ship, they sent her £10 for the family's needs for their voyage (**163**, **189**).

Her letters, and several hundred more, written by or on behalf of prisoners like her, are transcribed in this volume. They were written from gaols all over Britain, though mainly from London; from hulks lying in rivers and off-shore; or from ships about to depart on their long voyage to New South Wales. The recipients of the letters were the firm of Freshfields, solicitors to the Bank of England; a few were addressed to individual directors or staff of the Bank, or to friends who passed them to Freshfields. The letters, and other pieces dealing with legal matters, were later archived under the title 'Prison Correspondence', and have been kept ever since in the Bank of England archive, attracting only passing attention.

The heterogeneous and private nature of this collection of letters raises questions about the relationship between a powerful financial institution and 'its' prisoners, mostly poor and fairly ignorant, in extremes of difficulty and suffering. The relationship could produce significant acts of charity in response to abject pleading, which made all the difference to lives, mainly female lives, which had descended into squalor, fear and misery. Prisoners cajoled and manipulated the institution, provoking varying responses, sometimes cold, arrogant and distant, sometimes compassionate and kind to a profligate degree.

Pleas from many more of 'the Bank's prisoners' did not achieve the same degree of success as did Mary England. Women without children might be ignored, along with prisoners who continued their forged note trafficking in gaol, or who had refused to plead guilty to a non-capital offence in court when offered this option by the prosecutor, much vaunted as an act of mercy. Male prisoners' letters could be brushed aside unless they gave information leading to successful prosecution of others involved in forged note crime. The Bank of England and their solicitors responded with care, and with a rationale which fitted well their determined policy of ridding the nation of people engaged in the evil practice of currency forgery, a policy carried out professionally, doggedly and at great financial cost.[1] This collection of letters, revealing an often more compassionate underside to the Bank's single-minded and merciless activity allows an intriguing and important view of institutional charity.

The historical and legal context

The letters transcribed in this volume were written during the period known as the 'restriction' when the British government suspended the convertibility of cash (gold) payments. War with France, started in 1793, continued almost uninterrupted until 1815. Early in 1797, the British government became alarmed at the unprecedented levels of gold withdrawals from the Bank, fuelled by rumours of a French invasion. On 26 February, an order in council was issued to the Bank governor and directors prohibiting payments in gold. The order was regularized by legislation in May 1797, and renewed at intervals by further acts of parliament. This state of affairs lasted until 1821.[2]

At the same time as withholding gold payments, the Bank were encouraged to maintain currency circulation by various means,[3] particularly

1. Prosecution costs varied from about £114 to £150 per person prosecuted at times of high activity (1811–20) to £380 per person in times of low activity (1822). In addition, rewards for assistance in apprehension and giving evidence varied from around £200 each six months to £2,800 after the prosecution of 132 cases in May 1818. Records of these expenses were entered half-yearly in BECLS: M5/307–33.
2. For the period of 'restriction', see W. M. Acres, *The Bank of England from Within*, i, (1931), 275–90, 299–348; Sir John Clapham, *The Bank of England* (Cambridge, 1944), i, 253–72; ii, 1–16; B. J. Hilton, *Corn, Cash, Commerce, the Economic Policies of the Tory Governments, 1815–30* (1977).
3. The Bank also supervised the issue of silver coin. This included dollars valued at between 4*s.* 6*d.* and 5*s.* 6*d.* and tokens for 5*s.* 6*d.*, 3*s.* and 1*s.* 6*d.*; these were reused Spanish dollars captured from Spanish vessels, over-stamped at the royal mint with an impression of the head of George III on the neck of the Spanish king; several millions were issued from 1797 to provide coin for making small payments. From about 1811 to 1819, the Bank were also responsible for the issue of silver tokens, minted from melted-down French crowns and ingots; an even larger number was in circulation; Acres, *Bank of England*, i, 278–80, 299–310; E. M. Kelly, *Spanish Dollars and Silver Tokens* (1976).

through the issue of large quantities of paper money notes. For the first time, notes of £1 and £2 value were put into circulation.[4] The new notes were of poor quality and easy to forge, copy or alter. Soon, skilled forgers were at work. Using a large and complex network of dealers, they created a surge of forged paper money in circulation and, with it, public and institutional panic. The forgers used poorer, often ill-educated and illiterate people in their selling and uttering enterprises, many of whom handled paper money for the first time. Well-developed networks were set up by those who also dealt in counterfeit coin, mainly around Birmingham and in some Lancashire towns, to circulate forged notes. Within weeks of the suspension of cash payments coming into effect, the Bank found huge numbers of forged notes being returned to their cashiers by victims of utterers.

While forgery had been an ever-present challenge to the Bank's business, the extent of the threat, which gathered momentum from 1797, was unprecedented. Against it, the Bank mounted what has been described as the most extensive criminal operation of its day.[5] It is important, when considering the letters in this volume and the responses to them, to recognize the extent of this vigorous nationwide campaign of prosecution – its enormous financial cost, and the involvement of a wide range of existing law enforcement personnel, investigators and lawyers. The Bank may never have totally mastered the forgery epidemic, but they succeeded in keeping the lid on its worst effects. Local and national government lent them co-operation, but the Bank acted independently as a private prosecutor, endowed with vast financial and personnel resources. Between 1797 and 1821 (and beyond, as the impetus for vigorous prosecution outlasted the period of 'restriction'), the Bank, through the assiduous and single-minded work of its solicitors, Freshfields, prosecuted more than 2,000 people nation-wide for forged paper money offences.[6]

Forgery or fraudulent alteration of Bank of England notes had been a capital offence since 1697. In 1725, uttering ('offering, disposing of or putting away') of such a note was added to the list of capital crimes.[7] In 1800, the likelihood of a fatal outcome for a defendant prosecuted by the

4. These may have been seen as low value notes, but in the early nineteenth century a labourer's weekly wage could be less than £1. Thomas Sokoll (ed.), *Essex Pauper Letters, 1731–1837* (Oxford, 2001), 10, suggests a national annual income per head of £23; a woman prisoner (**164**) stated that her husband, presumably better paid than a labourer, had 30*s*. a week.
5. G.B. Mainwaring, 'Observations on the Present State of the Police in the Metropolis', *Pamphleteer*, xix (1822), 544. For the Bank's prosecution business, see Randall McGowen, 'From Pillory to Gallows: the Punishment of Forgery in the Age of Financial Revolution', *Past and Present,* clxv (1999), 107–40; 'The Bank of England and the Policing of Forgery', *Past and Present,* clxxxvi (2005), 81–116; 'Managing the Gallows: the Bank of England and the Death Penalty, 1797–1821', *Law and History Review*, 25/2 (2007), 241–82; Deirdre Palk, *Gender, Crime and Judicial Discretion, 1780–1830* (Woodbridge, 2006), 89–112.
6. In addition, they prosecuted about 1,000 counterfeiters and utterers of tokens and dollars, some of whose letters to Freshfields are summarized in this volume.
7. 8 & 9 Will.3, c.20; 12 Geo.1, c.32. These offences ceased to be capital in 1832.

Bank was much higher than for any other property offence. This was a fair reflection of the public fear of forgery, but at the same time it provoked horror and distaste. Further concern related to the comparative ease with which utterers of forged notes, the petty criminals, could be brought to justice and sentenced, rather than the major forgers behind them. Criticism, sometimes virulent, was directed at the Bank for this state of affairs. Their effectiveness and the apparent mercilessness of their prosecution strategy was attacked. By 1801, the directors of the Bank realized that the emergency measure of suspension of cash payments was likely to continue for the foreseeable future, and that a new weapon was needed to manage the situation without sending an 'intolerable' number of men and women to the gallows. It was the Bank solicitors who carefully drafted a bill, which was presented to parliament and became law in May 1801. This permitted prosecution for a 'lesser' offence, punishable by fourteen years' transportation, and became the most frequently used device in the war against forgery. It created a new offence of possession of instruments for making Bank note paper, or of possessing forged notes knowing them to be forged.[8]

Successful use of this new weapon required the Bank to offer to a defendant apprehended for uttering forged notes the opportunity of a 'plea bargain'. If he or she would plead guilty to a charge of possession, with a certain punishment of fourteen years' transportation, the Bank would not put the capital charge for uttering. It was an offer that most defendants could not refuse.[9] Many of the prisoners who wrote letters begged for this deal or gave thanks for being allowed it. This way of proceeding brought further criticism of the Bank. They were seen to be arrogantly manipulating the justice system and usurping the prerogative of the judges. However, the criticism was insufficient to deter the Bank and their solicitors from a strategy which successfully held capital sentencing at a 'tolerable' level.

The use of such prosecution procedures necessitated careful handling. In 1802, the Bank set up a Committee for Law Suits. It consisted of the governor or deputy governor of the Bank, five other directors and a secretary, and with a Freshfields solicitor in attendance to present documents and lead the deliberations. Most of the business of this committee was concerned with forged Bank note activities, but also, to a lesser extent, with matters such as Bank coin counterfeiting and other financial legal matters. Meticulous minutes of high quality were kept. They provide evidence of the size, cost and success of the prosecution enterprise, of the networks of policing and the use of lawyers dispersed throughout the country.[10]

In committee, depositions from magistrates' courts were read, decisions taken about whether to prosecute or not and whether a plea-bargain would

8. 41 Geo.3, c.39. See McGowen, 'Managing the Gallows' for this strategic move, the reasons for it and the drafting of the bill.
9. In London (to those tried at the Old Bailey), the plea-bargain offer was made by the Bank to 88 per cent of women, and 85 per cent of men, and was taken up by 88 per cent of men and women to whom it was offered. Plea-bargaining was a rare strategy in other felony trials at the time. See Palk, *Gender, Crime,* 99–101.
10. BECLS: M5/307–33.

be offered. Where there was to be no prosecution, reasons were given. Instructions to solicitors and senior police officers around the country were agreed. The minutes give further evidence about how many of the letters and petitions were to be dealt with. They recorded receipt of a letter or petition and whether the request made was to be granted or not, or the information offered by the writer to be followed-up. In this volume, information is given at the end of letters which were discussed in the committee as to the decisions made. However, many letters were not recorded as having been read in committee. It is much more likely that Freshfields made their own decisions to ignore them or to reply to them themselves, rather than that the committee secretary failed to record them.[11]

Old Bailey Bank note forgery trials between 1804 and 1834 produced 126 death sentences and 565 sentences of transportation. At this time, most death sentences for property crimes were not carried out, many convicts being respited to other punishments.[12] The vast majority of the sentences of transportation were carried out.[13] There are letters in this volume from sixteen prisoners awaiting execution. Most of the others are from those waiting to be transported. The wait for transportation could be long, particularly for women, and the condition of prisoners deteriorated in the grim gaols in which they were held for many months, and on the hulks where men were subjected to corporal punishment and hard labour.

The 'Prison Correspondence' archive

The archive (F25) is held at the Bank of England. It is part of a section of the Bank archives containing papers relating to work handled for the Bank by their solicitors, Freshfields.[14] F25 contains 1,167 separate documents placed in thirteen sub-groups. The majority of these documents are letters or petitions written by, or on behalf of, prisoners involved in forged Bank note activities. A few of these prisoners were being held for examination,

11. BECLS: M5/307–33. See Palk, *Gender, Crime*, 89–112, 118–19, 121–2, 131–5 for discussion of pre-trial and trial procedures and sentences in Bank of England forged note cases; and McGowen, 'Policing of Forgery' for the Bank's well co-ordinated apprehension strategies.
12. The numbers of those actually hanged for forged Bank note offences can be compared with the fate of those sentenced to death for the property crimes of pickpocketing and shoplifting in London and Middlesex from 1804 until the time when all three were no longer capital offences; (pickpocketing, 1808, shoplifting, 1823, forged Bank note crimes, 1832). Of eight death sentences for pickpocketing, and sixty-four for shoplifting, none was carried out. Of the 126 death sentences for Bank note offences, fifty-eight were carried out. Murder, not surprisingly secured the highest rate of execution in the early years of the nineteenth century; various forgery crimes were the property crimes where execution was most likely, followed by robberies, burglaries and other violent thefts. Palk, *Gender, Crime,* 49–53, 78–81, 106–7, 118–21, 125–35.
13. See Palk, *Gender, Crime,* 121–2, for London and Middlesex 'Bank convicts'. It is likely that similar outcomes relate to other parts of the country.
14. Freshfields' papers relating to work for the Bank were transferred to the Bank's Roehampton record office in 1909. Most files were heavily 'weeded' in the 1980s before being added to the Bank archive in the City of London. However, F25 appears to be intact; this is indicated by the fact that names on letters and petitions can be traced for nearly all women likely to have been in Newgate during the period of this archive.

some of whom were asking to be allowed to plead guilty to the lesser offence of possession. Rather more were being held after trial; a few in gaols awaiting their death sentences to be carried out; the rest awaiting transportation in gaols or on hulks; or on the transport ships as they made ready to leave British ports. Other pieces in F25 include copies of replies to these letters by Freshfields; letters to Freshfields from prisoners who were Bank debtors and bankrupts and other imprisoned felons seeking to give information about forgery activities; lists of prisoners to be arraigned or moved for transportation; and correspondence between Freshfields and the home office about particular prisoners.

The letters from prisoners vary slightly in form, but the majority adopted a standard letter-writing form of the time.[15] The letter sheets, varying in size, were folded several times to form a type of envelope; the text was on the inside and, on the outside, on what was in effect the front, was written the addressee's details. The open edges at the back were often sealed with wax. The recipient frequently noted on this part of the sheet the date of receipt of the letter (usually the same day if the letter came from another part of London) and the name of the sender. Sometimes the action to be taken would also be briefly noted there.

At least half the letters were committed by their writers to the postal service. The fronts bear post marks; for instance, 'Two penny post unpaid Newgate St. Jy 2 2 o'clock 1804 AN', or 'Newgate St. 2py. P. paid 10 o'clock F. Noon'. Other postal locations in London, where it is possible to decipher them, include 'Holborn Hill', 'Long Acre', 'Shoreditch', or further afield, 'Woolwich E.O.', and 'Gravesend 22'. Letters which did not bear post marks would have been delivered to Freshfields' offices by hand. This method was adopted if an immediate reply to the bearer was required. Two women writers apologized for sending letters by post, since, they said, they lacked friends to deliver them **(309, 423).**

The letters are in good condition, suffering only slight damage, presumably when handled originally in the early nineteenth-century. Until recent cleaning and repair, they were somewhat dirty and slightly blackened with age. Some were slightly torn from the resistance of the wax sealing when they were opened, and holes appear in the paper for the same reason. The paper quality is good. All are written in black ink which has not faded. The entire contents of F25 were microfilmed some time prior to cleaning. It was from the films and copies taken from them that transcription for this volume was ordinarily done. It was then possible to check all the transcriptions from the newly cleaned and repaired originals, which had been re-referenced (whilst retaining the order of the original grouping of the documents) in the Bank archives and mounted in several book volumes at the Bank. Prior to cleaning, the pieces – letter, response, and other pieces relating to the particular prisoner who had written – had been folded together in a small bundle under one reference number. They have now been separated and each piece given its own number. In this volume, the

15. See Sokoll, *Essex Pauper Letters,* 44–70 for informative descriptions of letters which resemble many of those in this volume in their form and style.

relationship found in the earlier bundles has been preserved, indicating which documents were 'attached' to the original letter. When the letters were originally bundled into their thirteen groups, only a rough chronological order was observed; there appears to have been little method in the filing system, other than to scoop up a bundle of papers dating from a handful of years and put them away. The first nine groups were marked, some time ago, as having come from London prisons (including hulks in the Thames), the remaining four from prisons outside London. However, this is not strictly the case, each being likely to contain some letters from anywhere in Britain.

The layout of individual letters is relatively standard. The place and date of writing are written either at the top right hand of the (first) text page or at the bottom left hand; sometimes one or both of these pieces of information is missing. The salutation is set at the left hand margin, varying in form, but formal in type, such as: 'Hon. Gentlemen', or 'Hon^{d} Sirs'. Valedictions vary in placement, left, right or centred, and are often complex in the polite custom of the day, such as: 'I am, Gentlemen, with profound respect, your very humble servant', or 'We beg leave to subscribe ourselves, Sir, your most humble servants and prisoners', or 'And as in duty bound will ever pray'.

Apart from these standard formalities, the letter style and content varies widely. Some are in a fine hand, and are floridly expressed petitions and letters, written by hired professional writers, begging mercy in various guises. Some are fluently written letters, well-spelled, easy to read, written either by prisoners themselves (mainly men, although a few women wrote themselves) or by their educated friends and relations. Some are clumsy, badly spelled letters written by less educated, but nonetheless capable, scribes, such as turnkeys in gaols, paid for the task. Others were written by friends and relations, or by prisoners themselves, on the border of literacy, trying as best they could. Many of this last sort are interesting examples of 'oral writing', with phonetic orthography, sometimes exposing a local accent; for instance, Scottish (**63**), Irish (**575–6, 596, 672**), London (**215, 677**). The heavy accents of some of the scribes in Newgate come through clearly and help to identify, along with their handwriting style, the batches of letters they wrote for prisoners, mainly female prisoners (for instance, **54, 76, 78, 81**). Some of the orthography is idiosyncratic and difficult to read, but, with patience can be decoded. A few letters are wildly scrawled (e.g. **204, 386**); some writers realize their handwriting causes difficulty to the reader, and excuse themselves, like the writer who asks the recipient to 'Exceuse my Power ha[*n*]d' (**672**).

The recipients of the letters

Most letters were addressed to the Bank's solicitors, Freshfields. Some were addressed to the governor and company of the Bank, with a handful directed to their chief cashier,[16] or to investigators appointed by the Bank

16. From 1778–1807, Abraham Newland held this position, and from 1807–29, Henry Hase.

to assist in the apprehension of suspects and the accumulation and presentation of evidence.[17] Other letters were sent to lawyers acting for the Bank in various parts of the country,[18] or to police officers and magistrates who had been involved in the prosecution of the particular writer. A few were addressed to people who might be influential and able to petition the Bank on the prisoner's behalf. A handful were letters written to prisoners' wives, or friends, sometimes deliberately passed to Freshfields (e.g. **64–5**), but sometimes finding their way to the solicitors' office having been intercepted by officials before they left the prison (**400, 402–3**).

Freshfields' office was the point on which all correspondence converged, whatever its intention. Whether well-written or scrawled, whether merely a rough paragraph, or a ramble of several pages, all were attended to by Freshfields' clerks and partners. The ceaseless flow of information was encouraged by the solicitors, as they sought to make themselves the clearing-house and repository for all information about the crime of Bank note forgery and those involved. Control was tight, reaction was prompt, and decision-making was centralized, based on astute use of a network of lawyers, police, informers and investigators. The means of communication was almost entirely through pen and paper.

The law firm which came to be known as Freshfields was well-known and respected in the City of London from the mid-eighteenth century. Today it is internationally renowned and still acts for the Bank of England.[19] In 1734, the Bank first appointed an 'attorney or solicitor', Samuel Dodds, from the firm which became Freshfields. Partners in Freshfields continued to hold that appointment over the period of 'restriction' and well beyond. In 1797, the partners were John Winter, senior, and Joseph Kaye. Winter held the appointment until 1808 jointly with Joseph Kaye who continued in the function until 1823.[20] It is Joseph Kaye's control and decision-making which is most apparent in responses to the letters in this volume.

During the 'restriction' period, other partners included Joseph Cam Maynard, from 1797–1800, Francis Beckwith, 1801–08, James W. Freshfield, 1801–40, John Winter, junior, 1805–08 and Charles Kaye, 1811–25. In 1818, because of the heavy work load, Joseph Kaye persuaded the Bank to appoint two additional solicitors, James Freshfield and Charles Kaye. During this period, the firm's offices were at 29, St Swithin's Lane, (1788–1808), 7, Tokenhouse Yard (1808–11) and 5, New Bank Buildings (1811–97), all of these addresses close to the Bank of England in the City of London. Letters addressed to the Bank's solicitors reflect the changes over the years in personnel and location. Writers appear knowledgeable

17. The first investigators of Bank notes, appointed in 1804, were Thomas Glover and Thomas Bliss. See Acres, *Bank of England,* 332, for their tasks, pay and vicissitudes. Over time, they were joined by others, including John Lee(s), Charles Christmas and Charles Procter.
18. Among whom were William Spurrier in Birmingham, John Lloyd in Stockport, J. Ridpath in Bath, Moses Greetham in Plymouth.
19. Currently operating as Freshfields Bruckhaus Deringer in London and world-wide.
20. Winter's appointment was not technically terminated until 1830.

about the personalities they wrote to and about the changes in the firm. Some writers preferred to address their letters to the individual chief clerks at Freshfields, and sometimes appear to have had an almost personal relationship with them.[21] Others would write for the attention of one of the Bank investigators whom they would have seen in person as they visited prisons to collect evidence, take down statements or check on the veracity of claims made in letters about prisoners' personal situations.

Little is known about the background of Freshfield's central actor, Joseph Kaye, who, without doubt, set the pattern for energetic criminal investigation, meticulous attention to detail, efficient office work and the sometimes benevolent responses made by the Bank to those they had prosecuted. He was the son of a Huddersfield worsted manufacturer who came to London to earn his living. He became a highly respected attorney whose clients, besides the Bank of England, included the Royal Exchange Assurance and the East India Company. His private clients, who included the close relations of William Wilberforce, and his partnership with James W. Freshfield, may indicate something about his interests. James Freshfield, an Anglican, was well-known and respected in dissenting circles through his quaker wife and was close to the Clapham sect of evangelical Anglicans. Some of the Bank directors and their families also were members of the Clapham sect or were sympathetic to evangelical causes.[22] Many were also directors of charitable institutions in London and left considerable charitable bequests.[23]

The senders of the letters and their objectives

There are nearly 700 letters and petitions in F25, written by, or on behalf of, prisoners held for forged note offences. Some were written before the prisoner's trial, but most afterwards. They involved 425 different prisoners; 201 individual women and 224 individual men can be distinguished. Since women were about 22 per cent of those prosecuted for this crime during the period covered by this collection of letters, clearly the letter-writing was disproportionately a female activity. Women were also more likely to be multi-letter writers who sometimes established what seems to have been a surprisingly close relationship with the Bank solicitors. (See the series of letters from Margaret Spears (**250–5, 289–95**), Ann Storey (**281–8**) and Sarah Howell (**256–61, 330–1**).)

This letter-writing was also a London-dominated activity, perhaps because of the proximity of Freshfields' offices to prisons in London and the ease of delivery of letters, or perhaps because of the large number of 'Bank prisoners' held for long periods in Newgate gaol, where word-of-mouth networks would have encouraged prisoners to write when they

21. Until mid-1818, many letters were addressed to James Westwood; after that to Mr Rooker, frequently called 'Hooker' or 'Crooker', or to Joseph Maynard, jr.
22. Judy Slinn, *A History of Freshfields* (Guildford, 1984), 29–66.
23. D. T. Andrews, *Philanthropy and Police* (Princeton, NJ, 1989) lists charitable directorships and bequests; her list includes names of several governors and directors of the Bank who were members of the BECLS.

heard of the successful results achieved by some requesting favours.[24] About 93 per cent of the women held in Newgate awaiting death or transportation for forged Bank note crimes wrote at least once to their prosecutors; about 24 per cent of the men held in Newgate did so. Letters from prisoners apprehended and tried outside London were significantly fewer.[25]

It is not possible to be certain which letters were written in the hand of the prisoner him- or herself. It is probable that many of the men were able to write. This is suggested by the fact that, as some of them moved prisons, or transferred to hulks or on to ships, the hand-writing of their letters remained the same throughout. However, this is not necessarily evidence of their own ability to write, since the similarity of hand-writing could have been because they used the same scribes throughout the time. The numbers of different hands detectable in men's letters are fewer than in the women's letters suggesting that the men did not have the same frequency of need to pay turnkeys or to get others to write for them. Only a few women appear to have written their own letters. Many were able to write their own signatures, although many more could not, signing by mark. Jane Williams was a woman who could write, and write well. She did so on her own account and for other women in Newgate and on the transport ship, *Lord Wellington* (**309**, **377, 404–6, 408, 412, 424, 429, 433, 437–8, 451–2**).[26] These letters were fluently and neatly written and well-spelled. Mary Lenny, a 'school-teacher and lodging-house keeper' (**268–9**) and Jemima Burton (**756–7**), the latter a fluent writer, are other examples of this minority of women. Martha Bramwell, not herself a 'Bank prisoner' provides an example of an enterprising woman who could write particularly well, using this skill to write for others, to read their incoming letters and pass information to Freshfields (**175–7, 183**).

Large batches of letters, particularly from women, are in the same hand and with the same orthography and repeated use of specific phrases. These were probably written by turnkeys or guards. For instance, a turnkey at Newgate, identifiable by his neat, unusual hand and spelling of 'Libberty' clearly wrote letters **469–76, 478, 486–7.** On the transport ship *Northampton,* one scribe would have produced letters **184–9, 194–5**; and for the men on the *Retribution* hulk, a scribe who wrote with a fine flourish

24. Descriptions of Newgate at this time emphasize the over-crowded conditions. This had, however, been a long-term problem in all prisons in and beyond London. Women in Newgate were free to associate daily in the common yard outside the 'female side' of the prison; they slept and ate in close proximity in a series of relatively small rooms; Arthur Griffiths, *The Chronicles of Newgate* (1987), 344–7; Albert Crew, *London Prisons of Today and Yesterday* (1933), 63–6. Networks of information and continued criminal activity were actively participated in.
25. In F25 there are letters from 119 individual women and 112 individual men in Newgate. Letters from another thirty women and another twenty-two men in Newgate are not in F25 but are recorded in BECLS minutes; it is likely they were delivered directly to the committee. Letters from prisoners held in prisons other than Newgate number eighty-five from women, 102 from men.
26. Her first letter (**308**), written in Newgate while awaiting trial at the OB, was not in her own hand.

penned at least **97–8, 101–3**. Margaret Spears and Sarah Howell (see above) did not always use the same scribe for all of their marathon of letter-writing, presumably hiring whoever was available when needed.

When these prisoners engaged with the Bank and their solicitors, men and women had different objectives in mind. This was because they had different needs, and because they came to understand what sort of request would be successful. Both the letter-writing strategies and the responses to them were highly gendered. The table below indicates these gendered strategies. It is not possible to be sure of the purpose of every letter so the details given should not be regarded as any more than a guide to the tendencies. More than one request could be made in one letter and some requests were made several times by the same person or group of people. All have been included in the table.

Purpose of letters (where possible to deduce)
Figures given per letter, which may have more than one writer (particularly if from women), and some letters have more than one purpose

Purpose	Males	Females	Total
To request pecuniary relief in gaol or on sailing	84	287	371
To provide information on forgery (for reward or favours)	93	14	107
To seek mitigation of sentence (of death or of transportation)	51	16	67
To request spouse or family be transported with them	31	5	36
To request return of property or money taken on arrest	26	5	31
To give thanks for pecuniary relief allowed in prison	1	26	27
To plead to lesser offence at trial	21	5	26
To speed up transportation	18	7	25
To claim innocence of crime for which sentenced	11	2	13

Purpose	Males	Females	Total
To seek permission to join army/navy/transfer to hulk	7	0	7
To seek recommendation to governor of NSW	3	0	3
To delay transportation	2	1	3
To be afforded protection	2	1	3
To seek privileges while in prison (e.g. visits)	2	0	2
To seek care for children left behind (by widower)	2	0	2
To be allowed to self-exile	2	0	2
Other (why son had to write for her; how to be witness in court)	0	2	2
(Letters to friends ending up with Bank solicitors)	2	5	7

Pecuniary relief was what nearly all the women desired, few writing about other issues. Men had varied strategies in their letter writing; many appear to have been financially independent, which few women were. They were also more able to acquire work in prison and on the hulks from which they received part of their pay for use while prisoners; there was little prison work available to women. A significant number of men wanted to obtain advantages for themselves by informing on others involved in forged note activities. They often told long and complicated stories about people they knew and where they were to be found and for this reason many of the men's letters were much longer than women's.

The misery experienced in prisons, especially in Newgate, provides for a litany of destitution which can be read in most letters. Little detail is given about the conditions in which prisoners were trying to survive; there was no need, since the recipients of the letters would have known well enough. There are very few references which are in any way descriptive of Newgate; one speaks of it as a 'maloncoley dwaling' (**74**), another of its 'Gloomey Warells [*walls*]' (**54**), another, after being held there for fourteen months, called it a 'gloommy, weary prison'(**431**). However, the penury, friendlessness, gross over-crowding, ill-health and hunger are endlessly appealed, together with the appalling difficulty of giving birth and nursing babies in this environment, and of keeping little children fed and clothed. This picture fits with a contemporary description of the women's side of Newgate:

> Nearly three-hundred women, sent there for every gradation of crime, some untried, and some under sentence of death, were crowded together in the two wards and two cells ... Here they saw their friends and kept their multitudes of children ... they slept on the floor at times one hundred and twenty in one ward, without so much as a mat for bedding, and many of them were very nearly naked ... Everything was filthy to excess, and the smell was quite disgusting. Every one, even the Governor, was reluctant to go amongst them.[27]

Prisons at this time were still being run by 'entrepreneurial' gaolers. Some were paid a salary (as was the keeper of Newgate) but all of them had to find ways of covering operating costs and making a profit. Thus, as many prisoners as possible had to be charged fees for as many things as possible – for admission, for food beyond the gaol allowance, for straw to lie on, for coal and candles, for leg irons to be removed. Prisoners with some money were targets for the greed of gaolers and made to pay well for 'comforts'.[28] A tiny handful of letters from male prisoners are marked as having come from writers in the 'Master's Side' or the 'State Side' of the prison where they would have paid for better treatment. The vast majority were unable to pay. The women in particular had to scrape around for every penny, notably obtaining resources from pawning any object they had, particularly their clothing. Some prisoners continued trading in forged currency. This did not recommend the women who did so as 'fit objects for mercy'.[29] Hence their appeals went straight to the point; money was desperately needed, whether in exchange for useful information, or merely because 'the Gentlemen of the Bank' were known to be benevolent.

Life for men on the hulks was an appalling experience. Some sought to avoid it, or pleaded to be transported quickly. In the Thames and at Portsmouth and Plymouth, the convicts were employed at hard labour, on river and harbour cleaning and other construction work, driven like slaves and inadequately fed. Only two prisoners give a glimpse of the degrading and dangerous nature of life on a hulk (**64–5, 110**).

27. T. F. Buxton, *An Inquiry whether Crime and Misery are produced or prevented by our present System of Prison Discipline* (1818), 113. Newgate in the first decade of the nineteenth century held between 500 and 1,200 (felons and debtors, remand prisoners and convicted felons, youths and adults, all unsegregated); 300 debtors were often held in the space for 100, 120 women in the space for sixty. This was not only a London problem; in 1818, 100 gaols across the country, with places for 8,545 prisoners, were holding 13,057; Griffiths, *Chronicles*, 343–4, 389–90. A useful source for conditions in prisons at this time is A. D. Smith, *Women in Prison: a Study in Penal Methods*, (1962).
28. The Gaol Fees Abolition Act 1815 signalled the decline of this system, but it was many years before it was entirely disposed of, particularly at Newgate. Fees on the 'Master's Side' or the 'State Side' of Newgate could include payments of between 3*s.* and 3 guineas for admission, 13*s.* 4*d.* a week for extra food, coal and candles, 10*s.* 6*d.* a week for a bed; Crew, *London Prisons*, 61–6.
29. Description commonly used in BECLS minutes and in annotations made on letters by recipients.

Responses to letters[30]

Many of the letters were annotated on receipt to show the decision taken on their contents, whether positive or negative. Where the letter itself was not annotated, the BECLS minutes might record the decision made. Information from both these sources has been inserted after the text of the relevant letters. Where evidence of a response is not available, it is likely that either none was made or that the Bank and their solicitors had their reasons for keeping their decisions under cover, for instance when they were planning to follow up information given about forgery activities, particularly if they were going to use witnesses whom they wished to keep anonymous.

Negative responses were always made to prisoners awaiting execution. There was never the slightest intention of supporting a request for mercy to be made to the Prince Regent or through the home secretary. These men and women had been prosecuted with single-minded efficiency and at great cost. The Bank felt the ends of justice had been served and a few executions might well prove a high-profile deterrent to others. In these cases, a terse reply would be made to the prisoner or to their prison keeper, stating that 'consistent with their duty to the public' the governor and directors of the Bank would not interfere (**300, 440, 446, 513, 672, 673, 747**). A response of this nature to Charlotte Newman who wrote an impassioned letter on the eve of her execution is a chilling example (**305**).

Such responses can be seen as an appropriate extension of the massive prosecution enterprise, as are the responses to those who said they had information to give. Sometimes these offers were ignored, since the Bank solicitors knew, through the efficiency of their own networks of police, lawyers and investigators, that the informant was not trustworthy; sometimes their response would show irritation towards those they felt were only seeking reward or revenge and who had no new or useful information to give (e.g.**743**). Payments to some prisoners for information which led to arrests and successful prosecutions were commensurate with the Bank's prosecution strategy whereby large rewards were paid out to all and sundry who assisted in the apprehension of forgers and members of their networks and in giving evidence against them. The few payments that were made to a small handful of male prisoners were mostly of this nature, whether one-off amounts or a weekly allowance while they were held in gaol. These payments were recorded in the BECLS minutes, not in any written response to the informant. Sometimes the Bank preferred the payment to go to the informant's wife or family. To the wife of informer William Henningham, there was a payment of £5; £10 for the wife and family of Charles Games to assist with their expenses when they sailed with him (**158**); £25 for Maria, widow of executed Daniel Davies, so she might open a chandler's shop to support her three children; £20 for the

30. For a fuller discussion of the responses made to prisoners' requests, see Deirdre Palk, '"Fit Objects for Mercy": gender, the Bank of England and currency criminals, 1804–1833', *Women's Writing*, 11/2 (2004), 237–57.

widow of executed Edward Harland, to maintain her family; £5 for Ann Dale (**153**), wife of transported informer, Henry, for a mangle to do laundry work to support herself; and £25 for Mary Gilbert, wife of Samuel, another transported informer, to set herself up in service to support her four small children (**674**).[31] Otherwise, charity to men was significantly lacking, and their requests were usually ignored. The Bank's policy on 'charitable donations' was made clear in Freshfields' response to two men who suggested that all prisoners were allowed £5 on embarking the transport ships. They were informed that they were mistaken; such money might be given to some women as a matter of charity, but never to men (**663**).

However, what is surprising, since it does not sit easily with the harsh story of prosecution, was the response to very many of the women prisoners, particularly those in Newgate. 'Relief', 'subsistence', 'allowance', 'a trifle for necessaries' (like tea and sugar)[32] was the incessant demand from these women, and this they received in abundance. In 1806, half a guinea (10*s.* 6*d.*) a week until they left to go on board the transport ship was the amount normally paid. The Bank decided by 1810 that this level of generosity could not continue when they saw how numerous forgery cases were and how long was the wait for women in prison while ships were made ready for them. The amount paid then dropped to 7*s.* a week. From 1811 until 1821, when the Bank intended to cease all these payments as the period of restriction ended, the payments could be 5*s.* a week for childless women who were found to be in extreme distress, 7*s.* 6*d.* for women with one child and sometimes 10*s.* 6*d.* for women with more than one child. In addition to this surprising generosity, there was usually a payment of £5 (in a few cases rather more) to virtually all women as they embarked on the transport ships. This embarkation money would also be paid to women from prisons outside London if they applied, having met up with women from London and learnt what might be on offer. It is worth remembering the high cost to the Bank of the prosecutions of these prisoners and the fact that they had faced charges of uttering notes of £1 or £2 value.

When pleas for subsistence money or for money to redeem clothes from pledge came in to Freshfields' offices, generosity was not blind. There were women to whom 'relief' was not paid; a few did not even merit the embarkation money. Those whose husbands were still in the

31. BECLS minutes: Henningham, M5/311, 25 Sept., 4 Dec. 1811, 19 Feb. 1812; Games, M5/313, 12 May, 1 Dec. 1813; Davies, M5/312, 9 Sept. 1812; Harland, M5/315, 12/13 Apr. 1815; Dale, M5/314, 20 Apr. 1814; Gilbert, M5/316, 29 Feb. 1816.
32. Tea and sugar were much desired both while in prison (**218, 232, 463, 481**), and when embarking on transport ships (**28, 34, 38, 191, 637**). Female prisoners boarding the *Lady Juliana* in 1789 had complained that the allowance of beef was too much for them and they wished it to be substituted by tea and sugar. An allowance of a quarter pound of tea per week between six women, and three pounds of sugar per week between six was then made. This tallies with the information given to the writer of **34,** an amount which she felt insufficient. Such an allowance was not made to men; Wilfrid Oldham, *Britain's Convicts to the Colonies* (Sydney, 1990), 158–9, from information in home office archives.

country, even though themselves incarcerated, were refused until the men had been transported. Women who had been notorious sellers and utterers, especially those who continued to trade in prison, were refused all pecuniary relief.[33] Relief payments were not usually made to women who had refused the offer of a plea bargain in court, although they received money on sailing. The Bank had also been severely criticized by the home secretary and the Prince Regent in cases where they had been judged to be manipulating the courts with their advice to defendants on how to plead; somewhat embarrassed by the criticism, they were reluctant to accede to these women's pleas.[34] Investigators were sent to Newgate to report on the genuineness of the requests; were the prisoners really in special distress, without friends, pregnant, had recently given birth or were ill? Sometimes the keeper passed his own (usually negative) views on the applicants. The investigators might agree with him, but in many cases often reported sympathetically to Freshfields, allowing many single women in particularly difficult situations to be generously paid (e.g. **356, 360**). Some women seem to have regarded the relief payments as their due, calling it the 'fortnight money'. Some were even prepared to argue about the amounts received; one woman said she had received only enough for one child when she had three (**265–6**); others upbraided the Bank for being overdue with their payments (**261, 264, 267**), another thought she had been forgotten since a gaol mate had received money and she had not (**330–1**).

Nevertheless, a sense of gratitude was more often than not present in the letters. This may, of course, have been an aspect of begging strategy, but the benevolence of the Bank meant a great deal to many prisoners. They were also grateful for the opportunity to plead guilty to a lesser offence and thus avoid the chance of being sentenced to death; certainly Freshfields presented this device to them as an act of great mercy on the part of the Bank. Letters speak of 'philanthropy [*which*] saved me from an ignominious death' (**61**), of 'having been mercifully spared thro the humanity' of the Bank (**377**), of being 'deeply impressed with gratitude for the lenity shewn us' (**394**), and thanks for the 'Great mercy Extended to Me in my Life being Graciously Spared' (**433**). Many of the women's letters express thanks and some were written with this sole purpose (e.g. **359, 399, 585**).

This collection of letters and responses suggests an unusual relationship. Some of the requests may fit the standard categories of charitable donation in the early nineteenth century. However, it might be appropriate to see many of the responses as exceptional examples of benevolence shown by

33. Among them, Elizabeth Hayselden, BECLS: M5/317, 11 & 25 July 1816; Elizabeth and Rebecca Bamford, Mary Bradney, Anne Dicken, Amelia Hines, Sarah Orton, M5/322, 19 May 1819, described as 'very notorious wholesale dealers and unworthy of the liberality of the Bank to afford relief'.
34. For example, Hannah Polley, Elizabeth Wingfield, Susan Farmilo. BECLS: M5/320, 2 July 1818; M5/321, 10 Mar. 1819.

prosecutors to criminals whom they had energetically pursued through the system of justice.[35] The Bank seem to have been motivated by a style of philanthropy which harked back to an earlier generation. Their benevolence was not determined by the moral deserts of the seeker of charity – far from it. What appears to have mattered to the Bank, to Freshfields and to those they sent to investigate appeals for charity, was whether the supplicant really was distressed, ill, in need of clothing, or food or whether children were suffering.

There could hardly have been more distance between two sides of a relationship. On one side was a powerful financial institution and its competent, professional legal advisers and agents. On the other were the miserable wretches who had, according to prevailing notions, placed their country in danger by their traitorous behaviour and who were now justly suffering as they awaited disposal to an inhospitable penal colony, far from their native country, leaving all they knew and loved. This was not a simple relationship of the powerless to the powerful. Conventions for requesting and receiving charity were presumably well-known to these supplicants who also knew a great deal about the motives and responses of the rich and powerful. They were not addressing an anonymous entity, as the language and address of many of the letters shows. The Bank may have had the upper hand in this relationship but, although they and Freshfields were in control,[36] prisoners knew how to use their knowledge of the rich and powerful to try to obtain the means of survival or to make an intolerable life more tolerable. Through this letter-writing, the voices of the poor were both listened to and heard, some of them to an extent that surprises, given the nature of the relationship between writer and recipient of the letters.

Editorial method and acknowledgements

Each document in this volume has been given a consecutive number (in bold print) which is followed by the reference number now used in the Bank archives (in italics). The renumbering of the archive at the Bank of England took place during my work on it. I have set out the letters in the order in which they were filed in their bundles (letter of request, responses and other documents relating to the request). Some transcribed letters are therefore indicated by a group of Bank archive reference numbers covering the letter and responses that go with it. The reference renumbering of F25 preserved the somewhat chaotic way in which these papers were originally put together. That order has normally been kept, although this may sometimes make the 'story' difficult to follow. An

35. For a discussion of charity and its changing nature in this period, see Andrew, *Philanthropy and Police*; Hugh Cunningham and Joanna Innes (eds), *Charity, Philanthropy and Reform from the 1690s to 1850*, (Basingstoke, 1998), 87–107.
36. This control is clearly signalled in the response to a proposal for a 'better use' of the Bank's charity from Elizabeth Pryor of the committee of ladies for regulating the conduct of females convicted of felony (**553**).

exception has occasionally been made where adjacent pieces in the files have been put into chronological order to make the 'story' easier to follow. As the vast majority of the letters were addressed either to Freshfields solicitors, or to the governors and company of the Bank, this has not been mentioned in the letter headings. An indication of the intended first recipient of the letter is given if this was not the Bank nor Freshfields.

Letters and petitions from prisoners held in connection with forged Bank note offences have been transcribed in full, except in the following three circumstances:

i) where formal petitions were sent in standard format, asking to plead to the lesser offence of possession of forged notes, and where the decision to offer this plea to the prisoner had already been taken by the Bank, the petition is summarized (in italics); ii) where a formal petition format was used to communicate in any other case, the standard introduction (e.g.'To the Governor and Company of the Bank of England, The Humble Petition of ... ... a convict in His Majesty's Gaol of Newgate Most Humbly Sheweth) has been omitted in each case and the transcription commenced with the petition paragraphs prefaced by the word 'That'; iii) where a prisoner sent a further letter at about the same time as an earlier letter and the later letter merely reiterates what had already been said, the subsequent letter has been summarized (in italics). All other documents in F25 have been summarized (in italics), be they letters from debtors, bankrupts, prisoners convicted of other offences, arrest warrants, lists of prisoners for arraignment or transportation, bills or receipts, or correspondence with the home office. Where a letter was annotated by the recipient or where, subsequent to receipt of the letter, other correspondence ensued (for example, responses from Freshfields, reports of Bank investigators, letters to solicitors acting for the Bank elsewhere in England, or to the home office), this information is presented after the letter concerned. Where the letter was recorded as having been discussed at the BECLS, this information is also given.

In the transcribed letters, spelling, punctuation (or more often the lack of), capitalization and abbreviations have been left as written. This does not normally cause difficulty in understanding and allows a closer relationship with the original writer. Where the writer has in error repeated a word, the duplicate word has been omitted. Where a word has been inserted in the letter by the writer at the time of writing, this has been included in the text without remark; only insertions made by annotation at a later time, usually by the recipient, have been noted in the brief editorial comment following the letter. Where the writer has crossed-through a word or words, usually making it unreadable, the deleted words have been ignored. Editorial comment has occasionally been inserted in the transcribed text, in italics and in square brackets in order to clarify information about a person mentioned in the letter or to note that a word(s) has been impossible to read. The layout of the transcribed letters has been modified to eliminate unnecessary 'white space'. The salutation, usually appearing on its own on the first line, and the valediction, occupying several short lines at the end, have been absorbed into the body of the letter text. However, where the writer broke up the rest of the text by the use of different paragraphs, this structure has been retained.

Acknowledgements: The editor would like to thank all who have helped her prepare this text for publication; in particular, Sarah Millard, archivist at the Bank of England for her help in handling my questions about the archive and for her welcome to me at the Bank; Bridget Kirk for managing microfilm copying at the Bank; the staff of the Archives Départmentales de l'Yonne in Auxerre for assistance in microfilm reading; Tim Hitchcock, Peter King, Vanessa Harding for advice on introductory material and indexing; Robin Eagles for his thoughtful oversight of the volume; the partners of Freshfields Bruckhaus Deringer; Richard Palk for his enduring help and support, generously, wisely and patiently given.

PRISONERS' LETTERS TO THE BANK OF ENGLAND

1. *[F25/1/1] J. Marshall, Clerkenwell prison, 1 March 1796*
Sir, When I was desired to withdraw yesterday I thought it only temporary or I should have convinced you & the Directors that I meant (to use your own words) "to be candid" – & have given you the Information you have justly sent for and have only to lament that you should have been so precipitate as to plunge myself and my poor wife who I can most solemnly assure you is perfectly innocent into Disgrace & Wretchedness such as I never could have suppose existed in this Country had I not experienced the Cruelty of it last Night by being obliged to stand all Night in a cold damp Stone apartment & denied even Straw to lie on – I hope & trust that she has met with different Treatment. Had Voltaire ever visited this place He would have written
'Un est le Sommeil, l'autre l'Espérance
Deux Etres benefiques meme aux Sein d'Indigence'
For the poor can get no Sleep here in the Winter I am sure. I beg therefore that you will allow me to have my Razor to shave & a Change of Linnen brought me – and you will add to the obligation if you will send a Permission for Mr Willey attorney in Basinghall Street to visit me as I have some Business to transact relative to my private affairs which I shall be materially injured by the Delay if I do not see him immediately.
The Information here inclosed I got by Chance and have for several weeks been trying to get the Plates but hitherto without Effect for tho' the Parties at one time offered to sell them I am persuaded they are not using them themselves
I am with great Respect Sir your most Obed^nt^ Hle Ser^t^, J. Marshall
Addressed to William Addington Esq.

2. *[F25/1/2–9] J. Marshall, Clerkenwell prison, 1 March 1796*
The late Laurence Jones who died in Newgate was I believe the first contriver of the present Forgerys of 10. 20. 50. & 100^L^ Bank Notes in conjunction with Idswell who was executed for forging stamps – Idswell married Jones's widow when he died and Jonas, a Jew, now in Newgate (brother in law to Idswell) became possessed of the Plates, Moulds etc Jonas being soon after committed for the Rescue of Idswell's Brother – agreed with Mrs Idswell to sell the whole lot, but when an offer was at last made for the Purchase She prevaricated & there is no doubt has found it more advantageous to use them and I firmly believe that the present Forged

Notes are from her Plates. The Mother or Mother-in-Law of Jonas who lives near Nightingale Lane Tower Hill is privy to the Transaction & I should imagine its probable that some of the Materials or Notes are concealed at her House.
Mrs Idswell visits Jonas & if She was stopped in Newgate in all Probability something that would lead to Discovery would come out. J. Marshall
Annotated by Bank solicitors, 5 Mar. 1796, that there was insufficient ground for holding Mr and Mrs Marshall; he had given useful information. Attached: letter and covering note from Marshall to acquaintance, Matthias Koops, debtor in Fleet prison, explaining his arrest on suspicion of uttering forged notes, asking Koops to confirm his innocence; letter from Koops to Bank attempting to blacken Marshall's name; notes from Bank solicitors to Bow Street magistrate requesting Marshall's discharge; acknowledgements from Bow Street magistrates' court.

3. *[F25/1/10] P*[eter] *Catapodi, Clerkenwell prison, 20 November 1797, held on suspicion of forging promissory note, gives Bank information about engraver whom he suspects of forging Bank notes.*

4. *[F25/1/11–14] Three bills for prisoners' upkeep from George Smith, keeper of Tothill Fields bridewell, with covering letter, 23 August 1781.*

5. *[F25/1/15] Samuel Mayner, Tothill Fields bridewell , 23 August 1781*
Honor'd Sirs, I am sorry to be so troublesome but Mr Smith [*prison keeper*] will not advance me one Shilling more till his Bill be paid, he give me 5.5.0 from your Notes you was Pleased to send, and stopp'd the rest for my Lodgings, as I have nothing to subsist on, either me or my wife, wich obliges me to trouble you a second time, but Mr Smith says that he knows one of the Directors, and purposes speaking to him, and waiting upon the Governor therefore took the Liberty of writing to know, if it would be agreeable to you weather Mr Smith should, nor not, Sir Please to send an answer will much Oblidge Your Hub^{le} Servant, Saml Mayner

6. *[F25/1/16] A. Mayner, wife of Samuel Mayner* [**5**], *29 August 1781*
Sir, Sensible of your Worthy Disposition by your former proceedings towards my husband makes me hope you will excuse my taking the liberty of writing to you again as it is with great reluctance I trouble you. I have Deferred it till I have not a Shilling left to help myself with except I sell the bed from under me wich I flatter myself you nor the Gentlemen dont wish. Mr Smith dont not chuse to pay him any more therfore what your Generosity pleases to allow him I hope you will appoint some place where I shall most thankfully go to receive it. I will wait on you tomorrow Eveing when I hope your Goodness will Condescend to give me an answer from your most obedint H^{le} Servt A. Mayner

7. *[F25/1/17–19] Bills for prisoners' keep in Tothill Fields bridewell from keeper, George Smith, and letter from his widow, undated in 1785, requesting outstanding payments from Bank.*

8. *[F25/1/20] Sarah Walker, debtor in annuities' lawsuit, King's Bench prison, letter, undated in 1785 about her case.*

9. *[F25/1/21] Note of expenses at Poultry Compter, undated, unsigned, in 1784, in respect of lodging, coach hire, providing turnkeys.*

10. *[F25/1/22] Bill from keeper, Alexander Fenwick, undated, probably 1780s, for expenses at debtors' prison (unspecified) in respect of William Roydhouse, debtor to Bank.*

11. *[F25/1/22–33] Papers, 1787 re: Sophia Pringle, charged with forgery of power of attorney for Bank stock, concerning her expenses in Newgate and Bank's disbursements to witnesses, etc.; complaint from Joseph Kaye, Bank solicitor, about rudeness of a turnkey towards him.*

12. *[F25/1/40–42] Misfiled copies of 1812 custody order, charge sheets and depositions for Maria Franklin, remanded in Coldbath Fields prison, shortly released uncharged.*

13. *[F25/1/43] Savile Robinson, New Prison, Clerkenwell, 17 March 1783, held for unspecified offences wishes Bank solicitor to call on him as he has information to give.*

14. *[F25/1/44] Humphry Potter, prisoner in New Gaol, Borough, detained on burglary charges unrelated to Bank, undated.*

15. *[F25/1/45–89] Folder containing typescript copies of 42 letters, correspondence between Bank and Parson Edgcumbe, inmate of Wood Street compter, 1783–4, unrelated to Bank note forgery.*

16. *[F25/1/90–1] Misfiled papers about raising money to build Bridewell prison, 1844.*

17. *[F25/1/92] Mary Charlton, prisoner in Horsemonger Lane gaol (unspecified charge) about Bank stock in her name; misfiled from 1844.*

18. *[F25/1/93–7] David Old, pin-maker, Poultry compter, imprisoned for debt of £95, together with petition and discharge note, 1794.*

19. *[F25/1/98] Order for discharge of John Walker, debtor in King's Bench prison, 1796.*

20. *[F25/1/99] Warrant for arrest of J. Angers, debtor, detained at 30 Wych Street (spunging house) 1800.*

21. *[F25/1/100–1] Arrest warrants for Mr Thomson in custody of Mr Hindon, 24 November 1798, then of Mr John Janson, 2 January 1799.*

22. *[F25/1/102–4] Thomas Coe, butcher, Kennington, formal petition on behalf of his son, James, undated in 1799*
That your petitioner is the Father of James Coe now in confinement on the prosecution of your Honorable Board on suspicion of uttering a counterfeit Note.
That your petitioner's Son for some time previous to this transaction lived Shopman with a Mr Turner of Fore Street London Linendraper. That Mr Turner having taken the note in question in the fair course of Trade and having paid it away the same was afterwards returned to him as being counterfeit. That your petitioner's son took this Note by mistake from the place where Mr Turner had laid it, and paid it away with other Notes, without knowing at the time that it was the Note that had been returned to Mr Turner and for which offence he is now in Prison.
That your petitioner can with the greatest truth and confidence state that his son is wholly unacquainted with any of the parties who have wickedly counterfeited the Note and that he has innocently become the object of prosecution by passing the Note in the manner stated, without the least intention of committing any fraud.
That previous to this unfortunate affair, the Son of your petitioner has preserved an unblemished character for Honesty and Sobriety, as appears by the certificate at the foot of this petition signed by the said Mr Turner and other respectable persons, some of whom have known him from infancy.
Your petitioner therefore most Humbly prays that your Honorable Board will be pleased to order your solicitors to stop all further proceedings against your petitioner's son and that proper directions may bee given for his immediate discharge.
And your petitioner as in duty Bound will ever pray
Attached: page of 19 signatures in support; letter from James Coe to Mr Windsor to whom he says he unwittingly paid the note.

23. *[F25/1/105–6] Two letters from Captain W. C. Davis, debtor to Bank, King's Bench prison, asking for early trial, 1800.*

24. *[F25/1/107] Letter from Moses Harby, prisoner in Wood Street compter, 1799, asking to see Mr Acton, Bank solicitor; offence unspecified.*

25. *[F25/1/108] Rev. B. Forde, Ordinary of Newgate prison, 1799, offering information on forgers.*

26. *[F25/1/109] H. Row, New compter, 7 June 1799*
Sir I having been detaind here a long time without having received any assistance except the half Guinea I recd I believe from you I am under the Necessity to apply to you for some little reliefe as I am at present in great distress I was led to hope their would have been some small allowance to witness detained by there suite but having received nothing hope your goodness will take my case into consideration as I am informed I am to be removed soon

I remain your Humble ser[t] H. Row
Annotated: June 1799 Bank Commissioners from Mrs Row, Give her a G[*uine*]a

27. *[F25/1/110–12] Receipts for payment of doctor's fees for attendance at inquest on prisoner, Benjamin Clinton, who died in Poultry compter in 1801.*

28. *[F25/1/113] Ann Macarthy, Newgate, 2 July 1804*
Hon Gentlemen, Impressed with sentiments of the greatest respect I should be wanting in gratitude, I should be divested of every principale of duty I owe for the many favours I have received, Favours which I (from having acted wrong) had no reason to expect; – It is these sentiments, flowing from a heart not un-mindful, not callous, or lost to a sense of the sacred Obligations it owes to kind and generous Benefactors has stimulated me to obtrude these lines to your humane Consideration, hoping they will be received with favour in your sight.
Gentlemen, there is I am informed a Ship taken up to transport the Female Prisoners in Newgate to some one of his Majesty's Settlements, and as I have long been burthensome on your hands, it is from these motives that has induced me to acquaint you that I should be happy to be sent abroad, to avoid those reflections which the unthinking and ill-natured might cast on me: – Could I gain permission, from the Hon the Governor and the Hon. Court, it would be the means of my spending the remainder of my years in peace and happiness. – Should you be inclined to grant this my humble Prayer, (as my Life has not been led in scenes of profligacy, vice and immorality) and be graciously pleased to allow me a trifle (should I be sent away) to procure tea and sugar and a few common necessaries, it will be most thankfully acknowledged and applied to the best purposes, as your bounty ought to demand and expect.
Endeavouring to follow then as I ought the rule of good Living, reflecting daily on the liberality you have shewn, with grateful esteem do I subscribe myself Your much obliged and Respectful Humble Servant Ann Macarthy

29. *[F25/1/114] Ann Macarthy, Newgate, 30 July 1804*
Hon Gentlemen With the greatest humility do I take the Liberty to address this Letter hoping I shall from the humanity and kindness extended to me have the redress I most humbly crave, my situation Gentlemen, you who are possessed of the noblest feelings of humanity can picture to your minds the anxiety which persons experience in a prison, especially when they keep themselves select from the Lower Orders of Society, and owing to this reason I have been most cruelly calumniated it being daily asserted that I was the cause of the death of the unfortunate men who suffered the sentence of the Law last Thursday, and this assertion cruel as it is, is accompanied by threats from the Traducers of my Character, that when I go on board of Ship, I shall be treated with the greatest severity and like-wise abroad, I hope Gentlemen you will believe me when I assert that I had not the least knowledge of the two persons: therefore though I am immured

in Prison for my act of indiscretion from the Kindness you have shown me I most humbly hope that the Gentleman who kindly comes to me will have the goodness to speak for me to Mr Kirby which will prevent their ill usage in future and confer a great favour, added to the very many obligations conferred on Your much obliged servant, Ann Macarthy

30. *[F25/1/115–18] Ann Macarthy, Newgate, July 1805*
Hon Gentlemen Thankful indeed might I be for your unbounded Generosity to me, without your benificient aid I and my dear infant would have suffered the greatest distress
Since my confinement I have endeavoured to behave myself with becoming propriety sorry for any misconduct
As I am now going to be sent away at two o'clock this afternoon I humbly implore a small Relief as in your Goodness may seem meet Ann Macarty
I hope I shall ever keep in mind your goodness
I Sirs have signed this supplication to certify that the Bearer George Bridgemen is sent from the unfortunate Ann Mcarty [*illegible signature*] Turnkey Newgate
Attached: copy letter from Bank solicitors to Moses Greetham jr, their agent, Portsmouth, 13 July 1805, enclosing letter to captain Boyce of transport ship William Pitt, *Spithead, asking to know when delivered; annotated to show acknowledgement received 19 July 1805; letter to Boyce requesting he lay out £15 for items to contribute to comfort of Ann Macarthy and her child, giving her remainder on arrival, since* she has conducted herself with great propriety since her conviction. Afford her all the protection you can.

31. *[F25/1/119] Ann Macarthy,* William Pitt *transport ship, Portsmouth, 13 July 1805*
Honrid Gentlem [*illegible word*] parden me taking the liberty of writing to you I have pact up my things in Newgate an directed them as I thought to go with me But I have lost them I Begd of Mr Shuter to send me them if he could find them. all my Child's Cloas is in the Bundle I left Behind like Wise all my own things. If you will have the goodness to see Mr Shuter baut them an send me some small Relieaf to the Capt, I shall for ever be in Dutey Bound to Pray for your goodness your most obedent humble servant Ann Macatey
Annotated: Mr Suter Gaoler.

32. *[F25/1/120] Sarah Whiley, Newgate, 19 October 1804*
Gentlemen, If the contrition of an unfortunate woman can have weight in my favour to induce you to have compassion on a misguided and deluded Female, mine is truly sincere.
I have never pleaded in anyway in extenuation of my offence, though it is well known I have fallen a prey to delusive and false persons, being unacquainted with the dangerous tendency to Society or fatal Consequences of the crime I now justly suffer for.

I am now, through distress, reduced to the painful alternative of imploring your Benevolence for a small Relief – I am well aware of your goodness towards the Unfortunate – I have no Friend to help me through my misconduct. Alas! But a few years ago I lived in honest and good repute, now lost to the world – through ignorance, – am I plunged in the lowest ebb of misery – pray have pity on me, and your Goodness shall not be mis-applied – My Prayers and my nine innocent Children shall join with me in Gratitude for your Benevolence extended to Your humble Applicant, Sarah Whiley

33. *[F25/1/121] Sarah Whiley, Newgate, 29 October 1804*
Honoured Gentlemen, With Grateful Respect do I return you my sincere Thanks for your Generous Relief to me, and I hope you never will have occasion to think me unworthy of your kind Benefaction; through the inhumanity of my husband have I involved myself in distress but my Contrition for my imprudence my sorrow for the Crime I committed has been such that I trust you will still kindly think on The Unfortunate Person who implores your Pity, who humbly subscribes herself Your Great Obliged Servant, Sarah Whiley

34. *[F25/1/122–4] Sarah Whiley,* William Pitt *transport ship, Falmouth, 5 August 1805*
Oh most Honrable Gentlemen Your humanity and goodness I humbley hope will Please to Pardon the Leberty taking by me to Return you my sencear thanks for the Benevolent kindness you have shewn me sence my Confinment for without your Generous aid and Support I should have been reduced to the greatest misery and want and it behaves me ever to be mindful of the gracious bounty I have received, and Gentlemen as I am so well Convinced of your fellings for the Destressed eaven of those who have been guiltey of so base a Crime the heniousness of which indeed I was not aware But I Bag Leaff to informe you kind Gentlemen that we are going to Saill from hear in a Day or tow and as its not in my power to Procure me a Little Tea and Shuger for the voige has emebolden me to aske the favour for a small trifle for that Purposs for thare is no more Aloude tell we go to Sea and then onley half Ounce per Wick and quarter Pound of Shuger for Eatch Person
So Pray Gentlemen with your wanted goodness take Compassion on the Unhappy Mother who has left nine children forever to Lament her Case Oh how great is my Trouble none is like to Mine Leave so many infant Children never more to see them But I hope God will protect them from all Bad Company from for that as Ben my Ruen
O most Hon^{d} Gentlemen I hope your Goodness will Please to Excuse this Liberty taking By me and Sirs I am in Duty Bound for ever to Pray for your kindness while Life Remains Sarah Whiley
Attached: copy note from Bank solicitors, 8 Aug. 1805, to agent, James Tippet, in Falmouth, enclosing £5 for small necessaries *to be given to captain of* William Pitt *for Whiley, to be used to contribute to her comfort; annotated:* £5 30th July 1805 No. 5563 put into the post on date; *note to*

Bank solicitors from Tippet stating he missed boat by 8–10 hours and was returning money.

35. *[F25/1/125] Ann Foss, Newgate, 22 October 1804*
Hon Gentlemen I hope it will not be thought impertinent in me, in imploring your Benevolence or inquire those to whom you are kind; I have incurred your displeasure, have merited the punishment I receive, and am convinced that what I suffer is justly inflicted on me, but after the sentence I have received, the little I had is expended, and in hoping you will excuse the Liberty, I may also, if it is but a small Relief, have reason to thank with heartfelt Gratitude my Generous Prosecutors and endeavour as I have hitherto done, while in this Country, and also, should I be sent abroad, to prove myself deserving (by a sincere atonement) of his Majesty's Gracious Mercy and your Charitable aid. I would plead in extenuation of this intrusion on your Charity that in the unfortunate Pl where I am confined your generous Goodness soon transpires, and having now no husband, who can help me, through his misconduct. I am inclined to hope that if it is but the smallest sum I may be a partaker of your Goodness.
Should this humble request which I pray to God may not hurt those in the same Prison who consider themselves under the greatest Obligation I humbly subscribe myself Your distressed Humble Servant, Ann Foss – Though shame indicted by the name of Ann Haynes

36. *[F25/1/126] Ann Foss, Newgate, 30 October 1804*
Gentlemen Pardon the Liberty I take, I sent a Letter to you acquainting you of my distress, imagining you might not have received my Humble Application, I once more presume, though I hope without Offence, to intreat your Benevolence, I know I have been Guilty, the Laws of my Country have proved it to my disgrace, but Gentlemen, am I more guilty than my Companion [*Sarah Whiley*] implicated in this offence for which we are both in Prison. I therefore most humbly intreat and with the greatest submission, hoping you will consider an unfortunate woman, subscribe myself Your Distressed Humble Servant, Ann Foss

37. *[F25/1/127] Ann Foss, Newgate, 14 February 1805*
Hon Gentlemen Pardon the Liberty I take which distress alone impels me in thus humbly imploring in your known Goodness a small relief, the last time I humbly addressed you you were led to believe I did not stand in need of your Generous assistance, but keen Necessity has once more stimulated me to humbly request a small relief as in your Goodness may seem meet. I have not any friend in the world, or I would not have supplicated this great favour. In pity then, Gentlemen, good and kind as you are be graciously pleased to grant me a trifle, sorry am I that I should have incurred your great displeasure and daily do I in secret deplore my past misconduct. I have no Friend to render me assistance or I would not dare to trespass on your Liberality. I have been guilty of a Great Fault but I am truly sensible & convinced of my error and would wish that it were in my power to call back the days of happiness I enjoyed before I was guilty of a crime which

has brought on me such great disgrace. Pray have compassion on me and in your willingness to do good even to those who have offended I most fervently intreat you to take into your human consideration the distress of Your humble Petitioner, Ann Foss

38. *[F25/1/128] Ann Foss, Newgate, 11 May 1805*
Mr Bliss [*Bank investigator*], Sir I hope you will Pardon ther Liberty of Riting to you. But Real Nessety oblige me to rite to you Hoping Your goodnes will Pardon me for ther Lebty I take I have ben heare one year and all my clothes is gone Sir I Hunderstand som Body hes bin so good to Tell Messrs Winter and Keas I have got a great deal of monee to send I had it I wold not take yor monee in name Sir if I did But no my wants you wold pity me I rote to them and thea sade I did not want anea I have not anea body to give me a Singel things Sir if by yor intersehon thea will give me triful to By me some tea and sugar for I hunderstand We are a geoing a Broard in a short time. Mrs Whiley has got a husband and dauters to help her I ham by my slef no frend in ther world o Sir if you will put in a werde for me god will Bless you and your Sir your Humbel Srnt, Ann Foss

39. *[F25/1/129] Ann Foss, Newgate, 9 July 1805*
Gentlemen In Expectation of being sent abroad in a few days I humbly implore you to have pity on me, it is well known in the Prison that I am reduced almost to poverty not having sufficient to pay for a Bed to sleep on.
Pray then Sirs have compassion on me the smallest trifle will be acceptable and will be received with gratitude by an unfortunate, an unhappy Woman, with the greatest respect, in the deepest sorrow, subscribes herself Hon. Sirs, Your Most Respectful Humble and Obedient Servant

40. *[F25/1/130] Elizabeth Ware, sick ward, Newgate, 20 August 1803*
Gentlemen It is with the greatest humility I venture to obtrude my supplication praying that your Compassion may be extended towards me for the sake of my Destitute and very Distressed Infants, trusting that their unhappy case will aid their captive mother by meeting those Benevolent feelings, which have often been the means of restoring the penitent offender to a grateful family.
My Sorrows, Gentlemen, under my Dilemma are great and I really deplore the Fatal Error I have fallen into; fatal indeed to me, having deprived me of every comfort of domestic Life, and left me with three helpless children (the eldest being not above Five years) and an Increase in Expectancy – entirely friendless and fatherless, having never heard, nor received the least Assistance, from my Husband since my Confinement, and who will be truly Orphans unless, Gentlemen, your Condescension and Humanity should alleviate my Condition – by interceding for some Mitigation of my dreadful Sentence – to be transported for the long and dreary space of Fourteen Years.
Be assured, Gentlemen, that I shall ever most gratefully feel and acknowledge your great goodness, and look upon you as the instrument of the

Mercy of Almighty God in raising me from the Lowest Depths of Sorrow and Misery to Joy, Comfort and Happiness, and ever most ardently pray that you may receive the due reward of Compassion to the Penitent and distressed.
I most humbly beg leave to subscribe myself Gentlemen Your dutiful and devoted Servant, Elizabeth Weare Her mark
Please turn over
PS I beg pardon, Gentlemen, for further intruding to mention that the threatening Expression, said to have been uttered by me towards my Husband must (with great Reverence and Humility I signify it) have arose through a misunderstanding as it was ever my Advice for him to speak the Truth when questioned on the greatest of all consideration Vize that of his Family.

41. *[F25/1/131] Elizabeth Ware, Newgate, 20 September 1803*
Gentlemen I very humbly beg Pardon for the Liberty I take in again obtruding on your Notice; but the Distress of myself & Children & the Remorse and Anxiety I daily experience on account of my sad Situation, will, I trust, be considered as some Apology for so doing.
I only beg, Gentlemen, in this to be permitted to draw to your Recollection an Intimation that some pecuniary aid would (on sending) be charitably bestowed on me & while I should acknowledge any, the smallest Donation with the deepest Impressions of Gratitude, my feelings would likewise teach me ever to pray that the divine Protection may attend on those who might be instrumental under Providence to soften my Affliction, by interposing for some Mitigation of my unhappy Doom before a Draught of Female Convicts should be sent from hence, which I am led to believe will shortly take place. I most humbly rest, Gentlemen, with the greatest deference, Your devoted servant, Elizabeth Wear her mark

42. *[F25/1/132] Elizabeth Ware, Newgate, 28 September 1803*
Sir, Having received your Charitable Donation, I catch the first Opportunity – very humbly- to express my sincere Regret of having been under the Necessity to make such an obtrusion and from the Receipt of your Bounty am convinced that Justice only was the Motive for prosecuting me – and being also convinced of the Necessity that absolutely exists for the Punishment of offences against Society, I humbly submit to my Country's Laws trusting under Providence to the Exertions of Humanity for an Amelioration of the dreadful sentence they have pronounced against me. In the meantime, Sir, permit me to say, that the comfort myself & Children have derived from your Bounty will ever impress on my mind sentiments of real gratitude by enforcing a Duty of always praying for the Happiness & Prosperity of my Donors Elizabeth Wear her mark

43. *[F25/1/133] Mary Ann Jenkinson, Newgate, 10 May 1805*
Hon. Gentlemen, Extreme distress impels me to trespass on your humanity. I would not dare to obtrude on your known liberality were I not bereft of Aparels, I hope my misconduct will be a warning to others not to commit

offences, which entail on them the sad appendages of misery and want, for myself I can assure you that I knew not the danger to which I have been exposed, acting like a foolish Woman, ignorant of the crime, I have become a victim to justice, yet now made sensible of my error I feel the sad effect of my duplicity and with Contrition would endeavour to atone for the Fault I have been Guilty. As I have lost almost all my Cloaths, if you would be so humane as to grant me a trifle, as in your Goodness may seem meet it will be received with Gratitude by her who ought always to acknowledge your humanity, and who subscribes herself Your obliged, distressed Servant, Mary Ann Jenkinson

I have several duplicates of cloaths in pledge, but have not money to take them out, or I would not obtrude on your Charity.

I should be happy to see Mr Bliss [*Bank investigator*] as I have something to Communicate to that Gentleman if he would be so kind as to Call

44. *[F25/1/134] Mary Ann Jenkinson, Newgate, 20 May 1805*

Hon. Gentlemen, In the unfortunate situation in which I lamentably am placed, it would certainly behove me to inform you of any Circumstances that would tend to my advantage, and from the mercy I have received from his Most gracious Majesty it would be a duty incumbent on me to acquaint you of any Person concerned in the nefarious Practice, I through ignorance am the unoffending sufferer.

I would inform you, that having seen Mr Bliss, whose Civility to me I am now thankful, has requested information of me respecting the persons who circulate bad Notes, but I can assure you I never was concerned with any person, nor knew not that Mr Holt was a vender of bad Notes.

In the business I carried on as a Japanner, Ann Adams who has changed her name to Portucie claimed an acquaintance, this woman was intimate with a man of the name of Whiley, whose conduct is well known, and as I have reason to believe that bad Notes are yet vended, though I do not practice such nefarious practices I will make it my study to apprize you of any such proceedings.

Trusting that you will (from the humanity you shew to Others known to be Offenders) grant me a small Relief to her, who with the greatest humility subscribes herself Your Distressed Humble Servant, Mary Ann Jenkinson

45. *[F25/1/135–9] Mary Ann Jenkinson, Newgate, 17 June 1805*

Hon. Sirs, I trust the Apprehension of Elizabeth Brown will not only tend to my advantage but be the means of developing the nefarious practice of issuing Forged Notes, and proving to you Gentlemen my ignorance of the Transactions in which I have been innocently involved. I should indeed be happy to see some of the Gentlemen of the Bank, whereby I might endeavour to exonerate myself as to what knowledge I have had of the woman, who perhaps has been the cause of my misfortunes- If I could be honoured with an interview it would confer a favour on Your Distressed Servant, Mary Jenkinson

Attached: two copy letters – 21 June 1805, in which Bank solicitors request sec./state (Lord Hawkesbury) for immediate transportation of Ann

Macarthy, Ann Foss, Sarah Whiley, Mary Ann Jenkinson and Elizabeth Weare, and 28 June 1805, in which they request from owner of transport ship, William Pitt, *letter of introduction to captain so they may get some money to Mary Ann Jenkinson; letter from Bank's agent, James Tippet, Falmouth, 23 Aug. 1805, saying his clerk had missed* William Pitt, *returning money, and asking Bank solicitors to recommend his son for legal partnership; copy reply from Bank solicitors, 26 Aug. 1805, acknowledging return of money,* which we are sorry for the sake of the Unfortunate object to learn reached you too late, *and stating they would be happy to help Tippett's son, but know of no lawyer needing a partner at the time.*

46. *[F25/1/140] Mary Prince, Newgate, 6 May 1807*
Hon. Gentlemen Your humanity I hope will excuse my trespassing on your known Commisseration, having had a Petition presented to the Right Hon. Lord Hawkesbury, in hope of a mitigation of my Sentence, humbly intreating your kind Recommendation. The length of Time I have been in Prison hath reduced me to great want, therefore I beg of you, having an infirm Husband, and Four Children with an aged Mother in her 89th year, to whom did your Petitioner tend to render Comfortable, considering Good Sirs that I was drawn into Error, be pleased to alleviate my keene Distress, which will ever be Gratefully acknowledged by Hon Gentlemen, Your distressed Servant Mary Prince

47. *[F25/1/141–3] James Clarkson, Newgate, 25 May 1807*
Gentlemen In my deplorable Situation I once more presume to intrude trusting my Application under all Circumstances may meet your Approbation.
I find it is shortly expected such Persons as are under sentence of Transportation will be removed when among that unfortunate Number my Name may be composed, with that view I now again Solicit Your Aid.
A Petition is afloat endeavouring to obtain a Conditional Pardon to Transport myself from this Country rather than be sent to any of the Hulks. The Respect for my Dear Wife & Children may in some Measure operate for the Prayer to be granted but a little Time is required.
I have therefore Gentlemen most earnestly to Solicit Your Kindness to send orders for my being detained in the Place until a decision is known, which from your hands I am Creditably informed is sufficient.
I humbly hope Gentlemen you are Sensible I am fully contrite & been erroneously led into this calamitous Affair and am persuaded you will in this Instance save me and my family.
Under the most assured heartfelt Obligation I remain, with utmost Respect Gentlemen your obedient, James Clarkson.
Attached: letter to Bank from J. Beckett, home office, 29 May 1807, transmitting Clarkson's petition for consideration by governor and directors; copy of Bank's reply, 30 May 1807 stating that since they allowed Clarkson to plead to lesser offence when they could have indicted him capitally, sufficient lenience already shown; their duty to public did not warrant further interference.

48. *[F25/1/144] Simon Boutell,* Retribution *hulk, Woolwich, 12 July 1807*
Sir Pardon the Liberty I Take of Addressing you – I have one favour to beg of you which is. That I may have the Opportunity of Going to New South Wales or Botany bay – with the first Draft. I hope you will undertake for me & your kind answer To this will be Thankfully Received. I am Particularly desirous of going out of the Country to Prevent further Trouble – which might Occur – I hope you will Supply me with a few Shillings To Purchase a Small Quantity of Sea Stores such as Tobacco &c as I am inform'd The Gentlemen of the Bank has been Very generous To Persons before. Sorry To inform you my friends has not been To see me Since I have been here – which I am in much Trouble About. I Ever desire To be Unfeignedly Thankfull for Preserving my Life from So Shamefull & Ignominious a Death as my Crime deserves – I freely Acknowledge The Justice of My Sentance & I hope in future To Return & be at Peace with all men – & a Usefull Member of Society. I Shall be Extreamly Thankfull if you would be So Oblidging as To Assist me in my Request & Shall be in duty bound to Pray for your Everlasting welfare. I am Sir your Most Ob[t] & Hum[l]- Serv[t], Simon Boutell
Pray return an answer if agreable to you I am on board The Retribution Hulk Woolwich, Kent

49. *[F25/1/145] Thomas Rushton, Giltspur Street compter, 13 May 1802*
Sirs, I arrived here last night from Chester In my way to Portsmouth, I was Convicted at the last assises Chester for having in my Possession one and two Pound Bank of England Notes, I had Some Conversation with Mr Ward Constable of Chester Castle about ten days Previous to my removal Respecting the one Pound Notes of the new curved Pattern that was hid in Liverpool and offered to disclose who are the Makers, on condition of having liberty to transport myself were I please. They are Persons not in the least Suspected they make the Paper and do all except the Plate one is now in London on this (I mean parting with notes) Business and the other in Dublin, they make Irish notes as well and will Surprise the Bank directors, they are in every respect equal to those issued from the Bank, it was my intention to write to you from Chester but was persuaded by Mr Ward to make the communication to him under Promise that he would transmit it to you, and as I have not heard any more respecting it Suppose Mr Ward has not made it known to you or the Directors of the Bank, believe I shall go from here this afternoon to the place of my destination if my Proposition meet your approbation I can tell how to put the parties into your hands
I am Sir respectfully your obe[t] humble Servant, Thos Rushton
NB I am now Chain'd to another Person and cannot think of conversing on this Subject but alone T.R.
I before mention'd in a Letter to Mr Ward Constable of the Castle Chester, that the one Pound Notes was hid in Liverpool, I mentioned the Place were the were hid and who I supposed found them, the particulars of that information in my Letter has I suppose been laid before you or the directors of the Bank of England – if these notes can be found, I can point out I conceive how the Person I had them from may be convicted, who is one of

the Makers and now in London, I have got the original note they were made from.

50. *[F25/1/146] Elizabeth Dudley, Newgate, 23 October 1807*
Gent^{n} Understanding it to be the custom of the B^{k} of Eng^{d} to allow a weekly Sum unto persons who are unfortunately confined at their instance, I take the liberty of troubling you upon that score & inform you I have not reced any assistance since yesterday was a month when I recd ½ Gua [*guinea*]. I therefore solicit your interference in my behalf being greatly Distressed, by communicating the same to the person in whose province it is to attend to this matter which will be gratefully acknowledged by Eliz^{h} Dudley

51. *[F25/1/147] Elizabeth Dudley, Newgate, 24 October 1807*
Gent^{n} Having been convicted last Session for hav^{g} in my possession a forged £1 B^{k} of Eng^{d} Note and beeing very much distressed & in want of the common necessaries of life and unable from Age & infirmity to do anything to assist myself, I am advised to apply to you for some assistance to which I am given to understand your humanity extends towards persons who are so unfortunate as to be confined at your instance without the means of support. Any small sum your clemency shall direct will be ever gratefully acknowledged by Gent$^{n.}$ Your unfortunate & Obed^{t} Serv$^{t.}$ Eliz^{h} Dudley
Annotated: 60 years of Age – much palsied, very distressed. *Further annotation by William Smith, BECLS secretary:* Present Mr Maitland & Mr Bowden [*Bank directors*] 27th October 1807, Bank – Mr Kaye is authorized to pay Eliz^{h} Dudley 10^{s}/6^{d} per Week until she is sent away from Newgate

52. *[F25/1/148] Mary Prince, Newgate, 24 October 1807*
Gent^{n} Understanding you assist those who are unfortunate enough to be here at your Suit without the means of support I beg to represent to you that I am one of those unfortunate persons, & have been confined here since January last that I am very feeble & near 60 years of Age my friends quite tired of rendering me that little assistance I first received from them & am in a very wretched state. I therefore solicit the extention of your humanity towards one who will ever gratefully acknowledge your liberality & am Gent^{n} with every sense of Gratitude,
Your very Humble Servt, Mary Prince
Annotated: Under Sentence of transportation for 14 years. *Further annotated by William Smith, BECLS secretary:* 25 Nov$^{r.}$ 1807 – Com^{ee} Law Suits. Mary Prince to be allowed ½ a Guinea a Week during her confinement in Newgate. Per Order of Eben^{r} Maitland Esq. [*Bank director*].

53. *[F25/1/149] James Strickland, unspecified debtor's prison, 4 February 1807, having heard of Bank's generosity, asks their help, reminding them that four years ago he helped them apprehend a forger. Annotated:* Bliss says this man has assisted him in enquires he has had to make.

54. *[25/1/150–1] Mary Pullen, Newgate, late September 1806*
Gentell Man of the Bank, Hope youre Goodness Will Pardon the Lerberty i take in Adreasing these few Lines to you But your known Huemaniety to A Manay unfourtunate Pursons imboldens me An fourtunate Woman to supplicate your Humaine Asistancens in Behalf of my salf Being on the vurge of Leaven my Native Countrey for ever o Most Honourable Gentellman if it tis your Plashour and my own unhapey that i should Goe i hope you Will huemaniley Greant Mee A treafall to Asist mee in My Peresant Rachied situaastuon to gat A few Nerscarys Wich is Rackqusite for so long A Voyage being intierley Naket havin Bin obleged to part With Evereything to surpourt my self and unfouretunat Children with this tan Months i have Bin Confine With in these Gloomey Warells. Gentellman i hope these Merscerable Lines Will have Wate in Huemaine hearts Like yours to Asist Anhapy Widow Whoe has disstrassed hir salfe to the Larest to halfe hir Racheid offens Whoe [*illegible word*] ourley in dread of Being torn from for ever As i ame too far Advanced in yares Ever to hope to Gat to the Eand of my voyage Much More to Return to tham on My Nees i humbley Bag you to Greant my Requst and shall thing mysalf Ever in duty Bound to pray for you Wile Life shall Larest youre humble pertictoner Mary Pullen
Attached: note from Mr Bliss, Bank investigator: Wednesday 1 October 1806, Sir, I called yesterday to see Mary Pullen but could not see her without Mr Brown's [*official, Newgate, from 1817 was keeper*] order. I have seen her this Morning and find her to be in great distress, all her things pawned and one of her daughters with her arm in a sling from a fall on the day of her trial – she says she will cause inq^{s} to be made after Willm Stone [**58**] and let me know, Your obedient Servant

55. *[F25/1/152] Sarah Pilcher, Newgate, 6 October 1806*
Gentlemen I hope you will pardon a poor lost woman the liberty she takes in thus addressing you, to request your kind interference with the humane Gentlemen of the Bank to make me some small allowance for my support and to purchase me some stores for my voyage – I understand a ship is about shortly to sail and I have no articles whatever to render me in the smallest degree comfortable as I have for several years been a Widow and in distressed circumstances, and have two children whom I must now leave unprovided, and who must as well as myself already have been without the means of subsistence but by the liberality of one person – I therefore most humbly beg you will condescend to lay these particulars before the Honorable Directors whose accustomed benevolence will I trust be exercised towards me, as I have felt every possible contrition for my misconduct Your most obedient & unfortunate servant Sarah Pilcher

56. *[F25/1/153] John Sly, Coldbath Fields prison, 30 September 1807*
Sir if you would make it convenient to call upon me I have something to communicate to you if you could get an opportunity to have me in private which you can if you think this worthy of your notice – what I have to say

is of no consequence to myself tho' much to the Bank. I am Sir your humble Serv[t] Jn Sly
PS I beg this may be kept a Secret even from the Keepers & not let it be known to them I wrote to you

57. *[F25/1/154] John Sly, Coldbath Fields prison, 14 October 1807*
Sir I am sorry it has not been in my power to send any further account to you before this but I can now let you know that there is a Letter went to Birmingham & I shall get the answer to it & will send it to you. I should esteem it a favor if you would be so kind as to give the Bearer a Line to the Governor to be so good as to let her in the inner gate to speak to me as tho' she is not my wife she would have been had it not have been for my Imprisonment & I have several things to say to her about my Business that I cannot say at the Gate for every one to hear. There is a number admitted by Bribing the Turnkeys but that is out of my Power as I have not a shilling to help myself & the young woman has done all she can for me. I am Sir, you most humble Servant, Jn Sly

58. *[F25/1/155] William Lawton Stone, Horsemonger Lane gaol, 4 April 1808*
Honoured Sir trusting your Goodness will pardon the Liberty I have taken in Stating the Situation of an Unfortunate Young Man and family whose Circumstances after Eight Months Confinement are left Destitute of Support and Sorry to say my self under Transportation for fourteen years at the thoughts of the Wretchedness of a Convictt Ship and being Separated from my Wife and dear Children my heart is broken and Attribute my Misfortune to being Ignorant of the fatal Consequences of my Crime and being treacherously Betrayed in hopes that Something may be done to Assist an Unfortunate Victim I have sent to the Bank of England and hope to be Enabled to better Means of Bringing to Justice those that are the Ruin of Many and trust in god for Mercy never to Offend the Laws of my Country any more and trust that Philanthropy and goodness that is Manifasted so Eminently that Character that my Family is Ever bound to Bless and with due Submission Subscribe my Self Your Most-Obedient and Humble Servant W L Stone
Addressed to Esq Goodenough 38 Hertford St.

59. *[F25/1/156] Joseph Hodges, un-named hulk,* [probably *Prudentia*] *Woolwich, 13 October 1805*
Gentlemen I have taken the Liberty of troubling you Beging the favour to have the Goodness to Interseed for me to have the trifling property Returned to me that was taken out of my Trunks at my Lodgings by Mr Bliss after I was taken into custody by him, which was a brace of pistols two Silver Crosses an one pocket Book. Mr Bliss Assured me I should have everything safe Back before I was Convicted at Croyden. I have since made Application for them to Mr Bliss an he informs me that he is is not allowed to Lett me have them. I have Gentlemen before My Conviction and since informed Mr Bliss of Different Shops where whar there has been

forged Bank Notes paid away and Likewise the people that pay them away which Mr Bliss has found to be true I discovered since I have been on Board the Hulks that this is found out by some people that is hear for the same Offence as Mine, people in the Country that Make them for sale an likewise pay them away I immediately Aquainted Mr Bliss of the same an Likewise whare the people ware to be found, therefore Gentleman as I have done Eavery thing to Serve the Bank I Hope you will have the Goodness to Interseed for me to have what trifling property belongs to me. As eaver so trifling will be a great help me in this Situation – I Beg to Remain your Most Earnest and Very Humble Ser[t] Joseph Hodges

60. *[F25/1/157] John Wood,* Prudentia *hulk, Woolwich, 10 December 1805*
Gentlemen After begging pardon for the intrusion permitt me to state, that I am an unfortunate person who was Convicted at Hertford Assizes in the month of March 1802 of having Counterfeit Bank of England Notes in my possession to the amount of one hundred and fifty pounds, for which offence I was sentenced to be transported to New South Wales for the term of fourteen years:- soon after conviction I was removed to the Hulks on the River Thames where I have since remained under order of transportation without the least appearance of having my sentence put in absolute execution, now Sirs as there has been ships gone out with prisoners from hence and no notice has been taken of me it seems cruel in a degree that I should be neglected, I have no desire to remain in England I acknowledge that I have had such bad connections in the line of circulating bad notes that I wish for a final seperation from; I am not at present warned of being one that is to depart the country in the present expedition to Botany Bay and I much fear I shall be left behind again. Therefore Gentlemen I humbly beg you will exercise your influence (if I am not at present in the Arrangement) that may facillitate my being efectually transported agreeable to the sentence I received, I know I am a usefull man in my present sittuation and that may have been the cause of my remaining here so long, but when I assure you that I wish to rid me of a connection so nefarious to commerce I repose my sanguine trust that you will promote my s[*p*]eedy departure for Port Jackson. I am Gentlemen with profound Respect &c &c &c your very Humble Servant, John Wood a Carpenter

61. *[F25/1/158] Thomas Young,* Royal Admiral *hulk, Woolwich, 30 September 1805*
Honourd Sirs Trusting in the well known benignity & humanity of your hearts I have presumed to become your Suppliant & I hope that as your Philanthropy saved me from an ignominious death, so will it preserve me from an hungry one, I have no friend to assist me I am in the extremes of need, & have no hope but in your benevolence, which I trust you will extend towards me, by supplying me with a trifle to purchase a few Stores for the Passage to Botany Bay, should you graciously condescend to comply with my request gratitude will engrave the obligation so deep, that time will never efface it from the memory of Your Most Obedient Most Obliged and Most Humble Serv[t] Tho. Young

62. *[F25/1/159] James Edwards,* Prudentia *hulk, Woolwich, 20 October, 1806, prisoner awaiting trspn, not Bank offender, received £2 note from friends in Cheshire which he 'changed' with chief mate of* Prudentia; *chief mate paid it to tradesman in London, who found it was forged, returned it to Bank, where, in conformity with usual practice, it was retained; chief mate had taken money in compensation from Edwards who was now desperate to get first note back from Bank*

63. *[F25/1/160] Matthew Bell,* Prudentia *hulk, Woolwich, 26 September 1807*

Sir I beg your parden for writen to you about the notes of bankes of England I was taken in scotland for them and sent to Jedborg and was eximened before Mister Henderson Mister Clever the shereief at Jedborg in scottland witch tha did make me a promes if I wad tell what way I got thes notes I shoud be set fre of them thare ware a thing that I never had on befor to understod any thing about – and I tould them the tim that I got them and the men whare I got them from and tould them all that lade in my pour a bout them and that I went of that pertence to take them but I thenk tha did not want to take them tha wonted to make money of yet or I am sure that might ben got at that time then I was taken from thare to morpeth Jall in Northumberland and was try at Newcastelsyes on the 5 day of august 1806 and now if yet ples you once to do any thing for me now I will be very much oblige to your sir I have got a wife and seven Cheldren all that I want in this world is my helth and leberty to go home gane to work for my wife and familey thare shal nobodey se me ever be scorned in any sich things gane I hope sir if you ples you will do som theng for me now if you plles won yer confinement is beter for a man than seven yeres is yet was the firest time that I ever sed won of thes notes or thar shall never wan of them com in my hand gane if I had my leberty if not I want to be sent from her if you ples Sir if you ples to send me anser Matthew Bell prudenhulk woolwich

64. *[F25/1/162] William Banister,* Retribution *hulk, Woolwich, to his wife, 12 June 1808*

Dear Wife and Children this comes with my love to you all. Hopeing it will find you Still in good Health. I recev[d] your letter on the 6 instant With a light heart to hear that you was all in good health and I trust in god this will find you the same as to my health it alters Every Day. Some times better and some times worse. But the lord's will be done for I trust hee will help mee in time I am sorry to hear of trade and other things being so bad for I Dought you will not Be able to get Bread for my little Children. But I hope that god will be with you and assist you in all things. I disire you will not fail to See M[r] Lloyd [*solicitor in Stockport acting for Bank*] and M[r] Baddley and if the can get my pardon I will do anything that lyes in my Power for them and for the good of my Country and Shall Ever be in Duty Bound to pray for them unto my lives End for if I had all the world in gould I would give it all that I might be restored to my liberty and be unighted

with my wife and Children to work and indavour to maintain my fear of god as I trust in god I could become a good member of Society
You wished to know how I was Situated. I will just give you a skecth [*sketch*] of it I am in a Ship with a Bout 400 men all as lowsey as Calves our Vitals is very Bad in the morning wee have some Barley and watter Boild thin without Salt and at noon Some Bread & Beef the Beef is Such as you never Saw most of it is such as Dyes of it Selfsh and Cows that are in a Decline and the Best wee get is leane Bully our Bread is a kind of Bran and Barley ground together just the Collour of ---[*writer's dash followed by illegible word*] and at night wee have some Barley Boild in the Broth that is made of the Beef but nobody will Eat that as it gives them the flucks and kills men Directly Every other Day wee have a Small lowance of Cheese to Diner in Sted of Beef. But you can Scarsely Cut it with nife – We Get our breakfast at six in the morning and then we are taken a Shore in Boats and work till noon and then goes a gain at one o clock and work till Six our work is Hardley fit for horses and there is men over us with Great Sticks and if we look off our work thay lay on us without mercy our legs is Cheand together Day and night and am amonghts nothing but thives and murderers and robers there is nothing But Blasting and Swearing &c-So you may be Sure I Cannot live Long here. I have not much time to Spare. But what leasure time I have I Spend it in prayer and I Disire you do the Same for if I was with you a gain wee could live a happy life in this world and Bring our Children up in the love of god which I hope you will Do you in Davour all at present from your Ever loving Husband, Wm Banister
NB plase to rite as soon as you know how things will be and let mee know how all my Children
Excuse my pen as I am hardly able to rite
Addressed to Mrs Nancy Bannister, Hempshaw Lane, Stockport, Cheshire

65. *[F25/1/161] William Banister,* Retribution *hulk, Woolwich, to his wife, 21 July 1808*
Dear Wife and Children I Rec^d^ your letter on the 18 instant With great joy to hear that God Continues to Bless you with good Health to work for bread for your Selves and our little Children that cannot help them Selves which I trust that hee will still keep you in the same for he has promised to be a father to the fatherless and to plead the Cause of the widdow. I have been taken with a very bad faver but through the timely assistance of medicine and the help of god I hope I shall get well in a little time. I got Bluded and took a filtre & other medicines which I trust put a stop to the Disorder. I was very poorly & then I recv^d^ your letter but when I came to read that you was in such good hopes of my pardon I was struck with such an Exstacy of joy that I had quite forgot my pain. So I kneeled Down to return my god thanks and then Went to rest and had a pleasent sleep that night. I am glad you have put my Son James to working [*illegible word*] you have done right in gateing him hee promised me the last time I saw him that hee would be a good lad and I have not the least Dought but hee will fulfil his promise & is being good to his mother.

You must Remember mee to Mr Lloyd and Mr Baddely – and let them know I shall be ever bound in Duty to pray for them as long as I live beSides rewards and all other things that Ever falls in to my hands which Will Ever be at there Service and will if I get my Liberty seek out that Villan of a morfey that brought mee in to this troble that all their rogery may be found out – there is men here get pardoned allmost Every week and I have great faith in god that through the merrits of his Son jesus Christ hee Will restore mee to my liberty that I may become a useful member of Christian Society if it fails this time it must not be Done away with But Dropt for a while and then tried again people here hav been Denied 3 times and got pardoned the 4 time but hope the will Do it now and Should it be my hapy lot to be restored to my Dear wife and Children in whom I plase[d] all my worldy Delight I should be the happyest man in the world for I could Imploy my leasure time in praising my god and teaching my Children so to Do and Shawing them good Examples to go by such has I have not Done before which I lament to my sorrow. When I am in the greatest Grieff I can ease myself with the thoughts of my Children being united together in peace and love with their tender mother which I hope is a comforth to you all. I find a Deal of Comforth in reeding the following Solms the 86 and 103 the 142 and 143 and Dear John I disire you to read these to your mother and Brothers and Sisters when you have leasure time and Do not neglect Church or Chapel – as many as can go for that is the first thing to do. As to mony as I Get better I shall want some kind of meals to raise my self with that will Nourish mee and what I had is nearly gone for I had 3g to lay out in a chest and other things that I was like to pay for and then you know I could not have much you may send mee a small trifle if you can spare any you know if it plase god that my pardon comes I shall want very little and I hope you will know be fore you need to rite. So I conclude with my Dearest Love to you and to all my Dear Children and May god rest his Blessing upon you and keep you in Safty from all Evil temtations unto your lives end Your unfortunate, Wm Banister

Written down side: You may let Mr Loyd or Mr Baddley look at this

66. *[F25/1/163] William Banister,* Retribution *hulk, Woolwich, 17 October 1808, to Mr Lloyd, solicitor for Bank, Stockport*

Dear Sir, I Beg you will Excuse mee taking the Liberty of writing these few lines to you as it is with an humble and sorrowful heart I write them it is to Humbly intreat your goodness that you will Soliset the Bank of England to Pardon my Distressed Condishion and to Shaw some mercy on mee for the Sake of my poor Distressed Wife and Eight Children which are Deprived of their tender father and laft to the mercy of the world peraps the greatest part of them will never Remember having seen their father and what must be their bringing up I Cannot tell but the Best of it will I Dout be hard for them tosed about from plase to plase I Can not tell where and often tould of their fathers misfortune while I may languish a few months more for them and then go in Sorrow Down to my greave. I think in my own Brest that it lyes in your power to get my pardon and if I Should meet your aprobation that your goodness will get my liberty I Shall Ever be in Duty Bound

to pray for you and will reward you as far as lies in my power and will Ever Do what I Can for my king and Country to Do them good I Durst be bound to be put to Death with out any mercy if I Do not find out murphey that Drow[d] mee into this Snare and Could in a few months Discover the Whole gang of them that is passing Some Hundreds Every week but I wil Do my in Davour to Do any thing that lyes in my power to make them amends all I Could wish in this life is to be restored to my wife and Children that I might live the rest of my Day in peace and Bring them up in the love and fear of god and repent my sins truly
Your Ever HS Wm Banister
Addressed to his wife for her to pass on

67. *[F25/1/164–5] J. Lloyd, solicitor, Stockport, to Bank solicitors, 12 November 1808***.**
States that he and his clerk found forged notes in Banister's garden; he has been pestered by Banister's wife to write to Bank on his behalf. He encloses **65–6**, *says he does not wish to say more, but asks Bank to mention in any reply that he has sent them as he does not wish to seem unhelpful.*

68. *[F25/1/166–8] William Banister,* Retribution *hulk, Woolwich, 18 March 1809*
Hon[d] Sir, I trust the necessity of my present unfortunate situation will apologize for the liberty I now take in thus writing you. If you'll recollect I transmitted a petition to you the 18th of last month addressed to the Hon[ble] the Governor & directors of the Bank of England, praying they would, in consequence of certain facts therein stated, be pleased to grant me a free pardon, a metigation of sentence, or allow me the privilege of transporting myself beyond seas, and, also begged that an answer might be condescended on & sent me when convenient.
To this petition you have never as yet been pleased to grant me any answer, I therefore hereby earnestly intreat of you to have the goodness to do so, as soon as you can. This, from your well-known humanity and compassion to the distressed, I am led to entertain the most fluttering hopes of a speedy deliverance from this my most miserable situation, which, if this should be effected, I shall always look upon it as the greatest of blessings, and as the highest obligation conferred upon Hon[d] Sir, Your most obed[t] humble Ser[t]
William Banister
Attached: petition stating that Banister lived in Stockport with his wife and children for most of his life, is of good character which can be attested to by gentlemen and principal inhabitants of the town, and that he was innocently led into harm by Archibald Murphy, Dec. 1807, who passed him forged notes in a mercantile transaction. *He pleaded guilty to possession although he believed he was innocent, not understanding that sentence would be fourteen yrs trspn. He now believed he should have pleaded not guilty and employed counsel at his trial. He asks pardon, or permission to transport himself; copy note to Banister from Bank solicitors:* The Governors and Directors of the Bank having interfered so far in your favour as to

relieve you from the Capital punishment to which your offence had subjected you, they decline interfering further

69. *[F25/1/169] John Bellairs,* Retribution *hulk, Woolwich, 29 January 1810*
Gentlemen, I most respectfully beg leave to submit the enclosed Petition for your approval, if it meets which I request that you will have the goodness to lay it before the Honorable Board to whom it is addressed, and if it is not presuming too far on your charitable goodness, I should be for ever grateful if you would favor me with a line by Post, intimating how far I may hope for the completion of my wishes therein contained, I am, Gentlemen, with the highest respect Your most obed[t] humble Servant John Bellairs
[*Petition no longer attached*]

70. *[F25/1/170] John Sly, Newgate, 25 January 1810*
Sir The person of the name of Braham or Abraham whom I mentioned to you before was (as he states to me himself) nearly apprehended at a Shop in Holborn in passing a 1£ note & had at the time 32 in his possession. he made his escape on acc[t] of the Shop man not being able to get an Officer to take him into Custody. I am at this time in the greatest distress of mind as the Convicts are now going off & I not knowing – whether I am to be so happy as to go with my wife or not & Mr Souter not being at home makes me request of you to give me a line in order to restore tranquillity to the mind of your unhappy Servant Jn Sly

71. *[F25/1/171–2] Elizabeth Ware,* [under sentence of death for returning from transportation], *Newgate, 25 December 1809, formal petition*
That your Petitioner in the year 1803, received from her husband, Thomas Ware [*prosecuted by Bank, May 1803*], sundry Notes, purporting to be good and lawful Notes of the Bank of England; that under the influence and direction of her said husband, she had sent a few into Circulation, previous to her discovery of their being Counterfeits; that on such discovery your petitioner, overwhelmed with the deepest affliction, under a just sense of the enormity of the Crime, remonstrated against the guilty deed, and but too truly predicted the fatal consequence which immediately followed. Her husband having fled from Justice, your Petitioner fell an innocent victim to the offended Laws of her Country, and after pleading guilty to her indictment she received sentence of 14 Years transportation to New South Wales as appears from the records of the Session, at which she was tried, and which was immediately carried into execution, leaving behind her two unprotected female infant Children, and a third, hanging at her breast, has shared the sufferings of its unhappy Mother. Considering her sentence to be for seven Years only, she embraced the only opportunity that might ever probably happen, to infold in her longing arms her long lost Children, but having been delivered into the hands of Justice, the awful Letter of the Law has been pronounced against her Life.

Your Petitioner filled with sorrow and contrition for the Crime, and oppressed with the weight of her sufferings, implores your forgiveness, and under a grateful sense of former favors, subsequent to her first trial and conviction, with the deepest humility, prays, gentlemen, that you will be pleased to take the circumstances attending her very singular case into your serious consideration, and, in your superior wisdom, be pleased to address the sacred person of His Majesty, the Fountain of Mercy, once more to restore to Society and the embraces of her Dear friendless Children, a poor creature who has been nearly seven years drinking the bitterest dregs, from the vials of human misery, for a Crime into which she became innocently involved.

Your humble Petitioner begs leave to assure the Gentlemen of the Bank of England, that should His Majesty be graciously pleased to grant the prayer of a Petition, signed by near fifty of his Majesty Most most dutiful and loyal subjects, and respectable householders, that the Death of her late husband gives her an opportunity of embracing an offer of marriage much to her advantage, with a person of the purest morals, and very respectable connexions, who only waits for the pardon of your suffering petitioner, to make her happy in the management of an extensive eating house.

Under the above circumstances your most humble petitioner prays you will be pleased to grant the prayer of her Petition, the most grateful sense of which, will ever be retained, and your Petitioner, with her Children, and probably Children's Children, will, as in Duty Bound, ever pray for their benefactors &c, &c Elizabeth Ware her mark

Annotated: Cannot interfere.

Attached: copy note from Bank solicitor: Mrs Ware's petition has been submitted to the Govr & Directors of the Bank who cannot interfere on her behalf 4 Jany 1810

72. *[F25/1/173] James Clarkson, Newgate (Master's Side), undated, 1810*

Honble Sirs With Due Respect I most humbley beg Leave to address you Respecting my Presant Situation about fifteen mounth ago I was tryed and Convicted of having forged Bank Notes in my Possession for witch I was Sentenced to fourteen years transportation since then I have bin Confind in newgate with a wife and two Infant Children who are in the Gratest Distress from my Long Confinement I am Reduced to the utmost not haven aney friends to Render me any assistance and I have a very Bad Rupture witch Gentlemen I am without the meanes of Percuring Nersessity for that Complaint yeasterday I was orderd to hold My Self in Redeness to go out to Bottany Bay by the first Ship witch will be in a feaw Days In Consequence tharefore I most fervently Solicit that you will Condescend to Concider my Case and that you will humanely Contribute Somthing Towards my Relief So far as in your wisdom it may be Deemed Providend I am Honble Sirs yours with Respect your most Oblig^{d} Humble Servant James Clarkson

73. *[F25/1/174] Sarah Davis, Newgate, 30 September 1811, formal petition*

That your Petitioner was Indicted at the last Old Bailey Session, for Uttering[1] as was alleged, in Company with another, a £5 Bank of England Note, to which Indictment She Pleaded Guilty, and was Sentenced to be Transported for the term of Fourteen Years.
That your Petitioner in her dreadful and much distressed Situation has ventured, (but in the most humble manner) to Solicit that Charitable Aid, which You have ever been pleased to afford to such Unfortunates as Your unhappy Petitioner; And She is the more emboldened to throw herself upon Your Benevolence, not only from the knowledge you have of her truly pitiable Case, but from the circumstance also, of her being absolutely driven to the most extreem poverty, and importunate distress; and which alas would have been truly indescribable, if Your Petitioner had not been enabled in some measure to alleviate it, either by the Sale, or Pledging of what little Wearing Apparel She had left
Your Petitioner therefore most humbly and ardently Implores your humane Consideration of her distresses, by condescending to make her what allowance you may, in your Wisdom deem meet And Your Petitioner as in Duty bound will ever pray

74. *[F25/1/182] Elizabeth Ware, Newgate, 25 March 1810*
Most Honored Gentelmen I most humbley bow down to you bagen your heuman harts will pardon the Liberty I take in thus Adrasing you was desird by Mr Suter to apley to you as he had sateld all acounts with you and that by your desire you would satel sume one to pay me a trifell weekley wich I have hard nothing about a fortinet is now relapst and I have recd nothing from aney one and being vary frendless Have taken the Liberty of bagen a trifell to suport me whilst Confind in this maloncoley dwaling and for every extreem kindness I have recd bag lave to return my most Gratfull thanks and most humbley Bow down to you kind Gentelmen praying for a Continuens of your kind benovlans and ever will as in deuty bound Constantly pray and bag lave to subscrybd my self Right honored Sirs your vary Obdant humbil sarvint Eliz^{h} Ware

75. *[F25/1/183] Elizabeth Ware, Newgate, undated*
Honoured Sir I humbley hope your Goodness will pardon the Liberty I take of riting as a munth is Now parst since I had aney relief hope your feeling harts have not withdrawn your kindness I would not take the Liberty of riting but being unwilling to part with those neserys wich I have bin [*illegible word*] with and further bag Lave to return my most gratfull thanks for those favors I have alredy rec^{d} and shall ever think my self in deuty bound to for ever pray in the meen time bag Lave to subscryb my self your most obdant vary Humble sarvint E. Ware

1. She was actually indicted of and tried for possession.

76. *[F25/1/177] Amelia Bellars, Newgate, undated, probably May 1810*
The Humble Petition of Amelyar Ballaiers humbley bow down to you honnared Gantlemen prayeng your Goodness will pardon the Liberty I take in thus Adrasing you haring the ship is redey wich is to Convay me and a maney more of my falow sufferes to a fare distant Country wich Gevs me grate unhapeyness being vary unprovided and my pore Child Likewise for so long a voiage most humbley bag your feeling harts will releve me with a trifell to redeem my Cloths wich through my long Confinemant I have bin obliged to part with and having no frends wich Cane rander me the smalest releff I thus take the Leberty of Adrasing you for such donatteion as it may plase you to bestow will be thankfulley Rec^{d} and as in deuty Bound will ever pray the unfertunet Ameler Ballairs Transpoart Newgate

77. *[25/1/175 & 178] Amelia Bellars, Newgate, 18 July 1810*
Gentlemen I humbly beg pardon for troubling you again, but hope and trust you will be Kind enough to forward my Memorial, to the Secretary of State [*Sir Richard Ryder*] that I may take my Departure from within those Dreary Walls, by the next Ship for New, South, Wales, which I understand their is one now a fitting out to receive Convicts on board, in August I trust you will do every thing that lays in your power for me, at the same time excuse the Liberty I have here taken – by complying with the above request – You will Much Oblidge an unfortunate prisoner Amelia Bellars
Attached: petition asking that she be sent on first available ship to NSW; she is truly contrite and would like a grant for her eight-year-old daughter to accompany her as there is no-one in England to protect her.

78. *[F25/1/177] Amelia Bellars, Newgate, 10 January 1811*
Gentelmen I humbley bag permishon to state to you that the ship wich is to Convay me and the rast of my falow suffers to a fare distant Countrey is redey and am given to understand that all are to be on bord in tan days most humbley hope that as nothing Cane be dun to extreycate me from this miserabl dwaling that your feeling harts will use your indavours to sand me a way in this ship bag lave to subscryb my self most honared Gentleman your vary humble sarvint Ameilar Balliers

79. *[F25/1/179] Elizabeth Ware, Newgate, 23 October 1810*
Gentlemen, I cannot sufficiently express my gratitude to you, not only for a former, but the present allowance of Seven Shillings per Week, you are so kindly pleased to make me, and which I have found of such essential Service to myself and Children, that I should think myself blameable indeed, were I not most gratefully to acknowledge such generosity, in the best manner I am able.
From the distressed state myself and Children were in, previously to your granting me the above allowance, I was of necessity, even for the common Necessaries of Life, obliged to Pawn or part with nearly the whole of my Wearing Apparel, which of myself, I shall never be able to redeem; I therefore have presumed (but reluctantly) to state to you, that in consequence of having received Orders to hold myself in readiness to be sent off to New

South Wales by the next Ship, which is expected very shortly to Sail; and having experienced your liberality on a former (but lamentable) occasion, emboldens me to ask permission to be allowed (and for the last time let my future fate be whatever it may) to again solicit, that you will with your usual humanity, be pleased to afford me such pecuniary assistance, as you have usually extended to such unfortunates as myself, on similar occasions.

I humbly beg leave to subscribe myself with a most greatful Heart Your most Obedient & very humble Servant Elizabeth Were [*own signature*]

80. *[F25/1/180] Elizabeth Ware, Newgate, undated*

Honored Gentelmen humbley bag permision to state to you that I am given to under stand that it is but a few day before I shall take my departure from this drery dwaling and most humbley bag pardon for thus Adrasing you being in extreem distress for what few articles wich my Long Confinemant have bin obligd to pawn most humbley pray as Mr Shuter tould me that you had heumanley ofered to remitt a trifell to redeem tham hope and trust what your feeling harts will plase to bestowe that I do not ofend in asking for it before I lave the prison as it will be imposebl to git tham whan on bord with out being defrauded of a part of the money and I will be ever Carefull to Lay it to the bast Advantedge and for such Goodness will as in deuty bound for ever Pray And bag lave to suscryb myself right honored Gentelmen your most obdant vary humble sarvant Elizabeth Ware

81. *F25/1/181] Elizabeth Ware and Amelia Bellars, Newgate, 9 February 1811*

Honored Gentelmen we unfortunet suffers Elizabath Ware and Ameliar Ballairs humbley bow down to you Craving Pardon in the Liberty we now take in troubling you but whan We had the hapeyness of seeing you yesterday we under stood that Mr Suter was to Give us the money your goodness was plased to Bestow we a Cordinly waited upon Mr Suter this morning in hopes from your Heumanety that he might have let us have the money to redeem our Cloths wich makes us both vary unhapey as Mr Suter seem to doute wether you would not be displased hope your Goodness will not think we take too grate Liberty in bagen you will be plased to sand to Mr Suter emidetly that we may Redeem our litle nessereys as with out tham our Cases will be treribly distrasing to be put on shore in a foring Country Naked and Distrast kind Gantelmen our time is vary short as Tuesday naxt is the day we expact to be put on bord and I hope and trust to have your anser by the barer wich will much alivate the sorows of the treuly unhapey Elizabath Ware and Amelir Ballairs

On reverse of page: We have bin just Cald to Mr Suter and by his desire we was to Rite to you emedtly as thare is not a momant to Loas at the same time we showd Mr Suter our Duplicats

82. *[F25/1/184–7] William Hitchen, Newgate, 13 October 1810, prosecuted for transportable offence (not against Bank), brought from Warwick gaol to Newgate, gives information on forgers, with affidavit and petition*

which Bank solicitors put before directors, who decline to forward his petition

83. *[F25/1/188–90] John Davis and John Downs, Newgate, 3 October 1810, serving six-month sentences for uttering base dollars, petition for return of property removed from them on arrest and for* some temporary relief. *Annotated:* Rejected.

84. *[F25/1/191–4] Joseph Palethorpe, 15 May and 15 June 1811, debtor in Fleet prison, demands return of mutilated note he submitted to Bank which was retained as a forgery. Bank investigator's office receipt enclosed. Copy reply from Bank solicitors instructs Palethorpe that he has no right over a forged note; the Bank always retains them.*

85. *[F25/1/195–6] Charles Cooper, Marshalsea prison, 15 October 1810, held for offence unconnected with Bank, offers to inform on dealers in forged notes; he includes list and descriptions of half a dozen he knows.*

86. *[F25/1/197] Thomas Swarbrick,* Retribution *hulk, Woolwich, 7 December 1809*
Hon^d^ Sir, It is a painful Subject which I have made bold to trouble you with a few Lines upon trusting you will have the kindness to excuse the Liberty I have taken.
The Circumstances of my Misfortune you are already acquainted with therefore it needs no comment here allow me Hon Sir to supplicate your kind interference on my behalf to enable me to procure the privilege to banish myself with my Family for Life to America, where I have Friends who will be happy to receive me and them, until I shall be able to provide for them, by my Own Industry which shall not be spared
Not doubting you will recollect having assured me and my Wife that you would not overlook my desperate situation, I have made bold thro' these means to remind you the length of Time I have now been in Confinement, experiencing the most severe hardship, and bereft of all the Necessaries of Life. I earnestly hope you will use your Interest with the Gov^rs^ of the Bank of England to induce them to grant me this indulgence, the completion of which will restore me to the greatest benefits at the Same Time fulfill the Sentence of the Law Upwards of two years Confinement will surely operate on their generosity and soften their Sentiments towards my misfortunes
to receive a Line from you acknowledging the receipt of these few Lines will confer on me a serious Obligation, and which I remain Confident you will not withold, allow Me, Hon^d^ Sir To Subscribe myself, Your Mo. Hum^e^ Servt, Thos Swarbrick

87. *[F25/1/198–9] William Banister,* Retribution *hulk, to Mr Lloyd, solicitor, Stockport, 19 March 1810*
Worthy Sir I trust my unfortunate Situation will apolligeize for my Bouldness in Riting you knowing that it lyes in your power to help mee in my

unfortunate Condishon I trust in god that you of your goodness Will speake to Mr Prescot [*Lancs. magistrate*] in my behalf to Disire him to Sine mee a petishon for liberty to Stansport my self out of the Country for the Space of my sentence as I have a friend in america where I Could live hapy the rest of my life that god permits mee to live. Sir my Situation here is bad but it is not my Punishment here that makes mee Repine it is the Loss of my poor wife and Children that I morn for look on my distress with an Eye of pity I Beg for Christ Sake and sufer mee not to remain in this [*paper torn, word illegible*] Where I am in Danger of loosing Soul and Body I am a monght 500 of the worst of men and hears nothing But Blastfaming of God's good name when I am offering up my prayers to god for my sins there is nothing but Cursing and Swearing all around mee and if I Could get out of the Country I Could in time Get my wife & Children to mee a gain and Strive to Bring them up in the love and fear of the lord that we might Save our Souls alive

my Wife will wait on you with this letter and the lord grant I may find favour in your goodness and Shall be in Duty Ever Bound to pray for you &c Your Humble St Wm. Banister

Addressed to his wife

Attached: note, 26 May 1810, from Mr Lloyd, 8, Norfolk St, Strand, passing letter to Bank solicitors without comment on content.

88. *[F25/1/200] John Bellairs,* Retribution *hulk, Woolwich, 23 March 1810*

Sir, The general Character which you bear for Humanity and benevolence encourages me to hope that you will not only pardon my giving you this trouble, but also comply with the request I am about respectfully to make – Having as you will be pleased to recollect been Sentenced to 14 Years Transportation for having Forged Bank Notes in my possession, I have been since that period (last July) confined on board this Ship, where my sufferings are very great, both of Body and Mind – As the nature of my Offence, for which I feel the utmost contrition, admits not the least hope of any mitigation of my afflicting Sentence, and as I feel I cannot possibly long survive the miseries peculiar to this horrid receptacle of the Guilty and the unfortunate, my only wish is that I may be speedily sent abroad, pursuant to the tenor of my Sentence, hoping that I may in that distant Clime by a Life of Rectitude and Industry obliterate the disgrace I have unhappily incurred, and in time retrieve that fair Character I once possessed in Society – I have heard it rumoured that a Ship is actually taken up for the purpose of conveying Prisoners to New South Wales, in the course of the ensuing Summer – Should that be the Fact, I most humbly entreat that you will in pity to my present sufferings be pleased to use your Interest in the proper Channel, that I may be included in the Number – Knowing the confidential nature of your situation, as to the Concerns of the Bank of England, and having no Friend to whom I can with propriety apply, I have presumed to address you, and earnestly hope that you will condescend to comply with my prayer – As my anxiety on this head will continue to increase, commensurate with my protracted sufferings, I have further to solicit the favor of a line in answer to this Letter, addressed as above, intimating whether I may hope for a compliance with my wishes. I beg leave to remain with the greatest respect Sir Your most humble but unhappy Servant John Bellairs

89. *[F25/1/201] John Bellairs,* Retribution *hulk, Woolwich, 9 May 1810*
Sir, I beg leave to express my heartfelt gratitude for your kind attention to my application, and for the hopes – you give me of ultimate success in your favor of the 27th March – After the assurance therein contained, I should fear you would think me presumptuous in again requesting your interference in my behalf, did I not trust that the anxiety of mind so natural to one in my unhappy situation, would plead my excuse – As the time of the Ship's Sailing for New South Wales, according to every report, is fast approaching, and knowing the multiplicity of similar applications which will no doubt be made at the Secretary of State's Office, I am fearful that mine my be overlooked, and therefore most respectfully beg that you will be so kind to take the necessary Steps in order that my name may be included in the List which I am informed will be very shortly transmitted to the Captain of this Ship –
I have also, Sir, to intreat your indulgence on another point, in which without your kind assistance, I feel myself incompetent to proceed – I have been given to understand that in certain Cases bearing a similarity to mine, the Directors of the Bank have, with their Characteristic humanity, generously bestowed on those persons, Convicted at their Instance, a small Sum of Money towards alleviating the miseries of the banishment, and to enable them to provide for their necessities on arriving at their place of destination – I therefore with the greatest deference and submission, request that you will if such a practice is not unprecedented, plead with the Honorable Company, that this their Bounty may be extended to me – as I labor under great privations, and am unprovided with the smallest matter for my future comfort – I beg leave to repeat my apology for this trouble, and am, Sir, with the greatest respect Your most obedient and obliged humble Servant, John Bellairs

90. *[F25/1/202] John Bellairs,* Indian *transport ship, Gravesend, 18 June 1810*
Gentlemen In presuming the liberty of addressing you I can only appeal to your kindness trusting you will be pleased to pardon the same
The purport of which is to acquaint you that I am on board this Ship bound for New South Wales in consequence of my conviction for Uttering forged Bank of England Bills. I do not presume to offer any thing in Vindication of my offence but with heartfelt sorrow and contrition bow down to the offended laws of my Country, at the same time acknowledge the Justice of my sentence, and humbly hope that if there is any acknowledgement made in consequence of my leaving the Country for the crime, that you will have the goodness to remit the same to me or to Captn Boulay of this Ship and address the letter on Rec^{t}. of this to Portsmouth or elsewhere, I remain Gentlemen Your Most Obt and very humble Servt John Bellairs

91. *[F25/1/203] John Bellairs,* Indian *transport ship, Gravesend, 13 July 1810*

Sir, I rely on your humanity and goodness for pardoning my once more troubling you to crave your kind interference in my behalf. Being now on the point of leaving my Native Country, probably never to return, and being destitute of Money, Clothes and every other necessary for my present or future Comfort, I have no hopes but from your known goodness of heart of which I have had such repeated proofs – About 7 Weeks ago, Sir, I took the Liberty of addressing you from on board the Retribution, respectfully entreating you to submit to the Directors of the Bank, my humble request that they would be graciously pleased (as I understood had been done in former instances to persons convicted at their Suit) to extend some little pecuniary relief to me, on my approaching departure, as the means whereby I might, with prudence and Industry make some provision for my future wants on arriving at my place of Destination – Not having been favored with an answer, I conceive it probable my Letter might not have come to hand – I now most humbly beg leave to solicit your Interest in my favor on that head, and hope it will not be thought a presumptuous or unprecedented request. I now Sir have to intreat your Charitable aid on another subject of the utmost importance to me in my unfortunate situation – At the time of my conviction I was possessed of a tolerable Stock of Clothes, which were consigned to the care of a Mr Nash, 6 George Yard, Whitechapel – On my removal to this Ship and subsequently I have repeatedly written to him, requesting that he would convey them to me without delay – A few days ago I received a decisive answer from Mr N. informing me, to my utter astonishment 'that my Clothes were pledged, and if I wished to have them, I might send the money for their redemption'. Dearest Sir, I have no Friend to whom I can apply to obtain me redress, therefore as I am confident you are an enemy to oppression and injustice of every kind, and that to your liberal mind, the pleasure of doing a good action in favor of a distressed object like myself will be its own reward, I most humbly implore that you will be pleased to take such Steps as your superior judgement may dictate, to inforce the restoration of my Clothes which are of such important consequence to me – We expect to Sail in the course of 10 or 12 days, I therefore take the liberty of hoping that you will with all convenient speed, do me the above essential favor, for which as well as all former ones received at your hands, I shall ever feel the most grateful sentiments, And am, Sir, with the highest respect Your most obedient and very humble Serv[t] John Bellars

92. *[F25/1/204] Robert George,* Retribution *hulk, Woolwich, 30 October 1810*

Sir in Consequence of me writing to you this is to inform you that I should much wish to see you to have a little talk concerning some questions that was asked me by M[r] Cristmas [*Christmas, Bank investigator*] and some other frends in Bedford and as there is a ship as I am informed to sail to new South Wales to take away prisoners from England I thus inform that by comeing or sending any person you think well to speak to me as a freind

very soon it shall be for the good of many at large I am your most Obedient humble S[t] Robert George
Annotated: No Notice or Minute

93. *[F25/1/205] Robert George,* Retribution *hulk, Woolwich, 8 November 1810*
Sir I again take the oportunity to inform you that in Consequence of the Last Letter I directed to you as I expected to have seen some of your people belonging to your Conextions respecting my Confindment Considering my heavy sentence pased on me at Bedford the tenth of last August for uttering or tendering down a note as knowing it to be a forged one tho' took it in payment being intoxecated with liquor on my return from Newmarket on friday the sixteenth of February altho I have had the sentence passed on me acording to law for the term of fourteen years its in your power to take in Consideration respecting of that business but I own that I have done very little mischief that you think I am deserving of what I have passed on me I will bear it with the greatest patience that man can do now Sir if you think well to endeavour to do me this favour I will open your eyes more than you by any means can imagine I am thoroly convincd that that unlawful Conextions ought not to be continued and by what I have to say to you that if you will bind your selves in a bond to liberate me from the sentance passed on me I will satisfy you in evry respect to the best of my knowledge as will much surprise evry reader
I am your most Obedient humble S[t] Robert George

94. *[F25/1/207] Elizabeth Leach, Newgate, 21 July 1812, formal petition*
That your Petitioner, driven to the greatest misery and absolute want, her Husband and Sister from whom She derived some little support Banished, added to a Twelve Months Imprisonment, and a very long and continued illness, with neither friends or relations to render her the smallest assistance, again ventures to humbly Implore Your generous pity and Commiseration of Your Petitioners truly deplorable Situation, & that you will be graciously pleased to grant her such temporary, or other relief, as to your humane Minds may seem most Meet And your humble Petitioner as in Duty bound will ever pray Elizabeth Leach [*own signature*]
Annotated: Petition rejected, 21 Aug

95. *[F25/1/206] Elizabeth Leach, Newgate, 2 September 1812*
Honr[d] sir I humbly hope you will not bee offended with this your unhappy petitioner has it is a unfortunate female who was convicted on the 13th of July 1811 on a Charge of uttering a one pound forged Note my husband was convicted att the same time for a simelar offence and sentenc[d] for 14 years transporttation and has Been sent away some months ago myself transport for the term of my Naturall Life and a Bad state of health prevents mee from being sent allso but am Left with these walls without a friend to assist mee or Commiseriate my unhappey Case who att the same time am Labouring under internall Complaints Deemed incureable by the faculty under these circumstances together with Extreem Distress hope you will

consider mee an object of Compassion and be humanely pleesed to Extend that generossity to mee as you have formerly done to unfortunates in my situation in what manner or as small as shall meet your approbation will be thankfully and gratefully Received by your truly humbled servant Elizabeth Leach
Hon[rd] sir I wish to add it is not my power to inform you where those fictious Notes came from for if I could I would Readily do so for the abolition of sush Nefarious practices but my husband Never would tell mee where hee had them from or who made them [*written in her own hand*]

96. *[F25/1/63/208] William Wicks, Horsemonger Lane gaol, 10 April 1812, not Bank offender, offers information on Bank note forgers which he hopes will win him favours.*

97. *[F25/1/209] John Smith,* Retribution *hulk, Woolwich, 13 September 1812*
Sirs, I hope your goodness will forgive the liberty I now take in addressing you. I am an unfortunate man fallen a victim to the laws of my country and cannot but acknowledge the justice of my Conviction. My sincere and unfeigned contrition is the only atonement I can make, but I fear my crime is of such a magnitude that it cannot be pardoned, and as I have a poor distressed Wife, and three Children, whom must in the event of my Banishment become a Burthen on my parish, I humbly beg to solicit your aid and attention to my case
I hope Gentlemen it may not be inconsistant for me to intreat you will interfere for me that my Wife and three healthy Children may be sent to New South Wales in the first ship with me – it would not only render me happy, but relieve the parish of a very heavy expence, and they would become useful to the Government.
You will I hope Sympathize with me in this trying and unhappy case, and render me the Necessary Assistance that may be in your power, to obtain the disired object – And if you would be kind enough to extend your charitable hand toward me, bearing me a little pecuniary help, I should be ever bound to pray for you – I am inform'd that a Ship is now lying at Blackwall nearly ready to Sail for that Colony as such I hope you will Gentlemen allow me to crave your early attention to this my humble Letter, which would ever be in my remembrance, and acknowledged with gratitude – I should Gentlemen be extremely glad and my mind easy if you would condescend to favor me with a reply – and remain respectfully Sirs Your most obed[t] Highly oblidged Servant John Smith

98. *[F25/1/210] William Middleton,* Retribution *hulk, Woolwich, 2 September 1812*
Gentlemen I take the liberty of writing to you on the subject of my deplorable condition which I hope you will be kind enough to excuse. I am Sir's fallen in to this Sink of inequity, yet the punishment I cannot but acknowledge to be just, but the heartrending pains for the welfare of my poor dear family is a burthen my nature can scarcely support – I have a Wife and

three small children without every means of Support – my property is consumed and nothing but poverty and distress stare them in the face.
Believe me Sirs this is a painful task, nor should I assume the liberty had you not extended your kindness already towards me and your phylanthropy so universally known.
I feel Gentlemen my crime to be of such a magnitude that it's not likely any thing should be done for me in this country, (notwithstanding I pledge this to be my only error) and as I am inform'd there is a draft shortly expected to be sent to New South Wales, I humbly intreat your influence to send me in the first Ship, so that I may by my Industry be enabled to send my Dear Wife and children a little support, but while I am confined here it is impossible, nor can I but feel a continual decay of health and strength. This I hope may induce you to comply with my humble solicitation and if you would be pleased to let your charity reach me, so that I may be enabled to purchase a few necessaries for the Voyage, and the immediate wants of my poor suffering family be relieved, I should be bound in all the ties of love and gratitude to pray for you to the latest moment of my life.
I'll not trespass longer but to beg you will condescend to favor me with an answer to this my humble Letter, which I shall ever hold gratefully in remembrance
I am Gentlemen very respectfully Your most humble and highly oblidged Servant Wm Middleton

99. *[F25/1/211] Elizabeth Morris, Newgate, 3 December 1812*
Honnoured Sir I hope you will Excuse the Liberty I have taken if you will be so kind to inform the worthy Gentleman of my Distressed situation having my Husband taken from me and has left me without any assistance with Two Small Children and in the family way now, and have not one Friend in the World to give me any Assistance hope your Goodness will Consider my Distress as I am under the Sentance of Transportation and Expcct to go away very Shortly and owing to my Misfortune we have made away with the whole of our Cloathes I hope the Worthy Gentleman will take in Consideration the Distress of the Unfortunate Wife of Tomas Slater who was found Guilty in November for Uttering A one Pound Forged Note and having one in his Possession that was also Forged the smallest assistance the Gentleman will Render I shall be for ever Bound to pray for them as I never Expect to see my Husband any more Your Humble Servant Elizabeth Morris

100. *[F25/1/212] Cathrine Watson, Newgate, undated* [*?December*] *1812, formal petition*
That your petitioner returns her most Gratefull thanks to the Gentlemen of the Bank in the liniency shewed Her in admitting her to plead guilty to the Minor Offence of having Forged Notes in her Possession in October Sessions last past at the Sessions House in the Old Baily
That your petitioner has two Small Helpless Infant Children Whom hitherto Scince her conviction She endeavoured to Support without craving any other assistance than Her own Means, but that now all her own

Resources were out She most Humbly Implores that the Gentlemen of the Bank will take her distressed Case Into consideration And Grant her Such Pecunary Aid As in thier wisdom And Judgement Seems Meet And petitioner in duty Bound Will ever Pray &c &c Cathrine Watson her Mark
Annotated: To be allowed 7/6 per week during her stay in Newgate

101. *[F25/1/213] John Smith,* Retribution *hulk, Woolwich, 11 February 1813*
Gentlemen, I now assume the liberty of addressing you with this Letter on the subject of my wretched and most melancholy condition, which liberty I trust the goodness of your hearts will forgive;
It is now upwards of Six Months since I most unfortunately offended the Laws of my Country, and was justly Sentenced to fourteen years transportation for the same;
The variety of miseries demanding and pressing upon me are more than I can describe, my pen is unequal to the task of representing the true Character of this horrible place;
In short my Life is truly wretched and would be insupportable, but that a Gleam of hope from your benevolent interference bears me up;
When I consider the goodness and generosity of your hearts (Susceptible of the feelings of humanity) I cannot but hope you will forgive this intrusion and interfere for me in any way your wisdom may deem meet, Should you condescend, and make application on my behalf with the Governor, and the Court of Directors of the Bank of England towards relieving my poor distressed Wife and Three Children who are at this time, labouring under the most poignant feelings of poverty and distress, being without protection, without Support, wounds me to the heart, but my sorrow can avail none,
You Gentlemen are aware of the unfortunate circumstance that led me here, therefore I need not trouble you with a detail of the event,
That I now presume to do is, to lay my Sufferings before you, humbly Supplicating your Kind Aid and Assistance towards releiving my distress, Should you Gentlemen intercede for me, and procure me a little Money from the Bank, towards assisting my poor distressed Wife and Children, whom I am afraid I shall never see more, when Drafted for New South Wales, which I daily expect, I most humbly beg leave to say that I shall bear the same in my memory to the latest moment of my Life and ever acknowledge the same with utmost gratitude
I therefore humbly hope you will condescend and give me a Line And have the honor to be Gentlemen Your most obed^{t} & hbl^{e} Servt John Smith
References Mess^{r} Glover & Lee [*Bank investigators*], Bank, whom I have no doubt will satisfy you respecting me
Annotated: 13 Feb 1813, Rejected.

102. *[F25/1/214] William Middleton,* Retribution *hulk, Woolwich, 10 February 1813*
Gentlemen I trouble you with another Letter and doubt not but you will allow my very wretched and distressed case to be sufficient apology more

especially when I inform you that my poor unhappy Wife is hourly expecting to be put to Bed – her case as well as mine I assure you to be the most miserable, its not in the power of my pen to describe it, nor can the heart of man conceive it, – those dire circumstances have given me the assurance of writing to you, humbly Supplicating your Sympathy
I have Gentlemen in my former Letter acknowledged with sorrow the enormity of my Crime which I shall repent to the last hour of my Life – I have followed that imprudent step but only in the event for which I am Suffering, and what little I had saved from my honest industry is now brought to nothing – In this very wretched state I almost daily expect to be removed to a Ship Bound for New South Wales, and leave my Dear Wife without the necessaries of Life, not even the smallest comfort or Support, in her present dangerous state
May I therefore Gentlemen beseech you to lend your merciful ear to my prayer and extend to me and my Dear Wife a little relief which Heaven certainly will repay you
It is unnecessary for me to trespass longer on you, therefore I beg leave to subscribe myself with all possible Submission and respect (holding most gratefully in remembrance your kind condescension in this particular) Gentlemen, Your most humble and devoted Serv[t] W[m] Middleton
PS. My poor wife is now a Burthen on the parish of Limehouse as also are my three Dear Children
Annotated: Rejected.

103. *[F25/1/215] John George Hearson,* Retribution *hulk, Woolwich, January 1813*
Sir, When I consider how universal your goodness and Phylanthropy is known I cannot but hope you will forgive the liberty I have presumed to take –
My Case Sir I trust have not been aggravated by anything perverse in me, I was Conscious of my guilt, and not willing to put you to the expence and trouble of prosecution, but pleaded guilty, and trust that you will thereby shew me a little lenity and mercy – I have prepared a petition addressed to the Right Hon[ble] Lord Viscount, Sidmouth setting forth my Case, praying clemency may be extended to me, which Petition I humbly beg to send you herewith for the favor of your Signature and Support – In the event of my being sent to New South Wales – I shall leave an only Child 12 Years of age without a friend – the very idea of which has induced me to become thus troublesome, trusting no other apology is necessary – You Sir, as an Husband – Parent – and friend, can have some idea of the state of my unhappy mind, therefore I hope you will not withold your kindness from me but in mercy to my Dear Child condescend to promote the prayer of my petition to the utmost of your power, which I should ever hold gratefully in remembrance and acknowledge with thanks – I am with every Sentiment of respect and obedience Sir, Your most humble & highly obliged Servant John George Hearson

PS I had forgotten to refer you Sir to John Lees Esq[r] one of the investigators at the Bank – that Gentlemen has known me and my Conduct some time and I have no doubt his testimony will be what you wish
To William Manning Esq[r] [*Bank director*]
Annotated: Rejected.

104. *[F25/1/216–17] John George Hearson and Hannah Hearson,* Retribution *hulk, Woolwich, 16 January 1813, formal petition*
That your Lordships petitioners were indicted at the last October Sessions held at the Old Bailey for having in their possession, Forged Bank Notes, purporting to be the property of the Governor and company of the Bank of England
To which indictment they pleaded guilty and were sentenced to be transported during fourteen years, by Sir John Sylvester K[t]
That your Lordships petitioners are most unfortunately fallen into the most miserable and Wretched of all conditions, whom with great humility begs leave to bring the particulars of their case to your Lordships view –
That they were Indicted and Arraign'd for having in their possession the said Fabricated Notes – That no other Bill could be found – and that they were induced to plead guilty to avoid the trouble and expence of a prosecution, trusting in your Lordships humanity and goodness for Mitigation of punishment – Those items they pray may come under your Lordships consideration, and render your petitioners worthy of your Lordships Sympathy
Further your Lordships petitioners begs leave to observe, that should their case be thought improper to be relieved by an extension of the Royal Mercy towards them, they pray your Lordship to send them together in the first Ship for New South Wales, and that their Daughter, 12 years of Age, their only surviving offspring may be allowed to go with them, whom from your petitioners Conviction is without every means of maintainance – Support – and protection – A Child, an Orphan without a parent, – a friend, property and Education, must be wholly dependant on the bounty of a generous public – What reflections for a parent doom'd to perpetual Banishment? Horror not to be described, nor scarcely endured when considered how very narrow is the thorny path of Virtue and Morality. It would be too presuming in your petitioners to expatiate on this most unhappy business, therefore they with all possible Reverance – Loyalty and Obedience prostrate themselves at your Lordships feet, praying most humbly Your Lordship to commisserate their case.
May it therefore please your Lordship to take this their humble Petition into your humane consideration, and in your goodness and mercy grant them such relief, as in your Lordships wisdom may be deem'd meet and your Lordships Petitioners will most humbly as in duty bound ever pray &c &c John George Hearson Hannah Hearson
Attached: further copy of petition.
[*BECLS: 20 Jan. 1813, petition read and rejected.*]

105. *[F25/1/217] Formal petition from Hannah Hearson, Newgate, 24 February 1813*
It is possible that she did not know of petition **104** *constructed by her husband, or may have believed, after a month, that she might be more effective in petitioning. She reiterates the earlier petition, but asks, through distress and several months imprisonment, for* 'temporary relief' *to maintain herself and here daughter.*
Annotated: 7/6 per week

106. *[F25/1/218–9] Richard Andrews,* Retribution *hulk, Woolwich, 4 November 1812, awaiting transportation for non-Bank offence, seeks favours from Bank by offering information about places in Birmingham and London where notes were forged and prices at which they, and counterfeit shillings, were sold. Best notes 12s. per £1 note, others 8s. or 6s.*

107. *[F25/1/220–1] William Simpson Henningham, Newgate, 12 February 1812*
Sir, if the Gentlemen of the Bank thinks they can make any use of the information I can give of the House of call for People that passes notes and Dollars &c with the name of the Person who sells them, also His hours of attendance at the said House I can also mention another Person who I Believe to be of Richmonds Party I know the street he lives but not the House or number Sir I hope if the Gentlemen of the Bank thinks the aforesaid will be of service that they will offer some conditions of pardon to me I should not wish any Person to be sent to me as there is a dout that I have informed already therefore my life would be in danger I should wish to write in Preference, I am Sir with Humble respect Yr Very Humble S[t] W. S. Henningham
Attached: copy reply from Bank solicitors, 12 Feb. 1812; they would receive his communication but no promise can be made to you as the inducement for you to give the information
[*BECLS: 19 Feb. 1812, his wife to be paid £5, and Henningham 7s. a week while in Newgate*].

108. *[F25/1/222] Note, 19 February 1812, of names and descriptions of persons involved with dealers in forged notes, a record of information of Michael Lamb, prisoner in New Prison Clerkenwell, on charge of handling 'Fleet notes'. Lamb states that, if set free, he could deal with all those mentioned.*

109. *[F25/1/223] Note, 19 February 1812, in same hand as* **108**, *records that George Payce, prisoner in Coldbath Fields prison, if set free, could deal with Burgin, a gingerbread baker of Old Street, London, and others, who deal in forged notes.*

110. *[F25/2/1–2] William Chrisford,* Retribution *hulk, Woolwich, 28 June 1813*

Sir, In the latter end of last week I saw Mr Charles Friend, he informed me that he had used his utmost endeavours to accomplish the business I promised should be done with Taverner, and has had several meetings with him on the subject, and I am sorry to say has never been able to do any thing with him, indeed I fear he has been put up to it and seems to fight Very shy – had I have been at my liberty he would not have been so cautious, and I am sure I could have accomplished it – However as the prospect of even accomplishing it appears very doubtful, and as there is a ship in all probability will be in readiness for the Bay in three or four weeks at most, and if there can nothing be done for me so as I may obtain my liberty, I would by all means wish to go to the Bay in the first Ship, and not remain any longer in this situation, I believe the most abominable place on Earth – I have also to pray of you as a particular favor, that Interest might be made with Lord Sidmouth, to permit Mrs Chrisford to go to the Bay also, as we have no child or any other incumbrance, and I am informed that His Worship is Rather favorable for Women's going with their Husbands than otherwise – My friend is to see Taverner in two or three Weeks again on the subject, but I fear it will be to no effect, however what can be done in the business, will be done – and remaining longer in suspense waiting for another ship is certainly what I do not wish and as I have used all the evidence as I can, or was in my power to accomplish the object of your wish I hope you will do me the Justice to believe it was not my fault that it failed – and that you will use your good Offices in procuring Mrs Chrisford to go with me in the same Ship, or by the first that goes after. I will thank you for a reply – I am Sir, Yo: Ob^{t} Servt Wm. Chrisford

Attached: Bank solicitors' copy reply, 30 June 1813: We received your Letter & we believe Mr Friend has used his utmost endeavour to detect the Person you mention but he informs us he suspects him. I will not deal with him at present – An application should be made by your Wife to the Secretary of State for leave to go with you & we are informed a Ship with female Convicts will sail in about a week

111. *[F25/2/3] George Barnes, William Chrisford, James Williams, Robert Johnson, George Russell,* General Hewett *transport ship, off Northfleet, 6 August 1813*

Gentlemen, We have been led to believe that the Bank in their Bounty and goodness has been so kind to Afford some little allowance of Money to those who have been so very unfortunate as to be Transported at their instance If this is the Case we whose names are to this letter signed are now on Board to make a long disheartning Voyage without a penny it would be most thankfully received if sent to us on Board the ship – We are Gentlemen your obedient humble Servants

112. *[F25/2/4] 'RW', Newgate, 24 May 1813*

Sir, I have Just been inform^{d} of a man that Deals Largly in Forg^{d} Bank Notes – his Name is truman he Lives at Birm^{m} in a Street Near the horse fair but the Name of it I Could not Learn the person that told me is a prisoner here
I am Sir Your Most Obedient Hum^{le} Ser^{nt} R.W.

[*R.W. likely to be Richard Walker,* **119–30, 190.**]

113. *[F25/2/5] James Williams,* Retribution *hulk, Woolwich 16 July 1813*
Sir, You may recollect that I was tried at Reading in Berkshire at the Suit of the Bank of England for having forged Notes found upon me, to which I pleaded guilty and Received Sentence of transportation for fourteen years – and am at present detained on Board this Hulk – The purport of this letter is to pray that you would have the goodness to endeavour to have me sent to the Bay in the Ship that is now in readiness for sailing which will take in the Convicts in the course of Eight days, and going in her would be of the greatest importance to me in my present unhappy situation, being here without One Single Shilling, and no hopes of any assistence whatever – and application from you would be immediately attended to. –
I humbly beg your forgiveness for this liberty I am Sir, your Ob[t] Servant
James Williams is the name Indicted in or now John King
PS: your answer will be thankfully received.

114. *[F25/2/6–11] Thomas White,* Savage *hospital ship, Woolwich, to Lord Sidmouth, 30 July 1813*
White, home office official working on the ship, asks Lord Sidmouth to pass information (received from prisoner, James Bartram, on Savage *for 2 years with badly ulcerated leg) to Bank about major note dealers in Birmingham. Attached: Bartram's statement; letter from Joseph Beckett, home office, forwarding White's letter to Bank solicitors; copy letter, 4 Aug. 1813, from Bank solicitors returning White's letter to Beckett, as they already know about Bartram's information; letter to Beckett from Bank solicitors, 21 Aug. 1813, saying they have sent investigator to* Savage *but expect to gain nothing.* [*Bartram sentenced to fourteen yrs trspn, Leics. summer ass. 1811.*]

115. *[F25/2/12] Henrietta Gregory, Newgate, 26 September 1813*
Hon[rd] Sir I hope you will pardon my troubling you with this a Liberty I truly hope will be overlook[d] in My Unfortunate Situation (and in My truly Distress[d] case for which I Sincerely Repent for having Committed an Error I am now Suffering for with my Poor Dear Six helpless Children who is all Unable to do any thing towards a Liveing and My Husband of a Bad State of health. I humbly Solicits your kind Benevolence and hope that My long Confindment of 14 Years Imprisonment will be taken into consideration and that During My Confindment in this Dismale Asylum you will be so Kind as to Contribute a Some thing towards Sirport of my family as My Presant Imbarestmint and Desparing is very Great. I do Earnestly hope in a little time I May be able to be of some Service to the Company – if Possiable I can with a Just foundation I will I Acknowledge the Unjustness of My crime and hope I Shall obtain Pardon from you and the Almighty I hope will Pardon me also having offended against the Laws of My country. Bleive me I never was Before ever Arraing[d] at the Bar of Justice and never did an Action to Disgrace My self or family But so Much to the Contrary my Greatest Ambission was to gain a Livelyhood for self and family By Honest Industry till this unforseen trouble Befell me – I thus State to you my Great Distress and hope you will not forget me in My Wretched and

Unhappy confindment it will not be till after Christmass that the Ship will go to the Bay. If I am to partake of your kind Benevolence to Sirport My Dear Children I shall be ever Bound to pray And am Hon[rd] Sir with Dew contrision Yr Unfortunate Prisoner Henrietta Gregory

116. *[F25/2/13] Henrietta Gregory, Newgate, 8 October 1813*
Hon[ble] Gentlemen You will Both I hope pardon me troubling you with this – having wrote to Mr Manning the Governor Stating to the Gentleman my distress Situation, with my family of Children having Six of them to sirport in my trouble Not having received any Answer to my Application I would Esteem it a very Particular favour if you will Be so Kind as to remind Mr Manning as possiable The Multiplicity of Business May have occur[d] to prevent the favour of an Answer which I truly hope will prove a favourable one in Consideration of My Great distress. I have related in My letter the Particulars of my Situation. Gentlemen I Beg leave to Apologise troubling You knowing that you are the Gentlemen who pays the Money which I sinserly hope my case will be duly considered that before I was in trouble and Sentenced for 14 Years was very Great – But being Deprived of Liberty I am no Able to Announce my trouble in Addishon to the former. When Mr Manning will do me the favour of an Answer which I hope will be a favourable in Complyance to My Humble and Submissive Regrets I shall ever be in duty bound to pray for the party conserned
I am Gentlemen With the Greatest Respect Yr truly Unhappy Prisoner Henrietta Gregory

117. *[F25/2/14] Henrietta Gregory, Newgate, 22 December 1813*
Honr[d] Gentlemen Your goodness will I hope pardon My Informing you that we have Yesterday had the overhall for the Ship and do expect to leave heer within to morrow or on Friday Morning and we are all Disire By Mr Newman that what Applications we have to Make to loose no time therefor hope Gentlemen that in consideration of My Large and truly Unfortunate family that you will consider My Distress[d] Situation Before I go away as I have many little Articles in Pledge at the Pawn Brokers which I should Be Glad to Embrace the opportunity of getting them to Day or to Morrow Christmas Day no Business will Be Done. I am Permitted to take 5 Children with me out of 6 Children which I have. I am Gentlemen with the Most gratefull thanks to you for all Past favours – and Sinserly wish you will not forget me in my Situation
I am Hon[d] Gentlemen with every dew respect Yrs Grateull & Obt Hum[le] Sert Henrietta Gregory
Annotated: 23 Dec[r] Five Pounds G. D.

118. *[F25/2/15–16] Henrietta Gregory,* Broxbournbury *transport ship, Deptford, 5 January 1814*
Most Hon[d] Gentlemen I Most Humbly beg your pardon troubling you with my Distress being truly thankfull for the favours already conferred on me I senserly hope I am not tho intruding on Your Indulgence By asking the

favour if you will Be so Kind as to Contribute to the Distress[d] family some thing More what you may think proper to Enable me to a few Necessery Articles for My five Small Children I am so Unfortunately as to be Oblige to take with me however My Unpleasant Situation is take them so Many thousand Miles and they are already very Sickly which require many little things not allowed By the Ship I hope I May be pardoned stating My case to You and hope You gentlemen will duly consider My Situation at the same time I hope not to offend
I remain most Hon[d] Gentlemen with Dew Respect Yrs very Oblige Hum[le] Sert Henrietta Gregory
Annotated: Mr Dorrien, Mr Smith 7th Jan[y] 1814 Ordered £5 more to be given her.
Attached: copy memo from BECLS secretary: Mr Smith begs leave to acquaint Mr Kaye that he has shewn Henrietta Gregory's letter to Mr Dorrien and Mr Smith and they have agreed to give her Five Pounds in addition to the like sum ordered by the Com[ee] for Law Suits on the 29th Ultimo – making it up Ten Pounds – Bank: 7th Jan[y] 1814

119. *[F25/2/27] Mary Walker, wife of prisoner in Newgate, Richard Walker, unknown address, 8 May 1813*
Sir I intreat your pardon for the great liberty I take in addressing you, and troubling you with the present state of my Familys situation. My own, your goodness has placed within reach of every necessary, yet how can I benefit by such indulgence, accompanied as it is by the recollection of my Childrens wants for these last two days Bread has been their sole support and that they are now without your unmerited kindness emboldens me to solicit your attention to them and supplicate your assistance and believe me yet, nothing short of actual necessity would compel me thus to intrude. With the most profound gratitude and respect I remain Sir, Your Much Oblided Obedient Servant Mary Walker

120. *[F25/2/17–18] Richard Walker, Newgate, 20 September 1813*
Sir I intreat my wretched situation may plead in extenuation of the liberty I take in addressing you to humbly solicit your opinion whether the Bank will approve any application made to the Secretary of State [*Lord Sidmouth*] for a mitigation of punishment my reason for this intrusion is that a friend imagines he possesses some interest which might serve me, but I declining his profer'd assistance until assured I was not acting with any disrespect towards the Bank, whose humanity to my Wife claims my gratitude and whose mercy would if extended towards me prove my salvation. Believe me Sir if the most sincere contrition merits pardon I am bold to say I might expect it, and suffer me to add the assurance previously made of necessity being the cause of my entering into such a traffic. My Family will I humbly hope be a powerful consideration in your determination I claim your pity and beg leave to assure my future life shall evince the just sence of the mercy shewn to Sir Your most Obed[t] Humble Servant Richard Walker [*in same hand as* **119**].

Attached: note of thanks to friend, J. Carless, warehouseman, who sent him £5 on day he was committed to Newgate (June 1813) with request for another £1 to pay his 'fees' [*although he was on 'Felons' Side' of prison*]

121. *[F25/2/19] Richard Walker, Newgate, 25 October 1813*
Hon Sir I humbly intreat your pardon for continuing to trouble you but hope my unfortunate situation will in a small degree plead my excuse, it is rumour'd some convicts are to go tomorrow, and if your goodness would extend so far as to prevent my being one of the number my obligations will be greatly increased.
If you could really be convinced of the treatment I have received, I flatter myself it would be considered some small extenuation of my offence – an offence nothing short of absolute necessity could have compell'd be to be guilty of – relying on your humanity only
I remain Hon^d^ Sir Your most Ob^t^ Hble Ser^t^ R Walker

122. *[F25/2/20] Mary Walker, wife of Richard Walker, 17 November 1813*
Hon^d^ Sir With feelings the most painful I presume to address you, and entreat your belief that nothing short of illness and poverty could induce me to take this liberty, but circumstanced as I am, am wholly unable to do the least thing towards my familys support, and among strangers who are pressing for their rent. With the most profound gratitude for your former benevolence, I remain with respect Hon'd Sir Your Much Obliged Humble Servant Mary Walker [*her son's writing; see* **126**]

123. *[F25/2/21] Mary Walker, wife of Richard Walker, 20 November, 1813*
Hon^d^ Sir I had hoped my continued illness would have not caused me to continue to address you, but truly unfortunate, have in addition to deplore that of three of my Children's illness with heartfelt gratitude for past favors, humbly entreat your relief this is the last time I dare presume to address you which nothing short of necessity could compel me now to do
With great respect I remain Hon^d^ Sir Your Much Obliged Grateful Servant Mary Walker [*same hand as* **121**].

124. *[F25/2/22] Mary Walker, wife of Richard Walker, 30 November 1813*
Hon^d^ Sir I have taken the liberty to acquaint you that Mrs Dale's name stands upon the List at Hick's Hall [*Mdx Quarter Sessions*] I understand she means to take her trial and am certain no pains will be spared to mortify and insult me. as I have acted according to your direction throughout the business, I beg leave to request your further instructions, being myself wholly unacquainted with proceedings of this nature and wholly unprovided should any expence attend it. If it goes to trial I imagine it will be necessary to request the attendance of Mr Abrahams who promised to come forward & state the assault as he witness'd it. From Mrs Dales known Character I am convinced should I be deficient, she will heartily exult waiting respectfully your commands Remain Hon^d^ Sir Your Much Obliged Ser^t^ M Walker [*same hand as* **123**].

125. *[F25/2/23] Richard Walker, Newgate, 20 December 1813*
Honor[d] Sir Fully sensible of the great liberty I take in addressing you I trust the unfortunate cause will plead my pardon, I am concerned to inform you my Wife has been confined to her Bed these ten days with Rheumatic Gout which has deprived her of the use of all her limbs and now lies in the greatest state of wretchedness and unable to procure the necessaries her state requires, under these afflictions humbly intreat your benevolent representation of her case hoping (tho without claim) that charity will prompt so opulent a Body to relieve the afflictions herein mentioned, with the most profound gratitude for favors already received I remain Honor[d] Sir Your most Obedient Humble & Unfortunate Servant Richard Walker

126. *[F25/2/24] Mary Walker, wife of Richard Walker, 23 December 1813*
Hon[d] Sir I am informed that it is your desire I should write a letter before I received the 5 pounds which the generosity and humanity of the governors and directors of the Bank have bestowed upon me I beg leave to state through the medium of my sons pen the unfortunate impossibility of my acceding to your desire as I am incapable of making the smallest use of either of my hands and that I am totally deprived of the use of all my limbs my son would have brought this himself but having an uncertain situation in the docks I am fearful if he Omits one days attendance he might be discharged the next with great respect and gratitude I remain Hon[d] Sir your Obedient Humble Servant, Mary Walker [*son's writing*].

127. *[F25/2/25] Richard Walker,* Retribution *hulk, Woolwich, 27 January 1814*
Sir, With the greatest reluctance I communicate to you my wretched situation and what renders it still more cutting. Mrs W. has not the powers to assist me in the least way having been confined to her Bed these last eight Weeks and upwards with the Rheumatic Gout under such melancholy suffering, I trust your goodness will pardon the liberty I have taken and allow me a trifle to procure a few necessaries this place and the severe season of the Year requires. I am now in possession of such circumstances that would render the Bk. the greatest service and had I my liberty could I am sure be acted on immediately relying on your generous Ans[r]. I remain Sir with the greatest Gratitude Your most ob't and very Hble Ser[t]. Richard Walker

128. *[F25/2/26] Mary Walker, wife of Richard Walker, undated*
Hon[d] Sir I hope you will Pardon the liberty I take in acquainting you that I have just received a letter from my unfortunate husband on board the hulk written in the most afflicting terms and earnestly requesting me to cause another petion to be presented in his behalf for which reason I take the liberty of troubling you for your Opinion on its utility with Gratitude and Respect I Remain Hon[d] Sir your Obedient Humble Servant M. Walker [*son's writing*].

129. *[F25/2/28] Mary Walker, wife of Richard Walker, 10 March 1814* Hon^d Sir Some weeks past you were kind enough to say you would present any Petition in my Husbands behalf which should come to your hands, but the doubts you express'd concerning its success and my severe illness prevented my taking advantage of your extreme goodness, but I cannot acquit myself of negligence without enclosing a part of a letter which he desired you might be made acquainted with. After thirteen weeks confinement, deprived of administering the smallest relief to his necessities, I have just heard he is going on Board the Somersetshire, for New South Wales, without a Shilling in his pocket, or Cloaths beyond those worn in the Hulks. You Sir will I certain commisserate my feelings and if I cannot procure the means of going to Gravesend to take perhaps an everlasting farewell I shall be the most wretched of beings. Pain & Want I have patiently endured but Shrink from the thought of never seeing him again. What I dare not solicit your humanity will I humbly hope suggest, and the obligations will be doubled Hon^d Sir Your Obliged and Obedient Servant M. Walker [*in hand used in Richard Walker's letters*].
Attached: two pages of letter in same hand, from Richard Walker to his wife, first page entirely crossed out, second partly crossed out.
First page: I will not distress you. Remember Mary, God is above all the world and knows all things, you must know. Spontaneously alias C. C--r [*Charles Cooper,* **145–6**] is dead, he departed this life poor Soul, on Saturday last in our Hospital Ship which lays close along side of our Ship he certainly was greatly indepted to me but he very cruelly and very ungratefully repaid me. I truly forgive him. I hope God will also forgive him there is one of my great enemies gone before me he has been at the Hospital Ship some time before I came down here. It is rather singular my other great enemy, Henry Dale although you know I never gave reason for him so to be went over to the Hospital Ship the day the other died with the Itch and being other a ways Ill. Therefore you see they were prevented doing me further mischief together being well matched for such wicked purposes. I Sincerely thank God for all his mercies, although ill I make no …
Second page: following request and informations I flatter my self be equally attended to as I have not the least doubt if so they will accomplish the design wished for. Viz. I am on the Word of a man and by all thats good and sacred in possessions of three Persons who was I at liberty tomorrow I could act on the next day. One has been selling for many years and is worth some thousands a man I can deal with at any time. The others also. I repeat to you again what I now write is no subterfuge but real facts surely my Dr Mary, M^r W--d [*Westwood, Bank solicitors' clerk*] should be seen properly and informed of it, he can do all if he thinks fit and observe the remainder of my life should be to their interest and my own imploy. Let me hear from you the moment you receive this but be careful how you write, its impossible for me to send my old things …

130. *[F25/2/29] Mary Walker, wife of Richard Walker, 5 White Cross Street, 5 September 1814*
Hon^{d} Sir, The condescending attention I have so repeatedly experienced induces me to hope you will pardon the further liberty I take of soliciting your interest. Having obtain'd permission for myself and Family to follow their Father to New South Wales, in a Ship expected shortly to sail, I presume through your means to solicit the Humane, and generous consideration of the Gentlemen of the Bank, without whose assistance I shall be unable to avail myself of the privilege extended towards me, my Family being destitute of common necessaries. I intreat your belief, Sir, that necessity alone could compel me to intrude after the obligations conferr'd, and for which my lasting gratitude is due, and with Humility beg your consideration of the Family for whom I plead, and that this last entreaty will fix their Fate, and I presume to hope satisfactorily to the feelings of those Gentlemen whose benevolence shall rescue them from Poverty, and restore them to a Parent. I beg leave to assure you Sir that the remembrance of your kindness can never be obliterated.
and remain with great respect Hon^{d} Sir, Your Obliged Humble Servant Mary Walker
[*BECLS: 8 Sept. 1814, Bank to pay £10 if her story true.*]

131. *[F25/2/30] Thomas Foss, Newgate, 21 September 1813*
Mr Harper, Sir, In my present unhappy situation I make bold humbly to request the favour of your kind interference in my behalf to the Governor and Directors of the Bank of England who I formaly had the honour to serve and shall be happy to give up the Engraver and every information that lay's in my power in mitigation of my punishment and what light I may be enabled to throw respecting bad Notes I hope will be satisfactory to the Governors & Directors of the Bank. It is also my I intention to apply by my Solicitor to the Court of Directors, but It is my opinion that your kind interference would greatly benefit my situation Sir with every relyance on your goodness that you will lay this before the Honble Court of Directors I remain Mr Harper an Unhappy Prisoner T Foss
[*BECLS: 29 Sept. 1813, rejected*].

132. *[F25/2/31–7] Thomas Foss, Newgate, 25 September 1813*
Mr Harper, Sir In my present situation it cannot be supposed that my recollection can be so clear as it otherwise would be I have humbly to request the favour of your laying this before the Governors and Directors of the Bank stating that if I give up the Engraver 3 or 4 Principles and 14 others which will lead to a discovery of the principal Makers in England also coiners. If the Governors and Directors would kindly extend mercy towards me so far as to mitigate my sentence to Transportation for Life would be all I should require of their Goodness. I have not the least doubt but I can give the Governors & Directors such information as I hope will surpass their expectations. Mr Harper Sir A Miserable prisoner Thomas Foss
[*BECLS: 29 Sept. 1813, rejected.*]

Attached: Foss's petition forwarded to Bank solicitors by Mr Price, 28, St John Square, 13 Oct. 1813; it asserts Bank's refusal to allow him to plead to lesser offence, his innocence of forgery though admitting possession, his betrayal by accomplice, who misled jury, and offers whatever information Bank requires about forgers and mentions another petition sent to Prince Regent for mitigation of death sentence to trspn for life. [*Petition read at BECLS, 20 Oct. 1813, and rejected*]*; letter from John Matt of Chelmsford complaining that Bank had not paid him expenses for being witness in case against Foss, requesting compensation for time lost and for his inability to take his horse to be sold on day of hearing in London; copy letter from Bank solicitors acknowledging receipt of Matt's letter, enclosing £2 for loss of time, adding:* You cannot expect the Bank to compensate you for the loss you may have sustained in not selling your Horse

133. *[F25/2/35] Thomas Foss, Newgate, 5 October 1813*
Mr Westwood, Sir, I am very much surprised to hear that you never saw the papers the morning last. Before my trial I requested Mr Price to solicit the Bank Directors to let me plead guilty which Mr Price informed me the Directors refused. The first week I was in the Cells I made the papers out with the intention of having them laid before the Directors in hopes of mitigation of punishment. I am sorry to hear was totally neglected, Sir be assured though I purchased the Press it was not for myself the plate was Engraved for the same party that the press was bought for. I was only employed to print out at [*two illegible words*]. Sir, I think the crime I have been guilty off my papers will atone for the capital tomorrow is Court day with the Directors if you will have the goodness to lay this before the Court I will esteem it as a favour Sir Your Unhappy Prisoner Thos Foss

134. *[F25/2/36] Thomas Foss, Newgate, 5 November 1813*
T. Foss's respects to Mr Kay and requests the favour to know that if information is given to the Bank for the benefit of the company and society in general I shall be happy to know if the Directors of the Bank will give a free pardon to two witnesses absolutely necessary for the conviction of others implicated in the Note trade be so obliging as to favour me with an answer in writing by bearer. If the above pardon is granted I will engage that every communication is made Sir Your Very Humble Servant, Thos Foss

135. *[F25/2/38] Elizabeth Jones, Newgate, 20 April 1813*
Gentlemen, Elizabeth Jones unfortunately convicted during the present Old Bailey Sessions, a poor widow, with three Children dependent on her for their daily support and having disposed of every thing she possessed to discharge the various expence of her confinement, destitute of every hope of pardon & of any means to procure further support for herself & her unhappy Offspring – it is her most ardent wish to be sent out of the Country as soon as possible. In the meantime she most humbly implores your humane attention for some pecuniary aid which may enable her to satisfy the wants of nature till that period of her departure shall arrive – for such a

favor your humble petitioner will ever bear the most lively sense of gratitude for so distinguishing a favor while she begs permission to remain With every degree of respect most gratefully Gentlemen Y[r] Obed[t] Serv[t] E Jones

136. *[F25/2/40–1] Elizabeth Jones, Newgate, undated early May 1813*
Gentlemen Nothing but the greatest Distress would have urg'd me to write to you, but at the same time Knowing of your Kindness to others who have been unfortunately plac'd in my situation, and at the same time having three Fatherless Children to Look to without any means of Support I am induced to write to you in this way – for the purpose of beseeching you to grant me some assistance During the Short time I may remain here
Your Kindness in So Doing will never be Effaced from the Mind of Yr. Hmble Sert. E Jones [*own signature*]
Attached: copy note from Bank solicitors, 8 May 1813, stating her letter laid before governors and directors of Bank who decline to make allowance.

137. *[F25/2/43–4] Elizabeth Jones, Newgate, 10 May 1813*
Sirs Your very indulgent favour in laying before the Governors and Directors of the Bank of England my application for their usual bounty is felt by me with the utmost sentiment of respect; and in humbly transmitting to your Disposal the respectful statement of my unhappy condition you will please kindly to make every allowance for the necessary importunities of a miserable sufferer. I am, Sirs, Your most humble and anxious petitioner Eliza Jones [*own signature*].
Attached: petition reiterating her distress; states she was unfortunate enough to have accompanied another woman [*Jane Smith, her servant,* **139**] *who passed the note; she was not in the habit of doing so.*

138. *[F25/2/42] Elizabeth Jones, Newgate, 15 June 1813*
Hon[d] Gentlemen I most humbly request your indulgence of this fresh prayer of your kind favor in my behalf, on the expected departure of a ship for New South Wales with those women sentenced to transportation; unaided by friends and sinking with the miseries threatening my three helpless infants, I implore the bounty of the worthy Directors of the Bank for some little assistance towards my unhappy outfit; and, though my added error has hitherto excluded me from their usual charity, perhaps your tenderness may induce you, in consideration of my distress and that from better circumstances I did not on the former occasion make any solicitation, to afford me an allowance at this melancholy crisis
I am, Sirs, Your most respectful and very Humble Servant, Elizabeth Jones [*own signature*].

139. *[F25/2/39] Jane Smith, Newgate, 20 April, 1813*
Hon[rd] Sir You will I hope pardon the Liberty I take in writing to you But having the Sentence[d] for 14 years I am truly very Much Distress and would

Be Very Much Oblige to you if you will take it into Consideration to Assist me – as I have no friends, or Relations only a Mother and not in her power to render me the least Assistance whatever as the Clothes I had when taken I have Been oblige to part with and as the Ship is Expected to go very Shortly it will Be Very Exceptable whatever you will please Remitt to me I am with Duty Honrd Sir Yr Very Obt Hum^{le} Ser^{t} Jane Smith

140. *[F25/2/45] Jane Smith, Newgate, 25 June 1813*
Honble Gentlemen Jane Smith presents her duty and hopes that the Honble Gentlemen will take it into consideration and Make an advance to Assist me to get a few things about me. Being so Much distress and finding that Mrs Elizabeth Jones [**135–8**] has received Money Yesterday from you I think it Extremely hard as I was lately led away and was Inosent in the Business. I only lived Servant one Month with her and to be drawn in and now be under the Necessity to be oblige to leave my Country for 14 Years is very distressing and to leave it in such a very distress manner I shall be oblige to do [*illegible word*] I have a little of your kind Assistance as Mrs Jones has not given me one halfpenny, I am convicted for the same Offence and I suffer the same as she does. A hard case its therefore my trouble is not to be describe having had no Assistance from any one But my poor old Mother that gets her bread By very hard Laibour – we go away on Monday and truly hope my Application will be look into with an Eye of pitty and compassion as my distress is beyond Discription that every one knows in the Prison I am Honble Gentlemen with every due respect Your Very Obt Hum^{le} Servt

141. *[F25/2/46] Hannah Hearson, Newgate, 14 April 1813*
Gentlemen You persume I have taken the Liberty to send to you for the Money I've received so far fm. the Hands of the Bearer if agreable to you will thank You to send to Day for the Bearer or in what Manner you think Proper I am Gentlemen Yrs Very Obt Hum^{le} Servt Hannah Hearson
Annotated: Paid 15/

142. [*F25/2/47] Cathrine Watson, Newgate 14 April 1813*
Gentlemen I have taken the Liberty to send to you for the Money that is dew and ask you Please to Remitt the Same to the Bearer will be thankfully Receiv^{d} from Your Most Obt Hum^{le} Sert Cathrine Wattson
Annotated: Paid 15/-

143. *[F25/2/48] Hannah Hearson, Newgate, 24 June 1813*
Honble Gentlemen This is no doubt the last Application I shall be under the Nessescity to write to you having this Afternoon got some final orders from Mr Newman to prepare for the Ship on Monday Therefore hope Gentlemen you will dewly consider our Situation of Being Banished from our Native land for 14 Years. I Senserly Return You Thanks for all favours I have Rec^{d} att your hands and that you will contribute some thing to Make me & My Child Comfortable This is my last application and hope not

trouble you any more I am Honble Gentlemen with evry dew Respect Hannah Hearson

144. *[F25/2/48] Cathrine Watson, Newgate, 24 June 1813*
Honble Gentlemen With Humble Submission I return you my senscere Thanks for all favours you have conferr'd on me and my Children. Mr Newman has this Afternoon Been round to inform us to prepare for the Ship on Monday therefore hope Gentlemen hope you will condescend to contribute some More to get a few things for My Children and self as The Voige will be some Months That will be Requisite and Nessesary and May every Blessing Attend you
This being the last Application I shall trouble you for hope you will comply with My Request
Hon^{le} Gentlemen Yr Very Obt Hum^{le} Sert Cathrine Watson [*same hand and on same piece of paper as* **143**].

145. *[F25/2/49] Charles James Cooper, Newgate, 9 June 1813*
Sir, Having no Friend but two sisters at a great distance in penurious Sircumstances and to stand as a mediator for me in my behalf – have most humbly to pray you will of your goodness & humanity be pleased Recommend the petition which the Bearer hereof will shew you & you by so doing will add one more great favour to him who is in deep distress having nothing but the [*gaol*] alowance to subsist on & is with the greatest respect Your Humble Pettitioner Chas Ja^{s} Cooper

146. *[F25/2/50] Charles James Cooper, Newgate, 5 July 1813, formal petition*
That he is now with the utmost contrition Justly suffering the sentence of the Law, being truly sensible of the inormity of his Offence, that he is in his sixty third year of his Age, and hath a Wife and two infant Children in the greatest distress, the oldest not more than Five years of Age, notwithstanding the Justice of his sentance, he cannot Divest himself of the Feelings of a Husband, and a Father, That the distress of my Wife and Children are more painful to him then his own suffering, they being inocent, and he Guilty, – that before his unfortunate confinement he used to pay, Eight shillings per week for his Eldest Childs support, that he has nothing but the Gaol Allowance, that his Wife cannot at presant get Bread for herself and Two small Children, he therefore most humbly prays and emplores you will of your Goodness and ~~bounty~~ heumanity be pleased to Assist her to Enable her to subsist until she can be relieved by the Parrish, praying humbly that you will of your liberality and Charity consider the Deep distress of his Wife and Family, and he and Family will as in duty Bound ever pray &c &c Chas. Ja^{s}. Cooper
Your Petitioners Wife will wait on you for An Answer she resides at No 1 Smiths Court Opposite St Andrews Church Holborn
[*BECLS: petition rejected, 7 July 1813.*]

147. *[F25/2/51] Edward Abell, Newgate, 4 May 1813*
Gentlemen I hope you will pardon the liberty taken in addressing you. I am sorry to say that my wife and 4 Children are in great distress, even want the Necessarys of Life – I need not Inform you that I was convicted last Sessions at the Suit of the Crown – and sentenced to 14 years Transportation – I have been Informd that some allowance has been made to the wife and family of Persons in my Situation – I therefore most humbly Implore your Interference in my behalf of my wife and Infant Children who are really distressed, your Kind Compliance – will very much Obge Gent^{n} your distressed & truly Unfortunate Hb St Edward J. Abell

148. *[F25/2/52] W. E. Hardy, Newgate official, June 1813*
Informs Bank solicitors that order received by Mr Newman (keeper of Newgate) for removal to transport ships of convicts Elizabeth Jones and Mary Roberts.

149. *[F25/2/53] Davenport Sedley, gaol servant, Newgate, 13 September 1813*
Reminds Bank solicitors that he had given information about George Barnes [**111**] *and Richard Walker* [**119–130**] *which led to their apprehension, trial and sentencing. He complains that Walker is still in Newgate and that Bank is maintaining him and his 'mistress' Mary Glover since they are providing useful information, yet he, Sedley, did not receive any money for his services. Offers further service in relation to Thomas Foss, bank printer* [**131–4**] *now in Newgate; he can find out from him more details of his network provided Bank delay prosecution; a further complaint is made that when Bank investigator, Lee, came to see him to obtain information, keeper of gaol was present:* private information should be privately received; otherwise, my life would be in danger in this place

150. *[F25/2/54] James Charlesworth, Horsemonger Lane gaol, 14 April 1814*
Fined and sentenced Oct. 1813 to twelve months in gaol for uttering counterfeit coins at Camberwell Fair, reminds Bank he gave them information on note forgers and complains he received no reward; he has new information from Mr Pritchard, overlooker of printing business, 31, Essex Street, Strand, who brought him lists of the Ladys with Indecent cuts in them *and knows identity of printer.*

151. *[F25/2/55–60] Set of papers from and about Edward Millson, various (non-prison) addresses in London, 6 June 1812 to May 1813*
Millson, apprehended June 1812 on suspicion of uttering a forged £5, claims against Bank for four days wrongful imprisonment before they decided not to indict him, for reimbursement of amounts he paid for keep in prison and to his solicitor (totalling £8 7s. 6d.), and compensation for insults received in the street since imprisonment, loss of job as book keeper to city firm, and conditions suffered on remand in New prison Clerkenwell. Papers comprise memorials and affidavits dated 8 July 1812, 10 Dec.

1812, and 9 Apr. 1813, and covering letter from lawyer, John Pownall of Staple Inn, emphasising Millson's current hardship. Also included is copy of Bank solicitors' response, 6 May 1813, that Millson not entitled to compensation as there was sufficiently good reason for arresting him.

152. *[F25/2/61] Henry Dale, Coldbath Fields prison, 12 May 1813*
Sir In conformity with your request I resume my pen for the purpose of communicating to you my Knowledge relative to Forgerys on the Bank, which I can be the means of detecting by going to Birmingham (Viz) the Engraver, Printer, Paper Manufacturer. If the Bank therefore with this assurance realized, I prescribe the following plan to go to Birming[m.] accompanied by Joseph Becket head turnkey to Mr Adkins in my own way of business, to apply to the partys alluded to who will readily serve me with what the Bank wishes me to purchase, for the said Joseph Becket to be in waiting at the time I pay for the Goods Ordered & at that time to make his seizure of the persons concerned. This I consent to do on the broad scale of humanity being most decidedly of opinion its the only branch of Forgery on the Bank of England in Birming[m.] (the detection of which is not at all improbable from the Am[t.] of Notes dayly executing) that it might save hundreds from falling Victims to the Gallows activated with a desire to serve community as well as restore myself to the sweets of liberty I am ready and willing to fall into the measures here laid down, conditionally that I am not again taken to any public Office for farther examination as it would defeat my plans in Birming[m.] moreover that on the partys in Birming[m.] alluded to having taken their respective Tryals, that I shall be at liberty to transport myself to any part of the World – Engl[d] – Ireland Scotl[d] & Wales excepted – for the term to be hereafter agreed upon & for the Bank of England to Furnish me with the means so to do allowing me 1 Mo. to arrange my Affairs in prior to my leaveing England – your Kind consideration as soon as convenient to lay before the Committee or whom you please will greatly – ObligeYour Obdt Hble St H. Dale
P.S. My motive for wishing Joseph Beckett to accompany me is I am acquainted with him & Mr Adkins has every confidence in his discharging faithfully any power the Bk. may invest him with

153. *[F25/2/62] Ann Dale, wife of prisoner, Henry Dale, 23, Tower Street, Westminster Road, 17 April 1814*
Most Hon[le] Gent Pardon the intrusion of an unfortunate and unhappy Woman, who with Two uneducated Children have been reduced by one fatal Act of a Wretched Husband and Father, to the deepest distress, permit me most humbly to Inform you, I am the Wife of Henry Dale now a convict on board the Somersetshire, waiting a conveyance to New South Wales.
A humble Conviction of your humanity so often extended to <u>others</u> placed in distressed Situations equal to my own, induced by a wish to support and Educate my now Fatherless Children, emboldens me to hope you will consider me as deserving your distinguished Consideration, and humanely induce you to afford me pecuniary Aid, to assist me in the purchase of a Mangle, or to place me in some way whereby I may be enabled to support

myself and Children – Permit me Most Honble Gent to inform you, that the little I once possessed have long since been sacrificed in contributing to the support of my unhappy Husband and Children – or I should not have presumed to make this appeal to your humanity. Praying your early answer, permit me to subscribe myself Most Honble Gent with the highest sence of gratitude Your most Obed^{t} Hum^{bl} Servant Ann Dale

Annotated: £5 [*BECLS: 20 Apr. 1814, confirms payment as not involved in crime*].

154. *[F25/2/63] John Vesey Low, unspecified prison, about 10 May 1813*

Hon^{d} Sir Tis with all that Diffidence which a Man in my situation must feel at Writing to the very Body that i have Injured, for his favour in this my fallen Condition, But it is the Boast of an Englishman, Tho a Criminal that in the humane Administration of the Laws of this my native Country, he the fallen Victim Draws upon his head the just sentence of the Law for the Crime he has committed is still Allowed the indulgence of Appealing to the feeling Breast of his Countrymen for that Mercy he in some Measure may Consider himself entitled to –

And so a Being truly Unfortunate I Beg with all humility, Not Wishing in the smallest Manner to be, by you Considered less Criminal nor for any Commutation in my just sentence for i was sensible i was Doing Wrong, many of the Wisest & Best of Men has been tempted to Commit wrong Which at Other times they would feel themselves Incapable of –

But Sir, I fear i am trespassing upon your time, have Duly Weighd in my Mind my situation and that of my unprotected family. It is the humble Prayer of my Wife and Self on the Behalf of my Children that they may be Allowd to Accompany me over to the place of my Destination for we each have but a miserable existence at present i hope to go the earliest Moment and if to go in the same Ship with them i should feel undescribable happiness, which i am informed is not Unusual by your humane Interference and shoud my Conduct in future when transplanted upon a foreign Earth intitle me to favour or Indulgence from the Governor or Superior placed over me Myself and Family for such Mercifull Grant will ever in Gratitude feel ourselves Bound to pray for such a Mark of your Goodness I further Beg to Subscribe myself Hon^{d} Sir, you very Humble Ser^{vt} John Vesey Lowe

155. *[F25/2/64] Petition on behalf of Sarah Fell by her parents, Charles and Anne Fell, countersigned by Charlotte Clarke of Islington who had Sarah's sister in her service. Fell held in Clerkenwell New prison on suspicion of uttering a forged note in City Road. They claim her innocence. Petition rejected by Bank. Acquitted at trial, OB, June 1813.* [*BECLS: 21 & 28 Apr., 9 June 1813; HO 26/19 records her as a* 'bad character'.]

156. *[F25/2/65–6] John Hopgood,* Retribution *hulk, Woolwich, 26 November 1813*

Sir The Convinceing proofs I have had of your Humanity and philanthropy, to alleviate the misfortunes of the oppressed, had induced Me now to take the liberty of addressing you upon the present unhappy and melan-

choly event as you are in possession of the Circumstances relative to my apprehension and Conviction I shall not enter into a long and labored defence, but can assure you I have been the Dupe of others who now laugh at my Credulity it is the most earnest wish of my unfortunate Wife as Well as Myself that She should accompany Me to New South Wales. I am Good Sir Destitute both of money and Friends, permit Me most earnestly to solicit your favour and Goodness to use your interference with the Govrs and C[o] of the Bank of England and thereby obtain permission for My Wife to accompany Me, and afford Me some small Pecuniary aid which will greatly oblige Yours respectfully, John Hopgood.
Attached: petition from his wife Mary, 1 Jan. 1814, permitted to sail with him, asking relief *since she was taking their child with her and had sold all her* 'things' *to support herself and husband while he was in prison. Mary given £5 on sailing.*

157. *[F25/2/67–8] Henry Russell,* Retribution *hulk, Woolwich, 23 November 1813*
Gentlemen Pardon the liberty I take in addressing you upon the present unhappy and melancholy events as you are in possion of the peculiar nature of the Case and likewise the Defence I made on the Day of my Trial when Baron Graham prisided at the Court I shall not presume to enter into the merits or demerits of the Case, but bow with due submission to the Sentence which has been passed upon me most solemnly do declare that I was grosely deceived and imposed upon with regard to the Notes, which has brought down such disgrace upon my Family, and misery upon my unoffending head I Received the notes in question from one Thomas Langley for a Debt due to me at that period conceiveing that the Notes were Lawful Money of Great Britan thus innocently did I become the Dupe of the above named Thomas Langley who has since been Executed for Forgery. It is the proudest moment of my Life amidst the difficulties which sourround me to make known to you Gentlemen that the Earl of Abingdon Lord Spencer Fenn Esq[r] Member of Parliament[2] and some of the finest Nobility in the Kingdom have kindly interested themselves in my behalf Permit me at the same time to represent that I have already endured nearly Five years solentary Imprisonment durcing which Period my sufferings have been Grate both in mind and Body, and my health is in consequence much impaired for these reasons as well as in Consideration of my Gene-aral Good Character and for the sake of my Afflicted Wife and Family most earnestly do I implore Gentlemen that you will extend unto Me your favour and Goodness and thereby obtain His Majestys Most gracious Pardon, or such mitigation of Sentance as in your Profound Wisdom you may deem meet – and should it not be in your power to Comply with this

2. The writer's use of these names is problematic. It seems unlikely that he knew the people to whom he refers. It is likely that he means three people: the earl of Abingdon; the Earl Spencer; and, possibly, Henry Fane (knighted in 1815), MP for Lyme from 1802-18 being the only parliamentarian at the time with a name which could have been construed as 'Fenn'.

my most earnest request and Intreaty permit Me to solicit the favour that you gentlemen with your known humanity will render Me some small assistance previous to my leaving Endland and as in duty Bound I shall ever pray

I have the Honour to be Gentlemen Your most Obd^{t} Humble Servt Henry Russell

Attached: copy letter from Bank solicitors, 25 Nov. 1813, stating governors & directors decline to interfere any further than they have already done.

158. *[F25/2/69] Charles Games,* Retribution *hulk, Woolwich, 23 November 1813*

Sir Your goodness will I trust pardon the liberty I take in addressing you, but the unhappy situation I am placed in, and the deep distress my Family and Respective Relatives are involved in will I trust plead an excuse for my so doing. Permission has been granted by My Lord Sidmouth for My Wife and Son to accompany Me to New South Wales since my Conviction my sufferings have been great, and are likely to be rendered stil greater, unless releaved in some measure by the humane interference of the Governors, and Company of the Bank of England; I cannot finish this Sir written under the pressure of many and harassing Concerns without begging You will accept my best Thanks and gratitude for saveing my Life which it was in Your power to deprive Me of and most earnestly do I implore that You will with Your known humanity recommend Me as disserving some small pecuniary assistance from the Govrs and C^{o} of the Bank of England previous to my leaving my native Country as I am destitute both of Money and Friends, and as in duty Bound I shall ever Pray – &^{tr}

I am Sir With the profoundest Respect Your Most Obdt Humble Servt Charles Games

Annotated: M$^{r.}$ Kaye be authorized to adv^{ce} him £ [*illegible amount*]

[*BECLS to investigate his request, 1 Dec. 1813, and if true give wife £5 on sailing.*]

159. *[F25/2/70] John Pearson,* Retribution *hulk, Sheerness, 10 July 1814*

Hon^{d} Sir, I beg the liberty of this letter Imploring your Humane attention in A Case so truly lamantable, As I am labouring under the most excruciating agony of Mind, attended with the several Necessities Occationed by my late Conviction and Sentence, Induces me to Solicit your Assistance in Causing to be Returned the Money that was taken from me and Eliz^{h} Pearson on the evening of our Apprehension, I Beg Pardon for attempting to Recover the Money which was taken from Eliz^{h} Pearson alias Wright as it is far from my Intention. But as we are as One, you will excuse me – And as we must enevatibly leave this Country very shortly, A little Money will be of an Infinite Service to One or both of us, therefore I beg you will be Pleased to Remitt to me on Bord this Hulk or to Eliz^{h} Pearson at Newgate, that Part of the Money which was taken from us, and not returned – Therefore I will give an Account of the Money that was taken from us and what we Received, which is as follows, Viz. from Eliz^{h} Pearson £3 3s- and from myself £1 14s 9½d, with 3s/6d from our lodgings which Amounts to £5 1s

3½d, and all we Received was £1 12s 6d therfore £3 8s 9½d remains. Wherfore should you be pleased to Cause the Above to be Returned as I have Above Directed, you will Hon^d Sir for ever Oblige Your Most Obedient Servant John Pearson

160. *[F25/2/71] T. Birch, New Prison Clerkenwell, 2 September 1813 to landlord of Admiral Benbow public house, Golden Lane. Awaiting hearing before magistrate at Worship Street for uttering counterfeit Bank tokens, he requests landlord to put in a good word for him.*

161. *[F25/2/72] William Holland, Marshalsea prison, 25 October 1813 Held for having half a forged £50 note in his possession, he explains his distress and asks Bank to get him out.*

162. *[F25/2/73] J. Atkinson, prison employee, Newgate, December 1813 Offers Bank useful information if they will call on him.*

163. *[F25/2/74] Mary England, Newgate, 29 April 1814*
Honred Sir I hope you Will Excuse the Liberty I take in troubling you With this I have Been so Unfortunate as to be in Newgate on the Account of the Bank Business Honred Sir I have Four Small Children and no one to Maintain them But my Selfe as my Husband has Left me and is Gown to Sea I Was tryed in February Sessions and I have been Obliged to Part With all my Cloathes and Every thing that I had to Support my Selfe and Children But I hope that God Will Punnesh the Wicked man that Braught me in to it and I Shall be Ever Greatfull if you Should be so kind to think of me in My distress and My Children if it is Ever so Small a trifle I Shall Be very thankfull I hope you Will Excuse the Liberty that I have taken in troubling you With this and if you should think of me I should be in duty Bound to Pray for you from your Humble Petitioner Mary England
Annotated: 10/6^d P^r. Week to be allowed

164. *[F25/2/75] Mary Beavitt, Newgate, 17 May 1814*
Honred Sir I hope you Will Excuse the Liberty I take in troubling you With this But it is through trew Necesity that I do it I have five Children and my husband has only thirty shillings p^r Week and it is out of my Power to Maintain More than two if it Lays in your Power to do any thing for me I Should Be thankfull to you as his money is Not Sufficent to Maintain me in a Prison and two Children as the Place is very Expenceive to Live in if it Lays in your Power to do this I shall Be Ever greatfull to you from your very Humble Petitioner and humble Servent Mary Beavitt
I should be very Much Obliged to Mr Foy [*Marlborough Street police officer*] if he Will Lett me have the Pocket Book he took from me

165. *[F25/2/76] Elizabeth Pearson/Wright, Newgate, 17 May 1814*
Honred Sir I hope you Will Excuse the Liberty I take in troubling you With this But my Husband is Left this Place to go Abroad [*left Newgate for* Retribution *hulk prior to sailing in Aug.*] and now he has Left this Place I

have Nothing to depend on But the Goal Allowance wich is very Little as When his friends Came to him I shared What he had But Now he is Left I have Nothing to depend if it Lays in your Power to assist me I Shall Be Ever thankfull if it Lays in your [*illegible word*] to do this a favourable Answer Would Much oblige your Very Humble Servent Elizabeth Wright

166. *[F25/2/77] Thomas Porter, Newgate, 12 June 1819* [*sic*]
Note about people he believes to be utterers of forged notes, transcribed from oral evidence by Thomas Glover, Bank investigator.

167. *[F25/2/78–80], John Schrouder, spunging house, 12 Fleet Lane, 26 October 1813*
Had given information about forgers to Bank investigator, Glover, received no answer and writes again to advise Bank.

168. *[F25/2/81–84] Jorgen Jorgensen, Fleet prison, October-November 1813*
Debtor writes three letters giving information to Bank about prisoner about to be discharged from Fleet, planning to deal in forged notes.

169. *[F25/2/85–6] Ann Anntwissell,* Broxbournbury *transport ship, Deptford, 10 January 1814*
Most Hon[d] Sir I rely on your genuine goodness of heart to pardon the great liberty I take in addressing you which nothing but my present melancholy situation should induce me to I beg leave to say that we are almost in hourly expectation of sailing and being in the greatest distress having no one capable of giving me the smallest trifle I do therefore most humbly intreat of you Sir to bring my melancholy case before the Hon[ble] Gentlemen of the Bank in humble hope they will be pleased to afford me some assistance for which favor I shall ever be truly Gratefull Your kind compliance will much oblige most Hon[d] Sir Your Obedt Humble Servant Ann Anntwissell
Attached: deposition of Thomas Barrett, deputy constable, Little Bolton, describing her arrest, escape from his house, pursuit and recapture.

170. *[F25/2/87–9] Ann Anntwissell,* Broxbournbury *transport ship, Northfleet, 9 February 1814*
Most Hon[d] Sir I most Humbly intreat you will pardon my taking the Liberty of troubling you to present the enclosed for me to the Gentlemen of the Bank I beg leave to return my most sincere thanks for the trouble you have before taken for me and with every sentiment of Respect and gratitude subscribe myself Your Obedt Servant Ann Anntwissell
Attached: two petitions re-stating **169** *in more formal terms. Second petition annotated with numbers of £1 notes, dated 8 Dec. 1813, totalling £5.*

171. *[F25/2/90] Catherine Kain,* Broxbournbury *transport ship, Deptford, 1 January 1814*
Most Hon[d] Sir,I take the liberty of informing you I was sent on board the Convict Ship which is to convey me from my native Country I do therefore beg of you Sir to be good enough to name my distressing case before the Honourable Gentlemen of the Bank in hopes they will be good enough to afford me some relief not having the means of providing for myself with common necessaries for so long a voyage I beg leave to say we expect to sail the first wind intreat of you Sir to comply with my request and with the highest Sense of gratitude for the trouble you have already taken I respectfully beg leave to remain Your Obed[t] Hbl Servant Catherine Kain
At top of page: Catharine Kane her mark

172. *[F25/3/1–3] Joseph Russell, Giltspur Street compter, 27 July & 18 August 1815*
Defaulter on Bank bills of exchange asks Bank to assist his release.

173. *[F25/3/4] Thomas Sharp, King's Bench prison, 22 May 1815*
Debtor imprisoned at suit of Bank asks to be discharged.

174. *[F25/3/5–7] J. A. H. Burden, King's Bench prison, 19 & 26 November 1814*
Debtor to Bank offers disclosures about utterers of forged notes in prison with him.

175. *[F25/3/8–20] Martha Bramwell, Newgate, various dates in 1814*
Set of letters from Bramwell, aged twenty-four, with four small children, convicted OB, Jan. 1814, for stealing from dwelling house; awaiting seven yrs trspn. In daily contact with female 'Bank prisoners' in Newgate. Her letters disclose to Bank their continued trading in forged notes; she requests relief and favours in exchange for information. She tells Bank, 4 Oct. 1814: You are much deceived in the objects of your Charity as there are some in Newgate that receive a weekly allowance at the same time they are living extravagantly by defrauding the Bank. *Between Oct. and Dec. 1814, she informs on forgery and selling networks in London and activities of female prisoners; also of some men. She thanks Bank for favours and pecuniary relief and asks more. She is to be held back from group of women about to sail, for her protection. Her little boy has just died of smallpox in prison, another of her children with smallpox is not expected to live; several other children in prison have died; she herself is unwell. Able to write herself, she writes letters for some women she informs on, sending copies to Bank; she says she reads letters received by other women, making copies of those for Bank; she also writes letters for some women to Bank.*

176. *[F25/3/21] Amelia Hatfield, Newgate, 3 December 1814*
Sir, as you was so good to intimate you would do something for me I return you my thanks for your goodness and should be for ever gratefull for

whatever you please to bestowe as I have so small a family it will be highly acceptable and Received with Gratitude by Sir your very humble Ser[t] Amelia Hatfield. [*in Martha Bramwell's hand.*]

177. *[F25/3/22–3] Ann Bailey, Newgate, 3 December 1814*
Sir, I humbly beg pardon for intruding on you beg leave to inform you I am much distress[d] having lost my little girl and have another child at this time very ill I hope you will not be offended if I soliset a little assistance I am humbly gratefull for what I have already received from the Generosity of the Gentlemen of the Bank and should be very thankfull for whatever you may be pleased to bestow on Sir your very humble Ser[t] Ann Bailey [*in Martha Bramwell's hand*].
Attached: earlier copy note, 24 Nov. 1814, from Bank solicitors to J. H. Capper, home office: Mess[rs] K F & K present their Complts to Mr Capper and take the liberty of reminding him that Amelia Hatfield & Ann Bailey may be sent in the Ship now about to sail to Botany Bay, the Husbands of these two Convicts are now in Custody for uttering forged Bank Notes & the Husband of Hatfield has been committed to Newgate for Trial & if these Convicts are suffered to remain in Newgate it will be impracticable to prevent their Selling forged Bank Notes there

178. *[F25/3/24] Sarah Watson, Newgate, 11 October 1814*
Sir I beg pardon for taken the liberty of trouble you with Letter but I understand from M[r] Hardy [*official, Newgate*] that I ham put down on the list for the ship Sir I wish much to be kep Back from this ship as my poor girl [*Mary Watson*] is still in confindment and I find that we shall go before the time of her coming out that esteem sir you will do me that k[*i*]ndncss to write for me to the setentary stats office to stop me from this ship as my daughter is all I wish to see before I go as she as no one to look to her I find by M[r] Hardy that it his in your power to do me this kindnys I trust sir you wil do me this favor sir for my poor girl sake and I return you the utmost thanks from your obednt and humble servt, Sarah Whatson

179. *[F25/3/25] Edward Harland, Newgate, 11 April 1815*
Sir Permit an unfortunate man to address you begging your intercession on his behalf, and intreating your favour by the presenting of the inclosed petition to the Governors & Directors of the Bank of England – I have stated, my request in a few words and leave the merit with them, may that mercy Implore, be bestowed, and may you Sir, in thus acceeding to my request Receive, tenfold for the trouble you take in thus complying, with the request from Sir Your Afflicted Devoted Hum. Se. Edw Harland
[*petition no longer attached*].

180. *[F25/3/26–7] Levi Andrews, Coldbath Fields prison, 22 May 1815*
Nearing end of twelve month prison sentence for counterfeiting Bank tokens, finding he cannot be discharged as Bank ready to prosecute him for another similar offence, he requests their clemency as he is young, with a wife and four children; signs in Hebrew. He appears to obtain bail.

181. *[F25/3/28–9] John Borrows, Coldbath Fields prison, 8 October 1814*
Hon[d] Sirs, I avail this oppertunity of inclosing a letter I received from my family and to shew the distressed case the are in and myself confined here without a penny to help and as to anything else I cant say a sillable to your Honors respecting the forgery I am confined for. I hope your Honors will take my case into consideration and allow a small Support for my family which are in the greatest distress and before I left London for Liverpool I went to M[r] Harriot of the Thames police and told him all concerning it and he desired me to go to the Bank and give my information there and they would well reward me for my information, and I was told there that they could do nothing before the note came into the Bank when I left the date and number and provided it came in, the Bank would apply to M[r] Harriot, of the Thames police and I hope your Honors will take my case into consideration and admit me as an Evidence against [*Jacob*] Isaacs [*sentenced to fourteen yrs trspn, Nov. 1814*] as to what I have said is the truth and that I mean to stand to I remain Hon[d] Sirs your most obed[t.] and Hble Sert John Borrows
Attached: letter, 2 Oct. 1814 addressed to Mr John Borows, Lambath Street Office London – if not there to be forwarded to him, *from Ann, his wife,* [*with surname* Emery *overwritten* Borrows] *in Liverpool, expressing extreme distress at his absence, claiming ignorance of where he is or what he may have done.*

182. *[F25/3/30–40] James Lloyd, Horsemonger Lane gaol, 13 February – 15 March 1815 & 12 December 1818 – 2 December 1819*
Lloyd, awaiting prosecution by Bank, writes three letters in 1815 offering information. No trace of trial; his offer was probably accepted as he writes five letters (1818–19), showing him active on Bank's behalf in entrapment of utterers and sellers in London and Surrey. [*See also Bank archive F34A/7.*]

183. *[F25/3/45] Elizabeth Pearson/Wright, Newgate, 19 October 1814*
Sir I hope you will pardon the liberty I take in addressing you nothing but the Great distress of my preasant situation could induce me to trouble you I beg leave to inform you I have no friend to assist me with the least trifle and am reduced to great distress in Consequence of not Had the Allowance the Gentleman were so good as to remit to me I understand the female Convict Ship is ready for our reception next week I have been obliged to Part with my Cloaths for Support having nothing but the gail allowance to live on and should be humbly thankfull if you would assist me with a trifle to releace them and your humble Petitioner will in duty Bound ever Pray &c &c Elizabeth Wright [*in Martha Bramwell's hand*].

184. *[F25/3/41] Elizabeth Pearson/Wright,* Northampton *transport ship, Deptford, 22 November 1814*
Sir Beg pardon for taking the Lirbairity of Addressying you but have bin infromed that thare is a trifull of money alowed when whe Leave ingland wich whe shall be verry thankfull for as whe are very much in Distress your

Humble pitionors Elizebeth Wright [*additional names Mary Hingland, Sarah Watson crossed through. Letter headed as coming from the* Northampton *'Convent' ship*]
Annotated: E. Wright a Pearson, No. 19705 22 Oct 1814 £5. £5 to be sent to her by Mr Kaye *and* The Mark of E Wright a Pearson 23 Nov 1814

185. *[F25/3/42] Susanna Blake,* Northampton *transport ship Deptford, 25 November 1814*
Sir I hope you will excuse the liberty for applying to you the Women on board that confest themselves Guilty have been allowed five pounds each. I was convicted and Andover – I am sent on board with one child I hope you will allow me the same as the women in the ship it will be of much [*illegible word*] as I am without any Mony I am Sir Your most Obd[t] Serv[t] Susana Blake
Annotated: £5 Winchester, *with numbers and dates of issue of 5 £1 notes:* total £5 Paid 6 Dec T. Glover' *and signature:* Susanna Blake

186. *F25/3/43] Susanna Blake,* Northampton *transport ship, Deptford, 3 December 1814*
Sir I hope you will excuse the liberty I take of informing you I was sent from Andover, for passng a bank of England Note being forged. I acknol[d] my guilt every woman in the Ship has received a sum of monny I am here with one Child veary much distressed I hope sir you will interfere in My behalfe I shall ever pray Your humble Serv[t] Susann Blake
Dear Sir I understand the ship will leave here on Tuesday

187. *[F25/3/44] Elizabeth Pearson/Wright,* Northampton *transport ship, 21 November 1814*
Sir I take the Liberty of informing you I have rote twice and have not got any answer the Gentlemen were on board from the Bank of England this Morning to pay some Women, they did not send for me – I hope you have not forgot me I am desperate you will not think me troublesome but necessity only causes me to make this application Your Most Obd[t] Humble Serv[t] Eliz. Wright

188. *[F25/3/46] Ann Downs and Ann Paul,* Northampton *transport ship, Deptford, 17 November 1814*
Mr Westwood Sir Whe take the Liberty of trobiling you as wee are In the Greatest Destress In this world Being Confined this 9 Months In the Castell of Lancaster and having No friends to help Us to aney think whe are almost Lost for Cloathing And Being Confined for the bank Business whe hope that your Hounour Sir will Consither Our Destress Situation and please to Relieve Us as whe are Now going On Bord of the Northamton Going to the Bay and in the Utrmos of Destress and Likewise I Ann Downs Leaving 4 Desolate Children Behind Mee Whe Remaine your Umbel Servant Ann Downs and Ann Pall

Annotated: Paul *under* Pall, £5 each; *number and date of notes to be paid and* Sunday 20 Nov 1814, *under which is Downs' signature and mark of Paul and* Mr Kaye to pay them £5 each

189. *[F25/3/47] Mary England,* Northampton *transport ship, Deptford, 16 November 1814*
Honored Sir I hope you will pardon the Lirbreity i take in writing to you but it is nothyng but the gratest distress that Obliges me to tack so grate a Lirbirty having three [four *written over*] Children to maintian uppon what your goodness has pleased to alow me wich i trust your goodness Wil be grate anouf to Alow me a smal trifull as i ham agoin to Leave My Cuntrey with four Children and have not seen my husband since i have bein in Confinedmint win I ham intirley trusting in your Mersey and goodness your humble pertitoner Mary Ingland
Annotated: Mary England is now on board the Convict ship at Deptford. £10; Mr Kaye to pay her £10, *with numbers of notes to be paid and date of payment* Sunday 20 Nov 1814 *with Mary England's own signature.*

190. *[F25/3/48] Mary Walker, wife of Richard Walker,* Northampton *transport ship, Deptford, 1 December 1814*
Hon[d] Sir, I feel the most painful sensation in addressing you after the repeated favors experienced, and other assurances given of no farther application but am so situated as to have no other hope of accomplishing the necessary end I have in view in this appeal than through your kind interest in my behalf with the Gentlemen of the Bank. The Captain of the Northampton has kindly permitted my Son to help to work the Ship but am wholly unable to procure him the necessary Cloathing and assure you no other circumstance of whatever necessity would have induced me intrude after the favors confer'd and for which my gratitude is unceasing. The Ship is daily expected to sail and should not have troubled you with a letter had not the illness of my Children prevented my personal attendance. With great respect
I remain Hon[d] Sir, Your much Obliged Humble Servant Mary Walker
Annotated with calculations, identification of £1 notes totalling £5.

191. *[F25/3/49] Mary Barnard,* Northampton *transport ship, Deptford, 20 November 1814*
Honnored Sir I take this Liberty of Riting to you to Enform you of My Destressed Situation at present being Confined this 15 Months In Heartford Gail for the Bank Business and quite at this present time destitude of friends hopes that your honour Sir will have Compashon On Mee and Let mee have Some Relief as I am Now On bord of the Northamton Going to the Bay In the Greates Destres In this World I have Applyed to you before and there Is Some Unfortuneate Whomen as Receved Great favour from you and I hope to find the Same Sir for I am in very Great Destress Sir I have Not One Shiling to by mee A Littel tea for my Sea Store and I the prisoner Marey Bernerd Shall be Ever In Dutey Bound to pray for you Sir

Annotated: £5 to be given to her, *numbers and dates of notes to be paid,* Mrs Barnard *and her mark on* 23 November 1814

192. *[F25/3/50] Ann Noble,* Northampton *transport ship, Deptford, 20 November 1814*
The humble petition of Ann Noble
This is to inform you that I have been confined in Exeter Goal for 15 Months on account of uttering a forged note upon the Bank of England and your petitioner being in great distress and no friends to releive her humbly solicits your benevolence in her behalf and your petitioner will in Duty bound to pray Ann Nobel
Annotated: £5 to be given to her, *Ann Noble's own signature and identification of notes given.*

193. *[F25/3/51] Charlotte Dixon,* Northampton *transport ship, Deptford, undated, probably November 1814*
Charlotte Dixon, not prosecuted by Bank, permitted to sail to NSW with her two infant children, to join husband, Thomas, [fourteen yrs trspn], May 1811. In great distress and hearing that Bank give money to women on the ship, she requests some. No reply recorded.

194. *[F25/3/52] Sarah Watson,* Northampton *transport ship, Deptford, 21 November 1814*
Sir Pardon the Liberty I take In writing to you. But seeing Mr Glover [*Bank investigator*] on Board yesterday making different presents to the Women from the Bank of England and my Name not being Call[d] I Beg you will think of me & take it into Consideration being quite at a loss for a few Necessarys From your Humble Petitioner Sarah Watson
Annotated: £5 to be given to her, *with identification and dates of notes, together with her mark on 23 Nov. 1814.*

195. *[F25/3/53] Rachel Sladen,* Northampton *transport ship, Deptford, 17 November 1814*
Honnored Sir I take the Liberty of Riting to you too Enform you of My Destressed Situation being Confined this 7 Months In the Castell of Lancaster and Leaving 4 poor Desolate Children Behind mee and taking One with Mee boath mee and It Is In the Utmost of Destress having No One to Send to Mee Either money Or cloathes Mee and My Child Is In Great Destress and Being Confined for the Bank Business I hope that your Honnour Sir will Consither My destressed Situation And Send me Some Relief as I am Lying On bord of the Northamton Going to the Bay I Remaine your Umbel Servant Rechal Sladen
Annotated: Rachael Sladen, Mr Kaye to pay her £5, *with identification and dates of notes to be paid, and her mark on Sunday 26 Nov. 1814.*

196. *[F25/3/54] William Webb,* Justitia *hulk, Woolwich, 12 December 1814*
Gentlemen, As an unhappy Man who has incurred the displeasure of the Law, and who most sincerely regrets having done so; I have taken the liberty of intruding on you this supplicatory address; in the fervent hope that my Contrite and decorous behaviour since Conviction as well as the Candid manner in which I acted with Mr Westwood [*Freshfields' clerk*] the Solicitor at Gloucester will awaken your sympathy and prompt you not only to lend a favorable Ear to my unutterable feelings, at the Idea of being exiled from my Native Country and from all that I hold dear, for the long term of 14 Years, but plead an excuse for my present presumption –
You will be pleased to recollect that I was Tried at the Assizes held at Gloucester in the Month of April last for having passed a Five Pound Note purporting to be one of the Bank of England Notes but which ultimately turned to be a Forged one – My Friends advised me to take the benefit of your humane offer to plead Guilty which I acceded to – Believe me Honorable gentlemen that no one can more sincerely feel the injustice of the transaction than I do, and I am most anxious to expiate my offence by demonstrating the Sincerity of my penitence – I humbly hope therefore that you will be pleased, in your great benevolence, to look upon me as a distressed object, on the Eve of leaving this Country to undertake a voyage of 18,000 Miles, without the means of procuring one single Article necessary for such an unhappy undertaking and in your humanity deign to Condescend to render me a small pecuniary assistance to enable me to undergo, the better, those sufferings which are the Consequent attendant on a Voyage of this description, and Condescend to make known to me your Generous intentions, thro' the medium of your Solicitor and be assured of the sincere penitence and fervent prayers for every earthly happiness to attend each and every of you – Honble Gentlemen Yr. mo hble. mo ob[t]. & very devoted Serv[t]. William Webb

197. *[F25/1/55–6] William Wilkins,* Justitia *hulk, Woolwich, 11 July 1815*
Gent[n] I some time past supplicated Mr Kay to deliver a Petition (which I enclosed) to the Bank of England Directors.
I intimated my unfortunate Case therein – and implored pecuniary relief – I also had the hope M[r] Spurrier [*lawyer acting for Bank*] would recommend me as a fit object of their Charity – You will in your humanity please to consider – that I was involved in this business without benefit to myself – to the disgrace of my character, and loss of liberty – After being as I am – It is my earnest wish to go to the Bay the next Draft – and endeavour to wipe away the impression of my disgrace – I therefore solicit your compassion to promote the prayer of my Petition – for assistance as it is expected the Ship will go in a few days. I am Gent[n]. Yr. Most Obt very Hble Ser[t] Will[m] Wilkins
Attached: copy note stating We submitted your Petition to the Gov[rs] & Directors of the Bank, who declined complying therewith. We are K. F. & K. London 11 July 1815.

198. *[F25/3/57–9] Joseph Scott,* Justitia *hulk, Woolwich, 30 May 1815*
Sir, I intreat you to pardon the liberty I take in supplicating your humanity by the intrusion of this and the enclosed Petition which I implore you to use your interest in supporting.
I before wrote a Petition but sent it erroniously to M[r] Hase [*Bank chief cashier*] instead of directing it to you – I therein expressed my unfortunate state as I now do – and which will I hope be compassionated by you and the Governors of the Bank for independent of the misfortune of the allotted punishment of the crime I have been convicted of – I am friendless – and those I most depended upon has in my misery rob'd me of my Cloths and all I had, so that I enter my Captivity in an unknown Country pennyless, friendless – unknown and not knowing any one – This I hope will create your sympathy in my favour – And I shall ever be Sir Y[r] most grateful Ob[t]. Hble Sevt Joseph Scott
Attached: petition repeating what is said in letter with additional information that he is twenty-four, a shoemaker, and copy note from Bank solicitors: I have laid your Petition before the Governors & Directors of the Bank, who decline complying with your request. I am, Yrs &c JK, NBB 2[d] June 1815

199. *[F25/3/60–1] Eleazer Lazarus,* Justitia *hulk, Woolwich, 26 May 1815*
Gentlemen I have no doubt but My unfortunate Situation will plead in my behalf in fact I am not only pleading for My Self but for Seven Motherless Children and in this my Situation I may Truly Observe they are Fatherless as I am Transported for the Term of Fourteen Years. No doubt you recollect my Case at last Darby Assizes – Gentlemen – I am Informed that the Governor and Company of the Bank of England frequently in Cases of real distress Extend Assistance by acts of Donation – and believe Me – I consider myself as likewise. My dear and Innocent Children fully comes within the Meaning of such acts of Charity. I therefore Implore you to be kind to represent me to the Hon. Gentlemen and for anything they may be Mercifully Inclined to bestow will be sincerely and thankfully rec[d] and for ever remembered
Gen[tn] I am Your unfortunate Humble Srt Eleazer Lazarus
P.S. Sir, I consider it my duty to observe that the Man who Impeach[d] against me has gone beyond the Truth in his statements to you and should you doubt it If You will honour Me with an Interview I will prove it to your satisfaction as I consider it of consequence
Attached: copy note from Bank solicitors: I have submitted your Letter to the Gov[rs] & Directors of the Bank, who decline complying with your application. I am Yrs &c JK, NBB 2[d] June 1815

200. *[F25/3/62–3] Edward Tayler,* Justitia *hulk, Woolwich, 17 May 1815, formal petition*
That your unfortunate Petitioner has been unfortunately drawn into bad Company, by whom he has been miserably involv'd in a labyrinth of trouble; out of which he has not been able to extricate himself, and a Sentence inflicted on him has been to be transported for fourteen years, to

which your Petitioner pleaded guilty at Kingston Assizes. That your Petitioner most humbly implores your kind and merciful Assistance to procure him his Freedom when he arrives at Botany Bay, being the Place he is so unhappy as to be Transported to. This being his very penitent and most humble request he begs Your merciful and kind Aid to enable him to procure his Freedom when he arrives at the Place he is Transported to, and in Consideration of the heavy affliction of his poor unhappy Wife who has lately been put to Bed, he most fervently begs that she may be permitted to go with him, which she is very desirous of, as it has pleased the Almighty to grant her recovery from her late Affliction. He humbly hopes thro' your kind Interest and favours to be enabled to go to the Place he is transported to in the first Ship that is to Sail there, and as in duty bound he shall ever pray Edward Tayler

In different hand, in pencil, at end of letter: Thomas Tayler 7 Somerset Street Aldgate Schoolmaster. *Petition annotated:* Rejected.

Attached: copy note from Bank solicitors: Your Petition has been considered by the Governors & Directors of the Bank who decline to comply with your request. K F & K New Bank B[gs] London, 30 May 1815

201. *[F25/3/64–6] William Wilkins,* Justitia *hulk, Woolwich, 5 May 1815, formal petition*

That your Petitioner was tried at the Assizes held at Warwick in the month of April last, 1815 for feloniously passing divers fictious Notes purporting to be those of the Bank of England when he was humanely permitted to plead Guilty, and accordingly sentenced to 14 Years Transportation

That your Petitioner feels the most accute pain and remorse at being led to violate the Laws of his Country and thereby degrading a Character, (however humble in life) was such as obtained him the respect of all that knew him

That your Petitioner is 27 Years of age and upward of 14 of that period has obtain'd his living by humble yet the most honest industry and which all those he has served will bear just and ample testimony

That although he might say and prove much in the way of extenuation but will only solemnly declare, that he was drawn in to commit the act for which he is doomed to suffer

That your Petitioner has been confined ever since the 1st of November 1814 which has been attended with great expence to him considering his humble occupation as a Servant and as his offence is of that nature as precludes him from all hope of a mitigation of his sentence in this Country. He most humbly throws himself on your Munificence Humanity and Mercy to extend your Benevolence towards him in granting him some pecuniary assistance as he is going to a place where he will not know or be known, and where he hopes by the propriety of his future conduct to atone for his past, which has blighted prospects which if not brilliant, might have been truly comfortable and happy

Your Petitioner therefore most humbly and earnestly implores your commiseration, to be pleased to take his unfortunate Case into your humane consideration and in your Munificence and Charity, bestow on him the Assistance he most humbly and respectfully supplicates.

And your Petitioner will ever pray. William Wilkins

Attached: Wilkins' covering note to petition and letter from high bailiff of Birmingham, emphasising Wilkins' excellent character and first offence.

202. *[F25/3/67–70] John Ivy Wilson,* Justitia *hulk, Woolwich, 20 June 1815*

Gentlemen, With the most profound and dutiful submission I lay this declaration before you. Considering it's a Justice I owe myself and Family to state to you my Innocence of what I am now suffering for. Gentlemen, my Case must be fresh in your memory as I was Tried last March at Derby. Charged with having uttered two Notes purporting to be Bank of England Notes, and was sentenced to be Transported for fourteen years and am now on board the Justitia hulk Woolwich Kent

Gentlemen, altho in this situation, I attach no blame nor Impute anything to the Court or you – altho in this situation I consider its truly proper the Laws should be Obey^{d} and do Consider Justice ought to have its Ends – If not no person nor public or private property would be safe I attach and Impute all the Blame to the Attorney I Employ^{d} My Case ought to have gone before the Court I should have pleaded Not Guilty and took my Trial Instead of doing this I received the Sentence of the Court untried and am thus situated, and in this my situation, I declare to Almighty God in all considering that he knows the secrets of all hearts, that I am an Innocent Man, and that I took the two Notes above mentioned in the regular way of Trade. I likewise Consider that it is the intention of the Law, or more properly explained, the Wish of those who sit at the head of it, that Justice and Mercy should go hand in hand and cannot help observing that no Man is safe under such circumstances as mine as in such Cases every man is in trouble. Gentlemen I consider it likewise a Justice I owe myself to state to you that previous to this most unhappy Event my conduct and character stood unimpeached I am upward of Fifty years of Age and can prove to the satisfaction of the World at large that I never was concern^{d} in any Illegal Transaction I therefore submit this to you previous to my leaving my Native Land well considering I shall never see it again I will submit myself to my most unhappy Fate and will put myself under the protection of the Great and Wise disposer of Events declaring to Almighty God and the World I am Innocent. Gentlemen I am your most unfortunate Humble Ser^{t} John Ivy Wilson

Annotated: Read in Comm^{ee} 22 June.

Attached: Wilson's cover note to petition, letter from James Whiston, keeper of Ashbourne gaol, Derbys., 25 July 1815, requesting reimbursement of expenses for apprehending Wilson, and Bank's reply, 4 Aug. 1815 saying if he will send someone to them in London, they will provide three guineas for his trouble.

203. *[F25/3/71] John Ivy Wilson,* Justitia *hulk, Woolwich, 27 July 1815*
Sir, Forgive the liberty I take, and trust my Situation will plead for taking the liberty. I wrote you some Weeks ago and Enclos[d] I sent a Letter to the directors of the Bank. I dont consider it required an answer and have no doubt but you was kind to lay the Same before the them – and as it may be some days before I leave England – If any of your Gentlemen should be coming near Woolwich I should like to have the honor of a Conversation. I am Sir your unfortunate Humble Sert J Ivy Wilson

204. *[F25/3/72] George Smith, address unknown, undated, probably mid-1815*
four about nine mounts ago i was takin up for pasen of bad note you was kind a noufe to give me the Libirty of taken the man that I had them off and it was not my faut it was the [*illegible word*] faut bout it Layes in my pour to take a Man iney Day that I Like that Sels 3 or 4 houndrs pounds a worth every wick Surs i pouts my selef under your proteshon and i hope you will not take eny [*illegible word*] of me i will tell you the [*illegible word*] when I see you If you will grant me my fre pardon i wil soun pout a end to bad notes ples to find a man cald [*illegible word*] the Coiner Whether you will grant it or not as i shall see the man that [*illegible word*] sels them Ples to send a not froum your ond hand righing what you will Don for me by the [*illegible word*] so i remain your Sarevent george Smith george smith to be left at the golden Lion Fore St London hold for me I shall not go for it my selef
[*This is a wildly scrawled note, difficult to read, addressed almost illeg ibly but showing* the Banck, Banck bilding]. *Unclear if writer is in prison.*

205. *[F25/3/73–4] Copy letter from Bank solicitors to Greethams, solicitors, Portsmouth, 22 July 1815 in which they request that the enclosed £5 note be passed to Mary Mazagora on transport ship,* Mary Ann, *for her and her children's use; the ship had left Deptford, and was believed to be nearing Portsmouth. If the ship did not touch Portsmouth, Greethams should return the note. Attached: Greetham's reply that they made every effort but were informed by the navy post office that the ship did not touch Spithead, thus they return the note.*

206. *[F25/3/75] Mary Watson,* Mary Ann *transport ship, Deptford, 26 June 1815*
Honoured Sir I hope your goodness will Send me a trifle of money I was Sent to the Ship on Friday morning and went away in grate distress and most of My cloths in Plege as I have Not a friend in London that Could give me a Shilling before I went away if your goodness will Send me what your think Proper the Ship Name is the Marey Ann and She will lay at Deptford a Short time your Humble Servant Marey Watson
Annotated: £5 each Paid 30 June 1815 T Glover

207. *[F25/3/76] Hannah Johnson and Mary Watson,* Mary Ann *transport ship, Deptford, 26 June 1815*
Honered Sir I hope you will Excuse Our Sending to ask you the favour of a Little Relefe as we are on Board the Ship and being Much distressed as What things we have are all in Pledge and wee Expect to Sail Shortly therefore Honered Sirs trusting in your goodness we Remain your Humble but unfortunate Pertitioners Mary Watson Hanah Johnson
Annotated: £5 each Paid 30 June 1815 T Glover

208. *[F25/3/77] Mary Beavitt, Newgate, 1 July 1816*
Honn[d] Sir I hope your Goodness will excuse the Liberty I take in Addressing you in my Unfortunate Case being ordered to prepare to quit my Country and now in the 55 year of my Age and Ruptured which is increased much in my near 3 years Confinement and with a Family of 5 Children unprovided for owing to the Illness of my Husband and a Rheumatic Disease (4 of which must go with me the other one my Friends support) if Sir your Kind interferance in my Favour in this Case to relieve me will never be erased from my Memory and hope Almighty God will bless you and for which myself and Unfortunate Family will in Duty bound ever pray from Sir an Unfortunate Crimanal Mary Beavitt

209. *[F25/3/78] Ann Taylor, Newgate, 7 July 1816*
Sir with humble sumition I beg leave to inform you that we are in daly Expectation of being Called to the Ship therefore have taking the liberty to solicet you to Extend you Well Known Goodness to me and my Child as I am in want of Many thing for so long a Voige and what I am in Want off Can be perchised much Cheaper than When we are on Board.
I am Sir with thanks for all past favours Your much Distressed and humble Petitioner Ann Tayler

210. *[F25/3/79–81] Elizabeth Hayselden, Newgate, 2 July 1816*
Hon Gentlemen I most humbly request your indulgence of this fresh prayer of your kind favor in my Behalf, on the expected departure of a Ship for New South Wales with those women sentenced to transportation – unaided by friends and sinking with the miseries of Leaving my friends and Native country. I implore the bounty of the worthy Directors of the Bank for some little assistance towards my unhappy outfit; having laid out what little Money I had; and, though my Added Error [*continued selling of forged notes in Newgate*] has excluded me from their usual charity, perhaps your tenderness may induce you, in consideration of my Distress and that from better circumstances I have never Applied before for any allowance, but my resources at this Melancholy crisis being exausted, I now humbly Crave for that Relief you have Granted before Towards other prisoners;
I am Sirs Your most respectful and very humble Servant Elabeth Hayselden [*own signature*]
Attached: much reworked draft letter from Bank solicitors to J. Beckett, home office, 8 Mar. 1816, explaining that since Hayselden had been an extensive note dealer, having £500 worth in her possession on

apprehension, and that Ann Taylor was one of her Confidential Agents, *it was imperative that both were removed as soon as possible; both were trying to be admitted to the sick ward at Newgate to delay departure. Same letter recalls Mary Beavitt* [**164, 208**], *overdue for transportation, also selling notes in prison, saying it would be useful if she were removed from Newgate to a house of correction. Further copy letter to Beckett, 20 May 1816, explaining widespread practice in prisons and hulks of sale of forged notes and counterfeit dollars.*

211. *[F25/3/82–3] Elizabeth Stubbs/Chamberlain, Newgate, undated, late 1816*
Sir I humbley hope your goodness will Pardon this liberty in writeing to you to beg a Continuance of your late bounty which I should not have presumed but have been Very ill for a long time and my Friends have it not in there Power to assist me for want of imployment and My Husbands friends is doing all in their power for him so I have nothing but What your goodness is Pleas to bestow on me I am Sir with Gratefull thanks for your Past favours your much Obliged and Distressed Petitioner Elizabeth Stubbs thirsday Even
Attached: undated petition with own signature, probably earlier than **211**, *requesting allowance, annotated on front:* 5/- per week

212. *[F25/3/84] William Cuthbert, Newgate, 24 April 1816*
Sir, I have most respectfully to apologise for the liberty I take in addressing, but the unhappy situation in which I have Placed myself Emboldens me so to do – not so much on my own account as for the sake of an amiable Wife and other distressed Relations who are rendered truly wretched by this my first deviation from the Path of Rectitude – The object Sir, I have in view is, that (as I have addressed a Petition to the Prince Regent, and also to the Honorable the Banks directers Praying their Honorable Board to order such a favourable Report to be officially made in my Particular Case as to them in their great mercy shall seem fit) you will be Pleased to further the object of my Petition so far as you can in your official Capacity, under the Particular Circumstances of my Case, Permitt me only to add that should your humanity be Pleased to interceede in my behalf such intercession will Ever be most Greatfully remembered and acknowledged by Sir Your Humble and Unfortunate Servant William Cuthbert
[*BECLS*: *3 May 1816, his petition for mitigation of sentence, not in archive, rejected.*]

213. *[F25/3/85] William Cuthbert, Newgate, 18 June 1816*
Gent^{n}, As I am now in hourly expectation of being removed to the Portsmouth Hulks from this place, and have every reason to believe that this evening will be the last of my stay I take the liberty respectfully to state to you that my long imprisonment has exhausted all my means of living and the resources of the few friends I have and that I am in consequence wholly destitute of ability to procure the trifling comforts allowed and which appear necessary as well on board the Hulks (where we are likely to wait at

least two three months) as on board the Transport on the Voyage. Gent^{n} Having stated this I most humbly beg of you to represent my situation to the Honble Court of Directors of the Bank and solicit for me the little assistance usually granted by their humanity on such occasions.
If Gent^{n} through your goodness I attain this favor would you also be kind enough to solicit it in specie and inform the bearer when to wait upon you for an answer to this.
Gent^{n} I hope the occasion will be my apology for the liberty and I am Your most humble and most obedt Servt Wm Cuthbert

214. *[F25/3/86] Thomas Brock, Newgate, undated probably September-October 1816*
Coiner, prosecuted by royal mint, sentenced to death, OB, Sept. 1816, writes to ask Bank for money to enable him to get petition written for Prince Regent; he argues they owe him something as he assisted in apprehension of two forgers.

215. *[F25/3/87] George Blaker, Newgate, undated, between September and November 1816*
Honerd Sirs I Return My Sincer Thanks and hever Shall think My Self in Dutey Bound to Consider you the Perssever of My Life and My Unfortunet Wife [*illegible word*] in the Sitewashon that the Lawes of My Countery will Premit Me and My Wife and I Solemny Declare to you that My Unfortunet Wife knew not but wat the Notes was Gud I Geve them to her I heard yestady that thare was a Man Tacking in Custidy and as not Give is Right name by the Infermachon that I Can Git is names Is Thomas Macklanine and that is the werey Man that those Peapul had them of Exeapt My Self and one the Woman that Was Tride
In the Case of a Few Days I Shall be habel to in Form you ware you May Discover I beleve ware the Maker of Sum of This Notes but Raley Carnt Say that this Pursen that Is Tacking hup is the Maker of them for God Sake Do not Late it Be none for I Surtiny Shold be Minded and you May Depend that having Intres I Will be Marke for I have Bin heden in it [*illegible word*] and did not Think of the Concqence of It But I Solemy Declare to you that I Never Did Change but that mone and that Ware at the Robin Hud Pubek Hous and as For the 2 Pond Note Solomy Call My God to Witenes that I ham Innence it is more Intres to the [*illegible word*] So I hever Remain your humbel Sarvent George Blaker

216. *[F25/3/88] William Chamberlain, Newgate, 30 September 1816*
Mr Westwood Sir, I beg pardon for Troubling you with this but it is real necessity that press upon me so hard that I cannot refrain any longer. If there is any thing that can be allowd by the Bank for the assistance of my poor creature [*his wife, Elizabeth Stubbs, also in Newgate*] and me I hope if it is in your power Sir you will allow it to us. I assure you Sir we have nothing but the Jail allowance and that is very Trifling indeed my friend Mr Edmonds Says there was a one pound Note in my Pocket book, if it is Consistant and if you will have the goodness to return it to mee I shall be

very thankfull – I cannot Say any more but Shall beg the favor of my friend M[r] Edmonds to say the rest I am Sir your very Oblgd hble Serv[t] W Chamberlaine

217. *[F25/3/89] Isaac Greenslade, Newgate, undated 1816*
Sir My Attorney M[r] Buckland called upon me yesterday and informed me If I send down this morning to you you would send me the Money which was taken from me by M[r] Gammon the Constable of Chiswick. With Respect I am your Obedient Humble Servant Isaac Greenslade

218. *[F25/3/90] Jane Brown, Newgate, 4 November 1816*
Sir nothing but reall distress Could have induced me to trouble you but as I have no Friend to Assist me hope you will not Withold your late Bounty from me as relying on your Well Known have Contracted a Small debt for Tea and Sugar and Cannot get any more till that is Paid hope you will pardon this liberty which nothing but reall want Could have made me trouble you I am Sir Your much obliged and humble Petitioner Jane Brown

219. *[F25/3/92] Jane Brown, Newgate, March 1817*
Sir With humble Submision I Most humbly Beg your pardon for presuming to solicit your Extenseve Goodness and Charity to Me I have Contracted a few Little Depts in prison and am Not abel to pay it Without youre Continued Goodness as I have Not a friend to Render me the Least Assistance Nor have Not Sence I have Been Confined here Sir I am quit Distrest that only has Induced me to Troubell you I shall Be in Duty Bound to pray for your Goodness in hopes to Make Amends for My future Conduct Sir With the Greatest respect and humbell Submicone I am your Humbell Petitioner Jane Brown

220. *[F25/3/91] Jane Brown, Newgate, 11 April 1817*
Sir I hope you will pardon the Liberty I take in Presuming to rite but being in great Distress and have not a friend to give me Any Assistance to support [*illegible word*] only my Goal allowance Sir I hope you will take my Distress into Considaration and bestow a litle of your benevolent charity on me and I will be ever bound to pray, with Submission I Remain your humble Petioner Jane Brown

221. *[F25/3/93] Benjamin Johnson, Newgate, 11 October 1816*
Johnson, under sentence of death for unstated offence, not against Bank, is an 'officer', perhaps a constable, who says he has many times in the past assisted Bank in apprehension of forgers; he insists he is innocent of the crime for which he is condemned and asks Bank to let him have money to get a petition drawn up to send to Lord Sidmouth or the Prince Regent in order that his life may be saved. See **228**.

222. *[F25/3/94] William Bagnell, sr, William Bagnell, jr, Thomas Bagnell, and John Riley, unknown address, undated, but probably May/June 1816.*

Bagnells, Birmingham die-sinkers, successfully prosecuted by Bank, Nov. 1815, for stamping silver Bank dollars. William Bagnell, jr, pardoned, offers Bank his services to go to Birmingham to detect people engaged in coining 3s. tokens and supplying them to Jewish connections in London. Writers enclose details of a plan [*not now with letter*] *which Bank accepts, June 1816.*

223. *[F25/3/95] Anonymous, Newgate, undated, probably September/ October 1816*
Prisoner, not Bank offender, offers information about fellow prisoner, Robert Harris, awaiting seven yrs trspn for theft, who is dealing in forged notes.

224. *[F25/3/96] R. Hooper, Newgate, October 1816*
Hooper, sentenced OB Sept. 1816 for stealing from dwelling, about to be transferred from Newgate to hulks, offers Bank information on sellers and utterers of forged notes, in hope of being pardoned.

225. *[F25/3/98] Elizabeth Fisher, wife of prisoner Frederick Fisher, unknown address, undated in February 1816.*
Honourd Sir With Humble Submisshon I Beg Leave to Intreat the Favour Of your Goodness in Be Pleaseed to Present My Petision to the rest Of the Gentlemen and to Speake A favourable Word for Me Being Drove to the Greatest Distress insamuch that I Am Desstitute Of Common Necesarys I do Purpose Going to Service in Case the Gentlemen Should Be So kind As to Assist Me in redeeming My Cloaths My Child Wich is Eleven Months Old I purpose putting Out to Nurse Honourd Sir Hopeing You Will be Graceousely Pleaseed to Speake for me to the Gentlemen A Without There kind Assistance I Cannot tell What Must Become Of Myself and Baby The Favour of Wich Will Ever Be Greatfully Acknoledgeed By Honourd Sir your Obedient Humble Servant Elizebeth Fisher
[*BECLS: 15 Feb. 1816, to send her £20.*]

226. *[F25/3/97] Elizabeth Fisher, unknown address, undated, probably July/August 1816*
Honourd Sir Humblely Hopeing You Will Be Pleaseed to Pardon the Liberty I have takeing in Again trobleing You it is to request the Favour of your Goodness if You Would Be So Kind As Favour me With A few Lines to Mr Capper [*home office*] in Order to forward My Departure in the Ship that is Going this Month As I Cannot have the happyness Of Provideing Myself A Sittiauation to inable Me to Get Bread And if I Could I Should Be Miserable Nothing Ever Will Give me A Moments Comfort But following My Hussband Honourd Sir I Beg Leave to add that Mr Hardy [*official, Newgate*] Presents his Complements and Says he Shall Feele Himself Much Oblidgeed to Mr Westwood if he Will Be So humane As to interfere in My Behalf As he Says there Will Not Be Another Ship Go for twelve Months Honour^d^ Sir Humblely hopeing you Will Be Graceousely Pleaseed to Concider My Unhappy Sittiation in Favouring Me with A few

Lines to Mr Capper As I Understand it Would Be to Great Effect the favour of Wich Will Be Ever Greatfully Acknoledged By Honourd Sir your Most Obedient Humble Servant Elizebeth Fisher

227. *[F25/3/99–100] W. Menzies, unspecified prison, probably Newgate, 8 October 1815*
Menzies, not Bank prisoner, offers information about sellers and utterers of counterfeit Bank tokens and forged notes.

228. *[F25/4/1] Benjamin Johnson, Coldbath Fields prison, 2 August 1816*
Asks Mr Westwood, chief clerk to Bank solicitors, to call on him. [*See* **221**]

229. *[F25/4/10] David Reading and Benjamin Morris, Coldbath Fields prison, 6 September 1816, to a work colleague. Neither a Bank prisoner, possibly informants, requesting shoemaker, William Grasby, their 'shop-mate', to send them their shirts and to raise a small 'subscription' from work mates.*

230. *[F25/4/2] Thomas Erstwaite, unspecified prison, 13 October 1815*
Sir, I would be very much Obliged to you if you would be so good as to call here and see me as soon as you Possibly can, I have got something to say to you very Particular Indeed
Thos Erstwaite

231. *[F25/4/3] Elizabeth Morris, unspecified prison, undated probably 1812, to a friend*
My Dear Friend, I am sorry to inform you I am in the House of Correction but I hope you and Celia is safe and tell Mrs Mor to take Great Care of herself and tell her not to be afraid of me for thea shall get nothink out of me the Officers of Bow Street ask me about her but I told them I did not no such a person, so if she minds it will be all right I am along with Mrs Slater and M^r^s tool can come and see her at any time but thea must ask for Elizabeth Morris – transtport let somebody come as soon as possable for I Long to know how you all are I am not to Go to Bow Street today if you send me anythink put My Name on the parcel Dont make yourself unhappy about me for thea can not hert me So Remain Yours
Addressed to: Mrs tool at the Back of the Ball Long Alley Moorfields

232. *[F25/4/4] Margaret Spears, unspecified prison, undated October 1816, to friends*
Dear freinds I Am in the House of Correcktion and Will Not have Any Heareing Wesanday please To tell My Brother [*illegible word*] to By Me a trunk and Wat Cloths I have Got about your House I Hope you Will take Care of Be So Good As to Send Me Some tea an Sugar And a pece of Meet put My Name on it and Leve it at the Gate and I Shall have it Send My pockets [*illegible word*] and Hearings Margate Spears
send them by Mrs Spink
Addressed to: Mr Grant, Shoemaker, George Street, Black Fryars Road

233. *[F25/4/5] Benjamin Prichard, Horsemonger Lane prison, undated, probably last half 1816*
Sir Mr Griffes caled on me and told me that you could not cum to see me nou sir i Be glad you cum hear for i have maded it my studey to tel you all i noe i can tel you more than ever you herd of Befour there more mackers of nots then one in Brummingham and i can Let you noe the coyners of tockens and other silver Yours Benj Prichard
sur i hope you concider me i have got a very Bad cold and i ham Ruperd Both sids and ware a duble trus and my iorn mackes it wors

234. *[F25/4/6] Samuel Hale,* Retribution *hulk, Sheerness, 21 March 1817*
Honar^{d} Si^{r} I hope You will pardon me with they Libertey I heave now teaking, In writing But As I am they man that you prossecuted, In December last for they notes I hope and Beg and pray of you Si^{r}, that you will pleas to teake it in to Consideration to advance Me a Litle Money, so that I may Be able to get me a Few Cloathes, to teake with me as I shall Indeavour If please god, to meake myselef as a usfull as my employers May requier of me, and if you dont heave they goodness, I heave not a friend in they world to fley to, as my Pore Wife, with three small Children she [*two words illegible under repair to letter*] Obleige to goe to a parrish, unless you Goodness Would of thought proper for hur to of [*illegible word(s) under repair*] As its hur wish, and mine as well, if you could But Get that favour granted, I heave wrote to my Sister In toune and if You Will pleas to write hur to call On Monday and Releive me with what you think proper As I heave understood you allways was kinde a nuf To releive others when they was sent away, we earspecket To goe everey day, and I Heartley Beg you will pleas to releive Me As I shall Be for evour Bound to pray for Your Charratey
Saml Hale abord they Retribuation Hulke Sherness

235. *[F25/4/7] Eleven female convicts,* Lord Melville *transport ship, Deptford, 22 July 1816*
Gent^{n} We the undermentioned unfortunate females having been prossecuted by the Bank, and Now about to be Transported to New South Wales most humbly solicit for that relief Generally given to unfortunate Convicts We beg leave Gent^{n} to remain your Most Obe^{t} Humble Serv^{ts} the Under Signed Hannah Doods, Mary Duncan, Mary Henshaw, Ann Evans, Ann Stiles, Mary Ann Allen, Sarah Holiwell, Eliz Dunn, Esther Ashby, Esther Turner, Eliz^{h} Hazelton [*each signs by mark*].
Annotated: Mary Beavitt, Mrs Blackstone [*prisoner's wife,* **236**].
[*BECLS: 25 July 1816, to pay each woman, except Hazelton, £5.*]

236. *[F25/4/8] Mary Ann Blackstone,* Lord Melville *transport ship, 18 July 1816*
Formal petition from wife of William Blackstone [*transported May 1816 for Bank note offences in London*], *asking charity to make purchases for her voyage to NSW as she has received permission from sec./state to join husband.* [*BECLS: 25 July 1816, petition refused.*]

237. *[F25/4/9] Susannah Courtney, Newgate, 22 April 1817*
Sir Being informed of your Kind alowance to your prisoners, prermett me humbley to solicet the same, as I have no friends that as it in theire power to assist me, and having been in prison for this tow monthe I have been oblidge to part with a many of my Cloathe to suport myself but relying on your goodness I RemainYour most obe^t^ Humb Ser^t^ S. Courtney
Annotated: in great distress & pregnant

238. *[F25/4/11] Charlotte Harrison, Newgate, 10 April 1817*
Sir I hope you will excuse the Liberty I am taking in asking the favour of the money you are so kind as to alow your prisonors, as I have offended all my friends by my late conduct they have all forsaken me and I am in Great Destress having nothing but the Goal alowance, your attention to thes few Lines will much oblige Your obe^d^ Humb^e^ Ser^t^ C. Harrison

239. *[F25/4/12] Robert Roberts, Newgate, 4 June 1817*
Tried OB, 3 Apr. 1816 for simple grand larceny of large number of high value promissory notes, acquitted, but remanded in custody for trial for conspiracy, informs Bank of forgery activities of prisoners recently discharged from Newgate.

240. *[F25/4/13] Samuel Newman and Benjamin Brown, Newgate, 29 June 1817*
Mr Westwood, Sir Wee Understand from you by Mr Humphryes our Attorney that you Granted us the favour of pleading Guilty for which wee humbly Acknowledge Your Goodness in so doing. There fore, for the Goodness wee have receiv'd from You wee think proper to Acknowledge from Whome wee Receved them From Wich is Mr King at N° 13 Duke Street Bloomsbury where he resides at Mrs Westbrooks Your Most humble & Obe^t^ Ser^s^ Saml Newman, Benjn Brown

241. *[F25/4/14] Samuel Newman, Benjamin Brown, William Harrison, John Bamber and John Grigg, Newgate, 17 July 1817*
Sir We the under mentioned Petitioner, humbley implores your indulgence for the contineau in the above Prison untill their may be a Ship ready to convey we the unfortunate Petitioners to the Bay
We further humbley solicete your indulgence to contineau in the above Prison assureing you Sir:- their hang a greater dread on our Unhappy minds to be removed to the Hulk, then the whole of the suffering we have hitherto undergone.
We further crave your indulgence assure you we men haveing families in distress and haveing no means to supply their craveing wants nor haveing no other support then Gail allowance, under the above circumstances we humbley implore your humain Assistance has far as may consistant
We further most humbley solicete to be sent on board the first Ship that may be sent to the Bay
Remain^g^ Sir with humble Submission your unfortunate Petitioners Willm Harrison, Jn Bamber, Saml Newman, B^n^ Brown, J. Grigg

242. *[F25/4/15] Samuel Newman and Benjamin Brown, Newgate, 27 July 1817*
Sir Your goodness will excuse the liberty of this request understanding thare is something allowd by the bank to Persons convicted we Sir are much distressd and my Cloths are all in Pleage if you will send me something it will be verry exceptable as I expect to go away every Night an answer will greatly Oblige Sir Your Most Obedeint and Humble Servant Benjamine Brown, Samuell Newman

243. *[F25/4/16] George Robinson, Newgate, 9 July 1817, formal petition*
Your Petitioner having a Wife and Eight Children wich have heretofore been Suported by him, and having been a man in Better Circonstances in Life, But through the Preasure of times and Losts in his buisness have Reduced him and his family to very Lowe Circumstances and am Sorry to Say that My Abillilitys have been So Weake as to Suffer Myselfe to Innocently Led into this Dreadful Sittuation in wich I am Placed and that by a most Intement Acquaintence not Considering My Danger
under these Circumstances your Petetioner most Humbly beg your Indulgence to be Permited to Plead to the Lessor Offence for wich your Petetioner Will Ever Pray The Mark of George Robinson Witness John Banks

244. *[F25/4/18] William Harvey, Newgate, 22 September 1817*
Gentlemen I conceive it to be in justice due to myself and the information may not be unacceptable to you, (tho' perhaps you may think me not entitled to the credit of your belief) for me to detail the facts which has placed me in my present wretched situation; I shall therefore commence from the period of my liberation from White Cross Street Prison on the 29th of April last, at which time my circumstances and situation was very needy and necessitous, tho' previous to the conclusion of the war I lived in good repute as a Licenced Navy Agent at Portsea, but on the peace being ratified I was ruined by the parties (Petty Officers and Seamen) to whom I had advanced considerable Sums of Money on their Prize Money, being paid off out of the Service and revoking my claims. When Liberated from White Cross Street Prison my Wife was within 10 Weeks of her Accouchment, we had a few valuable trinkets and a little plate which I disposed of for our support, and I tried every possible means to procure a situation as Clerk in order to obtain a Livelihood for my family, but without success – When my Wife was put to Bed on the 10th July I had not then in the House in Money or Goods 2 Guineas worth, nor did I know where or how to procure for her those Comforts her situation required – to the best of my recollection it must have been a fortnight or more after my Wife was put to Bed that a person whom I had known for some Months, seeing my distressed situation, tempted me by offering me Counterfeited Bank of England Notes – steeped as I was in poverty to the very lips, I closed with his offer – my situation was too desperate for reflection, and thus for momentary relief, I plunged myself and family into irremediable ruin – I declare to you Gentlemen that it was nearly the latter end of July when this occurrence

took place, and not 'till then had I ever seen to my Knowledge a Forged Bank Note – My detection then Gentlemen almost immediately following the Commission of the Crime

I cannot conclude Gentlemen without declaring to you most solemnly by all my hopes of pardon for my offence when I shall appear before that dread power who shall Judge you, me, and all the world in righteousness, that I never was in the Shop of Mr Prosser, or Mr Lockyer in my Life, nor did I ever utter a Note to either of these Gentlemen or to their Shopmen, as sworn by them before the Magistrate at Worship Street – As I am in great distress, I hope that you will be pleased to give to my Wife the two pound you have of mine, and I am also to beg that you will be pleased to intercede to get her a Passage to go with me to New South Wales for which purpose, and to receive the 2 pound detained from me, she will call on you Gentlemen on Wednesday morning. I am Gentlemen, with the greatest respect your most obedient humble servant William Harvey

245. *[F25/4/17] William Harvey, Newgate, 29 September 1817*

Gentlemen A circumstance has occurred which induces me once more to address you not to beg for mercy but to request that you will do me that justice which in the occurrence I am about to relate I conceive myself to be entitled to – A person of the name of Read alias Spence I am informed was apprehended on Saturday last in Holborn uttering Counterfeited Notes of the Bank of England – I have also been told that this Read alias Spence is the person who uttered the Note on Saturday the 16th day of August to Mr Elliot in Mr Lockyers Shop, Tottenham Court Road, for a Box of Loda Powders, and gave his address "Roberts 31 Howland Street" Elliot before the Magistrate swore that I was the person; I have already asserted most solemnly by all my hopes of eternal happiness that I was not the person, and I again assert it – I therefore request that you will in consequence of the intelligence I have obtained, cause Mr Elliot to be sent for, and that he may see Read alias Spence that if he should be satisfied that he was mistaken with a similarity of person, or in his Zeal for his masters interest (that is to recover the Money cost) and regardless to whom he affixed the Guilt; in either case should it be satisfactorily made out that I am not the Man, that the note taken from me to repay Mr Lockyer, may be returned, and the circumstance receive from you that consideration which I must presume it deserves. I am gentlemen your very respectful & obedient humble Servant William Harvey

PS. I must inform you Gentlemen that I wish the subject of this Letter to be kept Secret, for should it be known here (to use the Language of the Newgate inhabitants) that I had nosed tho' for the most justifiable motives, my life would be sacrificed by the Wretches with whom I am compelled to associate.

246. *[F25/4/19–20] John James, Newgate, 30 September 1817*

Sir, I take the Liberty of Sending these few Lines by the bearer who is my wife hoping you will put her in the way to follow me as she has no trade to get a honest living by and as its not in the power of her friends to Support her and as it is her wish to go out of the country if, Sir, you would have the Goodness to put her in the way – it will be the means of not doing that which brot me here or worse as I should not wish her to go out of the Country as a Convicted person if it could be avoided by Leaving the country Free. I am Sir Y[r] Humble Servant J James

Attached: letter, 14 Feb. 1818, to Bank solicitors from Ann, John James' wife, sent from Birmingham, asking their help to get permission from Lord Sidmouth to go to NSW; she says that if she cannot go, she has choice of starving or doing what her husband did in order to be transported.

247. *[F25/4/21] Edward Egan, Newgate, 22 September 1817*
Egan, sentenced to death, OB July 1817, for burglary, offers information about some gentlemen *of the Bank who are supplying bank note paper to forgers.*

248. *[F25/4/63] John Brooks and Isaac Greenslade, Newgate, September 1816*
Hon[d] Sir We most humbly hope you will excuse the liberty we are taking in thus troubling you, but when we were apprehended at Hammersmith last August, the constable M[r] Gammon of Chiswick took from our Persons the sum of £16 and some odd Money, since which, We have received from him at different times and at our different Examinations Four Pounds only so that there now remains a balance of £12, some odd cash, in his hands. We therefore most humbly beg and entreat you will give him directions, immediately to return Our Property in question, as we are much distressed having no other means of subsistence than the Gaoel allowance. Trusting you will grant this favor, most earnestly solicited by Your most obedient humble Servants John Brooks Isaac Greenslade

249. *[F25/4/22] Susannah Courtney, Newgate, 27 May 1817*
Pardon me sir for intruding on your goodness has i am in Great Destress and most humbly Begs to be Partaker of your goodness the same as my fellow Prisoners has i have Parted with What few things that i had and i have got any Freinds to help me an i have been 4 months in Confinement and i am in Great Destress and i shall be in duty Bound to Pray for your goodness to me Susanah Courtney
Annotated: Sus[a] Courtney convict £5

250. *[F25/4/23] Margaret Spears, Newgate, 24 March 1817*
Sir I hope you will excuse the Liberty I am taking in riting but being in Greate Destress and near the time of my Confindment and having not a thing prepared I shall take it a favour if you will send me a small sum of money as it is ten weeks since I received the last, theas few lines I humbley submit to your Kind Consideration and Remain youre obe[t] Humb[e] Ser[t] Margaret Spears

251. *[F25/4/24] Margaret Spears, Newgate, 10 April 1817*
Sir Pardon the freedom I am taking in Riting but as I am in Great Destress and without a friend in the world and exspect to be put to bed in a few Days and have not a thing in the world provided and in Debt in the Goal theas few Lines I humbley submit to your Kind Consideration and Remain yours Margaret Spires

252. *[F25/4/25] Margaret Spears, Newgate, 15 May 1817*
Sir I take the Liberty of informing you I am Delived of two fine Girls and hope you will extend your Goodness toward them, I was deliv^d^ the 6th of this month, and with the Children am likely to Do well, relying on your former Goodness I Remain your Obed. Humb^e^ Ser^t^ Margret Spires
Annotated: 5/- a Week is paid to her

253. *[F25/4/26] Margaret Spears, Newgate, 23 June 1817*
Honoured Sir I hope you will Pardon the Liberty I Presume in troubling your Honour, but in Consequence of me Layinginn I want more Nourishment than usall and two Little Babes is Verry Expencive washing and Nursing them, Sir I hope your humane Goodness will bestow allitle of your Benevolent Charity on your Humble Petioner and her two Dear Little Babes Sir I Remain your Humble Petioner Margrett Spiers

254. *[F25/4/27] Margaret Spears, Newgate, 6 September 1817*
Sir I am sorry to truble you so soon but as I have not received any thing since the 9th of Last Month and having had one of my Children ill Ever since and is now Dead I hope you will Pardon my riting so soon, but as I have been att a Great expence with it I hope you will Call as soon as Conveient till than I Remain your most obed Humbe Ser^t^ M Spires

255. *[F25/4/28] Margaret Spears, Newgate, 16 September 1817*
Sir I hope you will excuse my being so trublesome but it is my Great Destress that Compels me, as I have been att a great expense with my Child that is Dead as I was oblidged to have a person with me night and Day for some weeks before she Died and if you will Call as soon as Conveint it will much oblidge your humble Ser^t^ M. Spires

256. *[F25/4/29] Sarah Howell, Newgate, May 1817*
Honoured Sir I humbley beg your pardon for the liberty I now take in righting to you but I ham in great distress for the want of a littell suport for in my sitruashon it is very hard to have nothing but the gale alouance and I have nothing hels for I have no one to send me a peney and it dos not lay in my husbands power to do haney thing for me for whilst he weas in confinment he lost hall his work and all his tools and he his now in want of bred honoured sir I hope you will take this our aufull situashon into your considerashon as we are a unfortunat pair and inesent dron into this our aufull sitruashon and I have the sentence for hit and I never knoad the mening of such a thing nor did I know what my sisters husband weas gon for till I hared you say when I came in the ofis and till then she tould me he

weas gon for smugled guds and then I found the horror my sister had lindit me in and then I well knew my aufull situashon but I putt my trust in the lord and I hope he will be my gide and I hope honoured Sir you will not send me hout of my cuntry but hit is my sisters wish to go and all her children as tha are here with her honoured Sir I hope you will pardon me for the liberty I now take in trubling you but my Distress is grat and my husband is the barer of this to you I ham your humbal servant Sarah Howell

257. *[F25/4/31] Sarah Howell, Newgate, 24 June 1817*
Sir I hope you will please to excuse My liberty in troubling which I should Not Do but I am lying in at present And am very much Distrest as I Have not Got a farthing of money To Get any necessary thing that I want And should be very thankful to you If you will have the goodness to Let me have A little money and Sir your humble petitioner As in Duty bound will ever pray Sarah Howell

258. *[F25/4/32] Sarah Howell, Newgate, 3 July 1817*
Honnord Sir Pray Pardon the liberty of my Addressing these few lines to you but Sir having been Put to bed this fortnight Past and totley without friends that Can do Eany think for me I am totley distrest in Duty Bound Should Ever Pray if your Honnor Could make it Convent to let me have my Money Should not think of being so Extremly troubelsome but being so Very Much distrest Your Very Humble Servant Sarah Howell

259. *[F25/4/30] Sarah Howell, Newgate, probably July 1817*
Sir I hope you will excuse the Liberty I am taking in riting again but it is necessity that Compels me, as I have been Deliver^d of a Girl three weeks and have had nothing but the Gaol alowance to live and through this unfortunate busyness my husband as Deserted me and having been in pris Prison four months I have been oblidge to part with my C[*l*]oaths to suport my self these few lines I humbly submit to your kind Consideration and Remain your oben^t Humb Ser^t S. Howell

260. *[F25/4/33] Sarah Howell, Newgate, 8 September 1817* [*written as 1871*]
Honered Sir I ham very sorey to trubel you with this butt beleive me I ham verey much distresed indeed as my child has been very hill and so have I my self and it is for want of suport as I have no one to give my child haney thing but what I have from you honered sir beleive me my puneshment is more than I can discribe to you as it was the lest of my thoughts ever to be in such a place as this and all my Mrs and Mr will tell you the same I allweays felt to much hurt to let them know were I was but I have had one of them here to see me and she was more surprised then I can mentchon but I should never of been here had it not of been for my unfortnat sister honered sir I hope you will pardon me A most miserebel and unfortnat woman and look into this my aufull situeation and I will let you see that the remaner part of my days that your clemecy is not bestoed on the undeserved and if you think proper to refer for my caracter you may refer for hit

hat is 26 M[r] Smiths Wood stret Ceepsid and I dont feear but hit will beair the stricets investegashon – Honered Sir plees to pardon your Most obedent and unfortnat and Humbel Sarvant Sarah Howel in distress

261. *[F25/4/34] Sarah Howell, Newgate, undated*
Honored Sir I ham very sorry to be so trubelsom but believe me I ham very much distressed in deed for I have my child to suport and no one to Asist me and I have not reseived haney thing from you sinc the 8 of august and I ham in grat Distress plees to pardon me as I ham in grat trubel as my child has been very hill and Mrs Spirs has lost one of hers from your most obedent and humble sarvent Sarah Howel

262. *[F25/4/35] Grace Blaker, Newgate, 14 May 1817*
Sir I hope you will Pardon the Liberty I Presume in troubling you, but being Distressed through me Confinement and the Absence of my Husband Obliges me to Solicit for A little of your benevolent Charity, Sir the Ship Doctor have Inspected the Prisoners for the Purpose of going Abroad and Informs us that the Ship will Sail before the first of June I am Very Unhappy, Concerning Some of me Cloaths I was Obliged to Pledge, which I Shall be at a great loss for them, if I do not get A little of your benevolent Charity to Release them, I Remain your Humble Petioner Grace Bleaker

263. *[F25/4/36] Grace Blaker and Jane Brown, Newgate, 29 May 1817*
Sir I hope your goodness will pardon the liberty I take in writing to you but we have had orders this morning for the Ship & we are going on Saturday Morning and humbly Begs you will please to Consider My Present Distress as I have Contracted A few Triffling Debts in the Goal and I have A Desire to pay what I owe as I Dont wish to Go away in Debt to any person and By so Doing you will very much Oblige your most obed[t] humble serv[ts] And Humble petitioners Grace Blaker & Jane Brown
Annotated: £5 has been ordered to be paid to Grace Blaker. 5/- a week has been paid to Jane Brown, Convict £5

264. *[F25/4/37] Grace Blaker and Jane Brown, Newgate, 31 May 1817*
Sir I hope your Goodness will please to Excuse my troubling you but there is a Mistake in our payments as we have not Recd any money for this 7 weeks and we Have found the 5£ Pound we Recd little Enough to Redeem our Clothes out of pawn And pay our Debts in the prison and I hope Sir you will have the Goodness to let us Have the Remainder as we want to get Necessarys to take on Board with us and Sir you will Greatly oblige your humble Petitioners Grace Blaker and Jane Brown

265. *[F25/4/38–9] Martha Thatcher, Newgate 26 May 1817*
Sir I hope you will Excuse me Soliciting you Sir I understand their is an allowance for all me Children and you Only gave me for One and I have three Children if your Dispute me word you may Refer to governer I have no person to give them a shilling only for your Benevolent Charity I do not

know What would become of me and them Sir I hope will take me family into consideration and bestow a little more of your benevolent Charity on them by so doing your Humble Petioner is in Duty Bound to Pray for you Martha Tatcher
Attached: earlier formal petition, Apr. 1817, on behalf of Martha Thatcher and Sarah Howell [**256–61**] *asking to plead guilty to lesser offence.*

266. *[F25/4/40] Martha Thatcher, Newgate, 30 May 1817*
Sir I hope you will pardon the Liberty I take in troubling you but I am Ordered to get Ready to go to the Ship and the Other women have Received their 5 Pounds, and I am Distressed with three Children and have the best part of me Cloaths in Pledge, Sir I hope you will Consider me Distresed Situation and me Large family and bestow a little of your benevolent Charity to Enable me and me family to get me Cloaths, by so doing your Humble Petitioner is in Duty Bound to Pray Martha Tatcher
Annotated: Martha Thatcher to pay her £5.

267. *[F25/4/41] Sarah Gardener, Newgate, 10 April 1817*
Sir Having rote and received no answer I take the Liberty of once more riting as I am in Great Destress as my husband is out of employ and as been for this six month and as it not in his power to help me and as it is now ten weeks sence you gave me the Last money I am in Debt in the prison and have no prospect of paying it without your assistance these few remarks I humbly submit to your Consideration and Remain your obed[t] Humb Ser[t] S. Gardener

268. *[F25/4/42–3] Mary Davis, Mary Lenny, Margaret Sellars, and Barbara Oliver,* Friendship *transport ship, Deptford, 4 June 1817*
Honered Sir the Humble Pertition of Mary Davice who was tride at the County Gaol Notingham and Cast for Death But now Going to Leave my Country Leaveing 9 Children and quite Destetute therfor hopes you will Be So Kind as to take into Concerderation my pitifull Case Likewise Mary Lenny who was tride at the Winchester Last March and was Sentence to 14 years and as Left 6 Children fatherless and Destetute likewise Margrate Selars who was tride at Carlile Last August widow Sentense for Life Likewise Barbery Oliver who was tride in the City of Drurumn Sentence for 14 years Tranceporttation the Smallides Danation will Be Gratefuly Received By your Humbly Pertitioners Being all quite Destetute.
Annotated: Petitions from Mary Davis £10 Mary Lenny £10 Marg[t] Selars £5 Barbara Oliver £5 Convicts
Attached: petition 6 June 1817, in identical terms, on behalf only of Mary Davis and Mary Lenny. Both appear to be in Mary Lenny's own hand, addressed to Henry Hase, chief cashier of Bank.

269. *[F25/4/44] Mary Lenny, Winchester gaol, 15 May 1817*
Sir Embolden by the Lenity you was pleas to Shew Me at my trial & hope you will Be so Kind As to Grant Me My Humble Request that Is that I May not Be Sent out this Country From my poor Children I have Six and four

Of them intirly unprovided for having no Relation and very Young the Two Last is only one and four and the Other Two Years Old I was Left a Widow with five and young with Child of the Six. Mr Bear to whom my husband was Servent for near a Elven years Was so Kind as to raise a subscription for me wich enabled me to take A Lodging House and Day School By wich means I thought to Be able to Serport my self and family But I was unfourtunate Not Being able to let any Part of the House it Was very high Rent and By that Means I Became very Much in Debt wich I As Sure you Sir was the reason of My Altering of the Notes wich I am Now in the County Gaol Winchester Under the Sentance of Tranceporttation for fourteen Years and therfore humbly Beg that you will be Pleased to Let My Sentence Be Altered to inprisonment I asure you Sir that i have Never Ceased to lament My Misconduct wich as made my Health very Bad therfore the thought of Death cannot be more painfull that that of being sent abroad from my Poor Children Who have No refuge But the Workhouse
I hope you will Be pleased to take pitty on me and Grant my request that I may Be inprisoned and Not Sent abroad and me and my poor family Will Be in Duty Bound to pray for you as Long as We all Live your Gratefull Humble Servent Mary Lenny
Annotated: Mary Lenny convicted at the assizes at Winchester for altering Several Bank Notes of £2 each to £10 and uttering them – is a Widow with 6 Children was allowed to plead Guilty to Minor Offence to be Transported

270. *[F25/4/45] Mary Ann York, Newgate, 3 May 1817*
Honr^d^ Sir Permit me most humbly to address you with a few lines in which I beg to solicit your humane intercession with the R^t^ Honb^le^ Lord Sidmouth to divert my present stay in the Gaol, or to bestow upon me the happy Priviledge of being sent the House of Penitientiary. My motive principally for thus intruding upon Your Goodness is, should I be allowed time, I entertain a confident hope, I shall be able most satisfactorily to prove to You, my perfect, innocence upon the late unfortunate event, which has reduced me to the most Poignant sense of feeling and Distress, I am also induced Sir to persue this line of application from the experienced Kindness and attention you have been accustomed to show to every unfortunate person who has had occasion to address You on such Maloncolly subject And am Honr Sir Your unfortunate Hub^le^ Servt Mary Ann York

271. *[F25/4/46] Mary Hopkins, Newgate, 30 May 1817*
Sir I hope you will Excuse me Soliciting you, but I am Ordered to go to the petencly [*Penitentiary*] tomorrow Morning and I have contracted a little Debt here, to go away in any Persons Debt, it would hurt me feelings Verry Much, I would not Contract the Debt only Relying on your benevolent Charity, Sir I do not mean the 5 Pounds I only Mean the weekly allowance, Sir if I should be gone before you send you will be Pleased to give it to the Governer and he will Pay the Person I owe it to Sir its Six weeks since I Received any Sir by you taking me into Considaration I am bound Ever to Pray for you Mary Hopkins

272. *[F25/4/47] Thomas Simpson, Horsemonger Lane gaol, 16 April 1817 Condemned to death for forgery* [*not Bank notes*], *he petitions for mercy; petition rejected.*

273. *[F25/4/48] John Smith,* Justitia *hulk, Woolwich, 25 June 1817*
Most Honr[d] Sir The solemn reflections on my past lamented conduct, whereby I am reduced to my present unhappy situation, and my Wife and infant children to the Most severe distress, causes me to feel a difidence in addressing you, but imboldened by a sense of your characteristic humanity and christianlike Philanthropy, I am induced to hope your Pardon for so doing and for intreating a Compliance to my Humble request.
Having been tryed last Lent assizes at Nottingham County Jail, for uttering and passing Forged Notes of the Bank of England, and received the sentence of fourteen years Transportation Beyond Seas, and I am now on board this Ship waiting to be conveyed to New South Wales which I expect to sail for, in the course of a very few days, In consequence of having been precisely informed, you have made some provision for all the Females on board his Majestys Ship Friendship, now Lying at Debtford, that was prosecuted by you for the same offence, I therefore Most humbly & sincerely trust, you will have the condescending goodness to take my case into your Most serious and humane consideration & the distressed circumstances in which I am placed, and have your usual humanity and benevolence prevailed upon, to be pleased to grant Me Some assistance, as it will at this time greatly alleviate Me, and My family from the direful effects of extreme Misery and distress which we are now labouring under. I gave you all the information concerning the person of Isack Harwood of Lincoln, and my friends is now doing the same if possible to get him detected as he was the person who gave Me the Forged Notes, previous to my being taken into custody, and to whom I can ascribe all my present distress and Misfortune too, The extreme Poverty my Wife and family was in at the time I committed the fatal act, is beyond all discription, and indeed the Misery they are in at present, is beyond all conception, My Wife and five infant children now living at Bingham in Nottinghamshire, where they belong and all the support they now have is from the Parish, which is seven shillings & sixpence per week. And me in this unfortunate situation, waiting to be removed to a distant Country, without Money to aid or assist me or My poor family, The thoughts of which overwhelms my heart with the utmost sensation of grief and sorrow
It is therefore on that account I have to implore your benevolent and charitable assistance, that is if you will be pleased, to make some provision towards my support before I leave this Country and likewise I must humbly hope you will have the goodness to use your influence and exertions, towards getting My Wife and Children sent to New South Wales after me, as it is their Most earnest wish, and as I intend when I arrive at my destination, to remain in the Country and live hereafter a life, of the utmost decency honesty & industry and indeavour to retrieve the good character in another country I once enjoyed in this.

I sincerely trust you will have the decention to favour Me with an answer at your earliest convenience, In the Meantime, permit Me to subscribe myself Sir with the utmost sentiments of respect Most Hon[d] Sir, Your Most Obt Humble Sert John Smith

274. *[F25/4/49–51] John Dunn,* Justitia *hulk, Woolwich, 26 May 1817*
Honoured Sir haveing learnt from my solliceter at the time of my trial at Gloster that it would be to my advantage to give up those persons who I received those Notes from which I received the sentence of 14 Years transportation for. I beg to assure your Honourable Company of the Bank of England that I can prove of the greatest service to them and the Country at Large & that at a very Cheape rate I would therefore thank you to acquaint me with Your Disposition thereon and point out what you think would be granted me under those circumstances, and the answer to the same shall contain every oppertunity in the mane time I remain Sirs your most obedient and very humble Sert John Dunn
Please to direct to the Care of Captain Smith on Board of the Justitia Hulk Woolwich & sent for John Dunn
Attached: copy reply 28 May 1817, from Bank solicitors, stating that if he has information they will submit it to governors & directors, but cannot hold out assurance of mitigation of sentence even if it is useful; rambling letter 15 Apr. 1817 from Dunn in Gloucester county gaol prior to trial, to solicitor, Mr Shaw at R. B. McKenna, 3, Crooked Lane, Cannon Street, London, suggesting he knows forgers all over England, Scotland, Wales, Ireland and France and will help get them apprehended.

275. *[F25/4/52] Hannah Crampton,* Friendship *transport ship, Deptford, 26 May 1817*
Mr Key Honred Sir i ham infirmed by a respectabe Jentleman that the Convicts beloning to the Bank of England is intitled to the sum of 5 pounds Honred Sir if so i hope you will have that tender feeling towards the Distrest to forward it as soon as Possable Honred Sir i hope you will Pardon my Adresing you on this subject Sir i ham you Moast Obeident Humble Servent Hannah Crampton on Bord the Frenship
Annotated: Hannah Crampton convict £5

276. *[F25/4/53] Susannah Courtney,* Friendship *transport ship, Deptford, 7 June 1817*
Sir I am sorry to be so troublesome But my distress'd situation must plead my Excuse I recev'd 5 pounds but I never had any thing all the 4 Months that I were in Confinement [*5s. a week ordered from 24 Apr. 1817*] and I were so distress'd that I have not now one penny to help myself I had Borrowd so Much Money in the prison and I hope if there is any More Comeing to me that you will have the Goodness to send it to me and you will Greatly Oblige your Humble petitoner Susanah Courtney

277. *[F25/4/54–58] H. F. Horneman, White Cross debtors' prison, 3 October 1816*
Horneman, signing himself His Danish Majesty's Consul General in Great Britain, *in debt to Bank, requires them to intervene in an argument with his partner, Mr Rooke, which has landed him in this situation. Bank solicitors say they do not interfere in personal arguments.*

278. *[F25/4/59–62] Miscellaneous papers from 1816: draft bond and statements re Corporation of London's borrowing of £30,000 to build new debtors' prison in the City and repairs and alterations to Newgate.*

279. *[F25/4/64] John Christopher Dittmann, King's Bench prison, 22 August 1816*
Dittmann, debtor to Bank, wants to be freed as his partner, William Spunden, has been; he requires common bail *so he can get on with his* consular business.

280. *[F25/4/65–6] William Chapman, White Cross Street debtors' prison, 30 & 31 May 1816*
Debtor writes on behalf of ward mate, Alexander Man, who has had £20 stolen from his portmanteau. He thinks Bank may be able to help since it is alleged that the person who stole it is in Bank custody; this would relieve him and ward mates from suspicion.

281. *[F25/5/1] Ann Storey, Newgate, 30 January 1818*
Sir parddon me for again Intruding on you haveing before staded my Curcumstances to you and I ham at this time verey destressed I shall feel my self for ever thankfull to you if your Mercerey and goodness will reach so far as to think me Worthy of the support that from your kind Considerereation offenderes as me doue receve for wich Sir I shall be for ever thankfull to you I ham Sir youre Moast Obd^{t} Hum^{bl} Ser^{vt} Ann Storey

282. *[F25/5/2] Ann Storey, Newgate, 6 February 1818*
Sir I hope and trust that your goodness Will pardon and Excuse the Liberty I have again taken I dropt you a line last week to beg of you to plese to give me the Allowance that you have to otheres Sir I gave you everey Information that Lyd in my power I hope you will consider my Case I know that I have offended the Laws of the Nation Still i hope to find that favour from your Mercereyful goodness as i ham in grate Destress Sir if it is not two much Intruding pleas to drop me a line to Say if i may Expect the favour that i beg of you and when that i may Expect to see you and Sir by so doing I shall be in Duty ever thankfull to you I ham Sir Your Moast obd hum^{bl} Ser^{vt} Ann Storrey

283. *[F25/5/3] Ann Storey, Newgate, 26 February 1818*
Sir I hope and trust that your goodness will Excuse the Liberety I take to again rite to you but Sir i hope you will Considder that my Case is very hard I have not a friend in the World to help me to annay thing and through

my offence As my husband has lost his place and at this time it is not in his power to help me and i ham quight Destressed doue Sir Considder my Case for wich i shall be fore ever bound in Duty to thank you i hear Sir that the Whomans Ship is Expected to goue in the next month and if my fate is to goue I ham Moast Destressed for such a purpos pray Sir Excuse this intrushon and i trust to your kind humannaty that you will be pleased to relieve me in this my moast unfornaute and Deplorabel sittuion this is the sixth Letter that I have sent and if i was not so truley in want i would not be intrushon I ham Sir Your Moast Obd[t] and Hum[bl] Serv[t] Mary Ann Storrey Transport

284. *[F25/5/4] Ann Storey, Newgate, 2 March 1818*
Hon[rd] Sir I trust that you will pardon the Liberety i have taken I Address my Self to you as a moast Destressed whoman i have being triyed ever scence Decem[ber] Sentens I have repeatedly Aplied for the Favours that is Sumtimes Confered upon offenders as my Self but have not receved the smallest kindness none Sir i ham upon the point of leaving the Country for 14 years wich might as well have beeng for my life no one has ever Aplied to you in a moore Destressed State I have neather Friend Monney nor Cloths Sir I hope and trust that your goodness will be pleasd to Allow me sumthing before i goue for wich i shall be moast Humb[bly] thankfully for it so Sir I shall be glad to have it that i may have a oppertunaty to lay it out before i leve this place pray Sir Considder my Destress and think me a Object worthy of your relief for wich I shall be in Duty bound to pray I ham Sir your Moast Obd[t] Ann Story
Addressed to: Jeremia Harmer [*Jeremiah Harman*] Esq Governor of the Bank Broad Street

285. *[F25/5/5] Ann Storey, Newgate, undated March 1818*
Sir pray Excuse my Writing or trubeling of you but i Expect this day to receve the order for the Ship and I have not a friend in the world to doue annay Service i hope and trust Sir that you will Considder my Case and be pleased to give me Sum Ascestance as i ham sure of gouing and i ham in grate Destress and have nothing to goue to the Ship and i Expect from the govener that we are to be on Bord Eather on thuesday or Wedeniday and when i ham there i have not a friend that Can doue annay thing for me Sir whatever. you will be plased to give me i shall be glad to have the opportunity to lay it out while i ham hear as i ham Moast Destressed indeed fore Cloaths I ham Soririy to trubel you with so mannay Letters this beeng the Eaths time that i have rote i think that perhaps they have not all fell into your hands Sir pleas to say to the Bearer when i may Expect to see you I ham Sir your Moast Obd[t] and Humbel Ser[vt] Ann Storrey

286. *[F25/5/6] Ann Storey, Newgate, 24 March 1818*
Gentlemen I am sorry to troubl you but I feel my self hurt that I Cannot have any allowance from the Bank of England as well as my fellow prisnors –

I do assure you Gentlemen I am Drove to the most presing Distress I have made away with all my Cloths Except what I Stand up in & going out of my Country in that distress situation it hurts me much I was in hopes to have Rec^{d} something from your bounty that would have enabled me to have got anything as I might have apered not quite distressed in a forren Country, I hope Gentlemen you will take my Deep Distres in to your Consideration & I shall be bound Ever to pray for you Your Most Ob^{d} Sevt Ann Story

287. *[F25/5/7] Ann Storey, Newgate, undated March 1818*
Honoured Gentlemen I hope you will Excuse My Liberty in troubling you, but being far from me Native Contry, and Destined for a Climate where I do not know aney person I am Quiet Destitute of friends, Since me Confinement I was Flattered I would have five shillings a week, from you Gentlemen of your Charity Expecting it I Pawned Every Article of me Wearing Apearl I now being ordered for a Strange Country I have not as Much as a to Wear I am Quiet Distressed, and unhappy in Mind as I do not know what to do, but I trust Gentlemen, you will take me Distressed Situation into your humane Consideration and bestow me a little of your benevolent Charity in Order to Release me cloaths as I trust to your humane kind and benevolent Charity, I hope you will not Delay Answering this as I Expect to go on board Friday or Saturday and by your Gentlemen Considering my unhapy Situation your Humble petioner is in Duty Bound to Pray Anne Storry

288. *[F25/5/8] Ann Storey, Newgate, 26 March 1818*
Sir You will very much oblige a Distresed Woman if you will transmit this to the Board of Directors of the Bank as I am going to Leave my Country quite in Distress fully Expecting to have the same allowance as my fellow prisoners You will oblige your ob^{t} Sevt Ann Story

289. *[F25/5/8] Margaret Spears, Newgate, 29 November 1817*
Honered Sir, with humble permishion I have taken the Libberty of writing to you as I am in great distress & rely only on your mercifull bounty having know Friend to render mee the Smallest Assistance it is now too months since I Received any Money Sir I remain Your Humble Servant Margret Spires

290. *[F25/5/9] Margaret Spears, Newgate, undated*
Sir I ham Soririy to be Trubelsom but will be thankfull if you will pleas to let me know the Gentelmans Answer it is Necesetty that makes me Trubelsom wich i hope you will Excuse Sir we gou tomorrow so pray lett me know your Moast Obe^{t} Hum^{bl} Ser^{vt} Margrat Speares

291. *[F25/5/10] Margaret Spears, Newgate, 30 January 1818*
Sir I hope and trust that your goodness Will parddon the Liberty i have taken In Addressing my Self to you Intruding upon your Goodness Sir it is two months this day since I Recevd the Bounttyfull Allowence from you

wich is all the Support i have for myself ~~and Child~~ for wich i stand for ever Indetded to you for Sir may I persume to ask you for a Remitance as Soon as is Convenent for your Self as I ham in grate Destress at this time for wich Sir I ham in Duty bound to pray your Moast Obdent Hum^{bl} Servt Margreat Spires

292. *[F25/5/11] Margaret Spears, Newgate, undated March 1818*
Sir I trust that you will Excuse my Writing but we Expect to Receve the order for the Ship on tomorrow the last Monney that i Receved was from the 30 of Janr^{y} i would not be trubelsom but wen i ham gouing i will be very thankfull for what your goodness will be pleased to give me as it will be of grate use to me wanting to lay it out I ham Sir with gratefull thanks your Moast Obd^{t} and Humbel Ser^{vt} Margrate Spiries

293. *[F25/5/12] Margaret Spears, Newgate, undated March 1818*
Sir I ham Soririy to be trubelsom to you as to intrued upon your goodness but I Expect every Momment to Receve the order for the Ship as Mr Brown the Governer told us yesisterday that we shuld Receve the order as today Sir I have not a Friend in the world to help me to one penney and I ham very [*illegible word*] of to leave my Countery but hope and trust to your goodness as i Mentiond in my last the last Monney that i Receved was from the 30 of Jan^{ry} Sir If Convenent I hope you will call upon me upon what were you pleas to give me i shuld be glad to laye it out as i have not a friend to combe to me to doue one thing for me after i leave this place I ham sir with gratefull thanks your Moast Obd Margreat Speares

294. *[F25/5/13] Margaret Spears, Newgate, undated March 1818*
Sir I Returen you moast greatefull thanks for the kind Feavours i have recevd from you i will be moast infinetly oblighd to you if you will present this Letter for me Sir a Deal rest with you and i hope and trust that you will be pleasd to render me the Services that you Can i have not a friend in the world to give me one penney wich is hard for me and my Dear Childring i trust Sir from the kindnest that i have receved from you that you will doue all you Can to be the means of my haveing a littel monney for wich i shall be for ever thankfull to you Sir pray Excuse me but if you pleas to say to the Bearer if She shall Call upon you on Thursday afternoon or on Friday Morning or if you will be pleasd to Call upon me – I ham Sir your most Obd^{t} Margrat Spires
PS Sir dont think that we have not Receved the order for Mr Brown the Governer has told us that we goue on board on Friday pray doue what you can for me

295. *[F25/5/14] Margaret Spears, Newgate, 25 March 1818*
Honrd Gentelman I trust that you will pardon and Excuse the Liberty i have taken i return my moast gratefull thanks for the kindness that has been conferrd upon me wich has being a support for me and my Childring other ways i must have known grate want not having a friend in the world to help me gentelman i ham apon the point of leveing the Countrey and ame in

grate want of a few things has induced me to intrued apon your kind Concideriation hopeing that you will be pleasd to render me sum ascestaince my Leveing the Countrey and not haveing a friend to help me to one penney makes it moare hard for me i trust that my Applycation will not offend and whatever your Bountyfull goodness will be pleasd to bestow upon me will be receved by me with my moast gratefull thanks and a everlasting acknologement of your kindnest we Expect to be on board of the Ship on Friday and shuld be happy if i posibily can to provied a few things for my self and Childring before i goue from this place as i have not a friend to combe to the Ship to me Gentelman i ham intirely Depending apon your goodness for wich i shall be in Duty bound to pray I ham with gratefull thanks your Moast Obd^{t} and Hum^{bl} Sert Margreat Spires

296. *[F25/5/15] Catherine Brown and her sister, Louisa Kemble, Newgate, 21 March 1818*
Hon^{d} Sir. I most humbly presume your goodness will pardon the liberty taken As now three months since My sister and myself receivd sentence for fourteen years which priveledge you was so good to us I hope we shall ever feel sensible of, and with the warmest Gratitude we return you our most Humble thanks we have experienced the most severe distress since our confinement and what has added much to our trouble is the sudden Death of our father and haveing no friends whatever – we have informed we are to go abroad and have received notice to be in Readiness next Wednesday. We most Humbly solicit your Humane Consideration we shall Forever Be in Duty Bound to Pray Catherine Brown, Louisa Kemble

297. *[F25/5/16] Catherine Brown and Louisa Kemble, Newgate, 27 March 1818*
Hon^{d} Sir Trusting to your goodness and my very distressing circumstances I hope will Be an appoligy for the liberty I am takeing troubleing you I most humbly hope the Gentlemen of the Bank will take Our case into consideration being quite friendless and we are to leave here on Saturday morning. With your Permission the Bearer waits an answer We Remain with Respect your Humble Servents Louisa Kemble & Catherine Brown

298. *[F25/5/17] Catherine Brown and Louisa Kemble, Newgate, undated March 1818*
The Humble Petion of Louisia Cembell Catherine Browne Humbly Emplores the Humane kindness of the Governer and company of the Bank and take in to considaration that the are destitute of Father or Mother or any freind to give them the least assistance know being ordered to leave our country on Friday or Saturday we have no more time before we go to the Ship begs leave to Solicit your humane kindness and hope through our present Distress that you will bestow a litle of you benevolent charity on us both as we are in great Distress for cloaths or any Sea Store, Gentlemen we both hope you will Consider our Great distress and give us a little of your benevolent charity and by So doing your Humble petioners in duty bound to pray Luisia Cembell Cathearine Browne

299. *[F25/5/18] Copy letter, 12 March 1818, from Bank solicitors to John Ward, prisoner in Newgate, condemned to death for uttering in London, saying governors and directors of Bank decline to interfere in his fate. Ward's petition for mercy not in archive.*

300. *[F25/5/19–21] Harriet Skelton, Newgate 17 March 1818*
Hon^d^ Sir. The gentlemen who presented to you Mr Mannings [*Clements Inn solicitor, whose servant she had been*] letter on my behalf, [*petition earlier in March*] has stated to me that there is no hope of obtaining a change of my awful sentence of death to transportation for life, as my character is considered as particularly bad, and my case very flagrant. Will you allow an unhappy woman to state a few facts which I humbly hope will induce you to take a more favourable view of my case – Guilty as I am, and deservedly involved in disgrace. I am not guilty to the extent which is supposed. I most solemnly declare that I never lived in any house of ill fame kept by my brother, or anyone else, but the one in Leigh Street, out of which I was taken, and in that I lived only after it was opened as a bad house five or six weeks. Part of my time was employed in working at my business, in doing the upholstery work of the house, which was taken & furnished by my brother, not so much to be used, while in his possession, as to let to some other person, and it was not opened by him till the 20 dec^r^ last.
I further declare that I never was but in one house of that description with Ward [**299**] and that not for any lewd purpose, but in consequence of a violent quarrel between Parr and my brother, our only object was to make a noise, & thus expose the house as a bad house – I confess that my motive was not the good of the public, but to gratify a desire of revenge on the part of my brother whose advice I sincerely regret, that I followed. For this I was held to Bail, and on the 6 Novr last I was surrendered by my bail Mr Cooper of Eagle St Holborn, and was acquitted – and Mr Common Sargeant recommended the indictment of Parr, which was done at Hicks Hall I do most solemnly declare, that I never had a bad note to my knowledge in my possession, or ever passed one knowing it to be forged, till within the last four or five weeks before I came to prison, (now about seven weeks since) and as far as I can recollect nine notes only have been uttered by me, and not the number you supposed.
I am willing Sir to make every reparation in my power to the offended Laws of my country by disclosing all I know as to the person from whom the notes were procured, and by whom I believe they were made.
These few remarks will I humbly trust convince you that I am not so abandoned a character as you suppose, and that I am not guilty to the extent I am charged as to the notes.
Will you be so kind as to state this to the Gentlemen of the Law Committee, – My life being concerned I hope will supply an excuse for giving you so much trouble
I am Sir Your most obet and afflicted Ser^t^ Harriot Skelton [*own signature*].
Attached: copy letter, 19 Mar. 1818, from Bank solicitors stating her letter laid before governors and directors of Bank who still remain of the

Opinion that consistent with their Duty to the Public they cannot interfere in your behalf

301. *[F25/5/22] Richard Radford, Newgate, 20 March 1818*
Sir I am unhappily placed here for Trial for uttering a Forged Ten pound Note, which I have been most Villianiously entrapped into. I hope you will Condescend to call here I will give you Information of the Party, as I understand they are gone in the Country either to pass some or purchase some from the Makers and I every reason to suppose the Person who inveigled me sells them himself
I am Sir Yr Humble Srt Richard Radford

302. *[F25/5/23–4] Letter, with covering letter, from Mary Swain, Newgate, 20 January 1818. Sentenced to death for forging navy transfers, and reprieved, she suggests further mitigation of sentence, which Bank refuse to act upon.*

303. *[F25/5/26 & 28] John Hill, Newgate, 9 February 1818, formal petition*
That Your Petitioner is waiting to be Tried, (at your suit) at the ensuing Sessions held in the Old Bailey for having in his Possession Forged Bank of England Notes.
That Your Petitioner sensible of the Enormity of the Offence, as well as the Ignominy awaiting him, If Prosecuted to the full Extent, bows down with the utmost humility, and states, that he was driven by distress, for the Supplies of a Wife and four small Children to err from that Path of Rectitude which he now deeply Laments
That your Petitioner is informed it has ever been a Study of Your Honorable Board to Mingle Mercy with Justice, so that a Sinner may live to atone for his past Offences that as this is the First Time in his Life he ever had to do with such a Transaction
Your Petitioner therefore Prays you will be pleased to extend your mercy towards him by allowing him To plead Guilty to the Minor Offence and that you will in your infinite Goodness refrain from offering Evidence as to a Part of the Charge which affects his Life, so that by Banishment from this Country he may Live to atone, and amend the Remainder of his Life in due Repentance in hopes of Forgiveness hereafter
And as in duty bound he will ever Pray John Hill
Attached: covering letter for petition

304. *[F25/5/25 & 27] John Hill, Newgate, 20 February 1818*
Sir I beg leave to send the Inclosed to you And probably through your Interferrence With the Bank Directors. As I can Benefit them much by my Information. They may feel disposed to Speak to the Judge so as to Punish my Offence by Imprissonment in this Country allowing you to act as your Judgement may seem meet
I am Sir respectfully Your very Humble Sert John Hill
Attached: formal petition stating same point.

305. *[F25/5/29–30] Charlotte Newman, Newgate, 12 February 1818*
Hon[d] Sir I Most Humbly hope your humanity will Excuse the liberty I take to intreat your Consideration of my most afflicting situation I sometimes felt some hopes hearing of your great mercy towards those who have Been allowed to plead Guilty the last Sessions. I trust I feel most sensible the awful situation I am now in and the Justness of my sentence When I was at the Bar my Life was then in your hands and I now feel it more accutely Let Mercy Be blended with Justice it is yet in your power to save the Life of an unhappy sufferer which I most earnestly implore of you How sweet will be the hours of Reflection when you can rest upon your Pillow and commune with God & yourself that Life which if taken from one of Gods Creatures you have not power to Give A few days nay hours will Determine this awful Event I once more humbly beg of you to save my Life there is time yet for your Consideration. All depends upon you and a all wise providence the Just and Good God deigns to say he will Pardon & receive the true penitent whose sins are as unmeasurable as the sands of the seas. His promises are we shall live with him forever Can you then feel pleasure in the Death of a fellow Mortal that you are the means of saveing
I Once more intreat your Mercy to spare my life which will if I am allow[d] to hope for it be spent in the service of my offended God and prayers that you may Experience every Blessing he is able to Bestow From the Unfortunate Charlotte Newman
Condemn Cell half past 11 O Clock at Night
Pardon me if from the impulse of the moment I have said too much
Attached: copy note from Bank solicitors: Charlotte Newman, I received your Letter but I cannot interfere in your behalf. The Governor & Directors of the Bank have considered your Case & they also decline to interfere. JK Westwood, New Bank B[ds] 13 Feb[y] 1818

306. *[F25/5/31–2] John Morris, Newgate, 21 December 1818*
Sir I hope you will pardon the liberty I take in soliciting your Interest on the behalf of my Wife, for a Passage to my place of Exile, w[ch] I do beg will not be withheld as she did all in her power to apprehend and have W[m] Die taken and which your convinced of, the only recompense that can be wished is your kind intercession in her behalf w[ch] will ever be most gratefully acknowledged by Sir your Ms Obed Hble Serv John Morris
Attached: earlier formal petition to plead to lesser offence.

307. *[F25/5/33] John Morris, Newgate, 23 December 1818*
Sir From your general humane feelings for the unfortunate emboldens me to solicit the favor of a Letter of Recommendation to Major General Macquarie, Gov[r] of New South Wales. If you think I am deserving of such indulgence, you may be assured that I am far from being Old in Crime as I did not leave my Fathers Home until June last, when I came up here in order to obtain a situation as a Clarke, but was not fortunate enough to suceed, and unfortunately was induced to comit the crime for w[ch] I am about to suffer for, w[ch] I do acknowled the Justice of my sentence, I cannot say but I feel hurt at W[m] Die having got acquitted as he was the Man who

is the cause of my being here, and from the knowledge of his transactions has sold 400 forged notes each day, to regular Customers he Employed, three Carriers, Burn [*Byrne, cap. con. Sept. 1818*], Baker and Williams – and this Baker I understand his still an active Fraud – had I been admitted together with my Wife as evidence against Die, the Jury must have found him guilty, tis to be hoped that Die will not be suffered to carry on his nefarious Practices with impunity much longer and bringing so many unwary wretches to this place, I further beg leave to enclose a Petition to Lord Sidmouth praying a Passage for my Wife With me to my Place of exile and I shall ever most gratefully acknowledge your goodness. If you will be pleased to enclosed the said Petition to Lord Sidmouth as it will then be Complied with, had I not so short a time to Stop here I should have given the Bank some further information, as it is my wish to give them all the information I possibly can for their great Lenity in not prosecuting me Capitally – and am Sir Your most Obed Hble Serv[t] John Morris
PS I beg leave to state that I had no hand in the Petition to the Court for a Trial as I was satisfied with being allowed to plead to the Minor Charge, you will be pleased to understand that M[r] Brown Gov[r] was obliged to move me from the South Side of this Prison to the School as my life was Threatned and they still declare If I go in the same ship they will be my Death, such are my prospects, these Circumstances are all Known to the Gov[r] and how they mean to dispose of me I not yet aware of

308. *[F25/5/34] Jane Williams, Newgate, 11 August 1818*
Hounerable Gentlemen I hope you will excuse the Liberty I am taking in addressing these lines to you but as I am standing before you as a Criminal and am Commited to newgate untill the sessions and being entirely destitue of money or friends induces me to suplicate your humanity as I have had nothing since I have been Commited but bread and water nor have I any Prospect of reciving anything from any one if you would have the Goodness Gentlemen to take my Distressed Situation into Consideration I should for ever Pray the smallest trifle would be most Gratefuly Recived by your most unhapy and obeident Servant Jane Williams [*not in own hand*]

309. *[F25/5/35] Jane Williams, Newgate, 21 October 1818*
Honorable Gentlemen Embolden to address you as I am on the present subject by having mercy extended to me thro your Humanity and Goodness, and now entreats your Charity in the same Merciful and Benevolent manner having had no Friend to Assist me since I have been in Confinement and nothing to subsist on but the Goal allowance In hope you will take my Distressed situation in to your Consideration and extend a little of that Charity that is so kindly Distributed to some of my fellow Prisoners the truth of my assertions can be proved by enquiry at the Prison as my Distressed state is fully known.
With Humble Respect I remain Honorable Gentlemen your most Humble Servant and Prisoner Jane Williams [*letter in her own hand*]

Gentlemen Pardon A Letter by Post but being Destitute of a Friend to Deliver it and unable to Pay a Messenger is the cause of the liberty
Annotated: 22[d] Oct[r] Mr Christmas to give 5/- & to report further as to her situation. 29 Oct[r] Mr Kaye authorized to pay her 5/- per week during her stay in Newgate

310. *[F25/5/36] Clarissa Downes, Newgate, 25 July 1818*
sir I hope you will excuse me sending to you, – But thougt I had Slipt your memory as Mr Westwood used to pay me my money Every Month & it is now six weeks since I have Rec[d] any But my fellow prisoners have Recev[d] theirs Regularly wich induced me to take the Liberty to send to you Sir
I Remain Your Ob[d] Servt Clarisa Downs

311. *[F25/5/37] Mary Ann Reed, Newgate, 16 July 1818*
Sir I hope you will be so kind as to Excuse me troubling you but being distressed both me and me child through me confinement Emboldens me to solicit you Sir if you would be graciously Pleased to take me into considaration and bestow me a little of your Benevolent Charity it would be the greatest Charity Sir by you taking me into your Humane Considaration and by so doing your Humble Petioner is in Duty bound to Pray Mary Ann Reed

312. *[F25/5/38] John Owens, Newgate, 22 June 1818*
Sir I return you my most Sincere and Heartfelt thanks for your humanity and kindness towards me in allowing me to plead guilty, I am an unfortunate unhappy man and you Sir have it in your power to elevate my unhappiness by Shorting my Sentance as you knowing me to be an Iniasent man Seduced by a faulce Harted woman which taught to Sware my Life a way for Self gain, I do pray think on my unfortunate Situation, I am fearful it will be my lot to live this Country Should that be the case, I hope and trust Sir you will put my Wife in a way to follow me, and your petitioner will be in duty bound ever to pray for you and yours John Owens

313. *[F25/5/39] Thomas Coutts, Newgate, 4 June 1818*
Coutts, aged 17, requests to plead to lesser offence; Bank made this decision 27 May 1818.

314. *[F25/5/40] Richard Bennett, Newgate, 8 October 1818*
sir irite afew lines to you if you will have the profer that ican give you good satisfaction of two or three men which you have not got in Costody which Sells bank of England forged notes besides employing three of four every day to pas for them which they know are forged and one of them perticler puts amark on them which he said to mee that mark made them pas all the better beside he said there was not one in twenty which noes where that mark is but he said all that he had he put that mark on peticler and the other is men which i know as been going on that game for a great while ihave knone them myself for five months and iknow they have been seling forged notes ever since iknew them besides ican give you peticlar adress of

severel others which they sel to and iwil give you their names and adres which sells them if you can take them they will do you more good then twenty selers for they enploy so many in seling and pasing it is hard to tell you ibelieve there is several in this place that is took that as been pasing for one of them it is very seldom they go to pas any themselves but they go with them that pases for them and gives them to those who pases them when they get out from of about home Samuel Bailey are Seller Thomas Turner a seller Edward Dent [*cap. con. Jan. 1819*] those three are sellers of Bank of england Notes forged and if you will send any body to me as a friend iwill tell you more piticler about it iwil tel you what publick houses they kep

315. *[F25/5/41] Susannah Wilson, Newgate, 10 April 1818*
Sir I am Verry thankfull to you and the Gentlemen for all the faviours you were So kind as to bestow on me, in Allowing me to Plead Guilty, as I owe me Life to God and you Gentlemen, Sir I am ordered to be Ready to Embark on Monday Morning by Mr Brown, Sir I am no way prepared for My long and Weary Voyage, as my unhappy Confinement Distressed me, that I was Obligated to part all me cloaths, and I am Quiet distressed, Sir I trust your humane kindness will take my distressed situation into consideration and bestow a little of your Benevolent charity on me, Sir I have only to day and tomorrow to prepare and I hope you will be so kind as to give the bearer Answer Sir I Remain your humble Servt Susanahe Wilson

316. *[F25/5/42] Maria Wilkes, Newgate, probably December 1818, formal petition*
Your Petitioner was at the last September Sessions holden at the Old Bailey sentenced together with her husband to be transported for fourteen years she having pleaded guilty to an indictment for having forged Notes of the Governor and Company of the Bank of England in her possession. Your Petitionar respectfully takes leave to inform your Honourable Court that she is in absolute want having no means of support besides the Prison allowance. Your Petitioner without attempting to palliate her guilt or to object to the justice of her sentence humbly implores your Honourable Court to take into their merciful consideration the only circumstance which can plead in extenuation of her offence her extreme youth and the influence which a beloved husband must possess over the mind of a young and affectionate wife. Your Petitioner humbly but fervently entreats the Honourable Directors to extend some trifling weekly allowance to a young and helpless female sinking under the accumulated pressure of the severest privations and mental sufferings And your Petitioner will ever pray &c Maria Wilkes [*own signature*].
[*BECLS: 18 Dec. 1818, petition refused.*]

317. *[F25/5/43] W. E. Hardy, official at Newgate, December 1818, writes to Bank solicitors on behalf of Bank prisoners Mary Pendleton, Hannah Gilbert and Maria Wilkes, in great distress, deserving of Bank's attention. No requests from these women in Dec. 1818 were met.*

318. *[F25/5/44] Mary Hartnell, Newgate, 28 December 1818*
Sir I trust you will be pleased to Pardon the Liberty I presume, but being Distressed by my confinement both my Children and me in the greatest distress and Confined to my bed five weeks with the Feavour under Mr Bose care Sir I have one of My Children here in the Prison and the Second with My aged parents at 38 Saffron Hill in Great distress Sir I will be leaving My Country in the Course of six weeks both me and my Children Quiet distressed as I was Obliged to Part my Cloaths to support my Child Sir if you would be Graciously pleased to bestow on me a little of your benevolent Charity your Humble Petioner will be Ever bound to pray Sir I Remain your Most Obedient Humble Servt Mary Hartned
Annotated: has 2 Children

319. *[F25/5/45] Hannah Gilbert, Newgate, 2 December 1818*
Honored Gentlemen The distressed Situation in which I am at present Placed Emboldens me to take the liberty of again troubling you with an application to your Charity and Benevolence not having a Friend but and Aged Mother who is a Widow with 3 younger Children and reduced to the greatest distress without any assistance whatever but what proceeds from her Hands which are feeble and Infirm and Humbly assuring you that Distress tempted me to the Crime for which I stand convicted by offending the Laws of my Country and having your great Mercy extended to Me in so great a degree I now farther implore your Charity by having a little releif towards releiving my present necessities as I have parted with all my Cloaths since my long Confinement and having nothing but the Goal Allowance which can be certified by Mr Hardy at the Prison
Honorable Gentlemen I beg leave to Subscribe Myselfe With Humble Respect your Distressed Servant and Prisoner Hannah Gilbert [*letter written in prisoner Jane Williams' hand*]
Annotated: Bad character – Hoad a notorious Thief who kept her, has supported her in prison, but is now in custody himself

320. *[F25/5/46] Mary Pendleton, Newgate, 2 December 1818*
Honorable Gentlemen Hoping you will Pardon the liberty of troubling you in so repeated a Manner but being reduced to the Greatest Distress and having no Friends whatever to Assist me and having parted with all my Cloaths to Support me since my long Confinement and having a Mother who being unable to Support me and now reduced to the Greatest Penury thro my Imprisonment I now beg leave to implore your Charitable and Benevolent kindness to be Extended to me as you have Shewn your Mercy in so great a Degree and be pleased to Allow me a little of that Releif Which you have so Humanely given to my fellow Prisoners who are placed in the same Situation the truth of this may be Certified by the trouble of enquiring at the Prison I beg Leave Honorable Gentlement to Subscribe Myself your Humble and Distressed Servant and Prisoner Mary Pendelton [*letter written in prisoner Jane Williams' hand*]
Annotated: Bad character.

321. *[F25/5/47] John Riley, Newgate, 25 February 1818*
Mr Westwood, I John Riley do take the liberty in writing these few lines to inform you of these People which is Said the head in London for having These Bad Notes and it is Supposed no less than thousands goes thro their hands in a year as i been told since i Came to Newgate and the head man i know well & a few more of the Party and put you in the way of Ketching them with the Notes your Honor i have been 3 weeks in the Hospital and I am not well now i have nothing to Support me but the Gaol allowance and my wife is Starving in like manner And i hope your Honor will take pity on me my wife do not know what this letter is for, and if anything Can be done for me i want no more than to Send me to the Pententiary and i live for my time to be up ishall quit the Country and never to be seen in England no more Be so good as to Send an answer by My Wife if you send or Come to the Prison ihope you will keep this business as secret as you Can for if the Prisoners knew of this Business they Certainly Put an End to me if i dont put in the Right way of Ketching them in the fact i ill wan nothing done for me No more from your Humble Servant John Riley

322. *[F25/5/48] William Belcher, Newgate, 28 January 1818*
Hounoured Sir I hope that You will pardon the Liberty I have taken of Writing these few Lines to You hoping that You will take My Distress Case into Consideration at this present time under the Sentence of Being Transported a term of fourteen Years for Offering to pass a Bad One pound Note wich at this preasant time I Lay in Great Distress having a Wife and Child Who have nothing to Support them at this preasant time and having Made away with Everey thing that She had and his in Graet Distress wich I hope that Your hounour would Be Pleased to take my Destressed Case into Consideration I Shall Be Ever in Duty Bound to Pray for Your Honours Goodness William Belcher

323. *[F25/5/49] Elizabeth Stubbs/Chamberlain, Newgate, 26 September 1817*
Sir I trust your Goodness will pardon me troubleing you But being very much distress^{d} and in debt With persons here I shall be happy to see you the first Oppertunity you can make it Conveinant I am with Respect your Humble Servt Elizth Stubbs

324. *[F25/5/50] Catherine Brown and Louisa Kemble, Newgate, 29 January 1818*
Sir, with humble permishion I ask pardon for the Libberty I have taken in addresing thes few lines to you but I am in great distres at present as I have now Friends to come to me & our Father Died Suddenly since wee have been here & wee have no person to give us a Farthing & wee are only Depending on your Mersifull Bounty Wee Remain Sir Your Humble Servants Catherine and Emma Conner
Annotated: Louisa Kemble, Catherine Brown, £5 Note

325. *[F25/5/51] Thomas Smith, Newgate, 30 March 1818*
Request to plead to lesser offence as he is only 20 years old, has been to sea for 11 years, suffered hardships, three times shipwrecked and once taken prisoner by French. Bank took decision 11 days earlier to offer PB.

326. *[F25/5/52] Anne Pilkington and Mary Gillis, Newgate, 25 March 1818*
Honoured Sir I write you these few lines to Inform you we are ordered to go on board Ship Either Friday or Saturday and hopes your Honour will be So good as to bestow a little of your Charity on me and my Children as it is the Last time I will trouble your Honour me Children are in great want of Cloaths, and I hope you will Consider the long Voyage I have to take them as the will want Sea Store Mary Gilliss also hopes your Honour will consider her Distress and bestow her a trifle and by so doing we both are in duty bound to Pray Anne Pilketon Mary Gillisse

327. *[F25/5/53] James Law, Newgate, end of February 1818, formal petition*
Your Petitioner was suffered by your Honorable Board to Plead Guilty to an Offence of uttering Notes purporting to be Genuine Notes of the Bank of England and is now awaiting sentence.[3]
That Your Petitioner is now only Sixteen Years of Age and from his Youth was Ignorant at the Time of the Enormity of the Offence which he was led into, and never before attempted to utter such a Thing
That from the Indiscretion of your unhappy Petitioner, he is likely to bring down the whole of his Afflicted Family with Sorrow to Their Graves
That your Petitioner bows down with the utmost humility and Contrition having violated the Sanguinary Laws of his Country, by a just and Sincere Repentance in some one of the Asylums he might be brought to a due Sense of Religion, Taught a Trade and in his more Riper Years become an upright member of Society.
Your Petitioner therefore prays your Honourable Board will be pleased to Take into your humain Consideration his Tender Age, And by extending your Mercy Towards him, allow him to atone for this Offence by an Infliction of Punishment, Tempered with Mercy. That as he advances in Life he may by a strict adherence To a Virtuous Path proved himself not unworthy of any Lenity You may be pleased to Intercede before Sentence is passed in his behalf to be extended Towards him
And as in duty bound Your Petitioner will ever Pray &c &c James Law

328. *[F25/5/54] Mary Ann York, Newgate, 4 November 1817*
Sir I beg you will excuse the Liberty I take in writing to you weare I not very much Distrest I Should not Trouble you I have no Friends theave all Deserted me sence I have been Imprisoned I have no dependence but on

3. James Law was actually indicted and tried for possession.

your Bounty what I received last I owd the most of or I Should not trouble you now I received it on the 30 of the Last month
Your humble Servant Mary Ann York

329. *[F25/5/55] Mary Ann York, Newgate, 5 December 1817*
Sir I would feeld myselfe Extreamely oblidge to you if will pardon the Liberty I take in writeing to you weare I not so Distrest in the manner I am at present I should not have Troubled you I have Nothing to depend on by your Mersifull bounty
I have not receaved anny Mony sense the 03 [*30*] of September Last Mary Ann York

330. *[F25/5/57] Sarah Howell, unspecified prison, 7 October 1817*
Honoured Sir I ham very sorey to be so trubelsom to right to you again but belive me I ham in great distress for I left nugat in det for I have been very hill and so has my child and Mrs Spirs has rot to me for what I hoe her for she says you have been to her and told her you should come to me the next day I hope honered sir you will fulfil your promes as I ham in graet distress and my sufrings has been more all reddy than I was ever diserving of but the lord knows the secrets of all harts and I hope and trust that he will leed you to know that I ham not gilty I hope you will pardon me youre most obedent sarvint in distress sarah howal
Hat the hous of corection I hope honered sir you will think of me as well as the rest as I ham most weanting of it

331. *[F25/5/56] Sarah Howell, unspecified prison, 13 October 1817*
Honoured Sir I Most humbely beg your pardon for the lerbety I now take in righting to you but as Mrs Spires has resecived her Money I think hit hard that I have not as it is more then 2 months since I resevied Money and I shall be in ever duty bound to pray if you will permit me mine from your Most obedent and humbel searvant Sarah Howel the hous of Correction

332. *[F25/5/58] Margaret Watkins,* Maria *transport ship, Deptford, around end March 1818*
Sir Premit an unfortunate female to implore your Kind assistance in this time of my need, for having lost my liberty for Life and heaving found it is the Custom of your Company to assist those Convicted of paying bad notes when thay Leave their Cuntry I take the Liberty of soliciting the same as I have not a friend in the world and in great distress, and I Remain your Most Obt hble M Watkins
[*BECLS: 2 Apr. 1818, £5 to be paid.*]

333. *[F25/5/59] Alice Willcock, Ann Lord, Catherine Hardacre, Betty Wild, Mary Norman, Betty Healy, Betty Stott,* Maria *transport ship, Deptford, 30 March 1818*
Honoured Sir, We hope you will Excuse the Liberty We take in Adressing you in Respect of a little mony that is alowed by the Bank We the undersighned unfortunate Women is very Badley of for a little mony and will

thank you Sir if there is any alowance that your goodness Will Alow it to us Poor Women as most of us is destitute of frends and no mony as We understand the Women from Newgate Received it and We are all in Great distress and no mony to Buy any Sea Store by so Doing you Will oblige your Hum[b] Petitioners Alice Willcock, Ann Lord, Catherine Hardacre, Betty Wild [*Written in Alice Willcock's hand and signed by her; Ann Lord also signs, other five sign by mark beside their names written by Willcock.*] [*BECLS: 2 Apr. 1818, all to be paid £5.*]

334. *[F25/5/60] Alice Willcock, Ann Lord, Catherine Hardacre, Betty Wild, Mary Norman, Betty Healy, Mary Young,* Maria *transport ship, Deptford, 1 April 1818*
Honoured Sir We hope you will Excuse the Liberty We take in letting you know that We are all very ill Distressed for want of a few necessaries as there his 5 of us from Lancaster Castle that has Been upwards of 12 months in Prison and is very Badley of for a little mony We hope Sir you will Consider our distressed Situation as most of us is Destitute of Friends M[r] Capper was on Board to day and said We Must Aply to you and you Would relieve us, We are Sir your Humb[le] Servants, Alice Willcock, Betty Healey, Catherine Hardacre, Ann Lord, from Chester Betty Wild, from Litchfield Mary Norman, from Carlisle Mary Young

335. *[F25/5/61] Sarah Docker and Mary Young,* Maria *transport ship, Deptford, 2 April 1818*
Sir From the Despths of mesiery and want with banishment for life befor premit humbley to solicit you Kind assistance, for having heard from the Newgate transports that your goodness is extended to the unfortunat when they Leave England and having been in Confinement so long it as reduced us to great destress these few lines I humbley submit to your kind Consdi-cration and remainYour Destressed Servants
Annotated: Eliz[th] Docker was the name she was tried by; *by her name* Warwick, *by Mary Young's name* Carlisle

336. *[F25/5/62] Jane Taylor and Hosanna Thomas,* Maria *transport ship, Deptford, 2 April 1818*
Sir Premit tow unfortunate females to emplor your Kind assistance in this time of great Destress and having been informed that you assist the unfor-tunate when thay leave their Cuntry gives us Confedence in asking the same these few lines I humbly submit to your Kind Consideration and Remain your Destresed ser[t] Jane Taylor, H Thomas
Annotated beside their names: Worcester

337. *[F25/5/63] Johanna McCarthy,* Maria *transport ship, Deptford, 8 April 1818*
Hounared Sir I hope you will Excuse the Liberty i take in writing to you hoping you will have the goodness to alow me the Same pruvlage as the Newgate prisoners and Other Country prisoners also as i am quite

Destitude of Money and freinds and have Been Confined in Newgate in Bristol 13 months I Remain your humble Servant Johana M[c]Carty
Direct for me on Board the Maria female Convict Ship
Annotated: Bristol; *also* the Mark of J M[c]Carthy 10 April 1818 *signing for money.*
[*BECLS: 8 Apr. 1818, to be paid £5*].

338. *[F25/5/64] Sarah Turner,* Maria *transport ship, Deptford, 21 April 1818*
Honerd Sir I ham sorey to trubel you with this Letter But I did not know that I was leaving [*illegible word*] till to Day and I hop that your goodness will so kind as to fever mee with the seame Goodnes as you Did the rest with the [*illegible word*] mony as I have Left with out any thing of the kind and honerd sir the ship sail in aday or to and I hop that you will not Delay any time as tis so shart and Dear sir I hop that you will Be so God as to Let my Dear Gill come along with me if there is not any thing aginst her or not But if she is I Doe Declare to God that I Doe not know any thing about it for she kept it as a thing from mee and wat sever I tould you I Doe Declare twas nuthing but the trouef as you will find in time as I remain your unfortnet & humbel Searvant sara turner Detpoford

339. *[F25/5/65] Sarah Turner,* Maria *transport ship, Deptford, 25 April 1818*
Sir I hope you will excuse the liberty of my riting again so soon but as the ship sails on Friday the 25th and having nothing provided for the Voyage wich may be Long and being informe[d] it as been your goodness to give the prisoners five pound gives me hopes I shall not be one alone thea few lines I humbley submit to your Kind Consideration and Remain your obedent Serv[t] Sarah Turner

340. *[F25/5/66] James Armstrong, King's Bench prison, 6 November 1817*
Debtor to Bank, seeks information on imminently due sentence on his son prosecuted by Bank for uttering.

341. *[F25/5/67–8] Edward Thorp, Coldbath Fields prison, 26 December 1817 to his lawyer.*
Prisoner held for examination [*unspecified charge*] *asks to see his solicitor's clerk. Attached: letter from prison keeper refusing visit without permission from Westwood, Bank solicitor's clerk; letter on behalf of J Harmer of 29, Hatton Garden, requesting permission to visit Thorp.*

342. *[F25/5/69] Richard Twine, Horsemonger Lane gaol, 11 December 1818*
Formal petition from utterer of forged notes, expressing contrition and requesting to be allowed to plead guilty to lesser offence. Bank took decision 5 Nov. 1818.

343. *[F25/5/70] Catherine Gorman and Sarah Clowes, Horsemonger Lane gaol, 4 December 1818*
Formal petition expressing contrition, pleading their gender and requesting to be allowed to plead guilty to minor offence. Bank took decision 17 Sept. 1818.

344. *[F25/5/71] John Sayers, Horsemonger Lane gaol, 29 September 1818*
Formal petition expressing contrition and requesting to be allowed to plead guilty to minor offence. Bank took decision 1 Oct. 1818.

345. *[F25/5/72] Elizabeth Smith, Horsemonger Lane gaol, 29 September 1818*
Formal petition requesting to be allowed to plead guilty to minor offence. Bank took decision 1 Oct. 1818.

346. *[F25/5/73] William Grant, Giltspur Street compter, 1 April 1818*
In prison for assault, offers information to Bank on dealers in forged notes.

347. *[F25/5/74] Thomas Simcox, unspecified prison* [*probably in metropolitan Surrey*], *1 August 1820, unspecified addressee* [*see* **348**]
In consequence of my Trial Approaching so near if you will have the goodness to state at the Bank to know if you can postpone my Trial and please to Bring me a note signed by the Gentlemen to postpone it or else it will be impossible to get it done I will discover to them immediately where the Plate is that makes the Notes and also the People that makes them –
As they Told Wm Stevens [**500**] a Man in this Gaol if he would give up his Connections with it they would give him his liberty –
Now as to this Young Man I knew him a long time Ago I can tell you where he bought them and when they were made –
I have seen him Purchase them of a Man named Thomas Ashbey A Native of Birmingham At 3£ a Score the Wholesale Price This Man has them from his Aunt A Miss Smiths at Birmingham At Bordesly Street there is a Private room in her house with no road to it except by a Trap Door at the top of the House they have a Ladder by which they ascend up to this Room and then take the Ladder up after them They Notes are Signed in this Room and then put in Large stone Jars and then put under Ground in the Garden at the Back of her house Till Called for I also have seen them several Times at Birmingham
I can prove it – if they will give me time As I am A native of Birmingham this is all facts
There is also a Man at Solyhull Lodge about 2 Miles from Birmingham of the name of Bampton that Married Booths Daughter this Booth Suffered at Stafford for forged Notes a few Years Back and this All Bamptons family have been in the Bill way for Years at this House there is a Room Similar to that I have described to you with skylights to it In this Room there is the Plate Where the Notes are made And then send to Birmingham to Miss Smiths to be signed And this Thomas Ashbey Goes to Birmingham for

them he is living in London and Selling the Notes at this time and has for some Years
NB Please to copy this off before you go to the bank as I had no more Paper
There is Also a Great Many More men in that line near Birmingham I know they Formerly lived at Birmingham but on fear of being detected at Birmingham removed from the town To Handsworth of the Names of Brics a Whole Family and One Savage a Rope Maker by trade and his Family have been in that line for Years –
All This I can put the Bank in possession of if they will postpone my Trial and give me time as the Assizes are so near now. Please to send me an answer as soon as you can

348 *[F25/5/74 sic] Thomas Simcox,* Justitia *hulk, Woolwich, 26 August 1820, to Mr Scutts, end of the Albany Road, Old Kent Road, Surrey*
To Mr Scutts and Mr Palmer Gentlemen As in duty I am bound to Pray for you for your most zealous and arduos undertakings In my cause be pleased to accept these few ill written lines Which I now write to you and I hope the Lord will strengthen You In your undertakings which you have already began on my Part and should you succeed with the Blessing of God for me To be restored to society once more I should call myself one Of the happiest beings on Earth with my Family as you know From the information I have given you to understand I can Prove to be as useful a Member for the Bank as ever they employed And also for the Public good as the forged Note Makers Signify they shall make their Fortunes as soon as the Notes For his Majestys new reign shall get into circulation and the new Silver as they are making great Preparations for them in Birmingham at this time and there is not the least doubt but they will succeed in Counterfeiting them as some of them have For Years to my knowledge.
Now Gentlemen as you have been pleased to undertake That arduous task of restoring me again to my Family and as I hope the Lord will prosper your undertakings and also your Children as from your feeling for a Poor fellow Prisoner and My Family as I have no doubt you are Fathers of Families Yourselves according to the genrous feeling you have acted to me On Board his Majesty's Ship Justitia Hulk Woolwich
I also humbly crave that for the Sake of My Family that you will do the Best you can for me and I shall be Ever bound to Pray for You I am your Obedient and Ever Praying Humble Servant Thomas Simcox
[*See also an earlier letter* **501.**]

349. *[F25/5/76] William Pendray,* Justitia *hulk, Woolwich, 28 October 1817, formal petition*
Your humble Petitioner humbley solicites Your indulgence for the immediate inspection of his unfortunate conviction in the last Summer assizes for the County of Devon.
Your humble Petitioner unfortunately was convicted for uttering forged notes of the Bank of England obtained from Mr Arnold of Plymouth Dock in the County of Devon in exchange for two notes of hand to the amount of twenty seven pound odd Shillings the bank of England notes tender'd to

your humble Petitioner William Pendray was received by him not knowing the said to be forged on the Bank of England and passing them in the regular course of Business to a person of the name of William Radmore of Plymouth Dock in the County of Devon.
Your humble Petitioner further solicits your indulgence to state the whole of facts that cause your humble petitioners ruin and also his unfortunate Wife and four Children who by the sentance of the Law is compel'd to leave them in the utmost distress, and greatly acknowledges the indulgence of the Gover[r] and Company of the Bank to allow him to plead guilty.
Your humble petitioner further asserts the above William Arnold haveing been for many years in the habit of vending, uttering and selling to sundries of persons forged Bank of England notes and bass coins of His present Majesty King George the third in sundries of parts of his Majesty dominions to a great amount, haveing no other support and trappaning the innocent and unguarded causeing them to be thrown into a jail and causeing their utter ruin and shame assisted also by bribery and perjury on my acc[t]. in particular.
Your humble Petitioner further asserts the said William Arnold was tried at Exeter for a quantity of Cloaths wrongfully obtained the Witness against was prevented from appearing by the assistance of his money and a multiplicity of other Criminal transactions too numerous to insert.
Your humble Petitioner in the numerous of suffering he has undergone and the distress and ruinous situation he is plunged into by his perfidy Your humble Petitioner most humbly implores your humain and benevolent Aid allowed to the unfortunate persons in my unhappy situation.
Your humble Petitioner will not only thankfully receive the above mentioned stipulated aid but ever greatfully acknowledge the same and in duty bound will ever pray. William Pendray
N.B. Your humble petitioner begs leave to mention the particulars relative to Mr Arnold was unfolded to him since his trial which information having left a deep impression on his unfortunate mind even to be coupled with such a Character my acquaintance previous to my misfor[ne] was near to ten weeks at most

350. *[F25/5/77] Frances Morris, Stafford gaol, 25 July 1817*
Morris writes in support of petition from Oman Hall, formerly banker in Stafford, sentenced to seven yrs trspn for false trading. She does not appear in Bank records.

351. *[F25/5/78] Note of information, 21 August 1818, prepared by Bank investigator from evidence given by Timothy Lane, on remand in Giltspur Street compter for uttering forged notes.* [*Sentenced to trspn, Sept. 1818*]. *Names, addresses and descriptions given.*

352. *[F25/5/79] William and Maria Wilkes, Newgate, 1 October 1818, formal petition*
That your Petitioner is under sentence of 14 years Transportation for having unfortunately passed bad Notes and is now in very distressed

Circumstances, your Petitioner therefore humbly Solicitts your Honours will be pleased to Consider his situation and allow him the One Pound Note the Officer took from him on his Apprehension and if any small Allowance could be granted to Assist him, Your Petitioner has a Wife under the same Sentence in the said Goal without Friends, and in the greatest Distress who also Prays and hopes some Relief will be afforded on your Honours Consideration and your Petitioners will ever hope to be sensible and Penitent for their Offence and acknowledge whatever Relief may be granted with Gratitude – and your Petitioner be ever bound to Pray William Henry Wilkes, Maria Wilkes

353. *[F25/5/80] Copy note from Bank solicitors, 28 October 1818, to Mr Brown, keeper of Newgate, informing him when prisoners in his custody are to be arraigned before OB grand jury.*

354. *[F25/6/1] W.R.H. Brown, keeper of Newgate, 5 October 1819, to Mr Rooker, clerk to Bank solicitors; he will send off female transportation convicts in a day or two; if Rooker has money for them he should send it immediately.*

355. *[F25/6/2] John Storey, Newgate, 9 January 1820, formal petition*
That your petitioner have been arrested on the 14 ult^o^ for Tendering one pound Bank of England Note, which on investigating proved to be a counterfeit on said Bank, which he had taken as one perfectly good, and for which he had given its intrensick Value, That he have been since the above period, labouring Under the most callamitous difficulties, That he has an aged Mother, and an helpless Family, That he has not a friend in London to aply to for any assistance, his situation is therefore rendered distressing in the highest degree imaginable, He therefore
Humbly prays you^ll^ be pleased to consider his case & Grant that he may be so happy as to experience your kind interest, previous to, or at his Trial, at the ensuing sessions, to be Holden at the Old Bailey, for which he shall be truly Thankful, And as in duty bound will ever pray, & That prosperity in all your undertakings, and domestic Happiness may long continue to Gratify you and family, shall be always the most ardent wish of John Storey

356. *[F25/6/3] Esther Bevan, Newgate, 2 September 1819*
Honoured Sir I Humbly beg Pardon for this Intrusion and the Liberty I have taken in Soliciting A Little of that Charity So Humanely Extended (by The Honb^le^ Gentlemen of the Bank) to Those In the Like Situation As Myself I would Not have been thus Troublesom but was Obligated through Necessity Not having Any Friends to Render Me the Smallest Assistance And the Little Wearing Apparel I Possest have been forced to Pledge to Procure Subsistance And it will Not be In My Power to Redeem them Unless Kindly Assisted by The Humane Gentlemen of the Bank And Should it be Ever So Trifling they May Be Pleas'd to Bestow on Me Will be thankfully R^cd^ by their Most Hb^le^ And Devoted Servant Esther Bevan

Annotated: Esther Bevan is in a very bad state of Health and does not appear to have any Friends to assist her 13th Septr 1819 – £2 pd
[*BECLS: 15 Sept. 1819, to pay her £5.*]

357. *[F25/6/4a] Thomas Owen, Newgate, 28 September 1819*
Honored Sir, I hope you will not think me pre-dominent by taking the liberty of addressing myself to you it is to inform you I was Convicted at this present Sessions 1819 – for uttering a forged one pound Note and was by the Humanity of the Bank allow'd to plead Guilty which Sentenced me to fourteen Years Transportation I beg to State to you that having a Large family and no one to assist me in anyway whatever Induces me to Solicit you to render me some small assistance to provide myself with a few Necessaries to help to assist me on my Voyage to my place of Destination (Honred Sir) hearing of your humanity on all former Occasions Induces me to address myself to you hoping you will take my unfortunate Case into your Kind consideration and you may depend my prayers shall allways be offered up for you and yours It may be recollected before I was Committed I named to Mr Christmas the Inspector I would do everything in my power to place the man in your hands I had the Notes off at that time I thought it would be of very Essensial Service which I would have done but very likely you could not place that Confidence in me it was a Man that I am sure from what I have Collected in the prison and out Doors he is the principle Vender of them Diabolical things were so many poor Creatures are torne from the Comforts of there Wife and family wich is my unfortunate Situation but I hope providence will smile on me in another part of the World; there is a Man which at Certain times in the Week attends regularly at the Crown & Sceptre near Golden Lane and disposes of them to people at this time not the Man himself that I named to Mr Christmas but a Man from the same party you may depend I am not informing you wrong as I am sure of leaving this Cuntry but I do it for the Good of Mankind, I am sure and certain he is the principle Man in them and if I had been allowed at the time I would have put him into your hands I hope you will excuse the liberty I am taking in writing to you in such plain terms the Bearer of this is my Wife and she will be left with three small Children wich I hope and trust you will take into your Kind Consid-eration I remain with due submission your Obedient and humble Servant Thomas Owen
NB I hope you will not Communicate this to any one but whom it may concern or else I may be very much illtreated in this Place
Addressed to Henry Hase, Bank chief cashier.
[*BECLS: 30 Sept. 1819, request refused.*]

358. *[F25/6/4b & c] Thomas Owen, 4 October 1819*
Writes that his wife will call at Bank solicitors' office for answer to letter of 28 Sept.; letter from Elizabeth Owen [*written in husband's hand*], *repeating request for pecuniary help, since she cannot help him, having to apply to her parish for herself and children.*

359. *[F25/6/5] Sarah Ward, Newgate, 6 October 1819*
Honoured Gentlemen In Consequence of Receiving Orders to hold myself and family in Readiness to Embark On Friday Morning for New South Wales – I Consider Myself in duty Bound to Return My Most Grateful Acknowledgements for All the Unmerritted favours Conferred Upon Me During My Confinement here And Remain with the Most Profound Respect Your Most Hum[ble] And Devoted Sert Sarah Ward
Annotated on front: Not Known As Directed in Old or New Bank Buildings *as she addressed it to Mr Hooker, rather than Rooker, clerk to solicitors.*

360. *[F25/6/6] Elizabeth Rhodes, Newgate, 21 August 1819*
Sir I hope you will Pardon my Intrusion being verry Much distressed and best Part of my Cloaths in Pawn Since my Confinement through my health being Verry bad I could not live on the Strong Provision allowed here Sir I am ordered to be Ready for to leave my Country in the Course of a month, and have no friends to Relieve me but Relying on your Humane kindness to bestow on me a little of your Benevolent Charity by so doing your Humble Petioner will Ever Pray Elizabeth Roads
Annotated: Elizabeth Rhodes is in a very Ill state of Health and does not appear to have any Friends to assist her 13th Sep[r] 1819 £2 pd
[*BECLS: 15 Sept. 1819, to pay her £5.*]

361. *[F25/6/7] James Moore, Newgate, undated, November 1819*
Formal petition requesting permission to plead to minor offence. Bank made decision 11 Nov. 1819.

362. *[F25/6/8] Catherine Martin, Newgate, 2 February 1820*
Gentlemen Pardon the liberty I have taken in writing to you soliciting some relief from you has I have an afflicted Child to suport and my own health greatly impaired in consequence of confinement and having no friend to render me any assistance therefore absolute Distress induced me to ask this favour by complying with my request you will greatly oblidge your Humble Servant Catherine Martin
Annotated: 7/6[d] per Week to be allowed her.
[*BECLS: 9 Feb. 1820 records Glover, Bank investigator, visited her, found her child very sickly and, though three years old, unable to walk.*]

363. *[F25/6/9] Thomas Marr, Newgate, undated, mid-March 1820*
Formal petition requesting to plead to minor offence on grounds of youth [*aged 20*], *first offence, contrition, and heartbreak of his aged father were he to be executed. Three tradesmen whom he describes as his prosecutors sign petition; they do not wish to be involved in a death penalty. Bank took decision to allow PB, 1 Mar. 1820.*

364. *[F25/6/10] Lydia Hogan, Newgate, 17 November 1819*
Sir I hope you will pardon the liberty I take in troubling you, but having one of My Children verry ill not Expected to Survive Many hours, Obliges

me to trouble you as I am Distressed through my Childrens illness Sir if you would be Pleased to bestow a little of your Benevolent Charity on me your Humble Petioner will Ever pray Liddy Horgan

365. *[F25/6/11] Thomas McDermot, Newgate infirmary, 20 December 1819, formal petition*
That your Petitioner is under the awful Sentence of death in His Majesty's Gaol of Newgate for uttering a forgd One Pound Note purporting to be that of the Bank of England
That your humble Petitioner begs to represent to you that although found Guilty by a Jury of his Country, that he gave his real address N° 24 Reeves Muse South Audley St. Grosvenor Square, when questioned by the Officer who took him into Custody, and that the latter mistook it for N° 4 on whose oath your unfortunate Petitioner was convicted.
Your Petitioner also begs to state that he has a Wife and three Children who will be now left to the dreadful alternative of begging or starving, and it being his first imprisonment that you will be pleased to take his case into your consideration and recommend to the Government that the awful Sentence pronounced against him may be commuted to fourteen Years transportation upon the ground of his unhappy family and the peculiar circumstances connected with his Most deplorable Situation
And as in duty bound Your humble Petitioner will for ever pray Thomas M^c^Dermot
[*BECLS: 22 Dec. 1819, petition rejected.*]

366. *[F25/6/12] Maria Williams, Mary Anne Croft, Hannah Green, Anne Hall, Newgate, 24 February 1820*
Sir your Humble petioners emplore your kind and benevolent Charity as they are verry much Distressed and Deserted by their friends and also in a bad State of health which the Surgeon can Sertify I maria Williams is Confined to my bed and Mary Anne Croft also Sir beg taking Our distress into your humane Consideration and allowing us a little of your Benevolent Charity your Humble Petioners will Ever Pray Maria Williams, Mary Anne Croft, Hanah Green Anne Hall Sentenced 14 years
[*BECLS: 1 Mar. 1820, requested investigation of these women and three others; 8 Mar. 1820, relief refused; investigator reported that keeper of Newgate said they were* women of the worst description, unworthy of the Bank's bounty and to give them anything now would be a kind of encouragement, *they were employed and received part of their earnings every Saturday.*]

367. *[F25/6/13] Clarissa Downes, Newgate, 21 May 1818*
Hon^d^ Sir I most humbly beg of you to Except my Sincere thanks for your goodness towards me in permiting me to plead for which I hope I shall ever return a grateful sense of. I again intreat your forgiveness in presumeing to trouble you but haveing no friend & my husband gone abroad I have no prospect but starveing in a prison at present. I was in hopes to have gone with this ship I hope this will meet your Humane Consideration and your

Good disposition will Extend your Charity towards an unfortunate Individual Who will be forever in Duty Bound to Pray Clarissa Downs
Annotated: The Prisoner is in great distress & her Mother & Husband having been transported she has not any Person to relieve her, *and in hand of BECLS secretary,* 5/- per Week during her Stay in Newgate

368. *[F25/6/14a-d] Four similar copy notes from Bank solicitors, 27 October 1819, 1 December 1819, 12 January 1820, 16 February 1820 to W. H. Brown, keeper of Newgate, listing prisoners in his care who are to come up for trial at OB, asking him to inform them accordingly.*

369. *[F25/6/15] Hannah Polley, Newgate, 9 November 1818*
Sir I humbly Emplore your kind Entercession with the Bank Gentlemen to take my Distressed Situation into their humane Considaration as I am Confined here Since June in Great Distress as I have no friend but an Aged husband Obliged to go to the workhouse for relief, Sir the Gentlemen of the Bank were Graciously Pleased to Allow me to Plead guilty but I did not understand the law and I would Plead Guilty to any thing they ordered me in order to save my life as I was Ignorant of the Consequence, Sir if you would be Graciously Pleased to bestow on me a little of your benevolent charity your Humble Petioner will Ever pray Hanah Polly
Annotated: Rejected

370. *[F25/6/16] David Crawley, Newgate, 11 November 1818*
Gentlemen have wrote to before to try to get my wife and Children to go to New South Wales with me finding It not In your power to send her so by your advice wrote to Mr Capper [*home office*] and finding there she Cannot go as yet I beg leave to state to you that she has no other hopes but to retire to Birmingham her native place and In her unparrelld distress the Lord only knows how she Is to get there and at this season of the year with two small children should you Gentlemen be pleased to consider her distress and aleviate her present distress by granting her a trifle of the but part to defray her expences home you will I hope bestow it on a fit and worthy object of pity and greatly releave the distracted mind of him who remains your Humble prisoner David Crawley

371. *[F25/6/17a & b] George Velton, Newgate, 12 November 1818*
Gentlemen, Pardon the liberty I take by addressing you but under the present distressing circumstances having a wife and Infant Child I am compell'd through actual necessity. At the time of my Apprehension the officer by name Shaw thought it proper to take from my person The Sum of £1–13–10 which I need not add would in a great measure and very materially relieve me and helpless wife at this time. May I beg of you to interfere in this business by endeavouring to obliging Mr Shaw to repay the before-mention'd sum. I would be additionally obliged by your immediate interference on account of my being almost in Daily expectation of going off. The bearer my wife will explain more fully the

distress'd state we are in, and I rely on your compassionate disposition by thus far obliging me
I remain Gentlemen Your most obed serv[t] George Velton
Attached: letter, 11 Nov. 1818 from Velton to Brown, keeper of Newgate, asking him to look into same matter.

372. *[F25/6/18] Thomas Bowers, official at Newgate, 12 January 1820*
Introduces to Bank solicitors a Mrs Connolly, whose husband is a prisoner who can provide information on forged notes dealers.

373. *[F25/6/19] John Hearn, William Benham, John Riley, Thomas Watson, George Downes, John Rogers, James Butler, John Hill, William Downes, Thomas Smith, Richard Radford, Newgate, 2 May 1818*
Honor'd Gent[n], Most Humbly we Entreat your Forgiveness In Presumeing An Address to you, but acknowledgeing Our Past Errors and Offences, Particularly that of Defrauding your Honorable Company. We Once More Throw ourselves at your Feet; We Humbly Beg of you to except of our Sincere and Hearty thanks in extending your Mercy so far towards us as to Save our Lives. We further Hope your Mercy & Extensive Charity will Lean towards us in our Behalf, by Granting us that Donation which we Understand as Generally been Bestow'd to the Unfortunate Culprits who have been Convicted by your Honorable Company. We are Truly Distressed having No Friends that can assist us even in our Present Condition which is Truly Deplorable. (Some of us being even without Shirts to Cover our Nakedness). Much more in Provideing us with the few Necessaries of A Sea Stock, We therefore Hope this our Humble Request will meet with your Tender Mercy, and the Unfortunate Sufferers, who here sing their Names, will be ever in Duty Bound to Pray, and by their Future Conduct Shew themselves Deserving of your Donation [*each signs own name*].
Annotated : 11 Male Convicts in Newgate – Pray[g] relief.
[*BECLS: 7 May 1818, rejected.*]

374. *[F25/6//20] Samuel Dell, Newgate, 1 October 1819*
Honored Sir, Permit an unfortunate miserable Man to beg your interference on his behalf toward his detention in this Country either to get him to stop in this Prison or the Penitentiary. Pray hon[d] Sir feel for my Situation Imagine the horrors I must feel when I reflect on leaving a Wife and three dear Children whom I most tenderly loved, and in particular what remorse when I reflect it is my own fault that has plunged them also into the Whirlpool of Misery Let me beg of you Hon[d] Sir if you should decline any Assistance to put the Bearer M[rs] Dale in some way that she may obtain relief as to her Sufferings, any thing that I can do in the mean time I shall feel happy in doing and beg to say that if I had my liberty I could have placed Dye and other most Notorious Dealer in your Power, as I hinted to Mr Foy [*Marlborough Street police officer*], however as that is not the Case I am as I ever have been ready to serve the Bank in any shape

whatever as far as lies within my Power I remain with Every Sense of Gratitude for every favor received Hon[d] Sir Your very humble Serv[t] Sam[l] Dell

375. *[F25/6/21a & b] John Branley, Newgate, 23 September 1819, formal petition*

That Your Petitioner is a Prisoner in Newgate, and has been found Guilty of having a Forged Bank of England Note in his possession for One Pound and being allowed to plead Guilty to the Minor Offence has subjected himself to be Transported for Fourteen Years and has received Sentence accordingly.

That Your Petitioner has a Wife and Five Children, all of them in an helpless state of Infancy, and with their [pregnant *inserted then deleted*] Mother incapacitated of contributing to their mutual or individual support and are by his Your Petitioners conviction driven into the Sink of want wretchedness and despair.

That Your Petitioner has been a resident Housholder in the Parish of Stepney Nineteen Years during which time he maintained a good Character for honesty, industry and a strict regard for Moral rectitude of conduct and until this misfortune (which he has in common with his Wife and children to lament and deplore) is conscious of having never in one instance infringed the Laws of his Country, or received the least Mark of its displeasure.

That Your Petitioner is happy to have it in his power to say, that he is borne out in his Statement relative to his Character by the testimonial of his many and respectable Neighbors, whose Names they have been so good as to subscribe hereunto, and whose good wishes accompany his, that Mercy may be extended towards him Your Petitioner in mitigation of Punishment, whereby Your Petitioner may have not a very distant prospect of returning to the Bosom of his Family and Friends.

That Your Petitioner has been emboldened from the recollection of this being his first Offence to Petition his Royal Highness the Prince Regent and should Your Petitioner be so happy to prevail of upon You to give but the least support thereto, Your Petitioner will have confidence to hope the Royal Clemency will be extended to him, in lessening the term of his exile. His Wife who is pregnant of her Sixth Child, will take the liberty of presenting this Petition, with the one for his Royal Highness, praying Your support thereto

And Your Petitioner will every Pray.

Petition signed by his landlord, churchwarden, rent collector, two overseers of poor and eighteen other residents of Mile End and Ratcliff.

Attached: note to Bank from William Anderson and William Tyler, surveyors of highways, hamlet of Mile End, Old Town, Stepney, certifying that Branley had long worked for them honestly and industriously.

[*BECLS: 30 Sept. 1819, support refused.*]

376. *[F25/6/21c] John Branley, Newgate, 4 October 1819*

Sir, I am a Prisoner in this Place under Sentence of Transportation for 14 Years for having been concerned in uttering a forged Bank of England Note for One Pound.

On Monday the 23d of September last I took the liberty of leaving a Petition at your Office to be laid before the Director of the Honorable Company of the Bank of England with a view of obtaining their Interest to
Not having since heard whether my Petition has met with the reception desired and as the time is fast approaching where my Sentence must be carried into execution I cannot avoid feeling particularly anxious to obtain the answer of the Directors to the Petition
Your would therefore confer a lasting obligation Sir, on a wretched husband and a consequently distressed Wife and family consisting of 5 small Children, by making use of your interest to obtain an answer to my Petition as soon as possible and
I am Sir Your infinitely obliged and most respectful humble Servant John Branley [*own signature*].

377. *[F25/6/22] Jane Williams, Mary Pendleton, Hannah Gilbert, Sarah Hyland and Maria Wilkes, Newgate, 5 November 1818*
Honored Sir We beg leave to address you hoping the liberty will be forgiven as our Distress is the cause of troubling you we having being Mercifully Spared thro the Humanity of the Governor and Company of the Bank of England We further entreat your Charity to be extended to us as we are now reduced to the greatest Penury not having a Friend to assist us but entirely Depending on the Goal Allowance our Cloathes being all parted with and being quite Destitute we beg your human Intercession in our Distressed State in hope that Charity my be extended in some Degree as it has been to our Fellow Prisoners who are in the same Situation The truth of our assertion may be proved by the enquiry at the Prison. We beg leave to Subscribe Ourselves Sir your most Humble Servants and Prisoners [*Jane Williams, writing in own hand, signs, writes others' names, who sign by mark.*]
Annotated: Sarah Ireland 10/6 per Wk fm 8 Octt, Jane Williams 5/- per Wk. fr. 29 Oct.

378. *[F25/6/23] William Jasper, Newgate, undated, about November 1818, formal petition*
That your Petitioner was sentenced to Fourteen years Transportation at the last Old Bailey Sessions for having in his possession a forged Bank of England Note, for the Payment of One Pound.
That Your Petitioner having been informed that it has been customary for you to allow a small sum of Money to the unfortunate criminal, in order to furnish himself with a few Necessaries, before he leaves this his Native Country humbly hopes you will not think him altogether undeserving of being allowed the same.
That Your Petitioner humbly begs to state that his relations are so Poor and distressed that they cannot assist him in the smallest degree.
Your Petitioner therefore most fervently Prays you to take his case into your consideration And that you will be pleased to allow him such sum as

in Your goodness shall seem meet And Your Petitioner will ever most Sincerely Pray William Jasper his mark
[*BECLS*: *12 Nov. 1818, rejected.*]

379. *[F25/6/24] Thomas Kirby, Newgate, undated, about November 1818, formal petition*
That Your Petitioner was convicted at the last Sessions held at Justice Hall in the Old Bailey of having a Forged Note in his possession and received sentence of Transportation for Fourteen years.
That Your Petitioner bowing with the utmost deference to the Verdict of the impartial and honourable Jury by whom he was tried, humbly begs leave to intreat your attention and benevolence in his forlorn and destitute situation.
That Your Petitioner having been informed that in many instances it has been your custom to extend your Bounty towards the unfortunate criminal prior to his leaving this Country so as to enable him to furnish himself with a few necessaries requisite for so long a Voyage.
That Your Petitioner having no friends who can provide him with the smallest article, and being now in daily expectation of being removed from his native Country most humbly hopes that you will not think him altogether unworthy of your notice, but that you will be pleased to commisserate the unhappy situation into which he has unfortunately plunged himself, by allowing himself to be made the dupe of an artful and disigning man.
Your Petitioner therefore most ardently craves that You will be pleased to allow him the same Bounty which you have heretofore allowed (as he has been credibly informed) humbly assuring you that the smallest sum will be most gratefully and thankfully received, as his friends are all of them so poor that they have not the means of sending him the smallest assistance, should you be pleased to grant this Prayer of this his most humble yet ardent Petition that it will always be remembered with the most lively gratitude And Your Petitioner will ever most sincerely Pray. Thomas Kirby his mark
[*BECLS: 12 Nov. 1818, rejected.*]

380. *[F25/6/25a & b] William Turnbull, Newgate, 3 October 1819, to Mr Serjeant Bosanquet, 12, Montagu Place*
Formal petition to be allowed to plead to minor offence, sent to Bosanquest, as Turnbull's sister, Rebecca, was housemaid to Lady Bosanquest. Bank had already taken decision, 23 Sept. 1819. Attached: note from Bosanquet's clerk, J. Gibbs of Lincoln's Inn, forwarding petition to Bank.

381. *[F25/6/26] Thomas Carter, brother of prisoner John Carter, unknown address, 13 February 1820*
States he has been 20 Years at Messr Enies & Barnard Goldsmiths Ave Maria Lane St Pauls *and requests his brother be allowed to plead to lesser offence. Bank took decision 19 Jan. 1820.*

382. *[F25/6/27] Francis Whitby, Borough compter, 19 December 1819*
Sir As Being a prisnor in the Borrough Comter for atempting to pass forg^{d} notes I take Liberty of Writeing to you wishing a private Intervew With you or the other Solissiters of the Bank as I have paid But few a way and Detest the Concerne But trust I Can Give you that Information that Will Give you Sattisfastion and be a Great Service to the Bank Pleas to Let Mee have an answer as Soon as posable or the Partes May Hear of My Confindment and not to Be found Sir I Never ad a note from aney person But the Man I alude to wish I Can prove By the Man to Whom Introduced Mee to him for I have Been But Latley out of Business through Misfortune and a Large family of 5 Children on Seeing you I will Explain Better than By penn Your H S, F. Whitby

383. *[F25/6/28] Joseph Kaye, Bank solicitor, to Sir John Eames, magistrate, 5 February 1820, warning of an attempt to be made to enable prisoner, committed by Eames for further examination, to escape from Borough compter.*

384. *[F25/6/29] William Davies, Clerkenwell New prison, 1 March 1820*
too the Bank inspector saing that the man of wom I had the nots is name is samewell McLaud and is I bee live is now in horse Monger Lane for A resque But I doo not now of aney one elce for I have not Been Aquainted with them Not A fort knight so that I doo not now but verey Litell A bout them for wen hee gave mee the nots it was in A publick house that whe used and I paid 5s A note
Wm Davies by the Name of Wm Young Clarkenwell New prison

385. *[F25/6/30] Mr Atkins, keeper of Coldbath Fields prison, January 1820, submits list of 131 persons committed to the prison for uttering or possessing forged notes between 1 Jan. 1819 and 1 Jan. 1820. Annotated:* 131 persons £20

386. *[F25/6/31] Joseph Davis, Giltspur Street compter, undated, September/October 1818, to Peter Percy, sr, Bow Street public office, via Bank*
Mr Percy I am affrade you will consider me neglectful as you did not See me before the reason is I have a Companied Brown to Birmingham as I thought it would be the Shurest way to find out the Sellers at the preasant time for althow formerly I new maney of them things are verey much altered since I have bin aways. Whe have bin Entertained a several of thare houses & have had an opertunety of seeing everey thing I could wish but Cannot give an acount of the perticulars at this preasnt being verey pooreley with the fatiges of the gurney The Best way would be for you to put of my Exammenation & will Disclose that wich will be of the gratest Servis to the Bank & be a Means of Stoping in a grate measur the allarming traffick in this business for thare absolutely sold by Brown & Edwards & now Davis & maney more of the gang wich I Know well and wil due Everything in my power to give Everey Information for no man In England

Can have the opertunety of bringing it as I Can be trusted by aney of them with thare most private Consurns as I have all my lifetime bin Considered a good man Therefore frend Percy you may Rely on my integurety I beg you wil go to The Bank & she[*w*] this, & get my Examenation poseponded til I give them further Information wish I wil due to thare Sattisfaction The note I bin here fore I took a gambeling with them Thay absolutely put them in So much when at play wich you Know I gambel verey much I gave my rite plase of aboade & am not a tol affrerd of aney thing coming of it an I remain your truly Jos[h] Davis

The Business appened last nigh & I am in gilsper St Comter & for Examanation tomorrow I suppose

On front of letter, Davis writes: Mr Peter Percy Sen[r] Bow Stree publick offis to the Care of the Clark please to Let him have it Emedeatley it being of Importance; *and along side of front of letter:* frend Percy I Distroyed your Card for it wose not propper I should have it about me

387. *[F25/6/32a] Elizabeth Brown Owen, Horsemonger Lane gaol, 27 February 1820*

Sirs, I hope that you will excuse the liberty that I have taken in writing to you but I Wish to State to you the particulars of my Unfortunate Situation untill the time that I Sufferd Myself to be Led in to the Error that I have I had Allways Worked hard and Maintained My Family by my Own Industry I had four Children and the Parish only Allowed me Eight Shillings per week to Support them and What I Could Earn myself and I had no Father no Mother nor Freinds to Advise or Assist Me in my distress I am very Sorry for What has happened and I pray to God Almighty to Support me and to Spare Me for the Sake of my Dear Children and I will Strive for them Again as I have done and I Declare to your Sirs that I have worked hard for three Days and had only one penny Worth of Bread to Eat and Distress Drove me do What I have But I was Drawn in to it quite Inocently not knowing the Consequence and Trouble that it would Ocasion and My prosecutor says that he taken his Oath that I Said that My Name was Bowen Which I did not for I Said Brown Owen and I thought that the place of my Abode was named Carlisle Court Instead of which it is Called Carlisle Place but I was not Aware of that for there is no Name up at the Corner of the place and if you will take the trouble to Come and Speake to Me that I will Inform you Wheare these Notes are Made and the Name of the person that Comes Constant to the Bank to See if their is any Alteration in the Notes but if I do so I hope that for the Sake of My poor Children that he will try and get me my Liberty as they Will have no Freinds in this world When I am go[*ne*] to look to them but God Almighty and all My Troubles now are from being parted from them and Should I be Bannished in to Another County [*sic*] I Would Certainly Break my heart to leave them and I pray to God Almighty Night and Day to Let Me have them with me once more let me Suffer Any Hardships to Maintain them hoping that you will take pity on me for the Sake of my Children and that you will excuse this Liberty

I Remain Sir your humble Servant Elizabeth Brown Owen

388. *[F25/6/32c] Elizabeth Brown Owen, Horsemonger Lane gaol, 18 March 1820*
Sir, I hope that you will Consider my Distressed Case and take pity on Me for the sake of My four Fatherless Children. I have no Father nor Mother and My Children has no one to look to them but Myself having no Father I was Left very young in the world to strive for them which I Did working in the Fields and have not had but one penney Loaf in three Days for Myself that I might be able to give to My Children as I had but 8 shillings pr Week from the parrish at that time I was 8 Weeks Laying on a bed of sickness Which overwelhemed me in New Trouble and having no freinds in the Whole World to assist me or Mine but the Almighty God in whom I still put My trust with every hope in his Goodness I shall not be Cast or Leave my Dear Children I unfortunately entred into a se[*c*]ond Marrage with a hope of getting a home for My Children but as most unfortunately turnd out otherwise that I expected for I am now in More Trouble and Distress with the throughts of parting with My Dear Children. I am sincerely sorry that I suffered myself to be Drawn in to the error that I have but I Did not Consdred the Consequnce Before but I hope that If I get My Liberty with the Blessing of God Almighty I shall be able to support them by my own Industry as I have Done before I hope sir you will spare me and Consider my unhappy situation for the sake of My Four poor Dear Children. I have no Friends to Consult or Advise me for the Best, for belive me I was Innocently Drawn In to it as my Husband took the Notes for a Horse which I had no Idea the Notes where bad. My husband being frghtened and told they where bad, he whent away and I have not heard or seen him since I have been in Confinement which I take much to heart. therefore Sir I hope and Trust you will be kind enough to Do all that lays in your power for a most unfortunate and Friendless Woman, I pray to God night and Day that I may not be parted from my poor Children
Sir I remain your very humb and Obedient Servant Elizabeth Brown Owen
P.S. Sir I forgot to Mention that the Officers as sworn faulsely against me and the prosecutor most wrongley

389. *[F25/6/32b] Elizabeth Brown Owen, Horsemonger Lane gaol, 20 March 1820*
Almost identical letter to **387,** *penned by different hand.*

390. *[F25/6/32d] Elizabeth Brown Owen, Horsemonger Lane gaol, 28 March 1820*
Sir I hope you will not be offended at the Libberty I have takeing in riteing to you concerning My Drisstrees case as I am cast for Foureteen years Sir I hope you will Do all you can to set me free for I was inosent of the crime For I do not know a good and Bad one apart and I took the notes of my husband wich he told me he took for a horse I am sorry that I entered the second time of Marrage but i did it for the best thinking to have a home for my Childeren for if I am sent out of the Cuntterry I Shall Leve 4 Childeren Without a frind in the world

Sir if will take the trobble to come to Speek to me I can inform you of A Great Deal
I am your umble Servant Brown owen

391. *[F25/6/33] Elizabeth Redgrave, Horsemonger Lane gaol, 13 March 1820*
Sir, I hope you will pardon the Liberty I have taken in Troubling You with these few Lines as I before stated the facts to you, but If any further profes are required I could mention a few more perticulars If Sir you or any other Gentleman of the Bank would be kind enough to Call on Me, I have been Led away to Commit the Crime I am now suffering for, being Drove too it by the Greatest Distress having a sick Childe and A Husband at Sea, the Childe I have wholey to Maintain. I am suffering here while those escape unpunished that as brought me and many more and are still Doing so and will bring them to the same fate, therefore Sir, I shall feel myself much Honord by an answer to the above request.
Sir, I Remain your very Humble and Obedent Servant Elizabeth Redgrave

392. *[F25/6/34] Thomas Fuller, Horsemonger Lane gaol, undated in March 1820*
Honourd Sir My knowing your goodness induces me to wright to you hopping that youl forward this petetion to who you think Proper to ask them the favour to Let Me pleade Guilty to the Lesser offence of uttering forged notes[4] as i well no Myself Guilty of the Same and By so Doing youl Much Oblidge me your humble S[t] Thos Fuller
I would have related Something to you Concerning the affair But i Cannot Wright Myself
Addressed to Mr Warwick Bank
[*Bank had offered PB Aug. 1819*].

393. *[F25/6/35a & b] Mary King, Horsemonger Lane gaol, 10 March 1820*
Sir, I hope you will pardon My Liberty in writing to you to beg the Favour to be Allowed to pleaid to the Minor Offence, and Sir, If you and the other Gentlemen of the Bank will take into Consideration of My Distressed State It Will at once releave frome the Lowest Depth of Misery a Wretched Woman who as no Friend or Relation in the World to Do anything for her, and If the Gentleman will Comply to My Pettion, I should be for ever Bound to pray and If it is not to grate a Request – I should esteem Myself Much Honord by an answer to the Above, and in so Doing Sir you will Much Oblige Your very Humble and Obedint Servant Mary King
Addressed to Mr Freeman Bank Inspectors' Office.
Attached: letter 17 Feb. 1820, from Bank solicitors to clerk to magistrates, Queen Square, explaining that bill against King thrown out by Mdx. grand jury, OB Feb. Sessions; they request magistrate to issue warrant to Brown,

4. He clearly means possession of forged notes.

keeper of Newgate requiring him to continue holding her in Newgate for offences in Surrey.

394. *[F25/6/36] Jane Wilson and Elizabeth Miller, Horsemonger Lane gaol, 17 November 1818*
That each of us are deeply impressed with gratitude for the Lenity shewn us on our respective Trials – but having no Friends whatever to render us the least Assistance during our continuation in this Prison – and no means on our own part to assist ourselves – are reduced to the Gaol allowance of 24 Ounces of Bread for each Per Day – we most humbly entreat Your Kind interference with the Honourable Directors of The Bank That in their humanity they will please to alleviate our present suffering in such measure as they may think meet and as in grateful Duty bound will ever Pray &c. &c.
Inserted in margin by writer of letter: Convicted at the Assize holden at Guildford the 6th of August 1818
Annotated beside Miller's name: with one child
[*BECLS : 19 Nov. 1818, Miller to be paid 5s. a week in consideration of her having a child to support, Wilson's request rejected*].

395. *[F25/6/37a-j] William Eyre, debtor in King's Bench prison, in a series of correspondence with Bank solicitors between 3 Jan. 1819 & 8 Mar. 1820, asks for the signing of his discharge licence; he cannot pay Bank's expenses. Bank solicitors finally send discharge for him to marshal of prison.*

396. *[F25/6/38] Printed bankruptcy pro forma, completed 6 September 1819 in name of Edward Russell, hop and corn merchant, debtor in King's Bench prison, claiming discharge as insolvent debtor.*

397. *[F25/6/39] John Paulyn* [*or Pullein; see* **503**] *Coldbath Fields prison, 29 December 1819, formerly held in Tothill Fields prison on Bank charges, then released, writes concerning debts incurred in prison. His parents paid 3s. 6d. a week for his bed. Paulyn not prosecuted but admitted as evidence in another Bank case.*

398. *[F25/6/40] Lydia Astell and Mary Horne, transport ship* [probably *Janus*], *Woolwich, 19 October 1819*
Honnoured Sir, Pardon The Liberty Of me An unfortuneiate Feameal In Addressing my Senelf To your Honnour But From The very meney Hart Brakeing Sencetions I Now Feel In This Fountain Of Miserey I Have Involved my Senelf In to Though more Through A misfortune Then A Crime Oblidges me To Solessiet Your Kindness And most Humbly Begs That you Will Not Send Me out Of The Countrey Without Bestowing Your Charrity On me For The Sake Of My Dear Babs I Leave Behind – Honnoured Sir, I most Humbly Implor your Goodness To Look Down On me An unfortunate Young Wooman With An Eye Of pity So As To In Able me To Cloath my Children In A few things Of Which Am In grate Need –

Sir Some Heare From Newgate Have taken The Bennefit Of Five Pounds Which give me grate In Curradgement To Think your Honnour Will Kindly Take It Into Concederation And Extend your Goodness to Wards me, Likewise A Fellow Sufferer Named Marey Horn Joins With me And Humbley Prays For your Goodness To Extend towards her
Sir By Complying With The Above Requet Will Mutch Oblidge me An unfortuneate Feameal And In Duty Bound Will Ever pray Lydia Esden, Mary Horn
Sir, By The Advise Of Mr Caper [*Capper, home office*] – Have Indus me To take This Liberty In So Doing Hopes No Offence
[*BECLS: 14 Oct. 1819, already agreed £5 for these and eight other women*].

399. *[F25/6/41] Cathrine Wells, released prisoner, 119 Old Pye Street, Westminster, May 1818*
Sir, to Pass unnotised so great an Act of your Goodness and Benevelence Would be the hight of ingratitude in me I therefore beg leave in the best Manner I am Mistress off to return my most Greatfull thanks to you for restoreing me to my long lost Husband and Children Who has been Partakers of my Wretched situation Dureing my late long Confindment which has Exauesed every thing we had in Supporting our large Famaly 2 of our Children Died since my absence and to Add to our troubles the Dockters gives little hopes of my recoverry being in a decline and Traid Very bad for Want of Money to Carri it on Yet Sir in this situation I am thankfull to you for my Liberty and trust in God Whos never failing Goodness that has Protected me these last three Years to bring me through my present difficulty and may that Gratious God Ever Protect and Bless you With a long and happy Life and When he thinks fit to Call you may you enter into Everlasting Bliss is the Prayer and Ever Shall of me and my Famaly I am Sir with all Gratitude your most Obedent and Dutyfull Servant Cathrine Wells

400. *[F25/6/42] Catherine Leeson, unidentified prison* [probably Ilchester gaol], *November 1819, to friends*
I have sent you this to let you know I have been informd by A Gentleman that if I get a Coppy of the Affidavids that was sworn against me before the Grand Jury and take them before A Magistrate and the witnesses that is in my be half to come also and proave what you meant to do hear at Sizes it would be sent before the 12 judges and no doubt but I shuld get my liberty and pardon if so you must get another person as well as Marsh and the yong man
I will speak to Mr Bridal [*Bridle, keeper Ilchester gaol*] about it and then I will write to you when you write say nothing about it untill you hear from me as it is not known that I mentioned this to you –
you had better buy 13 yards of stuff like yours and lining when you receive some money for me for fear we should be sent off and if mother will let me have the Cloak send some purple lining and binding for it if you send 2 pairs of boots let them be my size and Mary shall have them and you had

better buy a lot of needles and Cotton for us to take with us at the fair of Bristol – there is a parcel of tickets in a purse mens Cloths some of them might do for Marsh and sell the rest Mothers blue gound is in pawn with my pelice what ever is in pawn if any get them out if you Can and and make us some pockets and send them to us I have some hopes yet but if I Cant get of I am Resign'd to My fate We join in love to you and mother and tell her it is no use to fret about us nor there is nothing that trouble us but parting with her and ye both but the time will Come when we shall meet never to part again
God bless you all C. Leeson

401. *[F25/6/43a & b] Mary Kelly, Newgate, 22 February 1820*
Gentlemen Pardon the liberty I have taken in writing to you soliciting your relief from you has I am in absolute Distress having no freind to render me any assistance my Mother being extremely poor and also being oblidged to pledge my Cloaths for subsistance and to Bury my Child while under examination therefore I am in that Distressed state respecting nessaries the Jail does not afford and Cloathing that I have not a change of apparrel and my health being greatly impaird by the long time I was under examination and having to attend to a sick Child therefore I hope you will think me an object worthy your consideration by complying with my request you will confer a lasting obligation on your Humble Sert Mary Kelly
Attached: note from Thomas Glover, Bank investigator, 24 Feb. 1820, confirming all that Kelly says, adding that her mother is in workhouse. His note annotated: £2 to redeem her clothes.
[*BECLS: 1 Mar. 1820, records this and award of 5s. a week while in prison*].

402. *[F25/6/45a] 'H.C.' (female), 'London', 26 July 1819, to her mother, Mrs Marsh, 18 Claverton Street, Witcomb, Bath*
Dr Mother I Received your Letter and am Glad to hear you are all well I am but very Indifferent the Poor Children are all Tolerable well thank God – I am Very happy to hear Poor Peggy is Comfortable and has got a good Husband I hope God will give them both a Blessing – I am Surprised at your not Mentioning any Thing about Kitty or Mary dont omit it in your next and Let Me know if Mary is Married and Let me know all the Pirticulars of Every thing – you need not be Uneasy about the things in the bed they are all Safe they are only Put down in the Ticket that way for Shortness. Tom Porter [**166, 445, 740**] and his woman are both don for fourteen Years And Expect to Sail for the Bay In Course of 5 or 6 weeks at farthest there is a womans Ship going and God Only Knows but it may be My Fate to go if it should I Must Resign Myself to the will of the Allmighty God who I hope will Protect Me by Sea as well as by Land but I have One Great Consolation That is that I can take My Children with me John Now does what he can for Me and Says if I go he will com up to Bristol and Sell his share of The Property coming to him and go with me I hear Jim Hall is doing very well There Durham is Married to a Settlers Daughter and does well also I can give No answer about sending Mary to you Until I find how

things will turn out with Me Should I Remain here I will send her to you if not She must go with Me She is grown a Fine Stout girl. Poor Little Margaret is Sent out 5 Miles in the Country with Som More Little Children to Nurse – Poor John and Mary is both together In the House I have the Youngest with Me I Mean to Send a Petition to the Secretary of State but God only Knows what Effect it May have however I will be able to Let you know More In My Next Let me hear from you As Soon as Possible and if it Should be In your Power to Send me a Trifle (but don't Distress yourself) you may Send it to Smiths John Still Lodges with them it wont do to send it me Everything is Opend here If you could Send Me a bit of Muslin to make a cap or two I should be thankful for it – Keep My Unhappy Situation as Secret as Possible and dont Say anything about it to Carpenter John has now got Nothing to do his Business Is all over Untill Christmass again John and the Children Joins in In Love with Me to ye all and May God Bless and Protect ye all are the constant Prayers of Your Unhappy and Dutiful Daughter – till Death H…C…r

P.S. Dont Omit writing to Me as Soon as Possible and Let Me Know all you can and Direct as before then John will get it and bring it to me it was a Travelling woman told Me She saw Peggy at Cheltenham

On front Margaret Marsh *is written below address, together with three other attempts at writing* Margaret. [*Unable to trace writer; may be false initials*].

403. *[F25/6/45b] 'H.C.' (female), 'London', 22 August 1819, to her friends at 18 Claverton Street, Witcomb, Bath*

My Dr Freinds I Now Embrace this oppertunity of Writing to you In consequence of not having an answer to my Last Letter and am very Uneasy at Not hearing from you I hope all is well with you and Let Me beg of You to answer this as soon as it come to Hand I have Not Heard anything as yet Respecting a Mitigation of My Sentance but there are Mitigations Expected down Every Day and Likewise orders for those that are to go to Botany Bay but I Trust in god it will Not be My Fate to be sent away – tell Kitty Leeson is In London John often sees Him he says he has been to Sea and Wanted to Know Where ye are as he should Like to See Kitty More, but John did not tell him where ye Lived – I expect John will be Obligated to go to Bristol in the course of a Few Days to See If his Father will assist him for he has nothing to do here and of Course he cant Live on the Air he will Call on ye In His way to Bristol dont Omit Writing by Return of Post And Let Me Know all Pirticulors Should I be mitigated I may be sent away to another Prison from here I have No More to add but hope ye are all In good Health and Conclude with My Love and Sincere Wishes for your Welfare and Remain Yours Affectionately H.. Cr

404. *[F25/7/25] Elizabeth Brooks, Newgate, 13 January 1819*

Honorable Gentlemen Pardon the Presumption of my thus Addressing you but Embolden by your well known Benevolence and Goodness of Hearts to those who Unfortunately have brought themselves under the Just laws of their Country by a violation of them being thro the Mercy of God and the

Royal Clemency Spared to once more throw Myselfe on your kind Consideration in imploring your Charity to be in some degree Extended to Myselfe and 5 Helpless Children who has no other Friend to look to for Protection or Support having since My long Confinement parted with every Article of wearing Apparel and every necessary In my Possession to suport Myselfe and them and now reduced to the Greatest Penury Expecting to leave my Native Country for ever without A hope of returning In hope Honorable Gentlemen you will take the Destitute Situation of My Distressed Children into your Consideration and Grant whatever Relief your Goodness and Charity may think Most fit and your humble Petitioner will be ever in Gratitude Bound to Pray For the Charitable Hand that would be extended to Relieve the Distress of an Helpless Family, I beg leave to Subscribe Myselfe with Humble Respect Honorable Gentlemen your very Humble and Distressed Servant Elizabeth Brooks [*written in the hand of Jane Williams*]

405. *[F25/7/26] Elizabeth Brooks, Newgate, 27 January 1819*
Honored gentlemen I hope the Liberty I take in Addressing you will be Pardoned but venturing to entreat your Charity to be in some Degree extended towards me as having got 5 Children who look to me for Support which I am unable to give them thro my long Confinement if Worthy Gentlemen you Should think me Deserving of your Charity as I have been obliged to part with every necessary I have had to Support Myself and them and Should it be my Fate to leave my native Country I have not got any thing but what is in Pawn to keep me nor any thing but the Goal allowance the truth of this can be ascertained by enquiring at the Prison Should I be Deemed Worthy of your Notice Honored Gentlemen entreating you to take this my Distressed Case into your Consideration and hoping you will be induced to extend a little of your Goodness to Myself and Children which would be most Thankfully and Gratefully accepted by your very Humble and Distressed Servant Elizabeth Brooks [*written in the hand of Jane Williams*]

406. *[F25/7/1] Elizabeth Brooks, Newgate, 1 February 1819*
Honorable Gentlemen I once more take liberty of addressing myselfe to you entreating a little of your Charity to be extended towards me as I am very much distressed myselfe and 5 Children which I have now got the Grant of them to accompany me to a Foreign Country 2 of them are at a Factory and I expect every Day to have them in town on purpose to be the companions of my voyage 2 of them are in London Friendless and unprotected altho I never had them in the Prison but since my long confinement which is now nearly 9 months I have parted all my Cloaths to Support them and is reduced to the Greatest Penury without a Friend to assist Me the 5th is in the Country and will not be any trouble to me as a Friend has taken her to provide for her and when my other 2 comes the will literally speaking be without Cloaths or anything that is necessary for them the 2 that is in London can be seen at any time one of them is the bearer of this

Honorable Gentlemen I take the Liberty of enclosing the Letters that come from my Children as a testimony of the truth of what I assert and Should you be induced to grant me a little of that Charity that has been so mercifully extended to my Fellow Prisoners who has stood in the same Situation of my Selfe Mr Hardy at the Prison can testify the truth of what I Say and your Humble Petitioner will be ever bound in Gratitude to Pray Elizabeth Brooks

Honorable Gentlemen should you be induced to read my Letters if you would have the goodness to return them it would oblige yr humble Servant and Prisoner [*written in the hand of Jane Williams*]
[*BECLS: 5 Feb. 1819 agreed £5 but only when she sailed*].

407. *[F25/7/3–4] Elizabeth Brooks, Newgate, 8 February 1819*
Gentlemen I am under the Nesesity of Appealing To your Well known Humanity and Feelings Humbly Hoping you will attend to The Humble Supplication of an unfortunate prisoner Eliz Brooks who was convicted of uttering a Forged Bank note Value one Pound in Last September and I am Now under sentance of Transporting for Life and of course Expect shortly To Leave My Native Country for Ever – and Having Obttaind Permission of His Majesty Government To Take My Four unfortunate children The Bearer who is one I Humbley crave your assistance To Enable to get My Two Children up From The Country so That I May Quit My Native Land Not Destitute and Pennyless Leaving Gentleman To your well know Generosity I shall Ever be in Duty Bound to Pray Elizabeth Brooks
Attached: copy letter, 13 Feb. 1819, from Bank solicitors to Nathaniel Pryor, 20, Gracechurch Street [*whom they call* Matthew Pryor, a Quaker] *who forwarded Brooks' letter stating Bank governor and directors had authorised £5 on embarkation.*

408. *[F25/7/2] Elizabeth Brooks, Newgate, 18 February 1819*
Honored Sir I take the Liberty of Sending My Daughter the bearer of this Hoping you will have the Goodness to let her know the Result of the Honorable Gentlemen in regard of my Distressed Situation and to have the Goodness to give her the Papers Relative to my Children as they are of the utmost Importance to me in regard of Sending for them to accompany me in my Distressing voyage from my Native Country if Honored Sir you would have the Goodness to add this favor to the many received hoping they will be induced in their Great Clemency and Charity and thro your Great kindness to in some Degree Relieve my present Distressed State and Honored Sir I Shall be ever in Duty Bound to Pray Elizabeth Brooks [*written in the hand of Jane Williams*]
Annotated on front: Opened by Mr Rooker but not for him

409. *[F25/7/5–6] Susannah Leonard, Newgate, 17 February 1819*
Honeard Sir Excuse me for trublin you my Prisent Situation Is in the greatist Distress I am Left Distute and No frind to Come Neir me to Bring me Lest Relife I have a pour Child In the Work House allmost Naked and Not a show apon Hiss Feat to Kipe Him from the Cold Honeard Sir I Hope you

take my unhapy Case In to your Humane Consideration to Let me Have my Litle things as I am Naked When I sent a parson affter them Mr Cousins my Land Lord said that Mr Rooker [*Bank solicitors' clerk*] Ordared now wone to Have them Honerd Sir Would you Be so Good to Order the Sherif Officer to Dispose of them to Relive me and My Pour Fatherliss Child Honeard Sir I shall In Duty Bound Evear pray Susina Leanord
Annnotated: underlining of above words and marking with x, enquiry to be made respectg the Contents of this lter; *and:* Mr Rooker never gave any directions whatever respecting any property belonging to the Prisoner
Attached: report from Charles Christmas, Bank investigator, stating that landlord detained Leonard's furniture until balance of half a year's rent, £5 11s., was paid.
[*BECLS: 25 Feb. 1819, Bank would not interfere*].

410. *[F25/7/7–10] W. H. Brown, keeper of Newgate, 11 February 1819, forwards request from prisoner on hulk, John Green of Blandford, tried in 1818, sentenced to fourteen yrs trspn, for return of £4 taken from him at time of arrest. Bank solicitors reply that they used £1 to pay an informer on Green; they return remaining £3.*

411. *[F25/7/11] Elizabeth Wingfield, Newgate, 5 February 1819*
Sir I hope you will Pardon my liberty but being Verry Much distressed since my Unhappy Confinement both me and My Child, Sir I am Confined since May last and I have Pawned all my Cloaths to support my Fatherless Child as I was Obliged to Send him Out of the Prison through his health being Verry bad Sir I Expect to leave My Country before long and I hope you will take my distress into your humane Consideration and bestow on me and my Child a little of your benevolent Charity, to Enable me to Get my Cloaths before I leave My Country Sir as a proof of my Distress Inclosed you will see my Dublicates of my Cloaths Sir by you takeing My distress into your human Consideration your Humble Petioner will be Ever Bound to Pray Elizabeth Winfield
[*BECLS: 5 Feb. 1819, £2 to be sent to keeper of Newgate for her*].

412. *[F25/7/12] Jane Williams, Mary Ann Reed, Sarah Hyland, Newgate, 1 February 1819*
Honored Gentlemen We beg leave to address you in an Humble and thankful manner for the many Favors recd from you but particularly for the allowance you were kind enough to make us in the Distressed State we were in and enable us to leave our native Country with some degre of Decency and Hoping Kind Gentlemen that we have not in any manner Cancelled the Charity you were so Good as to bestow us as having a Months Money Due to us on Saturday the 23d of January out of which we recd 1 weeks pay on Teusday the 26th of January which left 3 weeks Due and on Saturday the 30th received 1 weeks more in hope that our Situation will meet your Compassion and we allowed to have what you so kindly and Benevolently said we should have and in hope you will Pardon our troubling you so often but writing before and receiving no answer we took the

Liberty of addressing you again we beg leave to Subscribe ourselves Honorable Gentlemen your most Obliged and Grateful Servants, Mary Ann Reed, Jane Williams, Sarah Hyland [*written in Jane Williams' hand*].

413. *[F25/7/13] Hannah Polley, Newgate, 1 February 1819*
Sir I hope you will pardon my liberty being Verry Much Distressed Since My unhappy Confinement obliges me to Petion your Worthy Gentlemen for the Smallest Relief the think proper to bestow on me Sir I am 54 years of age and had verry Bad health since my confinement obliged me to Pawn my Cloaths, and have no Means of Releasing them if your benevolent Charity is not Extended on me, as I Expect to leave my Country in a short time and have no Person to Relieve me but an Aged Husband in Great distress
Sir I am Confined Since May and was obliged to send my Cloaths to Pawn by Various Persons Occations them not to be in my Own name Sir as a proof of My Distress Enclosed you will find my Dublicates Sir I Trust you will not Consider me Entruding by Calling your Worthy attention to Peruse my Distress but Relying on your Humane Consideration gives me a hope of a little of your Benevolent Charity to Relieve my Great distress Sir I Remain your Most Obedient Humble Petioner Hanah Polly
[*BECLS: 2 Feb. 1819, agreed to send £2 for her via keeper of Newgate*].

414. *[F25/7/14] Jean Wilson, Horsemonger Lane gaol, 8 February 1819*
Honoured Sir I again take the liberty of writing to you, which I hope you will pardon, as I think my last letter has escaped your memory, I would not be so troblesome to you, if I was not in the gratest destress for, Cloaths, and other Necessarys – having no one for to come to bring me any thing, and being so long in prison, In my letter to you last month I informed you all perticulars of my situation, and destress, which I hope you will have the goodness to take into consideration, and grant me a little aid, as it is 6 months since I had my Triel, and I had been 3 months in prison privious to it – and during all the time had nothing but the Jaol alowance,
I was tried at Augest assises, and pleaded guilty for uttring a Forged Bank of Ingland Note and got sentance of 14 years transportation passed on me, I again mention those circomstances in case you may have forgot what I had wrote you befor, and I begg you will have the goodness to do something for me in my destress, as I have no one for to do any thing for me trusting in your goodness I begg leave for to subscribe myself Honoured Sir your ever Oblidged and gratefull Servant Jean Wilson

415. *[F25/7/15–18] Correspondence, March 1819, involving James Cowing, of Cowing and Sons, debtor, King's Bench prison. He owes Bank £500, says his furniture and effects are being sold and asks Bank to accept 3s. 6d. in the £. Bank reply they will do so if his other creditors do likewise.*

416. *[F25/7/19–20] Frederick Suthmier, debtor, King's Bench prison, 18 May 1819, offers Bank £247 10s. in payment of debt of £2,100; Bank refuse.*

417. *[F25/7/21–4] Bank lists of prisoners for 13 January, 21 April, 26 May, 7 July and 15 & 17 September 1819 to W. H. Brown, keeper of Newgate, detailing prisoners to be arraigned at OB, asking him to inform them.*

418. *[F25/7/27] J. W. Jones, on behalf of Elizabeth Brooks in Newgate, 27 April 1819. Jones restates all that Brooks has said about her distress in* **404–8** *asking Bank to let her have whatever relief they think proper and to pay some debts incurred to* Mrs Coventry and others. [*BECLS: 28 Apr. 1819, decision of 5 Feb. 1819 stands; they will pay £5 when she sails*].

419. *[F25/7/28] Elizabeth Bush, Newgate, 21 April 1819*
Bush requests permission to plead guilty to lesser offence. Bank took decision 5 Mar. 1819.

420. *[F25/7/29] Elizabeth Bush, Newgate, 3 June 1819*
Elizabeth Bush Prisoner being very much distressed and obliged to part with her Cloaths having no friends to assist her humbly hopes that the Governor will take her distressing case into consideration and kindly bestow a triffle from his Humane Charity. Elizabeth Bush is at this time ill and under the care of Mr Bose in his Infirmary

421. *[F25/7/30–1] Elizabeth Bush, Newgate, 17 June 1819*
Sir Once More I Emplore you to take My wretched Situation into your Consideration and bestow on me a little of your Charity, to Enable me to Release My Cloaths as Mr Brown Informed me I would be leaving my Country in a Short time Sir as a proof of My Distress I take the liberty of Inclosing my Dublicates hoping you will be so kind as to bestow on me a little of your kind Charity to Release them and by so doing your Humble Petioner will Ever Pray Elizabeth Bush
Attached: copy note, 17 June 1819, from Bank solicitors saying that directors of Bank decline to accede to her request; her duplicates returned.

422. *[F25/7/32] Mary Deal, Newgate, 25 August 1819*
Sir I hope you will Pardon my Liberty being verry Much distressed Emboldens me to Solicit your kind Enterference with the Humane Gentlemen of the Bank, to take my Distress into their Consideration and bestow on me a little of their Benevolent Charity and by so doing your Humble Petioner will Ever Pray Mary Deal
Annotated by BECLS secretary: To pay her Two Pounds; *and by J. Rooker,* pd 11 Sepr 1819

423. *[F25/7/33] Susan Farmilo, Newgate, 8 March 1819*
Honered Gentle men pleas to Exchuse me for taken the liberty of writing to you sin as i have had mercy extended on me to a degree [*resp. from execution to life trspn*] Sir i have been so bold as to ask you if you pleas to Extend your Goodness on me as to releve my Distress for i am goin out of my Contry for my life without money Close or afrend Sir i am in great

Distress in Deed inever troubled with aletter before and iam sorry to Do so now but Distress Drives me to it Honered Sir as you have Extended your marcy on my fellow prisnors ihope and trust you will on me apoor prisnor as i am and have no frend sence i have been in prason seven months hear and my frends for saken me Honered Sir ihope you will Exchuse me for senden by the post for i have no frends to send it by Honered Sir i make no Demand but ihope and trust you will releve me if it is but Ever such atrifle for we are goin soon to my sorrow Sussan Farmilo
[*BECLS: 10 Mar. 1819, request rejected*].

424. *[F25/7/34] Hannah Gilbert, Newgate, 7 January 1819*
Honored Sir I once more attempt to address you by begging of you to take my Distressed Case into your kind Consideration having been very ill as Dr Box can testify and having no friend whatever to assist me being entirely without Cloaths having parted with them to support myselfe and as the time approaches when I expect to leave my native Country I beg a little of your Charity to be extended towards me as it has been so Benevolently granted to my Fellow Prisoners and Honored Sir you will be ever Entitled to the Prayers of your very much Distressed and Humble Servant and Prisoner Hannah Gilbert [*written in the hand of Jane Williams*]

425. *[F25/7/35] Hannah Gilbert, Newgate, 13 January 1819*
Much Honerd Sir I ham Sory to troble You But my present Situration and my Distress once more beg for reliefe for Kind Gentleman I at the present time ham in the graitest of Distress for I have lost the only friend I had wich was my poor Aged broken harted Mother Wich now lay Dead and is left behind hur 3 Orphin unprovided for the Oldest is but 15th Years of age kind Sir if you will take my present Distress in Consideration I Shall think myself in Ever Duty Bound to pray Your most Obedent And Humble Servent Hannah Gilbert
[*BECLS: 14 Jan. 1819, agreed to send £2 to keeper of Newgate, for her relief*].

426. *[F25/7/36] Hannah Gilbert, Newgate, 18 April 1819*
Much Honour^{d} Sir I Most humbly beg Pardon for intruding But having no Mother nor Father nor any Person to Look up to for the least Suport and ham intirly Depending upon your goodness in wich I hope you will Extend to wards me I have giveing to hunderstand that thare was left in Mr Browns Charg £2 Pounds and if So I never Recev^{d} But one I have several times ask Mr Brown for the Other triful but he Sas that he as no more for he was Paid no more for me I must once more beg You will take my Distress in Consideration and Releve me with A triful or Interseid with Mr Brown for the Other triful And by so Doing I Shall think myself in Ever Duty Bound to Pray Your Most Obedent and Humble Servent Hannah Gilbert

427. *[F25/7/37] Hannah Gilbert, Newgate, undated May 1819*
Hon^{d} Gentleman I receved One pound Out of the 2 pounds You was so good & Benovlent to send for Me which I return You My Most Humble

and Sincer thanks for the same I having no Relations nor frinds to releve Me but your kind Benovelance thairfore Gentleman I throw Myselfe at Your feet in hopes You will Commiserat My Case and give an Order to Mr Brown to remitt to Me the Other 1 Pound as it will be the Means of Elivating My present Destress

I Am Hon^{d} Gentleman with due Respects Your Most Obd Hum^{l} Ser^{t} Han^{h} Gilbert

P. S. Newgate Prison

428. *[F25/7/38] Mary Ann Griffiths, Newgate, 7 July 1819*

Sir I Humbly hope you Will pardon the Liberty I have taken but bean Confind in the Sick Ward for this month past and not one frend to give me the Smalest Trifell I hope you Will Conseder my unhappy Case I Would not Troubel you Only my present Illness and the smalest trifell Will be thankfuly Receved by your Humble Prisoner Maryann Griffis

Annotated: Mary Ann Griffiths convicted with Henry Dart

[*BECLS: 14 July 1819, agreed to send her £2*].

429. *[F25/7/39] Mary Hartnell, Newgate, 6 January 1819*

Honored Sir Pardon the Liberty of my thus intruding on you begging of you to take into your kind Consideration my Distressed Situation and hopes you will have the Goodness to lay my Petition before the Honorable Governor and Company of the Bank and hoping thro your kind interest to have a little of their Charity extended towards myselfe and Children we being in a most Distressed state and humbly hoping the Liberty will be excused I beg leave to Subscribe myselfe with every Respect your very Humble Servant and Prisoner Mary Hartnell [*written in the hand of Jane Williams*]

[*BECLS: 1 Jan. 1819, granted her 7s. 6d. a week*].

430. *[F25/7/40] Hannah Polley, Newgate, 7 June 1819*

Sir, I humbly hope that you will kindly take my distressing situation into your consideration being an aged [*54 yrs old*] Woman and my Husband at this time in the Poor-House therefore I have no friend whatever to assist me.

I am in a bad state of Health and greatly in want of more support that the Jail allowance I have been in confinement now almost thirteen Months and therefore hope you will bestow a trifle from you Benevolent Charity and I shall be ever bound to pray for you Hannah Polley

[*BECLS: 9 June 1819, request refused*].

431. *[F25/7/41–2] Hannah Polley, Newgate, 16 June 1819*

Sir I hope you will be pleased to pardon my Entrusion but being verry much Distressed I having no friends able to Render me any Relief lying these 14 months in a Gloommy Weary Prison having no support in my old age of 54 but my Goal Allowance, only the two pounds the humane Gentlemen Remited, Sir I Expect to leave me Country in the Month of July as there is a ship taken up for us Convicts I have Pawned the best part of

my Cloaths to Get me a little Nourishment as I have Never been well since my Confinement Sir if you would be Pleased to Refer to M[r] Brown he will Inform you of my Illness since here and also my having no friends Sir Once more I Emplore you to take my Distress into your Humane Consideration and bestow on me a little of your Benevolent Charity and by so doing your Humble Petioner will Ever Pray Hannah Polly
Attached: copy letter from Bank solicitors, same date, stating Bank directors decline to accede to her request.

432. *[F25/7/43] Elizabeth Rhodes, Newgate, 29 July 1819*
Honred Sir I Humbly hope you Will pardon the Liberty I have taken Having None friend to Give me the Smalest Trifel and nothing but the Goal allowance I hope you Will take my Case into Consideration and be pleased to allow me a Small Trifell from your Benevolent Charity Witch Will be most Gratefuly Received from your Very Humble prisoner Elizabeth Rose

433. *[F25/7/44] Sarah Ward, Newgate, 12 January 1819*
Honorable Gentlemen Embolden to Address you by the Great mercy Extended to Me in my Life being Graciously Spared I now venture to throw Myselfe on your Benevolent and Humane Consideration being in a most Destitute Situation with 4 Small Children and nearly going to Bed of a fifth which renders my unfortunate Condition much worse being obliged to part with every necessary I had to support myselfe and Infants who has no other Friend to look up to for Support and Protection Honorable Gentlemen I take the Liberty of asking your Charity to be Extended to me in some Degree as your Great Wisdom and Humanity may seem meet. Should it be my Fate to leave my Country for ever I am entirely devoid of Cloaths or common Necessaries to be obligated to Undertake such a Voyage Entreating your kind Consideration on this My Distressed state and hoping you will Pardon the liberty of my thus troubling you and begs leave to Subscribe Myselfe with Humble Respect your very Humble Servant and Prisoner Sarah Ward [*written in the hand of Jane Williams*]
Annotated: She was Convicted at the Sept[r] Sess[ns] at the Old Bailey for utter[g] forged Notes
[*BECLS: 14 Jan. 1819, awarded her 10s. 6d. a week*].

434. *[F25/7/45] Sarah Ward, Newgate, 10 June 1819*
Sarah Ward hops that the Govenor Will Consider her Destrsing Case having fore Children and Nothing but Gaol allowance and not a frend to assist her Watever She therefore Relies upon his Goodness in Continueing her the allowance as he as so Kindey Don During her Stay in Newgate as will bee most thankfuly Recevd by your Very Grateful and Humbel Servant Sarah Ward

435. *[F25/7/46] Sarah Ward, Newgate, 15 August 1819*
Hon[d] Gentleman In Consequence of Not Reiceving The Charity you so Humanely Extended towards Me Hitherto I have taken The Liberty of again Soliciting for a continuance of the Same And Trust My Present

Distress (And Not having Any Friend whatever to Render Me the Smallest assistance) will be a Sufficient Excuse for the Liberty I have taken in troubling The Hon[ble] Gentlemen of the Bank And beg Leave to Subscribe Myself With the Most Profound Respect and diffidence Your Most H[ble] and Obd[t] Servant Sarah Ward

436. *[F25/7/47] Maria Wilkes, Newgate, 13 January 1819*
Sir I trust you will Pardon My Intrusion being in Great Distress since my unhappy Confinement as I have no frends but an aged Mother that cannot Render me any Relief since I was bereft of My Husband by his being sent on board the Retribition where he suffered Great hardship Since his absence I have Parted all my Cloaths and have Not anything but my Goal allowance Sir if you would be so kind as to Present My Letters to the Gentlemen it would be doing a Great Charity as I Expect to be Leaving my Country in a short time, and have all my Cloaths in pledge Sir if you would Refer to the keepers they can sertify My Distress Sir let me once More Entreat you to Consider my Great Distress and bestow on me a little of your benevolent Charity by so doing your Humble Petioner will Ever Pray Maria Wilkes
[*BECLS: 14 Jan.1819, agree to send £2 for her to keeper of Newgate*].

437. *[F25/7/49] Anonymous 'Bank Prisoners in Newgate', 26 April 1819*
Honorable Gentlemen We For the Last time beg leave to Address you and returns you Our Sincere Thanks for the Charity extended towards us which has been the Means of our Supporting Ourselves During our long and tedious Confinement and Farther Entreating your Charity to be Extended towards Us on our leaving our Native Country for Ever So that We May be Enabled to Go with Some Degree of Comfort During our long and perilous Voyage as we are Ordered for Embarkation on Wednesday or Thursday Morning
Honorable Gentlemen We beg leave to Subscribe Ourselves with Humble Respect your Obliged and Humble Servants and Prisoners
The Bank Prisoners In Newgate [*in Jane Williams' hand; Bank solicitor annotates it as coming from female prisoners*].

438. *[F25/7/48] Jane Williams, Mary Ann Reed, Hannah Gilbert, Maria Wilkes, Clarissa Downes, Mary Hartnell, Elizabeth Brooks, Elizabeth Winfield, Newgate, 3 May 1819*
Honored Gentlemen We Humby Entreat your Pardon For thus Importuning you in Regard of your Extending your Charity towards us On leaving our Native Country as having Contracted a Few Debts which we Depending on your Goodness to Repay by Allowing us the Usual Stipend which you have so Charitably hitherto Done Honored Gentlemen We beg Leave to Subscribe Ourselves with Humble Respect your very Humble Servants and Prisoners
[*in Jane Williams' hand; she and Clarissa Downes sign their names, others sign by mark*].

Annotated by Brown, keeper of Newgate: The Above will in a day or two be sent to the Ship now lying at Woolwich
[*BECLS: 5 May 1819, award them all £5*].

439. *[F25/7/50] David Austin, Newgate, 24 July 1819*
Gentlemen, Having Pleaded Guilty to your Indictment and expecting to leave this place in a few days I beg leave to Inform you that my Friends were very Respectable but reduced by various Misfortunes and I can assure you it was necessity only that Induced me to the act that brought me into this painful situation – which compels Me to solicit the Kindness, which I understand you have frequently Bestowed on Many in My Situation, a small amount would assist me to many necessarys for My Voyage, which I am now destitute of. Your Bounty will confer an Infinite obligation on your very Humble Servant David Austin
[*BECLS: 27 July 1819, refused*].

440. *[F25/7/51–2] John Adams, Newgate, about 10 March, 1819*
Gentlemen, John Adams, convicted in January Sessions last, for uttering Forged notes, feeling the awful situation in which he stands most humbly implores your interference in his unfortunate case, deeply impress[d] with a sense of his error and also admitting the Justice of his sentence, he begs for the sake of A Wife and aged Father & Mother, that the part which affects his life will be taken into their merciful consideration. At the same time he begs to inform the Governor & Directors should they feel disposed for information by what means the said notes came into his possession he is ready and willing to make a full disclosure of the parties from whom they were obtained, feeling sensible that such discovery will not only meet the ends of Justice but tend in a great measure to prevent the frequent recurrence of cases similar to his one, that of the Young & unwary being led into the commission of crime by old and harden[d] offenders who reap great benefits by those who imprudently become their victims.
Gentlemen, for Mercy[s] sake consider banishment for life, a sufficient punishment it is that he asks, thereby taking off the dreadful part of his sentence (Death) buryed with a hope that mercy will be extended to his earnest solicitations humbly craves their interference and your Petioner will be in Duty Bound to pray (John Adams)
He writes on front of letter: at the suggestion of His Grace the Marquis of Buckingham
[*Attached: copy letter from Bank solicitors, 11 Mar. 1819: request rejected, consistent with Bank's duty to public; Adams was executed*].

441. *[F25/7/53] Thomas Arnold, Newgate, undated end March 1819*
Requests permission to plead to lesser offence, stating he used to earn a respectable living until illness forced him out of employment; he can get many reputable tradesmen to speak for his good character. Bank made decision 24 Mar. 1819.

442. *[F25/7/54] Thomas Arnold, Newgate, 29 April 1819, formal petition*
That your Petitioner was indicted at the present Sessions for uttering Forged Notes, but being allowed the privilege of pleading guilty to the minor offence, received sentence of Fourteen Years transportation.
That your Petitioner having been informed that in many cases you have extended your benevolence towards those unfortunate persons who by offending in a similar manner have incurred the awful sentence of the Law.
That your Petitioner most humbly begs to assure you that his friends are so situated as not to be able to render him the smallest assistance, he therefore most humbly hopes that you will not think him altogether unworthy of your notice, but that you will be pleased to allow him such pecuniary assistance as you may consider proper for to procure him a few necessary articles to subsist on during his long and tedious voyage from his native Country.
Your Petitioner therefore most humbly Prays you to allow him the same Sum as you have before granted to Convicts in his unhappy situation. And your Petitioner as in duty bound will ever Pray &c
[*BECLS: 5 May 1819, request rejected*].

443. *[F25/7/55] Thomas Grosvenor, Newgate, 27 January 1819*
Most Honr Sirs Permit me most Gratefully to return my Bounding thanks for the Lenity shewn me in suffering me to plead Guilty to the minor part of my lamented Offence being now fully evinced of such a Mark of important favour, and if I am not too far trespassing on Your Benevolent considerations implore such little aid the Necessity of my forlorn Condition may in Your great Goodness seem Meet I beg also most humbly to state that I am Destitute of any friends and terrible for me by this Dreadful Event have lost my Pension being the reward I met for the services I rendered to my Country by Sea, these I supplicate may Opperate in my favour by your feeling Considerations of me and humbly pray I may receive such relief as has in similar Cases Distinguish'd your Laudable and Charitable Purpose
I am Most Honr Sirs your Most Obed^{n} hu^{ble} & unfortunate Servt Thomas Grovener
Addressed to: The Cashier or Governors *and* Mr Suter *at Bank solicitors*
[*BECLS: 28 Jan. 1819, request rejected*].

444. *[F25/7/56] John Jones, Newgate, 29 January 1819*
Honord Sir Deeply impress'd with a sense of your great mercy in allowing me to plead Guilty to the minor part of my lamented Offence, I am now most humbly imploring the benevolent consideration of your respectable body to further compassionate my forlorn condition and your accustom'd and usual relief to the unfortunate Delinquent look upon me as one not wholly unworthy of your charitable succor and relief, I am Sir the unfortunate Young Man of the name of John Jones late a Soldier in the 18 Hussars and until this first and unhappy event bore in my regiment and I trust the World, an irreproachable Character I beg to remind the Benevolence of your Considerations that only the Two one Pounds could appear against me, which assurdly was the whole of my Dread concern, suffer me the to

implore of you such relief, being truly Distressed without a friend, Dependant only on the scanty allowance of the Gaol for my support such a Mark of your humanity will be most gratefully felt by, Hono[rd] Sir Your most Obdt Hub[le] & unfortunate Serv[t] John Jones
[*BECLS: 2 Feb. 1819, request rejected*].

445. *[F25/7/57] Thomas Porter, Newgate, 10 June 1819*
Gentleman I Was Convicted Last Sessions for having 3 one Pound Notes in my Prossesson and if you Think Proper to Wait on me as Soon as you Can I Shall be Able to Give you Such Information as You Will be Satisfied With Respecting Some Forged Notes Thomas Porter

446. *[F25/7/58–9] George Price, Newgate, 7 May 1819*
Gentleman I take the liberty of writing to you most humbly craving your attention in the distressing Situation that I am now placed in, begging of you, Gentlemen, to Spare my life as I was totally Drawn into the Snare by those People whom sell and have them from the Maker and those people Employed me to pass them for them which I received 7 Shillings in the Pound for my Trouble Now Gentleman if you will be so kind as to Save my life I will give you up the People that I had them from and all the information that lays in my power Now Gentleman I hope and trust that you will take my Distressed Situation with your most kind Consideration and Spare My Life and I shall be ever Bound in Duty to Pray for your kindness
I Remain your most Humble and Obediant Servant George Price
Attached: copy letter, same date, from Bank solicitors stating that Bank cannot interfere.

447. *[F25/8/1] David Sharpe, Newgate, 25 June 1819, formal petition*
That your Petitioner was Convicted at the last Old Bailey Sessions of having a forged Note, purporting to be of the Governor and Company of the Bank of England, and was sentenced to be transported Fourteen years for the same.
That your Petitioner having been informed that in many instances you have made an allowance of a small sum of money to such as were considered not altogether unworthy of it, prior to their leaving their Native Land in order to furnish themselves with a few articles necessary to take during so Long a Voyage, most humbly begs Leave to inform you that his friends are utterly incapable of rendering him the smallest pecuniary assistance this compels him to solicit your benevolence not only in consideration of his distressed situation but also on account of his having become a dupe to more artful and designing men who made him subservient to their advantage.
Your Petitioner therefore most humbly Prays you to grant him the same allowance given to others in a similar unfortunate situation And Your Petitioner as in duty bound will ever Pray &c David Sharp

448. *[F25/8/2] John Murphy, Newgate, undated in May 1819, formal petition*
That your petitioner was Convicted at the present Old Bayley Sessions for uttering Forged Notes being well aware of his offending the laws of his Country Craves most humbly that you will take his distressed Curcumstances in your merciful Consederation being greatly Distressed and having no means of relief Excepting your Benevolence Charity which you usually bestow on prisoners in A Similar Situation having along Tedious Voyage to encounter and your petitioner will as in duty bound for ever pray John Murphy

449. *[F25/8/3] Elizabeth Bamford, Rebecca Bamford, Mary Bradney, Amelia Hines, Ann Dicken,* Lord Wellington *transport ship, Woolwich, 21 May 1819, formal petition*
That Your Petitioners are on the Eve of going out to New South Wales, in the Lord Wellington Convict Ship, that they were Convicted at Warwick Assizes in April 1818 and Pleaded Guilty to the Minor Offence of having Forged Notes in their possession for Sale – that your poor Petitioning Prisoners were seventeen Months in Warwick Jail and utterly destitute not having one farthing in the World – under their deplorable Circumstances they Humbly hope the Govr and Company of the Bank of England will take their Case into Consideration and Order them to be paid the five Pounds Each as they have been good Enough to pay some of their fellow Prisoners under similar Circumstances – and Your Petitioners will be in Duty ever bound to Pray.
Letter penned by E. J. Bromley, ship's surgeon and superintendent who annotates it to certify that all have behaved with propriety since being on board, and all are in extreme poverty.
[*BECLS: 19 May 1819, considered payments to prisoners on* Lord Wellington; *refused all the above since they* were very notorious whole sale dealers and vendors of forged notes, and unworthy of the liberality of the Bank.]

450. *[F25/8/4] Sarah Orton,* Lord Wellington *transport ship, Gravesend, 26 May 1819, formal petition*
That your Petitioner pleaded Guilty to the Minor Offence and was sentenced to transportation for Life[5] and Humbly hopes that the worshipful Govr and Company of the Bank of England will take her Case into consideration and allow her the same Privileges granted to Elizth Hancox a fellow prisoner Convicted under the same circumstances for which your Petitioner will be ever bound to pray, the mark of Sarah Orton
Penned by E. J. Bromley, ship's surgeon and superintendent, annotated to certify that facts cited are true.
[*BECLS: 19 May 1819, refused money as 'notorious' wholesale dealer.*]

5. Sarah Orton's sentence was for fourteen yrs trspn.

451. *[F25/8/5] Ann Dicken,* Lord Wellington *transport ship, Gravesend, 25 May 1819*
Honored Gentlemen Embolden to Address you by the Mercy Extended to Me From your Hands and Now Leaving My Country For a Long term of years and Reduced to the greatest Penury thro A Long Confinement being Convicted at the Warwick Assizes of March 1818 and Got the Awful Sentence of Death passed on Me when Being Conditionally Pardoned to Be tried in August the same year and Being Sentenced to Transportation For 14 Years[6] with an Infant Child not 7 Years Old who looks up to Me For Support and Protection Which I am now Unable to Give Her Not only thro My long Confinement but by being Deprived of Her Father these 3 Years Having left 4 at Birmingham being Unable to taken them with Me thro Want of Clothing or Friends to Assist Me In Hope Honored Gentlemen you will take My Distressed Case Into your Consideration and Extend your Charity to Me in Some Degree as you Have to Most of My Fellow Prisoners Who have Unfortunately Committed the Same Crime Which Had Brought us to the Unhappy Situation in Which We are placed and Should this Humble Request be Complied with your Humble Petitioner Would Be Ever Bound to Pray. Ann Dicken [*written in the hand of Jane Williams*]

452. *[F25/8/6] Mary Bradney,* Lord Wellington *transport ship, Gravesend, 25 May 1819*
Honored Gentlemen In Hope you will pardon My thus venturing to Address you But Being in the Greatest Distress thro a Long And tedious Confinement of 18 Months Being Convicted At the Warwick Assizes in March 1818 During which Period I have Suffered the Greatest Want Having being Obliged to part with all My Wearing Apparel to Support My Selfe and Infant Child Not 3 years Old and Which I Am Obligated to Leave Behind (Altho Having an Order to take Her With Me) For Want of Means to Bring Her to Town She being Left to the Care of A Friend at Birmingham And Being Deprived of Any Assistance From Her Father Who Has been Gone to New South Wales these 2 Years and Being in Hope of Going Free When I unfortunately Got into the Situation In Which I am now Placed Honored Gentlemen
In Hope you Will take My Unfortunate Case Into your Kind Consideration and Extend your Charity towards Me In Some Degree as you Have So Mercifully Done towards the Remainder of My Fellow Prisoners Who With Myselfe Committed the Same Crime and Also Pleaded Guilty to the Offence And your Humble Petitioner Will Be ever Bound to Pray. Mary Ann Bradney [*written in the hand of Jane Williams*]

453. *[F25/8/7–8] Two lists of money in units of £5 paid (£70 and £40) to convicts on* Lord Wellington *transport ship, 19 & 21 May 1819, with*

6. Ann Dicken was sentenced to death in Mar. 1818, in a case in which only the cap. ch. was put. The judgement was reviewed by the twelve judges on a point of evidence and she was granted a free pardon. The Bank held that the indictment for the minor offence still stood; she was tried for this in Aug. 1819 and sentenced to fourteen yrs trspn.

signatures for receipt for: Jane Williams, Clarissa Downes, Jean Wilson, Elizabeth Moore, Elizabeth Mitchell, Elizabeth Jane Hancox; and marks for: Mary Ann Reed, Hannah Gilbert, Maria Wilkes, Mary Hartnell, Elizabeth Brooks, Elizabeth Wingfield, Elizabeth Smith, Sarah Clowes, Catharine Gorman, Mary Steel, Letitia Wardle, Mary Smith, Elizabeth Berry, Mary McCormick, Mary Heylin, Ellen Saunders.

454. *[F25/8/9] Mary Steel and Letitia Wardle,* Lord Wellington *transport ship, Woolwich Harbour, 5 May 1819*
To Solisseter and gentlemen of the Bank of England We petitioners Mary Steel and Letitea Waddle are convicts who got our time and sentance for Bank of England Notes forged haveing pleaded Guiltey to our Crime we are informed by some of the Newgate prisoners that the prisoners who get there time upon this offence by applying to the Bank will reseave the Sum of £5 pound as some of them have reseaved the same we hope if it be given to one it will to all as we stand greatly in need of it at this pressent time there is several prisoners here wich have reseaved 5/s pr week since the time they was convicted but we have Never reseaved the vallue of one half-peney we was tried last March but one wich is Now 13 months Since wich is a Long time to be in confinement without any assistance we therefore Humble beg your pardon for the Liberty we have taken in trubling you with thees few Lines and beg for answer we Humbly beg Leave to subscribe our Selves your most obedeiant Servants Mary Steel Letetia Waddle

455. *[F25/8/10–11] Catherine Gorman, Horsemonger Lane gaol, 19 April 1819*
Honered Sir I humbeley Beg your parden for takeing this Leberley of trubeling you But I am verey mutch destrest throue my Long Confinement I have Been Confind Ever sence the 12 of agest have not got one frind to Asest me I have Been obleged To part with all my Close I have Nothing Left me know But the Bare Jale Alounes to Live on sir the smolest Relefe of your kindness will Be gratefuly Reseved By your Humbel sarvent Cathrine Gorman
Attached note: Catharine Gorman, now a Prisoner in Horsemonger Lane Goal. It is uncertain when she leaves, it may be in a fortnight or three weeks has conducted herself very well while in prison, is very poor, has no children, nor does she appear to have any friends. 24th April 1819. *This note annotated:* To enquire respect of her & report thereon, *and:* Sent Catherine Gorman £2 – 30th April 1819 by order of Law Committee.

456. *[F25/8/12] Elizabeth Smith, Sarah Clowes and Catherine Gorman, Horsemonger Lane gaol, 4 May 1819, formal petition*
That your Petitioners are deeply impressed with unfeigned gratitude for the mercy shewn them in the late proceedings so justly brought against them. And being in extreme indigence humbly Solicit Your Honours will in your humanity condescend to allow Your petitioners such subsistence during their Continuation in this Gaol as in Your Wisdom may seem meet And

Your Petitioners as in grateful duty bound Will ever Pray &c &c [*each signs by mark, witnessed by G. Dawson, clerk of county gaol, Surr.*].

457. *[F25/8/13] Jean Wilson, Horsemonger Lane gaol, 20 January 1819*
Honoured Sir I am taking the liberty of writing you which I hope you will pardon me for – as I am very much Destressed, having no friend to asist me, or to look to me, I beg leve to inform you of my Destressed situation which I trust you will take into consideration. I was Tried at the last Augest assizes for uttring Forged Bank of Ingeland Notes, at Gilford, – for which I pleaded guilty, and receved sintance, for forteen years transportation, I have been here since that time at Hard labour in the Bridewall Side and have had nothing but the Jaol alowance for to subsist on Bread and Water, and scarsly any Cloathing, as I had been under the Necessity of making away with my Cloaths for to suport myself with, privious to my Triel, and since then I have not had it in my power for to redeem any of them, as I have no friend to do any thing for me, or to give me a singel Sixpence – So that I am in very grate want, of Necessary Cloathing, as I am all in rags, also of something towards geting me a little more vituals as the Jaol alowance is not sufisent for to suport any one without something else – and I have been so long without any other suport ever since the 6 of Augest last, so I hope you will have the goodness as look into my Situation, and do something for me –
Honoured Sir I begg for to recomend myself to your generosity and goodness having no one for to speak for me, I trust you will not dispise my humbal petiation, but if you think proper aid and aleviate the Destresses of a poor femeal prisner who is now suffering for her faults and waiting for to leve her Native Country for the long periad of forteen years, at the early age of 19 years as I have only atined that age – If this humbel letter will obtain your notice and you take the troble of ansering it, you will obtain the constant prayers of a poor destressed transport. If I have wrote you any thing amiss I hope you will forgive it, and atribute it to my Igeronance, trusting on your goodness I beg leve for to subscribe myself Honoured Sir your ever Humbel and Obed^t Transport Jean Wilson
[*BECLS: 21 Jan. 1819, order £2 to be made to jailer for her benefit.*]

458. *[F25/8/14] James Wren, White Cross Street debtors' prison, 29 March 1819*
Asks for someone from Bank to call on him as he has information to give and has already given Bank useful information.

459. *[F25/8/15] List, undated in January 1819, of 192 prisoners committed to Coldbath Fields prison during 1818 for uttering and possession forged Bank notes.*

460. *[F25/8/16] Mary Pendleton, Newgate, 28 January 1819, formal petition*
That Your Petitioner Mary Pendelton was found gulty of parsing forge Bank Notes and sentance for Foreteen years Transportation in September

Sessions Eaghteen Hundred and Eaghteen Your Petitioner thairfore throws hirself at Your Honorable Gentleman feet in hopes You Honorable Gentleman will Commiserat hir Case and grant hir that Allowance Your Honorable Gentlman as Alloted to the Other Prisioners in the like Extrumety which will be the Means of Elevating hir Present Distress – as Your Petitioner as got now frinds to Releve hir Except An Unhappy Mother
And Your Petitioner in duty bound will pray
[*BECLS: 28 Jan. 1819, £2 to be paid to keeper of Newgate for her use.*]

461. *[F25/8/17] Mary Smith,* Lord Wellington *transport ship, Woolwich, 7 May 1819*
Honeard Gentleman pardin the Liberty of adr's'n you I am a pour Widow and Left 4 Helples Childern Behind now I am sent out of my Cuntiary for 14 Eyrs for Having In my peshin Bank of England Forged Notes and Never Having Had aney Relife for this Nine Manths I wass tried In July a Sizes at Durham In the County of Bishipbridg Hoping Honeard Gentleman You Extend your Charity By Givin me a trifle as I am In the Greatest Distress a Gown out of my Cuntiary With out one Shilling
Honeard Gentleman I Shall In Duty Bound Evear pray Mary Smith
[*BECLS: 12 May 1819, ordered £5 for her on sailing.*]

462. *[F25/8/18–24] Letters from Bank solicitors to W. H. Brown, keeper of Newgate, 12, 14 & 18 April 1820, 28 June 1821, 18 May 1822, 12 September 1823, 25 October 1824, listing prisoners to be brought up for trial for Bank offences, asking him to give them notice.*

463. *[F25/8/25] Louisa Thorn, Newgate, 17 May 1820*
Gentlemen Pardon the liberty I have taken in writing to you humbly soliciting you to relieve my distresses for I was under the Painful nessity of pledging my Cloaths in consequence of being 9 weeks in confinement before my trial and has not having a friend on Earth to render me any assistance if any one of the gentlemen will condescend to come to Newgate to make enquiry he will find what I have here stated is honestly true for I have now in my Possession 30 Dublicates of my apparel for I had no other means of providing my Tea and Sugar which is my chief support my health not admiting of me eating the Jail allowance I therefore intrust you gentlemen to take my case into your consideration and afford me some relief be it ever so trifling it would be truly acceptable and your Humble Petitioner will be in duty bound to pray for you to the latest period of her existance your very Humble Servant Lousa Thorn
[*BECLS: 24 May 1819, hear evidence from investigator, Glover, that Brown, keeper of Newgate, thinks she is* not a fit object for relief*; request refused.*]

464. *[F25/8/26] Louisa Thorn, Newgate, 14 July 1820*
Hond Sir I Humbly beg Pardon for Troubling you As I Am At Present in very great Distress Otherwise I would not have taken the Liberty of

Soliciting you and hope you will be Pleased to Recommend My Case to the Honble Gentlemen of the Bank Who I trust will be Disposed of their Known goodness and Humanity to be Extend a Little of that Charity they have been Known to Allow Others in A Similar Situation – I am Quite Destitute having No Friend Whatever to Render me the Smallest assistance And Every Article of Apparal I Possest is in Pledge – I Would be truly gratefull were it ever so Small a Trifle the Honble Gentlemen of the Bank would be Pleased to Bestow Upon Me And trust it will Not be deny'd As I Am to be Banished from My Country And have No Other Dependance to Procure a few Necessary Articles Preparatory to My Voyage And Redeem My Cloaths &c And as in duty Bound Will ever Pray Your Most H^{be} Petitioner Luisa Thorn
Annotated: Has been in prison since February last – no child
[*BECLS: 18 July 1820, again reject request.*]

465. *[F25/8/27–8] Sarah Carter, Newgate, 13 July 1820*
Honorard Sir, I hope you will Pardon the Great Liberty I have taken in Writing these few Lines to you for to State my truly and unhappy Case of Confinement in this Prison I am Sir without one frind in the world for to assist me and without a father and Mother therefore I hope kind Sir that you Will take it in to your Consideration as I have not any thing But what I stand upright in I hope Sir that you Will Render me a Little assistence as I have not so much as one frind in the World for to Helpe or assist me as Such Sir I have been in Prison 2 months having nothing but what the Geol Allows me and your Petitioner Will in Duty Bound Ever to Pray Sarah Carter
Annotated by BECLS secretary: Sarah Carter was ord^{d} to be prosecuted in Ap^{l} Sessions, but the Bill was thrown out by the Grand Jury. She was again apprehended & Ord^{d} to be prosecuted 7 June; *in another hand*: No Child
BECLS: 19 July 1820, again refused.]

466. *[F25/8/29] Sarah Carter, Newgate, 5 October 1820*
Honoured Sir pardon this Great Liberty I take in Addressing theas feaw lines to you but I Dont know when I May be Called to leave my Country I have no Friends whatever to assist me and am Entirely Destitute of Evry Common Necesarry it is Entire Necesity that Compels me to trouble you but if you will have the Goodness to Assist me with a trifle if Ever So Small and I will be In Duty bound Ever to pray Sarah Carter
[*BECLS: 11 Oct. 1820, hear that Brown, keeper of Newgate says her statement false; request again rejected.*]

467. *[F25/8/30] Sarah Carter, Newgate, 25 October 1820*
Honoured Sir I hope and trust you will Pardon the Libberty I take In writeing to you but Extreme Distress tempts me to solicit your kind Atention I have been in Confinment these Six Months I have not one Freind in the world to render me the smallest assistance I am Doomed to Leave my Country for fourteen years I hope you will take Compassion on my Miserable Situation and send me a Little Money If you are kind Enough to grant

me my Request I shall be In Duty bound to Pray for you my Cloths are all gone I know not what to Do from your Most humble Servant Sarah Carter
Annotated: See Ltr fm Mary Robinson 15th April 1820; *and in pencil*: petition 19 July rejected
Attached: note dating from Nov. 1820: Sarah Carter, Hart. Treemer [*her name inserted in another hand*] & Mary Robinson are both friendless, they sometimes earn 6^{d} to 1/ per Week but the Women being numerous they cannot all get Employ. T. Glover 1 Nov. See minute Law Commee 1 Nov/ 20

468. *[F25/8/31] Harriet Treemer, Newgate, 14 July 1820*
Honord Sir I hope that you Will not be offended at the Liberty I have taken in Sending these few Lines to you as Sir I am Placed in the aukward Situation and having no frinds to assist me but an aged and infirm Mother as it being out of her Power for to Render me any assistence what Ever I have taken the Liberty for to write these few Lines to you hoping kind Sir that you will take it in to your Consideration and Render me a Little of your assistence if it be Ever so Trifling as I have no Cloaths and Expects for to Leave my native Country for 14 years and having nothing but the Geol Allowance as Such Sir your Petitioner Will in duty Bound Ever to Pray Harritt Treemer
Annotated by BECLS secretary: Har^{t} Treemer alias Day – was discharged pr Order of the Court 15 March but again apprend^{d} and ordered to be pros^{d} 7 June; *another hand added:* No Child.
[BECLS: 19 July 1820, request refused.]

469. *[F25/8/32] Harriet Treemer, Newgate, 30 October 1820*
Honoured Sir reliing on your gennerosity to Pardon me for Persuming to the Libberty of addressing you requesting you will take compassion on my unhappy situation haveing no freind in the world am temped to solicit your kind favours I have been In Confinment this six Months without the Comforts of Life and am Doomed to Leave my Country for fourteen years my fate Is hard Indeed Beleive me Sir I cannot Describe my sufferings I hope and trust you will grant me some releif I shall be ever gratefull for the smallest sum and shall be Ever bound to Pray for you Your Most humble obedient Servant Harriett Treemer
Annotated: See a Lr from Mary Robinson 15th Oct. 1820
[*BECLS: 1 Nov. 1820, refused request.*]

470. *[F25/8/33] Mary Robinson, Newgate, 15 October 1820*
Honoured Sir I hope and trust you will Pardon the Libberty I take in writeing to you but Extreme Distress tempts me to solicit your favour I have been In Confinment Ever since february without A Freind to Assist me with the smalest thing It Is totally out of my Father and Mothers Power to Assist me I am Doomed to Leave my Country for fourteen years If you will have the goodness to take Compassion on me and releive me with the smallest triffle I shall for Ever Pray for you your Most humble Servant Mary Robinson
[*BECLS: 1 Nov. 1820, refused request.*]

471. *[F25/8/34] Elizabeth Clowsley, Newgate, 25 July 1820*
Honnoured Sir I hope you will Pardon the Libberty I take In writeing to you but Extreme Distress Oblidgees me to solicit your Atention I have been Confined In this Dreary Prisson without Money or Freinds I hope Sir you will take My unhappy Case Into Consideration and send me A trifle of Money I am Doomed to Leave My Country for fourteen years I have been In Confinement Ever Since the third of March without the Comforts of Life witch Is very hard belive me Sir the smalest sum will be Most gratefully Receivd by your Most humble Servant Elizebth Clowsley

472. *[F25/8/35] Mary Ann Smith, Newgate, 11 July 1820*
Honnored Sir I take the Libberty of writeing to you hopeing you will send me A Little Money Belive me Sir I am In the greatest Distress I have not A Freind In the World to relive me I Must Leave My Country In A Short time and I know not what to do unless your goodness relives me I have no Cloths nor Money I have been in Prisson this six Months my sufferings Is More than I Can describe I hope Sir you will take Pitty on A Poor Distrest girl from your most humble Servant Mary Ann Smith
Annotated: a pound Note to be given.

473. *[F25/8/37] Mary Ann Smith, Newgate, 10 October 1820*
Honnored Sir I hope you will Pardon the Libberty I take in writeing to you but Extrem Distress oblidges me to solicit your favour I am greatly oblidged to you for the Pound Note you was so kind to send me I hope and trust you will once More take Compassion on my unhappy Situation and releive me to Describe my Destress I Cannot I have been In Confinment this seven Months and I have not one Freind In the world to releive me Could you send me A trifle of Money I shall Ever be In Duty bound to Pray for you
Your Most humble Servant Maryann Smith
I hear the Ship Is not goin this six Months I know not what I shall do

474. *[F25/8/36] Mary Ann Smith, Newgate, 18 October 1820*
Almost identical letter to **473**. *Annotated by BECLS secretary:* Mr Smith begs to refer Mr Rooker to the Minutes of the 18th instant. Not complied with. [*Minute referred to gives Mary Ann Smith as Mary Ann Carter.*]

475. *[F25/8/38] Sarah Paley, Newgate, 12 May 1820*
Hond Sir I hope My Present Distress Will Plead A Sufficient Excuse for the Liberty I Now take In Soliciting Your Humane Interference In My behalf with the Honble Gentleman of the Bank who I trust Will be Pleased to take My Poverty Into Consideration As I Am Quite Destitute And have got A Child to Provide for without any means Whatever but the Allowance of the Prison And Every Article of Wearing Apparal I Possest being in Pledge And Must Remain so Unless kindly assisted by the Honble Gentlemen of the Bank who I Pray will be Pleased to Allow Me A Little of that Charity They have been known Humanely to Extend to Others in A Like Situation

As that will be the Only Means of Alleviateing the Dire Distress of Your Most H^{le} and Unhappy Sv^{t} Sarah Paley

476. *[F25/8/39] Sarah Paley, Newgate, 5 June 1820*
Hon^{d} Sir I Humbly beg Pardon for this Intrusion as Necessity has compelled Me to trouble you A Second time. Humbly hoping you will be Pleased to Exert your Influence In My Behalf with the Honble Gentlemen of the Bank That they May be Pleased In Consideration of My Extreme Distress to Extend a Little of Their Charity to Assist Myself And Child with As I Am in Very great want – having No Friend to render Us the Least Assistance and Totally depending on the allowance of the Prison were it Ever so Trifling the Honble Gentlemen of the Bank would be Pleased to Bestow it would be Most gratefully received by Your most Hum^{ble} and Unhappy s^{vt} Sarah Paley
[*BECLS: 5 July 1820, record that investigator, Glover, found her in great distress, but without a child; request rejected since £5 already authorised for embarkation.*]

477. *[F25/8/40] Sarah Paley, Newgate, 13 July 1820*
Similar letter to **475** *&* **476**. [*BECLS: same date records that further report received from Glover; she was granted 5s. a week since she was not to sail as she was too unwell to leave.*]

478. *[F25/8/41] Elizabeth Smith, Newgate, 15 July 1820*
Honnourd Sir I hope you will pardon the Libberty I take In writeing to you but extreme Distress oblidgees me to solicit your Atention I have been Confineed I this Prisson Many Miels from my home this six Months without Money or Freinds I know not what to do unless you have the goodness to Assist me I am Sentancet to Leave my Country for fourteen years and have no Cloths I am Almost out of my Mind not one Freind to bring me the smalest trifle belive me I Cannot Describe my sufferings to be Shut up In A Prisson without the Comforts of Life I hope Sir you will send me A Little Money and I shall be ever bound to Pray for you from your Most humble Servant Elizabeth Smith
Annotated: has been in Prison since Feby last; *and in different hand:* was in Custody a short time before & discharged

479. *[F25/8/42–3] Martha Lucas, Newgate, 29 September 1820*
Sir I hope you will pardon the Liberty I Presume, in Soliciting your kind Enterference in behalf of me who is verry Much distressed, in Consequence of My Mother being in betholnoly [*St Bartholemew's*] hospital for Some time and my Dear Child is in Great Distress, as my Mother Supported her Since my Confinement, and now through her Illness my Poor Child is Deprived of her last friend to give her Bread Sir I hope you will be so kind as to take my Distressing Case in to your humane Consideration and bestow on me a little of your Benevolent Charity and by So doing your Humble Petioner will Ever Pray Martha Lucass

Attached: note from Bank investigator: Martha Lucas is as she represents in a distressed situation. T.Glover 2 Oct^{r}.
[*BECLS: 4 Oct. 1820, records she was in delicate state of health; 5s. a week granted.*]

480. *[F25/8/44] Martha Lucas, Newgate, 5 October 1820*
Sir being verry Much distressed Obliges me once more to Solicit you to be so kind as to bestow on me a little of your Benevolent charity as my Poor Child is in great distress throug my Mother being in Ospitol whom supported her sinse my Confinement, which is Eleven Months Sir I have parted with all my Cloaths, to support myself and Child Since my Mothers Affliction as I have not the least assistance from any Other Person but her Sir as a proof of my Distress Inclosed you will find my Dublicates which I was obliged to pledge to sirport my Child Sir I hope you will Consider my distress and your Humble Petioner will Ever pray Martha Lucass

481. *[F25/8/45 & 47] Elizabeth McBride, Newgate, 17 May 1820*
Gentlemen Pardon the liberty I have taken in writing to you humbly soliciting you to afford me a temporary relief for I am in absolute distress or I would not have dared to trouble you I was a long time in confinement before trial and having no friends to assist me I was oblidged to sell and Pledge my Cloaths to procure me necessaries so that I have not a change of apparel neither will the Ladies allow me any more in such a case as mine even be they ever so distressed a course garb while I have them washed, I have on, I have not had assistance from any one whatever since I have been in confinement I therefore intreat you to take my case into your consideration and hope and trust you will afford me relief be it ever so trifling it will be truly acceptable for I have a long time to remain in confinement before I leave my own Country and in a short time my health will be greatly impaired not having tea and Sugar which would be my chief support so that if you Gentlemen refuse me relief I shall be a wretched operation by the time the Ship goes I therefore most earnestly beg of you to relieve my distress and your Humble Petitioner will be ever grateful for your Friendship your Humble Servant Elizth McBride
Attached: note from Bank investigator: Mr Brown of Newgate dont think these prisoners [*linked with Louisa Thorn's request* **464**] are proper objects for relief. T. Glover 24 May 1820.

482. *[F25/8/46] Mrs Grey, matron of Newgate gaol, on behalf of Elizabeth McBride, 12 July 1820, to Thomas Glover, Bank investigator*
Sir I am sorry I omitted when I saw you in the morning to mension Eliz^{h} Mc Brides Case to you – But thank you to present it to the Board as she have no freind on Earth to do any thing for her – she is a very Deserving quiet young woman & I believe did not know any thing of the notes till she was unfortunately drawn into them by Voss that suffered here If sir you will have the goodness to think of her she will Ever pray
If you will Confer a favour on My self Most Respectfully M. Grey, Matron

Annotated: Has been in prison Since beginning of February last – no child & not known before apprehended

483. *[F25/8/48–9] The Revd Robert Crosby, Hoxton Square on behalf of Elizabeth Brown, prisoner in Newgate, 24 October 1820*
My dear Sir, In the Case of Elizabeth Brown now in Newgate under Sentence of transportation, at the Instance of the Bank of England, I feel considerable interest. Her father is a respectable tradesman in this Parish: She lived some years in a place of respectable Service in Hoxton: Her Husband is very affectionately disposed towards her & She has Two Infant Children. Knowing well your feelings in such a Case, I have presumed to solicit your consideration to it. I have little hope, that She can be suffered to remain in this country with her husband and children. If that is impossible, may She not prevail on Government thro' the intercession of the Bank, to send out her husband & children with her to New South Wales? It would be a shocking thing in a moral point of view to separate her from her husband and to send her into a Country, where She would probably form connections, the remembrance of which would be grievous unto her as long as she has existence.
I am by no means desirous of advocating her case beyond what to me seems rational. She is a Modest woman & well behaved. She has also imbibed principles of piety and is very Anxious in regard to the future welfare of her Children.
If, for such a delinquent any favor could be found, I should feel peculiarly grateful. And I am fully persuaded that upon her Kindness would not be idly squandered.
With many thanks for your past acts of kindness to me I humbly requesting you to forgive this attempt to Serve thro' your interest a poor unfortunate fellow Creature, labouring under peculiar circumstances and feelings, I have the honor to remain, with sincere respect, My Dear Sir, Your faithful Servant Robert Crosby
Attached: statement from Elizabeth Brown to Revd Crosby, 25 Oct. 1820, admitting she was not innocent of crime, but committed it through need, having been ill for four months beforehand.

484. *[F25/8/50] Sarah Wright, Newgate, 19 October 1820*
Most Respectful Sir, My Present Unhappy Situation Urges Me to solicit a Favour which Necessity I Trust will Plead An Excuse for. I beg Leave to State I am A Bank Prisoner And Am at Present Confin'd in Childbed And being Without Friends And Money Am In Consequence of That Depriv'd of The Means of Procuring those Necessaries so Requisite for People in My Weak Situation – I Therefore Humbly hope the Honble Gentlemen of the Bank will be Pleased to take My Case into consideration And be dispos'd to Assist me With A Little of That Charity they have been known Humanely to Extend to Others in A Like Situation And as in duty Bound will Ever Pray Sarah Wright
[*BECLS: 25 Oct. 1819, grant payment of £2*].

485. *[F25/8/51] Mary Howard, Newgate, 14 September 1820*
Hon[d] I hope you will excuse me Troubling you with this as I am in the Greatest Distress possible in my Situation which is Extremely Distressing I hope you will have compassion for Gods sake on me and my Husband who is a Lame Afflicted Creature and I have had him on my Hands this 5 Years I hope you will hold out some [*illegible word*] or give your word you will use your Influence which I Know is great to get our Sentence Lessend If we plead Guilty and you will find it most Gratefully Acknowledge as we both will inform as all we know –
I informd M[r] Glover that I would see the Person I had them from which I took them entirely for Distress and not before I had been pressd Hundreds of Times we have heard a Great Deal about all A Certain Set of Peoples Affairs who are the Real Instigators of this Infamous transactions & have had me entirely to it
I humbly pray you will call on me and if you will Assist us to get our Liberty in a Little time we will inform you how to find them all out without much Trouble in hope you will not be Offended I am Hon[d] Sirs Y[r] Most Ob[t] Ser[t] M Howard

486. *[F25/8/52] Sarah Hewster, Newgate, 17 July 1820*
Honnoured Sir I hope you will Pardon the Libberty I take In writeing to you but Extreme Distress oblidges me to solicit your Attention I have been Confined In this Prisson this two Months without Money or Freinds and am Extremly Ill I am Doomed to Leave my Country for fourteen years Belive me Sir It is More than I can bear my health Is Declineing Every Day for want of the Comforts of Life I hope Sir you will have the goodness to send me a trifle of Money I shall be ever bound to Pray for you
Your Most humble Servant M Huster
Annotated: Hewster apprehended about 12 Months since & com[d] for trial a Memorial rec[d] & she was not prosecuted she is near 70 Yrs of age a very old dealer
[*BECLS: 19 July 1820, request refused.*]

487. *[F25/8/53] Sarah Hewster, Newgate, 12 August 1820*
Almost identical letter to **486.**

488. *[F25/8/54] George Thorpe, Newgate, 11 July 1820, to Thomas Smith, tap room, Kings Bench prison*
Hon[d] Sir, I took the liberty of addressing a letter in Answer to one you was so Kind as to send me
M[r] Davis [*prison officer accompanying transportees*] has informed me that I may expect to go away in a night or two and that if you wish to see me I had better acquaint you of the circumstance as you was so kind as to mention in your letter you would wish to see me before I go. I think if you was to see M[r] Davis it would be of service to me has he goes down with us – Hoping you and your father and all the family are in good health
I remain Hon[d] Sir Your obedient humble Ser[t] George Thorpe

Annotated: in Bank investigator's hand, with names, and some part addresses.

489. *[F25/8/55] J. Vickers, Newgate, 15 July 1820, sentenced for house-breaking, offers Bank information on Bank note forgers.*

490. *[F25/8/56] William Thomas Woodberry, Newgate, undated April 1820*
Formal petition to plead to lesser offence. BECLS took decision 29 Mar. 1820.

491. *[F25/8/57] Sophia Woodberry, Newgate, undated in April 1820*
The Humble Petion Of Sophia Matilda Woodberry Prayeth that the Honourable Directors and Governors of the Bank of England will have Mercy on their Humble Petioner now A Prisoner in Newgate and Permit her to plead Guilty to the Minor Offence your Petioner had not left her Fathers house but one month when she was Apprehended and it being her first Offence your Humble Petioner Implores Forgiveness of the Honourable Gentlemen and hopes that they will listen to their Poor Prisoners Petion your Petioner was Over persuaded to do it not thinking of the Dainger it would plunge her and her whole Family into She thinks it her Duty to Inform the Honourable Gen^{n} that the Notes was bought of Henry Capper 4 Charles Street Drury Lane Your Humble Petioner as in Duty Bound will ever Pray
[*BECLS: took decision 15 Mar. 1820.*]

492. *[F25/8/58] Samuel Longman, Newgate, 7 April 1820, to Charles Christmas, Bank investigator*
Sir, I Beg Leave to take Liberty of writing to you concerning beening confin^{d} here for the Bank Buisness there fore if you would have the Goodness to come In to Me and Give it to me from under your hand Not to Prosecute I will tell you where the Man Lives and his decripson and Been an old Sail Master in the trade and has sold them to me and Brought in to this trouble
I am your humble Sert Samuel Longman

493. *[F25/8/59] William Woodhead, Newgate, undated in April 1820, formal petition*
That the Honourable the Governor and Directors of the Bank of England will have mercy on their Humble Petitioner now A Prisoner in Newgate on A charge of passing A forged note and Permit him to plead guilty to the minor offence Your Petitioner haveing neither Father nor Mother liveing and being A long while out of Employment was betrayed into the offence not knowing the consequence and haveing previous borne a good character and being his first offence your Humble Petitioner implores forgiveness of the Honourable Governor and Directors of the Bank of England, and thinks it his duty to inform that the Note was bought of Henry Capper 4 Charles

Street Drury Lane, and hopes they will hear the prayer of their Humble Petitioner William Woodhead
[*BECLS: 29 Mar. 1820, had decided on lesser charge.*]

494. *[F25/8/60] Moses Bannister, Newgate, 16 October 1820*
Mr Rooker Sir, I Hope you will Excuse the liberty I Have taken in adressing you – but my Reasons are to aquaint you were we use to get the nots from – Sturgess & Overton & me use to by them of a man of the name of John dart [*sentenced to fourteen yrs trspn, OB, May 1821*] at the man in the moon noble St Goswell St but is now moved to the Coach & Horses Fann St Goswell St were he is still selling them to Explain to you in whate way Sturgess Pland it with the offiscers to apurehend me will be unnesacerey as I Shoul[d] soppose you are or soon will be aquaintend with as you have Sturgess allreddey in Custedey and I shoul[d] soppose you will overton befor Long – but above all I Hope you will not suffer the seller of them to go unpunish[d] – that is the Case of so miny Poor famaleys Comming to distruction – I Hope Sir you will Teake my Case into your Humain Concideraiton & grant me that Relife you seme best fit for belive me sir I never shoul[d] Have Pas[d] another note if I Had not been drawn into and my Praiears and that of my unfortunent wife and famaly will be Ever Liftend up for your welfare and Prosperty Pray Sir Look over my Case and be as Lining as you Can towards me and if you whant Eney information that is in my Power to Give I Ham quite Readey to Communecoat it to Eney Person you may think Proper to Send
I Remain sir your Humble Sr[t] Moses Bannister
Plese sir Excuse the writing

495. *[F25/8/61] James Downes, Newgate, 19 June 1820*
Sir, As I have been made the fool of a designing party and been, innocently on my part drawn into this dreadful situation, I am therefore fully determin'd for my own sake and for the happiness of my wife and family, (provided I can obtain my discharge) to inform you of a Man that has pass'd several bad Notes, as well as where they were pass'd together with the person they were had of, should you Sir think this worth your attention you will find that I have been the dupe of these peaple and that I have a claim to be exonerated from the base treatment I have experienced, I am Sir With great respect Your very Obed[t] Serv[t] James Downes

496. *[F25/8/62–3] George Seymour, Newgate, 12 June 1820*
Honoured Sirs, I the undersigned have unfortunately rendered myself amenable to the laws of my country, having been sentenced to 14 years transportation for having had forged Bank of England notes in my possession, & Notwithstanding this I can solemnly assure you honoured Sirs, that I was drawn into the Commission of the Crime by some of those harpies who go about to ensnare the unwary, and had I not accidentally met with them I should certainly never have contemplated any offence of the kind. These men frequent a house named the Brewer in Friar Street, Blackfriars Road, where all sorts of bad characters resort every day. All I ever had in

my possession was 8 notes, which I received at three different times. I paid 6 Shillings for each. There are to my knowledge 6 of those wretches that go about and entangle young men whose character yet stands good in the world. I have no doubt that the 8 notes formerly in my possession will in due course come to the Bank as my right name was endorsed on all except those given to Mr Harrison the Pawnbroker, on which the same name was written as appeared on the Duplicates of things which I had pledged with him. Many unfortunate and respectably connected young men are sent out of the country and brought to disgrace and ruin through those wicked men. I maintained myself long creditably and in Kentish Town I carried on the business of a saddle and harness maker, where I am sure the inhabitants will give me a good character for honesty and industry, though unfortunately losses in trade, not owning to negligence, compelled me to give up all to my creditors.
My father is a respectable tradesman in Reading in Berkshire where he has carried on a business for thirty years and stands in high credit, and I have also 10 brothers and sisters, most of them in trade and creditably married.
I therefore hope, honoured Sirs, you will take my case into consideration and interest yourselves to procure me some mitigation of punishment. I shall feel particularly grateful, and afford you such other assistance as you may think proper to call for. We expect to go hence daily and therefore an early answer will very much oblige me.
I have the honour to be, honoured Sirs, with the most perfect respect, Your most obedient and most humble Servant, George Seymour
Attached: copy note 15 June 1820, from Bank solicitors stating that governors & directors considered application but cannot interfere.

497. *[F25/8/64–5] George Seymour, Newgate, 14 July 1820*
Gentlemen, Deeply impress'd as I am with a sense of my Guilt and humbly penitent for the crime I have committed – I venture and I hope with confidence to lay before you the truly distressing situation in which I am at present unfortunately placed. Conscious as I am that I am making this appeal to the Humanity of men – whose generosity has been eulogised by a far better pen than mine – from those who have experienc'd your kindness – from those who have witness'd your benevolence. Destitute as I shall be for want of some working Implements in going over to the place of my Destination – I should feel truly and very sincerely obliged if you would assist me with a small supply of Cash to furnish myself with them a boon which I believe has been granted by you in several instances – and I trust by a strict adherence to the principles of Honor and Integrity I may yet be able to retrieve that Character I once possess'd and become a useful Member of Society – In the sincere hope this application will not be in vain permit me to remain with every sentiment of respect and esteem.
Gent^{n} Your truly obliged & very hble sev^{t} George Seymour
Attached: covering letter, same date, from Seymour requesting his letter be put before governor & directors.

498. *[F25/8/66] Ebenezer Bult, un-named prison, 10 April 1820*
Petition to plead to lesser offence. Decision taken 5 Apr. 1820.

499. *[F25/8/67] Catherine Martin, Newgate, 14 April 1820*
Honered Sir i hope you will parden the liberty i have taken of writing to you but i have a Child very eavy aflected and i shall be very thankful if you wold let me have the fortnight mony as i do expect to go away on monday or tuesday so i remain your humble servant Catherine Martin

500. *[F25/8/68] William Stevens, Borough Compter, 7 April 1820*
Sir I would be very Much obliged to You if time permits you to Come to the Borough Compter Mill Lane Tooley Street Southwark as I am Very much Desirous of seeing you Tomorrow being 8th of the above date And you will Much oblidge Your Humble Servant William Steevins

501. *[F25/8/69] Thomas Simcox, Horsemonger Lane gaol, 30 July 1820 to J. H Scutts, cooper, corner of Albany Yard, Old Kent Road, Surrey*
Sir I have taken the liberty to wright few lines to you hoping you will not be offended I have heard as you are a gentleman of feelings towards poor prisoners as you was so kind as to interfere with Friends in the Neighbourhood for Betsy Usher & Rachael Biddulph [*both acquitted Kent summer ass. 1820*] I hope you will do the same for me I am ashamed to beg such a favour from you as I am an entire stranger to you but your goodness been as such I will open my mind to you and any Friend you will appoint to come with you as I can give the Bank of England such information as will Astonish them if you and your Friend will interfere for me with the Bank of England I shall ever be bound to Pray
I am Sir Your Most Obedient servant Thos Simcox
[*written after* **347**, *before* **348.**]

502. *[F25/8/70] J. Appleton, Kings Bench prison, 23 May 1820*
Appleton who conducts the Bake House *in the Kings Bench prison has been given a forged note by a debtor appearing in bankruptcy hearings and wants Bank to look after his interests.*

503. *[F25/8/71] Printed pro-forma made out 26 September 1820 in the name of John Paulin Coats or Pullein Coates, tanner,* [*see also* **397**] *prisoner in Kings Bench prison, claiming discharge as insolvent debtor.*

504. *[F25/9/1–2] Lists from Bank solicitors to W. H. Brown, keeper of Newgate, of prisoners to be arraigned at OB, May and June Sessions 1821.*

505. *[F25/9/3] Martha Lucas, Newgate, 1 January 1822*
Sir Relying on your Goodness and Humanity to Pardon this Intrusion As My feelings in my Present truly Unhappy Situation Urges Me to Request

you will be Pleased to lay this Statement for the Inspection of the Hon[ble] Bank Committee – To Whom With the Most Profound Respect and Gratitude I beg Leave to return My Sincere thanks for the lenity that has been Hitherto Shewn Me And the Charity that has been Extended, And Humbly hope A Continuance of the same May be Granted being Solely Dependant upon the Humanity of the Hon[ble] Gentlemen of the Bank for the Means of support for My Child Who in being Deprived of Father and Mother is now left quite Destitute, having Now No Friend whatever to Render Me the Least Assistance having Recently lost two of My Brothers by Death and have Also An Aged Mother lying Dangerous Ill in St Barthalamews Hospital Under the Distressing Circumstances I trust the Hon[ble] Gentlemen of the Bank will be Pleased to Take My Case into their Most Serious Consideration And Not Withdraw that Charitable Aid they have so Humanely Extended And as in duty Bound I will ever Pray their Most Humble And Submissive Ser[t] Martha Lucas
[*BECLS: 9 Jan. 1822, refused continuance; felt it was government's fault that ships were taking so long to be prepared and did not wish to grant any more relief to those waiting in prison.*]

506. *[F25/9/4] Sarah Paley, Newgate, 2 January 1822*
Sir I hope you will Pardon the Liberty I Take in Requesting you Will be Pleased to Present these few Lines to the Hon[ble] Bank Committee to Whom I beg leave to Return My Sincere thanks for the Lenity that has been Hitherto shown Me And the Charitable Assistance Received but Humbly hope a Continuance of the Same May be granted As I have A Fatherless Child solely Dependant Upon Me for support And No Friends whatever to Render Me Any Assistance. Should the Hon[ble] Gentlemen of the Bank of their known goodness and Humanity be disposed to Extend Any Further Pecuniary Aid they will Not Only Confer a Lasting Obligation but greatly Alleviate the Distress of their Most Humble Ser[t] who as in Duty Bound will ever Pray Sarah Paley
[*BECLS: 9 Jan. 1822, refused continuance; see note to* **505.**]

507. *[F25/9/5] Elizabeth Brown, Newgate, 2 January 1822*
Most Respectfull Sir I hope you will Not Consider My Second Intrusion Presumptuous as Necesity Again Compels Me to Request you Will be Pleased to lay these few lines before the Hon[ble] Gentlemen of the Bank Committee Humbly Trusting they may be Pleased of their Known Goodness and Humanity to Take My Deplorable Case into their Consideration And be Disposed to Extend their Charity By Granting A Further Continuance of that Pecuniary <u>Aid</u> they have so Humanely Hitherto been Pleased to Allow Me (and for which with Humble Gratitude I beg Leave to Return My Sincere thanks) As I am very Much Distressed And in an Incapacitated State with two small Children to support having Now No Other Dependance but the Allowance of the Prison. My <u>Husband</u> being out of Employment Under these Circumstances I hope the Hon[ble] Gentlemen of the Bank will be Pleas'd to Grant that Assistance they have

Now Withheld and as in Duty Bound will ever Pray your Honors Most Humble Ser^{t} Elizth Brown

508. *[F25/9/6] Sarah Carter, Newgate, 24 September 1821*
Hon^{d} Sir Relying on your Goodness to Pardon this Intrusion As Necessity Urges me to Solicit Your Interference with the Honble Gentlemen of the Bank humbly hoping they may of their Known Goodness And Humanity be Disposed to Render Me a Small Portion of that Charitable Assistance they have been known to Extend to others in a Similar Situation As I Am Very Much Distress'd Not having Any Friends to Whom I Can Apply And have A Child to Look Up to Me for support And Am Quite Destitute of the Means of Procuring these Necessaries Requisite for Myself And Child Preparatory to our Voyage Should the Honble Gentlemen of the Bank be Pleased to Assist Me With ever so Trifling an Aid it will be Most Gratefully R^{d} and as in Duty Bound will ever Pray Sarah Carter

509. *[F25/9/7] Elizabeth Smith and Elizabeth Webster, Newgate, 24 September 1821*
Hon^{d} Sir Elizth Smith and Elizth Webster begs your interference with the Honble Gentlemen of the Bank in their behalf humbly hoping they will of their known goodness and Humanity be dispos'd to assist them with A small portion of the charity they have been known humanely to extend to others in A like situation as they are very much distress'd and not having any assistance since their long confinement and likewise quite bare of those necessaries so requisite for them Preparatory to their Voyage Elizth Smith has got A child to look to and Elizth Webster being in an Afflicted State and standing in need of more Nourishment than the Prison affords wich is not in her power to Procure humbly hopes the Honble Gentlemen of the Bank will kindly Assist them with A little Pecunary Aid wich if ever so small will be thankfully Receivd by Elizth Smith Elizth Webster

510. *[F25/9/8] Catherine Taylor, Newgate, 11 July 1821*
Sir I Humbly beg Pardon for this Intrusion As Necessity Urges Me to Solicit your Interference with the Honble Gentlemen of the Bank Humbly hoping they will of their known Goodness be disposd to assist Me with a Small Portion of the Charity they have been known Humanely to Extend to Others in A Similar Situation I would not have presumed to Trouble them were I Not Very Much Distress'd and in want of cloaths and have got no Means whatever of Procuring any Unless the Honble Gentlemen of the Bank will Humanely Assist Me And as in duty Bound will ever Pray Catherine Taylor

511. *[F25/9/9] Sarah Redding, Newgate, 5 July 1821*
Sir I humbly hope you will Pardon this Intrusion As Necessity Urges Me to Solicit your Interference with the Honble Gentlemen of the Bank in My behalf humbly hoping they may of their known Goodness be Disposed to Render me a small Portion of the Charity they have been known humanely to extend to others in a Like situation as I am quite Destitute of Friends of

Money and My Cloathes being in Pledge Must Remain so Unless Kindly Assisted by the Honble Gentlemen of the Bank as it will not Otherwise be in my Power to redeem them should they be disposed to Extend their Charity in ever so Trifling a Manner it will be Gratefully Received by your Most H^ble^ Sv^t^ Sarah Redding
[*BECLS: 11 July 1821, request not complied with.*]

512. *[F25/9/10] Frances Grey, Newgate, 5 July 1821*
Sir Relying on your Goodness to Pardon the Liberty I take in Requesting you will be Pleased to Lay My Case before the Honble Gentlemen of the Bank (as I am quite Destitute of Friends or Money) Humbly praying they will of their known Goodness be Dispos'd to Extend a Small Portion of the Charity they have Humanely to Extend to Others in A Similar situation As I am rather Bare of Cloaths and have no Means whatever of Procuring Any Unless Assistance by the Honble Gentlemen of the Bank who I hope will in Consideration of my Distressed Situation grant me some trifling Aid and as in duty Bound will ever Pray Frances Grey
[*BECLS: 11 July 1821, request not complied with.*]

513. *[F25/9/11–14] Josiah Cadman, Newgate, 28 October 1821*
Gentlemen, The awful situation in which I am placed has induced me once more to address you, and the knowledge that my fate is in your hands encouraged the hope that mercy may yet be extended to me.
When I learnt that it was not consistent with that resolution which you have taken, with respect to such offenders as myself, to suffer the plea of Guilty to the minor offence to be made, I preferred acknowledging my Crime to vainly contradicting it, [*guilty plea to cap. ch.*] and undergoing the form of a trial which could not have made my guilt more apparent or more hateful to me – I have in consequence received the appalling sentence of death, and now, standing on the brink of eternity, I make once more, an appeal for Mercy, to you, upon whose breath depends my existence, coupled, as my fate is, with that of a confiding heartbroken Wife [*Ann Smith, alias Sarah Cadman, cap. con.*] I have every inducement to beseech that you will spare our lives to give us an opportunity of amending them. That I have the stronger desire to do so, the confession I have made to one of your Officers, and my conduct since my apprehension, I humbly submit are sufficient evidences. I am moreover willing to do every thing in my power to detect and bring to Justice the hidden contrivers of the nefarious system which has been perfected by the blood of so many victims to whose number, unless your clemency shall avert my impending fate, I may soon be added. There is nothing that can be suggested that I will not assay, no enterprise however dangerous that I will not gladly undertake, to accomplish this object. I have no pledge to give for this, but the solemn assurance of a wretched man in too perilous a case to be insincere in word or thought.
The only ground (beyond those I have before mentioned) upon which I can lay any claim to your indulgence, is that my Case, guilty as I am, is not worse than <u>any</u>, not a tithe so bad as <u>some</u> of those which have received the Mercy I now implore; – None of them, I believe, had to bear the pangs of

famine and the agony of seeing a Wife perishing for want of the necessaries of life. Those only who have felt such Misery can tell how hard it is to suffer – upon this subject I hardly dare touch, but I beg humbly to remind you that the long continued practice of suffering offenders to plead to the minor offence, and the recent cases of Ross, Beresford, Smith and many others convince me that you have been merciful, and induce me to believe that you will be no less to me. I know that upon your Representation to the Government depends my Life or Death.
Gentlemen, I implore you by that forbearance you have so often displayed to other Criminals, and the recollection of which stands now like the Angel of Hope, between me and the Grave which is open at my feet – by those charitable feelings to which the discharge of your public duty does violence, by your domestic happiness, – by the reward promised to those who emulate the first attribute of Heaven, – Mercy! – by that Great and Good God on whose clemency all Men rely, and 'who desireth not the death of a sinner, but rather that he may turn from his wickedness and live', to weigh the awful condition in which I stand and when you consider the temptations to which I have been exposed and the misery I have borne to let the balance of pity incline in my favor – recollect I beseech you that I am not hackneyed in the practices for which I stand condemned, that the papers I annex prove that at no very distant period I enjoyed the approbation of Gentlemen whose praise could only be obtained by deserving it, and believe the solemn assurance which perhaps may be uttered with my dying breath, that if your Mercy should be extended to me, all that may be spared to me of existence shall be devoted to such worthy purposes as may evince my gratitude for your interposition. I am Gentlemen in the deepest affliction your obedient servant Josiah Cadman
Attached: letter, 23 Aug. 1821, from James Bacon, magistrate, Clerkenwell, informing Bank that Cadman had information to give; set of five testimonials for Cadman from high ranking naval officers praising his service as marine on HMS Censor 1815–16, and as clerk to lieutenant quarter master in Chatham division of royal marines 1813–15 & 1817–19; copy letter from Bank solicitors stating Bank would not interfere to prevent execution; letter from J. H. Capper, home office, 15 Nov. 1821, requesting briefs on Cadman and his wife to be sent to Lord Sidmouth.

514. *[F25/9/15–16] Sarah Stewart, Newgate, 11 July 1821*
Sir I Humbly beg Pardon for this intrusion I beg you will lay my case before the Honourable Gentlemen of the bank I am greatly distressed for wearing Apareel and totaly without friends having no one to asist me whatever I hope you will have the goodness to allow me whatever you may think proper if it is ever so small a trifle I will be truly thankfull on atending to this request you will highly Oblidge your humble Servent Sarah Stewart
Attached: note from Bank investigator, 26 July 1821, Sarah Stewart has no Freinds who call upon her. Sarah Johnson [**515**] ditto. Jane Carter [**516**] has Friends who call upon her. She cohabited with John Smith and was pros[d] with him for selling forged Notes. T. Glover; *further letter from Stewart, 5 Sept. 1821, identical with* **514**; *note from Bank investigator, C. Christmas,*

Sarah Stewart has One Son who was transported and she has no Person that relieves her. She is an old woman & was an old offender
[*BECLS: 8 Aug. & 19 Sept. 1821, refused relief.*]

515. *[F25/9/18] Sarah Johnson, Newgate, 26 July 1821*
Relying on Your Goodness to Pardon this Intrusion I have Presumed to Solicit Your Interference with the Hon[ble] Gentlemen of the Bank in My Behalf – Humbly Hoping they will of their Known Goodness be Dispos[d] Humanely to Assist Me with a Small Portion of the Charity they have been Pleased to Extend to others in a Like Situation As I am very much Distressed for Cloaths &c and I am Quite destitute of Any meanes whatever of Procuring any not having any Friends to Render me the Least Assistance Under the Present Circumstances I hope the Hon[ble] Gentlemen of the Bank will be Pleased to take My Case into Consideration And as in duty Bound will ever Pray Sarah Johnson
[*BECLS: 8 Aug. 1821, refused relief.*]

516. *[F25/9/19] Jane Carter, Newgate, 8 July 1821*
Sir I humbly Beg your Pardon for taken this liberty I hope the Gentleman of the bank will take my case into consideration I am greatly distressed having no friends and unfourtunately all my Cloaths are in pladge and I have a Child four years old intirly depending on the jail allowance I hope you will have the goodness to allow me a triefele to help maintan the Child and in so doing you will for ever Oblige your Humble Servent Jane Carter
[*BECLS: 8 Aug. 1821, refused relief, noting she was a notorious bad character, husband convicted five yrs before, two men with whom she since cohabited executed for Bank forgeries, and current accomplice was a house breaker and seller of forged notes.*]

517. *[F25/9/20a & b] John (alias George) Ellis, Newgate, undated 1821,* [*probably August*]. *Formal petition requesting to plead to lesser offence; attached note, 10 Aug. 1821, to Mr Maynard, Bank solicitors' clerk, to say examination of Ellis by magistrate to take place at noon next day; BECLS decided, 22 Aug. 1821, to prefer cap. ch. only as known as common utterer.*

518. *[F25/9/21–2] Edward Stamford, 10 Alfred Place, Kent Road, on behalf of John Wilkinson, prisoner in Horsemonger Lane gaol, 5 April 1821*
Respected Sir The inclosed will prove that my intentions are correct – John Wilkinson who by accident I heard was confined under sentence of fourteen yrs transportation for uttering forged notes – purporting to be of your Company – in fact by my serious requiring of him the manner he obtained them – his respectability formerly – being related to most respected connexions – induces me to believe the inclosed – it may I trust be of some service – at all events I think I am doing justice to the police – and hope I do not intrude upon your time, your immediate answer will oblige Yours respectfully Edward Stamford

Marked on outside: Sir immediate enquiry is necessary. Pay the Porter One Shilling ES
Attached: note from John Wilkinson, same date, promising to inform Stamford of every particular relating to his prosecution.

519. *[F25/9/23] Lydia Hogan, Giltspur Street compter, May 1821, formal petition*
That your Petitioner was in May Session 1819 convicted of the minor offence at the Old Bailey but mitigated in April 1820 to two years farther imprisonment as above, since which time, until within these last two months, your Petitioner most thankfully received from your Bounty and kindness the sum of 5/- weekly, which has greatly contributed to the support and comfort of five children in a great measure dependant on said releif – Your Petitioner therefore humbly entreats that the same may be continued to her, and will as in Duty bound ever pray Lydia Hogan
Annotated: Refused

520. *[F25/9/24] Lydia Hogan, Giltspur Street compter, 20 May 1821*
Sir i humbley bag to be Pardond for the Liberty i hav Took in adresing this Letter to You as i am much distressed i have Four Children out an one in Iv not a frend to Look to me But Gal an myself without your Goodness will pleas to alow me some Small triefeel to suscport Me an i have 11 munths to be confined yet i have a very bad State of hulth an thrust you will be pleas to sand me a triefeel of money I shall be ever thankfull to you For it I remain your Humbel Sirveant Prisoner Ledy Orgin

521. *[F25/9/25] Lydia Hogan, Giltspur Street compter, 19 September 1821*
Sir I hope you will pardon the Liberty i have taken in addressing myself to your notice for it is the height of distress that oblidges me to Solicit your favour be it Ever so small i have got a very sickly Child with me and have had a great deal of sickness myself and Child to Since last Christmas and i have nothing at all but the bare gaol allowance having no friends to Come to assist me with any thing only my poor Children and it is not in there power to do any thing for me humbly hopeing you will take my Case into Consideration and i will in duty bound to ever pray your most Humble & Distressed Prisoner Lydia Organ

522. *[F25/9/26–7] John Lomas, Coldbath Fields prison, 11 March 1822*
Hon^{d} Sir Under the Present circumstancese [*facing two cap. chs*] you can have no Objection to Return me the tickets of Several of my Cloaths as I am in great distress and would Be Glad of any little assistance in my Present dreadful Situation and I may Be able to turn Several of my things into money and great Part of them are not my Own
By so doing you will greatly Oblige your most Obedient Humbl Servant J. Lomas
Attached: letter from his father, 4 Mar. 1822, to Mr Christmas, Bank investigator, at Dog Lane [*Row?*]*, Mile End, asking for interview next*

day with Mr Maynard, Bank solicitor's clerk, as he has important information to give.

523. *[F25/9/28] John Lomas, Coldbath Fields prison, 14 March 1822*
Gentlemen In consequence of my not having been called on this day as I had reason to expect I must most respectfully beg the favor of your sending to me my pocket book with the duplicates &c which Mr Maynard took from the officer on the 7th inst – and which he promised to return to me today
I am Gentlemen your most Obt and most humble Sert J Lomas

524. *[F25/9/29–31] John Lomas, Coldbath Fields prison, 20 March 1822*
Sir I beg to acknowledge the receipt of the things through Mr Christmas junr and I cannot omit this opportunity to express my heartfelt gratitude for your politeness to Mrs Lomas and your consideration in having given her permission to have access to me. I have further to hope when I appear again before Sir Richard Bernie you will allow me to be sent to this place untill such time I go up to take my trial
I am Sir with great respect your most obet and Most humble Sert John Lomas
Attached: cover letter and letter, 1 July 1822, from Thomas Butts Aveling, manager of Truman's brewery, Spitalfields, to Bank on behalf of daughters of late Mr and Mrs Boreman, defrauded of £8 by Lomas [*by this time executed*], *asking for relief to be sent to them; copy reply from Bank solicitors, 5 July 1822, directed to pay them £10* out of commiseration for their destitute situation, *emphasising that this is not payment for loss since Bank never make such payments.*

525. *[F25/9/32] William Connell, Coldbath Fields prison, 23 March 1821, held for non- payment of fine; Bank wish to take him to Warwick as witness in one of their cases, but he says if he comes out of prison to help he does not wish to be sent back there.*

526. *[F25/9/33–4] Charles Shearer, debtor, Kings Bench prison, 3 April 1821 to William Mellish Esq.,* [*director of Bank*] *offering information in exchange for money. Attached: visiting card of Anderson & Shearer, commission agents, New York & 15, Little St Thomas Apostle Street London; Bank solicitors refuse offer 5 Apr. 1821.*

527. *[F25/9/35] William Morris,* Justitia *hulk, Woolwich, 3 May 1821 to Mr Oswell Milne, New Bayley, Manchester* [Salford]
Sir In a letter I Reseved from my wife She informes me that She as bean at You Respecting my time Being Migitead and She saise that if I will Tell the truth you will be afrind to me the truth I heave tould and am willing to Tell it againe I Reseved the two notes of aman at the Signe of the Blue Bell High Street Manchester on 14th March for Guingham But Did not know the man but he had Stockings to Sell and that is as true as I Can Speak But Mr Milln It is all Becase I went to York against the Radecills they heave done

all that as Lead in there Power befor to Ingure me but it never was in there power nor it is not posoble for aney neighbour that I heave to give me One ill word in Reguard of Honsty nor neaver had anething of the Cind Lead to my Charge in all my Life so I think it is hard to teare me from my Wife and fore Small Children as Insent as I am But it is all Middleton Reformers and they heav Rejoiced So much at me being transported they heave Publiched it in the Londen Peapers and it as Been in bord this Ship and I am thredned with Dearth before I get to the Bay as they are detrmend to heave none But good men they will not heave traters there – Mr Milln if Cornell taylor had been Living I should not heave Been heare I was youst to take all my Intelengence to Collen taylor it was me that Informed M[r] Taylor of the Burning of Manchester and Bamford Healy Plant Lancashire and Kent was Impresned for the saime – I am Very Badley thought of in Middleton for Being against the Reformers But if Ever it be my Lot to Com back you Shall Heave more Intelange at new bayley then Ever you heave had and you may Depend there will be Occeagon as soon as they get settled thay will be wars then Ever I heave spent plinty of money with them on purpos for news and it wood be the same again

Mr Milln if you will heave the Goodness to writ to Lord Sidmouth there is no Doubt But it wood be Done as it is the firs offence and as Insent as adove I Beg that you will Aply as Soon as you Reseve this as there is aship Expected here every Day and all that Lays in my power shall not be wanting In that Busness Onst I humbley beg that you will Keep me in Ingland as it is in Your Power and anething that I Can feavour you with Shall not be wanting Dont feale as soon as you heave Resev[d] this

From your Humble servant William Morris

I should Like your answer as soon as posable

Front of letter marked: With speed

528. *[F25/9/36] James Holman,* Justitia *hulk, Woolwich, 6 May 1821*

Gentlemen Could you but witness my wretched and deplorable situation I feel confident you would Interest yourselves in promoting my wishes namely of my being removed from here to the Penitentiary where I trust from an unexampled course of life and a knowledge of my unworthiness I might again become an Honourable and useful member to society and at a future period (which, I trust, would not be distant) be enable to provide for a Young and Unprotected Wife who without your generous and humane interference will be inevitably left destitute and unprovided for – I have given M[r] Christmas every information respecting Smith and female associate and would feel happy at all times in rendering every service to your most Hon[ble] Company. My former communication has been founded on a sure and firm basis – Truth – and in the case of Smith and companion part is verified.

I therefore again humbly presume to throw myself upon your most gracious mercy sincerely praying you may yet be pleased to grant my earnest request, anxiously awaiting the opportunity wherein (by your sanction) you shall see all my former proposals both verified and accomplished. On the contrary Gentlemen should you imagine from my knowledge of such characters that I am an unfit Object to Remain in this Country (which I [*hope*] you will not) I must fervently pray that your Philanthropy and Benevolence will induce you to assist me at this most melancholy crisis it has to enable me in a distant Land to support my dearest Wife (with your assistance and Industry Combined) and retrieve that Character which I have lost thro' my late and Unfortunate misconduct and folly – I make this appeal to your feelings under the grateful Impression that you will pardon the intrusion. I remain Gentlemen with the purest motives for your Most Hon[ble] Companys Welfare James Holman

529. *[F25/9/37–8] James Holman,* Malabar *transport ship, 14 June 1821 to Mr Christmas, Bank investigator*
Sir It is not without sanguine hopes of success that I make this appeal to your Benevolence – A few days now must terminate my sufferings in England – the heart rending Pangs of bidding Adieu to Wife – Friends – Country – and everyone dear to me – is now swiftly approaching to my Lot – I leave my Native Land destitute of common necessarys – I am not even provided with my exterior Clothing to make a Respectable appearance on my landing in New South Wales – It would be an act of real charity if the Hon[ble] Company of the Bank of England would remunerate my services (for so I may term them) with a trifle so that I may be enabled to furnish myself with such Apparel as would be most suitable to my views it might be the means of paving the way to my promotion and it would at all events confer an everlasting – grateful – and most essential – obligation on Sir, your Humble, Obt Servant James Holman
To Mr Christmas PS I have taken the liberty of writing to Mess[rs] Kay – Freshfield & Kay upon the same trusting real distress will plead for the presumptious liberty I have here taken. I beg leave to state that Saturday 16 In[st] as the date appointed to sail. C. Later [*sentenced to fourteen yrs trspn, Kent ass., spring 1821*] has been draughted on board the Malabar with me – but has returned on board the Justitia. I really thought Sir, that myself would have had a much better chance of a mitigation from the communications I made than Mr C Later
Attached: letter, same date, from Holman to Bank solicitors, containing same information as **529,** *annotated:* rec'd 16 June Spring assizes Maidstone minor offence
[*BECLS: 20 June 1821, relief refused.*]

530. *[F25/9/39] Bridget Slater, Newgate, 5 April 1821*
Honoured Gentlemen I hope and trust you will Pardon the Libberty I take In Addresing you I wrote to you once before, but received no Answer I hope you will take Compassion on my destressed situation and Grant me Some releif I have been In Confinment this seven Months to describe my suffering I cannott I have not A Freind In the world to render me the smallest Assistance my Parents being very Much destressed Could you have the goodness to grant me my request I shall Ever be in Duty bound to pray for you Your Most Humble Servant Bridgett Slater
Annotated: Refused

531. *[F25/9/40] Richard Burbidge, Newgate, 7 April 1821*
Sir being giving to understand by my brother who had some conversation with you upon the unfortunate situation I am placed in he informed me if I sent a note by my friend you would do me the favour of getting a ticket of a Watch & seals that was was taken from me at the time I was taken into custody hoping you will be so good as to give it to the bearer of this note I Remain Your Humble Servt R Burbidge
Annotated: Deliv^d it to Mr Corigan 7 April 1821

532. *[F25/9/41a] Fifteen 'out of London' women,* Mary Ann *transport ship, November 1821*
To the Humane and Honble Gentlemen Of the Bank The unfortunate women whose names are undersigned Humbey prayeth that the Directors of the Bank of England will generously and Humanely extend their Clemency towards them as before now they have done kindly towards others Jemima Burton, Hannah Whiteley, Mary Pimblott, Catherine Hilton, Jane Bridge, Isabella Hammill, Catherine Quinn, Maria Stevenson, Ann Williams, Clementina Rebecca Miares, Prudence Davies, Mary Wilson Wright, Elizabeth Montagu, Louisa Thompson, Sarah Prince

533. *[F25/9/41b] Twelve 'London' women,* Mary Ann *transport ship, November 1821*
We the Undersigned Prisoners of the Bank beg Leave to Present Our Most Grateful Acknowledgements for the Lenity That has been Shewn to Us And Humbly hope the Honble Gentlemen of the Bank Will of their known Goodness and Humanity As We are Now About to Leave Our Country be Pleased to Aid Us With that Charitable Assistance They have been Known Humanely to Extend to Others in a Like Situation And As In Duty Bound Will ever Pray, their Most Humble Petitioners Elizabeth Smith, Jane Carter, Sarah Johnson, Sarah Redding, Sarah Stewart, Frances Grey, Elizabeth Webster, Elizabeth Pascoe, Sarah Appleton, Catherine Taylor, Mary Stalker, Charlotte Thorn
Annotated; £75 Country £55 London £130 Eliz^h Smith was ordered to be p^d 2^d June 1821 – which has been res^d for her
[*BECLS : 12 Dec. 1821, realized they had granted £5 short, mistaking Elizabeth Smith in London list for an Elizabeth Smith previously paid; they had £5 each in hand for Sarah Paley and Martha Lucas who could not sail, so one £5 to be paid to E. Smith on current list and other £5 to be used to pay a witness.*]

534. *[F25/9/42–3] William Jervis, Horsemonger Lane gaol, 9 April 1821 Formal petition submitted on his behalf by twenty well-placed citizens of Camberwell, begging that his life be saved.* [*BECLS: 11 & 18 Apr. 1821, refused to interfere*].

535. *[F25/9/44–6] Lists of prisoners to be arraigned at OB sent by Bank solicitors to W. H. Brown, keeper of Newgate, 6 December 1820, 10 January 1821, 4 February 1821*

536. *[F25/9/47–8] Mary Ann Platt, unspecified house of correction, 7 November 1820*
Sir, May I solicit your kind attention to the information I am about to give assuring you it is Honest – I have been innocently ensnared into this unhappy offence by Mary Ann Kelly who is the sole cause of the approximating misery which must overwhelm me if you do not kindly extend your Lenity towards me – the young woman who was acquitted last week was ensnared in the same way that I have been – trusting to your humane interference in my behalf – and submitting my case to your kind consideration I am Sir Respectfully Your Obedient Servant Mary Anne Platt
Attached: letter from Mary Kelly to William Scrubbs at Black Horse, Vine Street warning him and friends to be careful since Mary Ann Platt had given information to Bank solicitor; annotated: 5 St Helens Place 7 Sept. 1818. [*Kelly and Platt indicted jointly.*]

537. *[F25/9/49] Phillis Johns, Newgate, 1 November 1820*
(Hon^d Sirs) I beg Pardon for the Liberty I take In Troubling you tis Necessity has compell'd Me to Request you will be Pleas'd to present My Case to the Honble Gentlemen of the Bank, to whom I Return My Most Grateful thanks for the Sum of 2 Pounds by the Hands of Mr Teague – at the same time I Most Humbly hope they will of their Known Goodness and Humanity be Pleas'd to Extend their Charity to Myself And three Helpless Children As I Am Quite Destitute of Friends or Money And have No Means Whatever of Procuring those Necessarys Requisite for our Voyage and a Great Part of Our Wearing Apparral &c being in Pledge which Must be Forfeited unless the Honble Gentleman of the Bank will Humanely assist Me in this My Distress'd Situation And As in Duty Bound Will Ever Pray Phillis Johns
[*BECLS: 11 Oct. 1820, £2 awarded as she had given birth pre-trial in Giltspur Street compter; 8 Nov. 1820, granted 7s. 6d. a week.*]

538. *[F25/9/50] Elizabeth Denham, Newgate, 13 November 1820*
Hon^d Sir I should consider My self Much Indebted to your goodness if you will condescend to call on Me Any time Most convenient As I wish to Speak with you Respecting the Unpleasant Situation I Am Placed in And should be glad to a Little of Your advice on the Subject I beg Leave to say I am at Present Waiting to take My Tryal at the Ensuing Sessions on a Charge of having A Uttered a Forged one Pound Note in so doing You will Sir Much Oblige Your Hum^le Sv^t Eliz^th Dent

539. *[F25/9/51a & b] Elizabeth Gould, Newgate, 8 November 1820*
Honoured Sir relying on your generosity to Pardon the Libberty I take In addressing you but extreme distress tempts me to solicit your kind Atention I have been extremlly Ill this two Months and have not one Freind In the world to render me the smalest Assistance I am Doomed to Leave my Country for fourteen years and am now wholy relying on your benovlence for relife should I be so fortunate as to meet the honourable approbation of

the honourable Gentlemen I should be ever bound to Pray for you with heart felt gratitude
Your Most humble Servant Elizabeth Gold
Attached: note from Charles Procter, Bank investigator, stating he found her in great distress.
[*BECLS: 15 Nov. 1820, rejected request; but next day, after report from Glover, Bank investigator, agreed to send £2 to Glover who should judge how best to use for her relief.*]

540. *[F25/9/52a & b] Sarah Carter, Newgate, 14 November 1820*
Honoured Sir relying on your generosity to Parden the Libberty I take In writeing a second time to you fearing you had forgot me tempts me once More to solicit your Kind Attention believe me Sir my distress Is greater than I can Describe I have not one Freind In this world to render me the smalest Assistance I am sentance to Leave my Country for fourteen years my feate is hard Indeed I hope and trust you will have the goodness to take Compassion on my Misserable Situation and grant me some releif honord Sir I have been in Confinment this seven Months without the Comforts of life Should you be so kind as to grant me my request I should ever be in Duty bound to Pray for you from your Most humble Servant Sarah Carter
Annotated: I believe the former application of this Pris^{r} was rejected by the Committee
Attached: note from Glover, Bank investigator, same date, saying no husband, child or friend visit her. [*BECLS: 22 Nov. 1820, refuse relief until she embarks.*]

541. *[F25/9/53] Sarah Carter, Newgate, 28 November 1820*
Identical letter to **540,** *believing Bank solicitors had not received it.*

542. *[F25/9/54a & b] Ann Prince, Newgate, 15 November 1820*
Sir I beg Pardon for thus Tresspassing on your Goodness As Necessity Obligers Me to Solicit Your Interferrence with the Honble Gentlemen of the Bank in My Behalf – Humbly hoping they will be pleased to take my Case into Consideration And be disposed to Assist Me with A Little of That Charity They have been known Humanely to Extend to Others in A Similor Situation – I Have No Friends to Render me the Least Assistance And have got one Child to Provide for Who With Myself is Quite Bare of Cloaths As I have been cruelly taken the advantage of During My Confinement by A Person who I Entrusted with the Care of them And Unless the Honble Gentlemen Of the Bank be Pleased to Extend their Charity Myself and Child will be Debased of the Means of Procuring there Necessaries Which are so requisite for us During our Voyage And Several Articles of Apparal which are Now pledged will be Forfeited it Not being in My Power to Redeem them – And I Remain with the Most Profound Respect Your Most H^{ble} Sv^{t} Ann Prince
Attached: investigator's note: Ann Prince a Prisoner in Newgate She has a Female Child about 4 Months & is in great distress. Sarah Ewster [*Hewster*][**543**] has no Friends or Family is in great distress. T. Glover 22

Nov^{r}; *also annotated*: Jane Cartwright [*Sarah Carter*] is in great distress – no Friends
[*BECLS: 22 Nov. 1820, granted 5s. a week.*]

543. *[F25/9/55] Sarah Hewster, Newgate, 21 November 1820*
Hon^{d} Sir I beg Pardon for troubling you again as I am so very Distress^{d} I am induced to beg you will in Pity to my years Present My Case to the Honble Gentlemen of the Bank humbly Hoping they will be Pleased to Extend their Charity to Me As there is No Object Stands More in Need of it than Myself – I have been in Confinement for five Months Past and have Not had any Person to give Me the Least Assistance during that time And have only had the Jail Allowance to Live on I would Not be so Intruding if I had wherewith to procure Me A Few Articles Necessary for My Voyage And to Redeem my Cloaths I Should feel truly grateful for the Smallest Act of Charity Bestow^{d} Me by the Honble Gentlemen of the Bank Who I Trust Will be Pleas^{d} to Grant Me some Pecuniary Aid As they in their goodness May think Proper And As in Duty Bound will ever Pray Your Most H^{ble} Sv^{t}
Sarah Ewster
Annotated: See ltr fm Ann Prince dated 15 Novr 1820
[*BECLS: 22 Nov. 1820, rejected request until she embarked.*]

544. *[F25/9/56] Harriett Treemer, Newgate, 10 October 1820*
Honnored Sir I hope and trust you will pardon the Libberty I take In writeing to you but Extrem Distress temps me to solicit your favour I am Domed to Leave my Country for fourteen years and I have not one kind Freind In the world to releive me I hope your goodness will take Compassion on my unhappy situation and grant me some Releife If you will be so kind to send me A trifle of Money I shall Ever be In Duty bound to Pray for you I have been In Prisson five Months and have not had A Penny from Any one but the Prisson Allowance
from your Most humble Servant Harriett Tremer
[*BECLS: 18 Oct. 1820, refused request; investigator said she was not distressed.*]

545. *[F25/9/57] Rachel Herbert, Newgate, 28 November 1820*
Honoured Sir relying on your gennerosity to Pardon me for writeing to you but Extreme Distress tempts me to solicit your kind Attention I have been robbed of all I had since I have been In Confinement I have Nothing Left not so Much as a thing to my back but what I have on what to do I know not unless you will have the goodness to Lay my Miserable situation before the Committee I have not one Friend In the world to render me the smalest Assistance my situation Is truly Distressing being under the Sentence of Leaveing my Country for fourteen years have no other Dependance than the honourable gentlemen of the Bank
from your most humble Servant Rachel Herbert
[*BECLS: 6 Dec. 1820, investigator, Glover, reported she was not a fit object for mercy, request refused.*]

546. *[F25/9/58–9] Henry Harris, Newgate, 1 December 1820*
Dear Sirs I take the liberty of Forwarding you the following lines being given to understand that their has been A Man Describing himself a Coachman and stating that he never had a note till I sold him one – but I solemnly declare to that Almighty God befor whos presence I shortly have to appear that I never in my life saw that man nor ever attempted aneything of the kind and I should esteem it as an extreme favour if I could be permitted to see that man and then I should Die in peace I do assure you Sirs that this unhappy catastrophy has come quite unexpected being allowed to plead to the Minor Offence having but two against me I most humbly lay my unhappy case before you Gentlemen and earnestly crave your kind consideration in my favour trusting that if their should be slightest possibility of my life being spared and being banished the country during the remainder of my Days I should be in duty ever bound to pray that God of his Infinite Goodness and Mercy would shower down his choisest blessings on your devoted heads Consider Sirs my undeserving Parents that quickly must drop with sorrow to the Grave and may your compassionate hearts feel but one pang For an Unfortunate Sufferer H. Harris
Attached: note from Mr Sheriff Williams, Smithfield, to Bank, 2 Dec. 1820: Mr Sheriff Williams with Compliments to the Govr & Comp^{y} of Bank of England feels it His Duty to convey the accompanying letter. *Note annotated:* Vide ltr from Henry Harris to the Gov^{s} & Comp^{y} dated 1 Dec 1820 *and:* Note the Evi^{ce} wanting

547. *[F25/9/60] Mary Ann Smith, Newgate, 11 December 1820*
Honoured Sir I hope and trust you will Pardon the Libberty I take In Writeing to you A second time but Extreme Distress tempts me once More to Solicit your kind Attention I received A one Pound Note four Months back witch I Ever shall be gratefull for I have been in Confinement Ever Since May and have not A Freind In the World to render me the smalest Assistance I am Doomed to Leave my Country for fourteen years I have Lost all my Cloaths what to do I know not I hope and trust you will take Compassion on my Miserable Situation and grant me my request and I shal be In duty bound to Pray for you from your most humble Servant Mary Ann Smith
Annotated: Rejected

548. *[F25/9/61] Mary Lambert, Newgate, 17 December 1820*
I hope and trust you will Pardon me for taking the Libberty of writeing to you but Extreme Distress tempts me to Solicit your kind Attention I have been in Confinement Ever since September and have not A Freind In the world to render me the smalest Assistance witch is so very hard for God Sake Let me beg of you to take Compassion on my Miserable Situation and grant some relief believe me Gentlemen to describe my distress I cannot should you be so kind as to grant my request I shall be In duty bound to Pray for you as it Is uncertain when the Ship will Sail I am Doomed to leave my Country for fourteen years
from your Ever humble Servant Mary Lambert
Annotated: Rejected

549. *[F25/9/62] Mary Jones, Newgate, 27 December 1820*
honoured Sir I hope and trust you will Pardon the Libberty I take In Writeing to you but Extreme Distress tempts me to Solicit your kind Attention I have not A Freind In the world to grant me the smallest releif my sufferings Is More than I can describe to be confined In A Prison without the Comforts of Life I hope you will take Compassion on my destressed Situation and Grant me my request I am Sentance for fourteen years transportation and have parted with all my Cloths beleive me Sir I shal Ever be gratefull for the smallest releif and be In Duty bound to Pray for you your Most humble Servant Mary Jonce
Attached note: Mary Jones is not a proper object of Charity T. Glover 28 Dec[r]; *further annotated in another hand:* How much £69

550. *[F25/9/63] Elizabeth Denham, Newgate, 11 December 1820*
Honour[d] Gentlemen relying on your gennrosity to Pardon me for the Libberty I take In Addresing you but Extreme distress tempts me to solicit your kind Attention my distress Is more than I can describe my husband suffered hear witch Left me unprotected on the wide world with two small Children Without A Freind In the world to render me the smallest Assistance I hope and trust you will take Compassion on my Miserable situation and Grant me some releife I am Doomed to Leave my Country for fourteen years Could you be so kind as to grant my request I shall Ever be In Duty bound to Pray for you from your Most Humble Servant Elizebth Dennam
Annotated: To be allowed 7/6 p[r] Week during her Stay in Newgate [*BECLS: 20 Dec. 1820, noted she had 2 children with her.*]

551. *[F25/9/64] Elizabeth Denham, Newgate, 3 January 1821*
Honoured Sir relying on your genrerosity to Pardon the Libberty I take In Writeing to you but being very Much Distresed So Much I know not what to do I have young baby sucking att my breast my triall Is More then I can bear I have Partted with my Cloths to help to support my dear Child I have not one Freind In the world to give me the smallest releif honoured Sir If you will take Compassion in my Miserable situation and Alow me A trifle of Money to releiv my destresed Mind to describe my destress I Cannott I hope and trust you grant me my Request and I Shall ever be In duty bound to Pray for you from your Most humble Servant Elizebth Denham
I have one Child att Nurse witch Makes me two Children and I owe A Sum of Money to the Nurse
Annotated: For Glover's report See Ltr fm Sarah Wright of same date. Not complied with [*BECLS: 10 Jan. 1821, noted a weekly allowance already granted.*]

552. *[F25/9/65–6] Elizabeth Denham, Newgate, 31 January 1821*
Honoured Sir I am truly Sorrey to be Under the painfull Nessasity of writing to You again but I am quite Destitute of Every Nessary of Life for my two poor Helpless Children only trusting on the know goodness of the worthy Gentlemen and you Honoured Sir I wold for Ever Acnolledge my thanks to you if you wold be Graciously pleased to Lay My Destressed

Case before the Committee As I am Entirely Destitute and Distress beyond discribing Having Nothing but the bear Allowance of the Geoal to subsist on which is scarce Enough to keep life within me My poor Child is very ill And Has been for this week past owing to the whant of Nourishment and it is oute of My power to obtain the least Comphorts for Eather of them only depending on Your goodness and Compassion I parted with the last thing I Had Before I wold trouble you but being Now Destitute again I wold Ever Acknolled my thanks to you if you wold take In to Consideration my Piti-full Case and I will be in Duty Bound Ever to pray Elizabeth Denham
Attached note: Mr Brown of Newgate says that neither of the Parties are Distressed, Bridget Slater, Elizabeth Denham, Mary Howard, C. Procter [*Bank investigator*] 1 Feb 1821
[*BECLS: 7 Feb. 1821, confirms weekly allowance.*]

553. *[F25/9/67–8] Elizabeth Pryor, (member of association for the improvement of the female prisoners in Newgate) re: Elizabeth Denham and other matters, 20 Gracechurch Street, 6 February 1821*
The Gentlemen Bank of England directors are respectfully inform[d] that Eliz[th] Denham, a Bank Prisoner in Newgate begs her case may be taken into consideration for a weekly allowance towards the support of herself and two Infant Children. E. Pryor has taken this liberty on the behalf of E Denham and at her request.
E.P. begs leave to call the attention of the Gentlemen to the consideration also, of the gratuitious allowance of the £5 which has been usually presented to them on board the Ship when about to be transported. From the observations E.P. has been capable of making she is apprehensive this act of great kindness is attended with no real benefit to them Individually in the way it is intended, because they presume upon it, and they will expect it; the consequence is, they lavish their weekly allowance whilst in Prison, still in debt, their cloaths in pawn, and they generally in a worse state than if they were not in expectation of the addition of the £5.
In stateing the above remarks, E.P. begs further to observe, that on board the female Convict Ships, she has felt peculiar interest for the better regulating the Convicts by Classification, Employment and organizeing a School for the Children in order measurably to prevent those disgraceful scenes which have too commonly prevail'd. These regulations are attended with considerable Expence, and the Bank Convicts share in common with the other women, in all the privileges which are thus dispensed among them.
E.P. does not ask for the £5 to be with held altogether, but if they could see no impropriety of throwing their gift into the general fund for the express purpose above stated, it would be put to a good and beneficial account, and prevent those perplexities which never fails to occur on those occasions.
E. Pryor hopes the Gentlemen of the Bank of England will excuse this liberty, more especially as it may appear premature, but she engaged to apply on behalf of E. Denham, and thought it right to throw the whole subject before them, in hopes it may have due place in their consideration.

Attached: copy letter, 15 Feb. 1821, from Joseph Kaye, Bank solicitor to Mrs Pryor: Madam, I submitted your Letter to the Gov^{rs} and Directors of the Bank, who have complied with your recommendation in favour of Elizth Denham. With respect to what is given by the Governors & Directors to Female Convicts previous to their departure for New South Wales, they think it is right to retain the Application of it under their own immediate control. I am &c J. K., NBB, 15 Feb 1821

554. *[F25/9/69] Sarah Wright, Newgate, 3 January 1821*
Hon^{d} Sir I humbly hope the Liberty I Take in Troubling you a Second time will not be considered Intruding as Necessity Compels Me to Solicit your Interference In my Behalf with the Honble Gentlemen of the Bank Praying that they will of their Known Goodness be Disposed to Extend their Charity by Assisting me a Little as I am very much Distressed And have got No Friends whatever to Render Me the Least Assistance And it is Not in My Power to earn Any Thing at Needle Work having a Young Baby to attend to
I Feel truly grateful for two Pounds sent Me Whilst Confin'd in Childbed and Were I Not so Embarrassed I would Not have been so Troublesom I am Quite Bare of necessary for Myself And Child And have got Several Articles in Pledge which I Can't redeem Unless the Honble Gentlemen of the Bank will kindly Undertake to have Pity on Me And as in duty Bound will ever Pray your most H^{ble} St Sarah Wright
Annotated: Not complied with

555. *[F25/9/70] Bridget Slater, Newgate, 31 January 1821*
Honnored Sir I hope and trust you will Pardon the Libberty I take In Addesing you but Extreme Distress tempts me to solicit your kind Attention hopeing you will take Compassion on my Miserable Situation I have been in Confinment five months and have been Extremly Ill for this last two Months and have not A Freind In the world to render me the Smalest Assistance haveing no other hope to depend on then your honnor I hope and trust you will grant me my request & beleive me sir I shall Ever be In Duty bound to Pray for you – should you think me worthy of your Attention & Send me A trifle of Money I shall Ever be gratefull for the Same from your Most Humble Servant Bridgett Slatter
Attached note [F25/9/71 double numbered, see below] 31 Jan. 1821: Vide ltr fr Elizabeth Denham (for Character) Pet^{ns} Eliz^{h} Denham Sarah Wright These Two women are in the same Situation as those before transported T. Glover 8 Jan 1821

556. *[F25/9/71] Mary Howard, Newgate, 30 January 1821*
Honoured Sir relying on your goodness to Pardon the Libberty I take In Adresing you but Extreme distress oblidge me to solicit your kind Attention and knowing your general Character and your sincere wish to do good beleive me Sir my triall is very Great more than I Can bear. I have been in Confinement Ever since the 1 of June and have Lost Every thing I had in the world. My husband is on board the Leviathan att Portsmouth and is

Extremly Ill and have been so Ever since he Left this Prison. My dear Child Left to the wide world deprived of both Father and Mother honoured Sir think for A Moment what I Must suffer to be robberd of my husband and Child and house and home all in one Fatal Day for God Sake Let me Intreat you to take Compassion on my sufferings and render me what releif you think proper as I am Intirely Friendless and deprived of Every Comfort witch renders my situation Miserable honnered Sir I hope and trust you will have the goodness to Intercede for me to be kept in my Country as my husband is very Ill and never Can bear so Long A voyage and beleiv me Sir Any information I can give you I will with the greatest of Pleasuar humbly Praying your honour will render us this kindness as I hope and trust In god you will and Crown your endeavours with success and I pray to God you will meet your reward sir in Heaven for your goodness. I have just received A Letter from my Afflicted husband he informs me the dockter of the Bay Ship tels him he is sure not to go to the Bay he has Lost the use of his side his suffering is More then I Can Describe honoured Sir Let me once More Intreat you Grant me my request and keep me in my Country for my poor husbands and Child sake and I shall ever be In duty bound to Pray for you Your Most Humble Servant Mary Howard
Annotated: Vide ltr fm Eliz[th] Denham 31 Jan[y]
[*BECLS: 7 Feb. 1821, notes she has child with her but is supported by friend.*]

557. *[F25/9/72] Samuel Evans, Newgate (Master's Side), 15 January 1821*
Sir I have been unhappyly the dupe of others without ever having the most distant intention of using the practice with which I changed to my own Emolument. Unfortunately my own trade of Boot maker made me the lodger of Mr Burns and consequently put me in the way of acquaintances which I should otherwise not have known. If in your better judgement & kindness any communication can be attended to from Me which may opperate in my favour I will most unreservedly make it if You will give Me the opportunity Y[rs] Respectfully Sam[l] Evans

558. *[F25/9/73] George King, Horsemonger Lane gaol, 26 March 1821*
In custody for seven months prior to trial for uttering, asks to plead to lesser offence; BECLS already decided, 9 Aug. 1820.

559. *[F25/9/74–5] Jane Gould, Horsemonger Lane gaol, 18 December 1820*
honerd Sir your humble pertikiner Jane Gould the Wife of Staven Gould how is a transport [*sentenced to fourteen yrs trspn OB, Mar. 1820*] now laying in horse monger Lane prison and I have bean hear a long time I was cometed in march last and I ham in great want at this time having no frands to do heney thing for me as my husband is gaown to the bay I hope your honer will have the goodness to asstist me I would not have troubled you if I was not in want but laying hear so lone and I do not know how long I have to Stop longer I hope your honer will take it in to considerrashen and sand

me something to halp me as I have bean hear So long I ham vary bad of from your vary humble sirvant Jane Gould

Attached: note from Bank investigator: Jane Gould a prisoner in Horse-Monger Lane Goal, is no worse off than other Women, who are in the same Prison for the same offence T. Glover, 22 Decr 1820

560. *[F25/9/76] Charles Carnegy, New Prison, Clerkenwell, 24 November 1820*

Gentl^{n} I most humbly beg pardon for the liberty I take in intruding myself upon your indulgence and merciful consideration of my distressed and unhappy situation in which I am unfortunately place. But Gentlemen if you would be pleased to allow me, I can satisfy you that I was completely drawn into the Snare while the Authors abetters and planers are suffered to remain at large and who I can inform you of provided you allow me when I am sure you will see that I am the dupe and Victim of the real Culprits I am Gent^{ln} Your Most Obdient and distressed Servant Charles Carnegy

561. *[F25/9/77] John Arnold, keeper of New Prison, Clerkenwell, 30 December 1820 requests remuneration of incidental expenses, including twice hiring coaches to transport Bank prisoners from Hatton Garden to Newgate.*

562. *[F25/9/78–81] William Hill, Newgate, 24 January 1824, to Mr Lees, Bank investigator*

Sir, In consequence of Death occurring in my family I have been prevented fullfilling my engagement with you this occurrence taking place rather suddenly.

As I purpose of Postponing my Trial (if possible) until the March Sessions every thing will be done on my part which I think will prove satisfactory to those who are humane to interest themselves I Remain sir Most Respectfully Your very Obed^{t} Humb^{le} St W. Hill

Attached: statement addressed from OB, Dec. 1823, unsigned, explaining that Hill wished to postpone trial until next sessions so he could discover real culprit; this annotated to request Hill to send information to Bank solicitors, who would send investigator to him; note on Hill's behalf, 31 Dec. 1823, from Newgate, requesting Bank solicitors send someone to him [presumably the appointment which Hill postponed by **562**]*; copy letter from Bank solicitors, 16 Feb. 1824, to Mr Foy, West India Dock police office, requesting information on Hill, due for trial in two days' time; they were* desirous to negative *his claim to be employed by the West India Dock company in Oct./Nov. 1823, and wish Foy to send evidence* in the course of tomorrow.

563. *[F25/9/82–3] John Smith, Newgate, 16 September 1823*

Sir, I have considered it my Duty to inform you that I have just heard that the person, Fidler & his two companions stand committed for trial at Hicks

Hall [*Mdx quarter sessions*] this Sessions for passing bad money, three of the most desperate characters in the Circulation of Forged Notes, two of whom are in feigned names, Sulbrook' name is Gust, Williams is Nash & Fidler [*cap. con. OB Sept 1821*] in his proper name.
Now having laid this before you I humbly trust you will have the goodness to endeavour to have as much lenity & mercy shewn me as will prevent the awful Sentence of the law being carried into Execution, I trust in Consideration of my Confession of this Circumstance my pleading guilty at the Bar also the Distress with which my Family & Connexions are plunged into will I trust have a consideration & excite a Sympathy in your Breast for the Sufferings of a poor fellow creature, trusting this will meet with attention I remain Sir Yr Mo: H^{le} Ser^{t} John Smith
Attached: copy note from Bank solicitors, 24 Sept. 1823, stating his letter laid before governors of Bank who cannot consistent with their duty to the Public *interfere.*

564. *[F25/9/84] John Smith, Newgate, 24 September 1823*
Gent^{n} Your Letter I received yesterday & altho' you express therein that the Govr & Directors of the Bank of England will not interfere in my Behalf I trust they may not be induced to add anything against me than what is allegedly done, so as to prevent my Friends interesting themselves to save my Life & as I have endeavored to disclose everything I knew I have in add^{n} to say that conversing with one of the Prisoners here, I have learnt that Black Harry, the Person who Fidler [*see* **563**] obtains the Notes, lodges in No. 15 Vine S$^{t.}$ Chandos St Covent Garden & further that He has been always living by the Sale of them, & keeps them in the front Cellar I cannot myself vouch for the exact Truth of this but am led to understand that it is correct and trust this will be an additional appeal to save me from a disgraceful End – & prevent others from falling into the same perilous situation, I am Sir, Y^{r} H^{le} J. Smith
[*BECLS: 1 Oct. 1823, read letter; noted no point in replying.*]

565. *[F25/9/85] Ann Layshaw and others,* Mary Ann *transport ship, Woolwich, 25 May 1823*
Honble Gentlemen We the undersigned Petitioners now on board the Mary Female Convict Ship having been unfortunate enough to be convicted for Uttering Forged Notes, as set forth in the enclosed statement taken from the Government Report, most humbly beg you will be pleased to grant your petitioners the same Donation you so very Humanely have done to others who have been placed in the like unfortunate situation. And your Petitioners as in duty bound will ever pray Eliza^{beh} Webb, Elizth Trindle, Ann Rummer [*these sign by mark*] anna Lasaw [*own signature*]
Annotated: See Minutes of the Committee 30th May. Ann Layshaw was convicted at the Summer Assizes 1822 of uttering forged Bank Notes for £5 – in the County of Essex. The other three Prisoners were not prosecuted by the Bank & with respect to two of them Trindle & Rummer it appears they were Not prosecuted for uttering Bank of England Notes – but Notes of the Norwich Bank as to Eliza Webb we have no information

566. *[F25/9/86 a & b] Maria Williams, Newgate, 20 August 1824*
Sir I beg pardon for this intrusion but I trust you will take me your humbel petitioner into your kind considderation haveing been a prisoner in this prison upwards of ten months and Laying for some time under the awfull Sentance of death but the Royal mercy was extended towards me for which I am unfeignedly thankfull, but as I am to leave my Country for life and much distressed haveing no Freinds whatever to assist me I hope your kindness will extend towards me and lett me have the bank money as I understand that Some have had it Sence it as been stopt and if it is allowed me it will be most thankfully received and be of the Greatest Help to me your Humbel Servent whome will ever be in duty bound to Pray trusting you will forgive every liberty you may think me Guilty of beg leave to subscribe Myself yours moste obedient Maria Williams
Annotated: frm the Prisoner with a recommendation from the Govr of Newgate
Attached: note, 28 Aug. 1824: The Governor of Newgate has been seen regarding Maria Williams who was convicted in January last for uttering Forged Notes, and he considers her a fit object for Pecuniary Relief on account of her having Conducted herself with so much propriety since her Trial. She has no Children, having never been Married. The Vessel in which she is to embark will sail this week. £5-0-0 [*sum in red ink*], Maria Williams *with her mark* 4 Sep 1824 *and witness signature.*

567. *[F25/9/87] Maria Williams, Newgate, 31 August 1824*
Respectfull Sir By your condecension in coming to make inquiries after me who confesses the unfortunate conduct I have pursu'd – feeling true thankfullness for the Mercy & compassion that has been extended towards me in sparing me from an ignominious death – likewise my gratefull acknowledgements to the worthy and every respectfull superiors of this prison for the lenity extended while under the awfull sentence of death. As the Honourable gentlemen have taken into consideration my destitute state, and your humanity in taking the trouble, trusting you will forgive this liberty in addressing you – may I presume to crave your interest in procuring me an assistance being utterly destitute to embark on such a voyage, having no relations to assist me & having a number of articles in pledge – which would require some repair, and little I had, could lay it out to some advantage than when in the prison. Humbly soliciting the Generosity of the Honourable Gentlemen in behalf of an ignorant and misguided Female will ever pray in their behalf – and with due respect remain your unfortunate Obliged Humble Servant Maria Williams The ship is expected soon to sail

568. *[F25/9/88–9] Completed insolvent debtors' relief pro-forma, 18 October 1827, summonsing to court, on 8 Nov. 1827, prisoner in Fleet prison, Thomas Claughton Esq., of Haydock Lodge, Lancs., also of Parliament Street, Westminster, and Bloomsbury Square, Mdx, with copy letter from Bank solicitors forwarding pro-forma to royal mint solicitors, Amory & Coles.*

569. *[F25/10/1] Joseph Ball, Warwick gaol, 27 February 1801*
Ball, a bankrupt, asks Bank for temporary relief and names and addresses of people who might assist him.

570. *[F25/10/2–6] John Hollins,* Fortune *transport ship, Portsmouth, 26 February 1801.*
Set of letters from Hollins, not Bank prisoner, addressed to Sir John Carter, Portsmouth, passed by Carter to Bank solicitors. Hollins, pardoned for his crime, wishes to offer information gleaned from friend on Fortune *about forgers. Attached: note of several names, made by Bank solicitors; copy letter from Bank solicitors to William Penrose, treasury official, stating they have received many letters from Hollins via Sir John Carter but Hollins never comes up with information.*

571. *[F25/10/7–9] John Pasmore,* Fortune *transport ship, Langstone harbour, Portsmouth, 1 September 1801 & 6 May 1802. Pasmore, friend of Hollins* [**570**], *not Bank prisoner, addresses letter to Sir John Carter to forward to Bank, offering information on forgers; attached: note from Bank declining offer; second letter from Pasmore showing he is keen to inform on certain gentry.*

572. *[F25/10/10–12] John Green, Ruthin gaol, Denbys., 4 January 1804*
Honored Gentlemen With great submission I take the present liberty of presenting my needfull address to the humane consideration of your Hon[d] persons, which I hope you will remember in mercy; I have great reason to praise the Lord for his past mercys and also to return you my most Humble thanks for the interfusion that hath been made by your worthy person, in behalf of having my life spared when it was so near a point. I still trust in your Goodness that you will remember how I was led from my original path of virtue to the punishment I now suffer by those that ought to have suffer'd in my stead; but the Lord is Gratious and mercifull; but he can bring the guilty to suffer. But now it remains on the contrary, that the innocent suffers and the guilty is set free; but the time will come when we shall all be Judged aright; which gives me hopes that I shall have Happyness for all my sufferings which are very great at this present I have this two months bore great afflictions in one leg that hath broke out with being so confined, which hath caused me to suffer much in such a Dreadful place; and being separated from a tender Wife and seven small Children, that are brought to the brink of ruin by this fatal seperation; which hath took place almost this two years past; I being the offspring of a reputable Family in all Circumstances, which makes my fate still harder; may the Lord incline the hearts of your Hon[d] persons to intercede in the behalf of me receiving Pardon for my past offences; which thing I hope will be a warning to many; I most Humbly beg you will except my thanks for what is past, and still trust in your Goodness & mercy for what is to come, for which your poor petitioner remains in duty bound to pray; J. Green
Attached: two letters to Bank from Humphrey Jones, keeper of Ruthin gaol; 23 Oct. 1803 and 7 Mar. 1804, asking for Green's sentence to be

mitigated further since his good character warrants restoration to his family.

573. *[F25/10/13] John Sumner, prison keeper, Birmingham, undated in 1804*
Sends bills to William Spurrier, solicitor acting for Bank in cases in Warws. and Staffs. for services rendered re Bank prisoners.

574. *[F25/10/14] John Baddeley, Stafford prison, 18 April 1808*
Hon[d] Sirs, Pardon me if I offend in writing to Your Honours as I now ly under Sentance of Transportation for haveing in my possession a quantity of Notes that was forg'd upon Your most Honourable Bank for which I very much repent not only for myself but the thoughts of many others I fear will come into the same situation or worse by those base Villains the makers of such kind of base Money which Induces many to their ruin and the thoughts of the large quantity of money it takes to prosecute those whom they notes are found upon, I hereby think it my duty to inform Your Houners that it's in my power was I at liberty to take up all the Makers in Birmingham and stop their Proceedings in making of all kinds of Base Money boath Notes Gould and Silver coin so if your Honners should take the above with Consideration and lend me Your assistance I will for Your Honor and the Countrys Good use every endeavour and bring them to Justice even to the hasard of my life which I believe wou'd be the case as they are well Arm'd at that time when they know they are in danger they sign the Notes at a Certin place and then takes them to a House where their Customers meet as they must be took betwixt the two Places when they have the Goods upon them as they are mostly alltogether You wou'd be surprised to see the quantitys they send of to all parts of England Ireland Scotland and to all parts of Wales I now am wise to the knowledge of the evil that attends it makes me very willing to have it all destroyed I can tell if I am in any Company if their is one amongst them that trades in the above goods in a few minutes. So if Your Honnors think proper to take me for the Business You may depend upon my Sincerity and I would loose my life in the Action before I would miss taking them as I am now Convinc'd of the evil Consequence of their Business my purposing this in hopes of saving the lives of many besides the vast expense attending – and I have another way I can take them as I dont wish to make publick if Your Honours shoud take it into Consideration it shall be my Study to render all the Assistance I can.
I am Gentlemen Your Most Humble Petitioner John Baddeley
P.S. I should take up a great many Makers of the aforesaid notes & Money and I have something Particular to say if I could see you
[*BECLS: 11 May 1808, request rejected.*]

575. *[F25/10/16] William Phillips, Warwick gaol, 5 April 1808*
Mr Kay Sir, I hope you and Mr Spurror [*Spurrier, Birmingham solicitor*] will have the goodness to take my distressing case in to consideration as I have no frends in the world but you and Mr Spurror as is well nown that is

throaw mee that Marsh Gulley [**590–1, 593**] and Baker was taken as I always suplied Suanah Criss with money to do the Bisness with tham and to go by the notes of them to send to utter at Woodbridge but could not tel witch way the mother sent them to him, witch throw Howell living with Criss thay have turned thair backs upon mee wich is well nown to Mr Spurrer that was don to Seaive mee but if Plase God I should wonce more be restored to my Libberty you may depend that all that I can do to Searve the Bank or the mint I will do to the best that I can wich I mack not the List Doubt but I could Put a nend to Som of the bisness in having B Patrick [*notorious forger*] at work at a Bank Plate or if you woud wish me to go with Mr Antony [*public office, Bow Street, London*] or any other Person to Ireland to have Mr Patrick taken at work for hee will do anithing for mee I would do, as I will now were to find him in Dubling or any others Persons that I now, but Sir I only wish I could See you and Mr Spurrer heair I could satisfy you more than I ham Able to rite at this time as I would be Bound in aney sum of monney to you to Purform what I have heair rote as I have no frend now Left as since my confinment heair I have Lost my Wife and my Father and Last Satterday night my mother dyed So you see that I have no frend Left and 5 children but if Plase God I should be at Libberty wonce more I ham Positif I could have Dry taken with the notes uppon him and King and W Foster but if you will plase to ask Mr Antony hee will inform you what I told him but Sir I have this time rote to Mr Spurrer and If I should See him I will Inform him my mind concerning of It Sir I hope you will be my Frend this time and I shall be for Ever bound to Pray for you and to Seairve you in anething at any time, So to conclude with my Prairs to you to be my Frend from your most obedent Humble Searvant Wm Phillips

576. *[F25/10/15] William Phillips, Warwick gaol, 17 April 1808*
Mr Kay Sir Plase to Excuse mee in takeing this Liberty of riting to you as I have no frend in the world but you to take my Distresing case in to concideration as since my confinment heair I have lost my Wife and Father and the first of this month my mother and now I have no frend Left but my children wich is not in thaire power to Assist mee in it nothing and if Plase God you will Step forward in my bealf this time I shall be in Dueaty bound to seairve you in anething that liese in my power to do for you and the bank and if Plase God that I should Get my Liberty I would go with Mr Antony to Irland to have Mr Patrick as hee would do anething for mee Eather in the notes or make a Plate for them or I would Go Anewere Else to seairve you or to have B Patrick first as I would be bound in aney Amount to you to Perform what I have rite to you as I ham well convinced that there is no other Person in Birmingham wich makes the Plates but him and concerning the Dealers in them I informed Mr Antony when I see him heair Last, Sir. I only wish that I could of seen you at the Asise I could of Satisfide you more then I ham Able to rite to you wich should of bin to your satisfaction Sir I hope you are convinced that throu my Intrest the Peple that was found Giltey at the Asise by Chrissmas [*Christmas, Bank investigator*] was for my beneficit Sir I hope for God Sake you will be my frend this time as I expect the peple to go Soon from heair to the Hulks an I ham verey unesey

about it as you must Expect Guley [Gulley, **590–1, 593**] not to be frends with mee throw is Wife and Likewise with the rest that is hear Sir I hope you will be my frend this time and if I should Get Liberty I would Eather com up to you or would go with Mr Antony and I ham sure that I could have B Patrick imedley but Mr A will Inform you so to conclude with my Praire to you to be my frend I remain your most obedint and Humble Searvent Wm Phillips

577. *[F25/10/17–19] Thomas Cribb, Chelmsford gaol, February, 1808*
In prison for horse-stealing, provides information about forgers; list of names written by Thomas Archer, keeper of Chelmsford gaol.

578. *[F25/10/20] Joseph Bridge and Michael Hughes,* Fortune *transport ship, Spithead, 6 January 1806*
Gentlemen Permit your unfortunate servants most humbly to take the liberty of intruding on your Wisdom by the brief statement of our unhappy Case and make an Appeal to your Humanity for an Amelioration of the Rigours of our Distress
When on Board the Hulks we voluntarily in conjunction with many of our fellow Sufferers volunteered our services to His Majesty in his Land Forces abroad, underwent Inspection before Justice Graham and the Colonels of HM African Corps wereby these Gentlemen approved and inrolled, but were afterwards informed we had been guilty of Aggressions towards You we could not be accepted and were in Consequence ordered on Board this Ship bound to N. S. Wales. We now in the most humble and respectful Manner implore your Clemency and that you would graciously consider to Permit us to avail ourselves of his Majesty's Army as consistent with our fellow Sufferers who are not yet gone to join there Corps or if this cannot be granted we most humbly intreat you to take our unhappy Case into your consideration and grant us such Amelioration of our Situation as you Gentlemen shall in your Humanity be disposed to grant which Favour will ever be acknowledged with the most heartfelt Gratitude and for your Felicity Hon[d] Gentlemen will be duly offered the Prayer of Your truly respectful unfortunate Servants & humble Petitioners Joseph Bridge Michael Hughes

579. *[F25/10/21] John Rimes,* Fortune *transport ship, Spithead, 5 January 1806*
Honoured Sir I humbly take the liberty of addressing You to request your acceptance of my most sincere and thankful Acknowledgements for the Favours you have so generously conferred upon me Permit me to assure you, I shall ever retain the most grateful sense of them
I could also wish to impress, if Possible, on an exalted Mind like Yours this conviction that tho' doomed to Banishment by the Law, I am in effect utterly innocent of the Crime for which I suffer, believe my solemn Parting Assurance that it is so notwithstanding which I now patiently submit to the Dispensations of the Providence and Severity of my destiny nor will the endeavours of those I leave behind be at any Time deficient if by them they

can be fortunate enough to render any Service to the Bank. In addition to the Favours already received Permit me Sir once more for the last Time to make an appeal to your Goodness: by every Account in the Country where I am going Letters of Recommendation prove the most signally serviceable had I one to present to the Governor on my Arrival it might prove the means of my being taken off the Hous and by working at my trade might insure A Competency and avoid that laborious Toil so irksome at my Time of Life can I Hon[d] Sir derive this benefit from your Generosity if therefore you will condescend to grant me this Request if sent to me by Post under Cover directed to me on Bd the Fortune B. Bay Ship Captain Shore Spithead or elsewhere Be assured Sir I shall never prove ungrateful for your Goodness but will Pray for your injoyment of every Felicity under heaven whilst life animates

Your highly obliged and truly respectful humble servant Jn Rimes

580. *[F25/10/22] Richard Westcoat, High gaol, Exeter, 16 September, 1807*

Honoured Sir I hope your Honour will not be offended with me for troubling you as I ham a prisenour and transported for 14 years and my Wife [*Jane*] Likewise I am a Baker By trade and have Ben enfortunate with the Busness that I have it not in my power to provide for my poor Childern and there wheare forged Notes found in a Saspan belonging to me I Do Declare to God I Never utered one forged Note in my Life to the Best of my knolage thearefor I hope your honours Goodness with your Intrust will Geet my sentence to some Impresenment or Aney other punishment your honours Gooness Could Impose on me so that in some Little time I may be Inabled to Support my Childern and it will be my Dutey to Informe your honours of all the makers of those Bad Notes and the utterers of them and Should I be so fourteneate to Geet my Liberty and should be put In power I will take Every one of them and Bring them to justeis this I hope will be kept as a scerecret or the Busness Cannot Be Done and I should be yoused hill by the Rest of the priseners and as I have No money Left and my Creadeit is Lost on this Sad Busness after I have Done what I have promissed I should be thinkfull to Sarve his majesty on board one of his Ships in the Best manner I Can

I hope your honour will feal for my poor Childern and I shall be in Duty Bound to pray from your humble Sulisutues Rich[d] Westcott

Addressed to Mr Abraham Newland, 'governor' [actually chief cashier] *of Bank.*

581. *[F25/10/23] George Jenkins, Lancaster castle, 30 March 1807 to Joseph Nadin, deputy constable of Manchester to forward to Bank*

Sir Acording to your Request I rite to you the judge as Bin most graciously pleased to Repreve me. thearfore I have duly Detirmaned to Make Evrery Restituion that is in my power for the Crime wich I have been Gilty of, and I ham well convinced that I Can Make a full Discovery of the Real Agants and Manufactors of forged Note and by that put a stop to Evrey farther Circulation of them, but that is not the onley things wich thay are Gilty of

for thay have the peapel that Makes the Bace half Guineys and Seven Shilings peces and Dolers of wich they Make Great Numbers and the Last time I was at Birmingham thay was going to Make a plate for Pontifract Bank and likewise upon One of the Hull Banks and I belive thear his One maid upon Leeds Bank wich will All Cum from the Same Place in Birmingham and thear his upwards of Twenty of those peopel in the Concarne wich I Could Discover if I Could have Liberty to go to Birmingham with you or any Other person proper to Haperend them I ham Serton I Could Discover them at work on the Said Notes &c but if I might be A Lowed I would Advise you not to Make Aney Search after them at presant so as thay may git to know for you may Be Sheur that as theare his so maney of thare Aquaintances in trubel at presant they will be very much upon thare Guard at presant for fear of Aney One Discovering them and thare procedings and Bringing them to justis. Charles Taylor is the persons name that Ingraves the Plats he Lives in Birmingham but I do not know his place of A Bode – But him and Miller Baker Willans Ernshaw and A person in the name of Kirkman wich is Distributed A Large quantity of Notes in Manchester and Round About it and he is A Great Aquantance of Kershaws and Bethels Likewise of Henery Mileses and Barters that as Long ben in the practis of Circalating forged Notes in Lancashire and if It be posable that I Can have the Liberty to go to Birmingham I have Determand to Make Recompenc for the Linety I have ad Shewn to me and the Injery I have Don to the Cuntrey thearfore if you Lay this my Reselution before the Majestrats of Manchester and thay will Indevour to Git me that Liberty wich is Nessery to Inable me to Discover the Real Agants of the above Evels I will be Bound to Cause them to be put An Intire Stop to thare procedings wich will Be best don in the Corse of the Month or Six weeks then thay will all be at Birmingham again folowing the same practises the Afore Named I Could Easey Cause to be Aperended with your Asistanc unless it is Kershaw for I Never hard of his being theare but James Bethel frequently goeth to Birmingham Amongst the Makers of the Notes to git them for other peopel and I think has done for Sum time thearfore if you think proper I will indeaver to Git Sum Farther Information from a person that is in heare with me that will be of Serves in regard to Aperending the Aforsaid peopel and if you will be so kind as to Ancer this Letter I will git it Every information I can But as I ham a Pore Riter I ham a fraid you will not be Able to Understand it, I have Nothing more at presant
From your Humble and faithful Prisnor Geo Jenkins

582. *[F25/10/24] John Hatton, Lancaster castle, 17 October 1806, to John Lloyd, solicitor, Stockport, forwarded to Bank*
Sir, I should have answered yours before this But ad sent to Manchester to See if I could get any more knowledge than I was in Possession of In regard to what I have to Say respecting the Interest of the Bank of England Is that I Can Inform them of the Person that I ad them from who ad the Plates for five & one Pounds likewise several persons that is in the abit of Passing them. One of them that was with the man that sels the notes the Same time I got them is in Prison at this time in here and the other at Manchester.

Every Information that I can give that will to the Interest of the Bank will faithfully give if that it will atend to giving my Liberty. This being the only Preis of Transaction I have Ever been concerned In Fighting the Interest of the Bank. I hope in your representing it to the Governors it will excite in there Breasts motives of Humanity to do away the Severity of the Punishment

I am Sir Yours Humble Ser[t] J Hatton

Annotated: 25 Oct Wrote to say he must tell Manchester – J Lloyd.

583. *[F25/10/25–6] John Hatton, Lancaster castle, 27 October 1806, to John Lloyd, solicitor, Stockport, forwarded to Bank*

Sir, Yours of the 25 Came safe to hand – return you my sincere thanks for all favours but Cannot think of giving anyone Names of any one unless I have a Promis beforeand, then will faithfully give any Assistant that Lies in my power if you Cannot do any thing in this shall apply in a nother manner Myself your favour to this will Oblige yours J. Hatton

P.S. It will be Poor satisfaction for me Providing I should Caus Others to be imured And to be Still in Bondage myself Yours JH

Attached: petition on behalf of Hatton, signed by Charles Prescot and Holland Watson, Lancs. magistrates, marked Rejected *by Bank solicitors.*

584. *[F25/10/27] Mary Burn, County gaol, Surrey, 7 November 1806*

Gentelmen Parden the Liberty of my Wrighting to you Gentelmen I return you my Humble thanks for the favours I have received from you had it not have ben for your Bountyfull favours I Must have starved in this Unhappy Place

Gentelmen as I am Going on Board of Ship and have a Shilling to help my Self with and am Greatly neceseated for a few things too take with me Gentelmen Permit me to ask you this one favour to assist me with a trifle to Get me a few things what I Greatly stand in nead of as I have not a friend in the world but you Gentelmen with thankfulness of heart I remain gentelmen your obediant humble Servant Mary Burn

585. *[F25/10/26] Mary Burn,* Sidney Cove *transport ship, Spithead, 20 November 1806*

Gentelmen parden me for taken the liberty of riting to you Gentelmen i should have rote to you before to return you many thanks for all the favours i have resieved from you and likewise for the 5 pounds i resieved from Mr Shooter [*Suter*] But Gentelmen i have been very ill ever since i have Been on Board wich has Been the occasion of my Not riting to you Before and in Great distress i should have Been had it not Been for your Goodnes So no More from Unfortunate Marey Burn

586. *[F25/10/28] William Peters, Gloucester City prison, 24 March 1809*

Sir As I am now in prison under sentencing of the law for having in my possession Bank of England forged notes and for fear others may fall into the same snare by the arts & Designs of such evil purposed persons. The Author of my presant misfortune which by their unjust practices I now labour under and that such artful and unjust persons should not lead others to become prey to their machinations and so unfortunately have been ensnared and I in order by Contrition to put a stop to their progress am willing to give up the names & places of a band who are the Head of such diabolic practice in order to stop further sacrifices that may be brought in like danger by the violation of our just laws as to bring disgrace as this I have done & being sentanced to fourteen Years transportation to prevent the execution of which as I have a Wife and five Small Children who entirely depends on your distressed Servt for support, provided I may be given my full liberty to My Family, I will impeach the said person as by that meanes it will not only releive my distressed family but stop the progress of further depradation and will be of great benifit to the Kingdom at large as well as to all Banks concerns, and Humbly hoping in further to prove his Majesty most dutiful and loyal subject William Peters alias Walker

587. *[F25/10/29–30] Edward Curran,* Portland *hulk, Langstone harbour, Portsmouth, 12 March 1810*
Curran, not Bank prisoner, writes via hulk Captain Blackman to offer information to Bank on forgers. Bank solicitor's copy reply, 20 Mar. 1819, asks Blackman to collect information but states no favours will be forthcoming.

588. *[F25/10/31] James Hickson,* Portland *hulk, Langstone harbour, Portsmouth, 1 October 1808*
Hickson, not Bank prisoner, writes to Joseph Nadin, deputy constable of Manchester, to offer Bank information on forgery and forgers.

589. *[F25/10/32] Jonathan Forbes,* Captivity *hulk, Portsmouth harbour, 23 January 1809*
Gentlemen The generous disposition you have ever Evinced towards the Unfortunate in my situation induces Me to hope you will have the Goodness to lay my Case before the Honble Directors of the Bank not doubting that they in their benificence will make some distinction between the hackneyed and the Unhackneyed offender
I am one of the three Unfortunate persons Convicted in feb^y^ Sessions 1807 of having uttered a two pound note – purporting to be a bank of England one upon the Evidence of a Man named Thos Kaye who at the time of giving Such evidence before the Magistrate did me the Justice to own he had given me but two of them which was almost a Month before I was apprehended – I do declare most Solemnly Gentlemen I never in my life to my knowledge saw a forged Note untill the aforesaid Thos Kaye persuaded me to take those two aforementioned and after the Unfortunate transaction of having the passed the one for which I now suffer I felt all the horrors of a Man troubled in Mind, followed my business which is that of a Taylor working at Mr Nunn's in Thayer Str Manchester Square untill the Saturd^y^ night when Thos Kaye with the Officer from Bow Str took Me in Custody.

I am a Man going on fifty years of Age of a weakly Constitution and have had an Incurable fistula these ten years
Gentlemen, I most humbly implore your Kind Mediation with the Honble the Directors of the Bank to procure some Mitigation of my sentence that I may not have so long and tedious a Voyage to Make which I am almost sure my poor weak frame would never be able to Acomplish Your Obed^{t} and Hble Ser^{t} Jonathan Forbes

590. *[F25/10/33–4] Thomas Gulley,* Captivity *hulk, Portsmouth harbour, 2 October 1808*
Sir Pardon me for trespassing on your time but I Conceive my Present Situation Calls Aloud for relief & also that of my Poor forsaken family. I have Six helpless babes the oldest not more than 12 Years & the Youngest not 2 years, which my Unfortunate Wife as with her [*Martha Gulley awaiting trspn*] Surely this must Excite Pity, when you consider the Distresses of a family – in this awfull Situation they having no friend on Earth to render them the smallest Relief & I there Father and friend Doom^{d} to Suffer for what I am not the Least guilty of – Summers & Fuller Certainly Swore falseley against me – I Can Appeal to Many Persons of Respectability for an Evidence, Even Mr Spurrier [*solicitor, Birmingham*] who as Been the Occasion of this Prosecution Against me well knows I am Innocent of the Charge – I had not the Smallest Concern Ever in Bills of Bad Money in the whole Cours of my Life or Any Connection with those Men that Suffered – Meredith & Francis. [*William Meredith and William Francis executed*]. Many Respectable Gentlemen Sign^{d} a Letter Sent to the Judge on my Account Saying and Declaring my Innocence in Matters of the Kind – Nor was there Ever any thing of the kind Brought Against me I can Positively Declare before God, Sir if you Recolect Summers Swore I had Francis House to fetch the Bills & when I Came to the Dog Publick House on Horse Back Francis House was in the Stable of Course must be a great falsity – Meredith Solomnly Declared in his Dying Moments that he fetch^{d} the Bills Himself & that I had no part in the Matter with them or Knew any thing of their Transactions no way I am Certain Sir Mr Spurrier Can fully Explain the Whole Business to you if he likes & trust he will make you Sensible this is the truth of the Whole Matter Sir, as this is my Unfortunate Case I hope you^{ll} Investigate the Business Thorouly & I am Certain you will Regret I am now Suffering without the Least Offence – I hope you will take my Case Into your humain Consideration & Also that of my Distress^{d} Children Left Fatherless & Motherless who are now Laminting & Suffering on Account of my Misfortune I Could be glad if I might Have the Opportunity of Enjoying them Again – But if you Cannot be truly Convinced of the Truth of what I have Before Observed – I should be Exceeding thankfull you will be so Kind as to Git me Inserted Among the Number of those call^{d} upon to Leave the Kingdom for NS Wales the next Draft that goes – as my Present Situation is so Afflicting to be in this Country & have a Distressed family Laminting in pain the Loss of an Efectionate Father & Mother –

Should be thankfull Sir if you will Condescend to Inform me if their is any probability of being Released – as I am Now concious it all rests with you & Should be glad to Know if you will do me the favour Above Mentioned – to see that I am Among the Number for New South Wales as we are inform[d] a Ship is Preparing & for that Destiney I hope in God it may be So if I cannot have what I so ernesty Intreat for which is Liberty to Assist a Disconsolate family Subscribe Myself Sir Your Unfortuate Serv[t] Tho[s] Gulley

Attached: copy note from Bank solicitors 4 Oct. 1808, stating they will ask sec./state to include him on next draft of transports.

591. *[F25/10/35–6] Thomas Gulley,* Captivity *hulk, Portsmouth harbour, 23 March 1809*

Sir I Receiv[d] your Letter date 4th of Octob[r] – Sorry to find that no Intercession Could be Made for me, have Another favour to request of you which I trust you will comply with as I have Now Been Confin[d] two years & four months I am by this Means Depriv[d] of Every Shilling of Money I was poss[d] of as trial proving so Expencive having Cost us 60 Pounds – I find that Phillips [**575–6**] is Liberated from Warwick Goal & he can Inform you of my Innocence in the Business for which I am Convicte[d] for, as he is well Acquainted of Every Circumstance & as to Signing the Notes I Assure you I Never did such a thing in my Whole Life & as to my Wifes Connection I am Unable to Speak to it – However I Conceive it a Preconceited Plan to Draw her into the Trouble – I Humbly Hope Sir you will have the goodness to Appear as a friend in this Distressing Time of Need & Remitt me a Little Money to Provide me a few Articles for a Long & Dreadfull Voyage, which I hope & trust will not be as Long just as you Promised me in your Last I should be sent in the first Ship that sails with Male Convicts

And Should Also be thankfull if you could make Interest at the same time so far to take one or two of the Unfortunate Orphans I have Left Behind may be permitted to go with me, as they are poor things Left Destitute of Any friend in this Country but the Parish, I should be Ever thankfull if you will Condescend to Apply for me – as I am Pursuaded it may be granted through your Interest, with thankfullness and Gratitude Ever Esteem it a favour – Remain Sir your Unfortunate Serv[t] Thos Gulley

PS Sir your Answer will be thankfully Received

Attached: copy note from Bank solicitors, 1 Apr. 1809, refusing application for money, referring him to Mr Graham, magistrate, Bow Street public office, to try to obtain permission to take children to NSW.

592. *[F25/10/39] Eight males,* Captivity *hulk, Portsmouth harbour, 5 November 1808*

Sir Pardon Us that we have intruded on Y[r] time by addressing you but our Situation Induced us to Do it hoping you will have the goodness to take care that Our Names are among the Number of those Destined to New South Wales as we are Led to believe a Ship will be Prepared for Male Convicts for that Colony in a Short time & and we having a great Desire to be sent to our Destiny rather than to remain Here – by Oblidging us in this

respect which we trust you will Do we shall ever consider you our friend & thankfully receive a few lines in ans^{r} To the Above. We are Sir your Most Ob^{dt} & Humble Serv^{ts}
Simon Boutell was Left Thro indisposition at this Place from the Admiral Gambier
Richd Westcoat, Benjn Maddocks, Richd Jones, Saml Hulbert, Wm Radford, John Johnson, S. Boutell Left as above, John Eastwood; All for Bank of England Notes

593. *[F25/10/37] Twelve males,* Captivity *hulk, Portsmouth harbour, 15 February 1809*
Sir, The Philanthropic Character you bear induces Me to hope you will not be offended at the Liberty I take in requesting you to Lay the Situation of Myself & fellow Sufferers before The Honble Company of the Bank of England
Being truly Sensible of the Goodness & Humanity of the Honble Company of the Bank of England We whose Names Are Hereunder Assign^{d} have taken upon us to address You, Hoping you will take our Cases into your Humane Consideration & Grant us a small remittance to Procure us Some Necessaries which we shall stand in need of on our Long & Tedious Passage to New South Wales. The Length of time we have been confin^{d} has occasion^{d} us to be without Money So much so that without the Assistance of the Honble Company I am fearful we shall feel much Distress
We therefore humbly implore your Benevolence in Such Distressing circumstances Being Led to believe The Honble Company has been good to many Prisoners of the same Description We trust therefore we may have a share of Their Benevolence as it will Greatly alleviate our Troubles & We shall ever Consider it our Duty to Pray For your Everlasting Prosperity & Subscribe ourselves their Ob^{dt} & Humble Serv^{ts}
P S We are all desirous of being moved to our destiny by the First Conveyance. Therefore Should be thankful you will have the Goodness to notify the same to the Honourable Company
Simon Boutell, Thomas Gulley, Jonathan Forbes, Richd Jones, Benjn Maddocks, Saml Hulbert, John Badeley, Richard Westcoat, John Davis, John Eastwood, John Johnson, John Townsend [*with dates and places of trials*].
[*BECLS: 23 Feb. 1809, request rejected.*]

594. *[F25/10/38] Richard Westcoat,* Captivity *hulk, Portsmouth harbour, 4 October 1808*
Sir Pardon Me for addressing you but I am Desirous of embracing an Opportunity should the Goodness of the Honble Company of the Bank of England be So gracious as to Permit which is That I May have the favour of going on board One of his Majesty's Ships of war as Baker or Pastry-cook which employ I have followed my whole life & I should now willingly extend my services if agreeable to Them I have a wife & Daughter which are Disconsolate & unprovided for at this time should be thankfull to have the Priviledge of Supporting them The Remainder of Life

I have Intreated that my case & Situation May be Laid before our beloved Soveriegn Hoping that I May be favoured with a Share of His Royal Clemency & Mercy, & I trust my future Conduct will be Such as will gain esteem among all Superiours of all Description – I hereby solicit your Kindness & Benevolence in this respect & I shall ever have Occasion To Subscribe Myself Y[r] Ob[dt] & devoted Serv[t] R[d] Westcoat

595. *[F25/10/40] George Griffin, keeper, Bath gaol, 3 November 1808*
Requests 26 guineas to be paid by Mr Atkins [Adkins?] of Bow Street police office, for board, washing and lodging for Mary Redford from Birmingham, held in Bath gaol as witness in Bank case against Joseph and George Enever in Bath. Griffin had, over twelve months, requested payment from Mr Ridpath, Bank solicitor in Bath, without effect.

596. *[F25/10/41–4] William Phillips, Warwick gaol, to Mr Antony, public office, Bow Street, London, 18 June 1808*
Sir I receved your letter this Day an to in form you that if Plase god I should get my liberty Mr Tatnall [*gaoler at Warwick*] and mee will com up to London the same Day and then wee can fix up on the bisness wish I ham quite Sure I can have the under menchon[d] peple apprended with the Notes upon them that is Wm Foster from Bath as hee takes a Larg Quanty of them besides base Silver and Jabis Dry hee lives in Yorkshire but I cannot tel the plase as I told you when I see you but hee always come to Birmingham for them and Robert King lives at the same plase, and Charles M[c]Quinn hee lives in scotland a very larg Dealer in Silver as well as notes but hee General gose in to Yorkshire with his Goods and there is Wm Bradbery [*cap. con., Warws . ass., spring 1811*] hee lives in Birmingham hee goese to all the fairs round this part of the Country with his goods and a mainey more People wich Deales in them as well as silver and concerning of the Hinshaws and Hall I think thay would be varry shi up on mee but I could find a man or two as never was in anney prison wich would Do the bisness with them but I now that thay would not with out being paid well for It wich I would soon setle that bisness with them and bring the men up to London to you and I would have B Patrick making a plate and I would Go to Irland with you to Mr Patrick as I ham Quite sure that hee would do anything for mee but posable I could have B Patrick at work with somebodey Eles as hee makes a manny and Sells them to the peple that I have menchined above and to Purform what I have heare rote if that I did not cause them to be taken up with the notes on them as well as Base Silver, I would be bound in aney sum of monney and I will sign a bound for five thousand Pounds to you or anybodey Eles if you will send a Bond down to me I will sign to that a mount to do all and Evereything wich lies in my Power to have them all apprended for notes, as well as silver and Haffey Jacobs in Midle sex street white Chappel London wich I can have him aney time I ham Quite sure in 6 month I could have neareley 80 peple and they would not now Did the bisness for them if things was to be Don Quite Snug and the way that I should Plan the bisness and I would make affey David never to Do anithing more wich is unlafull but if Plase God I should Inform

you more Particlars and Go with you to Mr Kay and then wee could setle the bisness but must not be Don in Quite such a urrey must be time for it Sir I hope you will give your self the truble to speck to Mr Kay for mee and at same time I return you manney thanks for the truble you have taken for mee and I make no Doubt but I shall be inabled to Show som of my Goodness towards the bank and the mint to all thair Satisfacsion for what I have Don time Past wich I ham Sure that I can in 12 month Put a stop to the bisness

Sir your anser to this as soon as convent will for Ever oblige your most obedent and Humble Searvant Wm Phillips

Attached: three further letters from Phillips in Warwick gaol, 15 July 1808, introducing himself to Bank solicitors, 25 July, summarizing **596**, *and 19 Aug. 1808, summarizing both the foregoing.*

597. *[F25/10/45–7] J. Bullock, unamed prison, probably Newgate, writes two letters dated 19 May 1808 to J. Sanderson Esq. of Brick Lane, London thanking him for his part in gaining him pardon from death sentence which arrived the previous night* [*unknown crime, not Bank offence*], *he has information on Bank note forgery and asks what to do about it; 22 May 1818, Bullock writes to Bank to say he is suddenly required to board ship to NSW so cannot compose himself sufficiently to write all that he told their investigator the previous day, but feels he has said enough to be of help.*

598. *[F25/10/48] John Biggs,* Captivity *hulk, Portsmouth harbour, to Mr Ridpath, solicitor, Bath, 15 July 1811*

In presuming the liberty of addressing you I can only appeal to your kindness trusting you will be pleased to pardon the same

As you are not unacquainted with the nature of my unhappy circumstances I need not state the particulars of the case but humbly beg you will be pleased to take my case into your humane consideration at the same time requesting your kind assistance in extricating me from my present wretched condition

I have already given you every information in my power and that the most disinterested, and sure I am you must perfectly see how innocently and inadvertently I have been drawn into my present unhappy and miserable situation, not knowing the danger and risk I ran emboldens me to hope for success and tis to you Sir that I can only look up too with assurance in hopes of being attended by the desired effect

I am inform[d] application must be made to the Right Hon Richard Ryder His Majestys Principal Secretary of State for the Home Department to whom all Petitions are addressed and sure I am if you Sir would humanely take my unhappy case in to your benevolent consideration I am firmly persuaded a mitigation if not a total release from my present degraded state would be the result as my former character as ever been unimpeachable and since the unhappy affair for which I am confined, I may look forward with certain hopes of being restored to my family and friends and to society and enable me to remember you with gratitude to the latest moment of my life

Resting entirely on your candour and in hopes of your benevolent interfearance towards the accomplishment of a termination of my sufferings in this miserable wretched and unfortunate situation and in hopes of being favor[d] with an answer when convenient remain Sir with profound respect Your &c Jn[o] Biggs
Annotated by Ridpath forwarding letter to Bank solicitors: On the other side I send you a copy of a Letter Received in my absence from Jn[o] Biggs & am, Gent[n] Your very obt sert J C P Ridpath, Bath 24 July

599. *[F25/10/49–50] John Biggs,* Captivity *hulk, Portsmouth harbour, 1 October 1811*
Gent[n] The many generous Accts of your benevolence towards the unfortunate induce me to trespass on your condecention of interference in my behalf which I hope you will Pardon. I am fully persuaded that you possess those feelings and pleasure in be coming an intercessor for those who have generally conducted themselves in a moral and sentimental manner
That I was innocently and unguardedly drawn into the error for which my sentence was denounced against me I do most solomnly declare The Note that Convicted me I took in the regular course of Trade not knowing it to be a base one and I did all in my power to have the Person who paid it to me brought to justice the truth of which assertion Mr Ridpath of Bath can testify to whom I have address'd a Letter in Answer to which he recommended me to apply to you Gent[n] who acct as Sol[rs] for the Bank of England My only motive for Trespasing on your goodness his to request your kind consideration in signing a petition in my favor to be presented to the Secretary of State in hopes of procuring me a pardon or such other mitigation of any sentence as may be deem[d] proper which his a very severe one to one who as conducted himself as a fair Member of Society for 30 years in the Parish of Sisson [?*Siston, between Bath and Bristol*] regularly attending the Bath & Bristol Markets as a Pork Butcher and supported an infirm wife and 7 children most of them reduced to the utmost poverty and want by my misfortune and who join in solicitations to you Gentlemen hoping you will be pleased to render their unfortunate Father your assistance to endeavour to procure his restoration. I should think myself an happy Man and confident no inducement whatever would prevail on me to deviate from the strict path of Virtue but conduct myself as a good and usefull Member of Society. Your kind compliance with my request and an early Answer would be esteem'd a lasting favor confer'd on your unfortunate and obed[t] S[t] Jn[o] Biggs
Annotated: Rejected
Attached: copy note from Bank solicitors, 2 Oct. 1811, confirming that governor and directors of Bank decline complying with his application.

600. *[F25/10/51] Hugh Pierce,* Portland *hulk, Langstone harbour, 18 June 1811*
Hon[ble] Sirs having by my late miscontuct so far incured the Displeasure of your Honors as to amount to a Dreatfull Sentance of Death and Still remain

for Life which is a Dreatfull Sentance more than I expected as I have acknowledge my Faults and was inorcent Drawd into the Secret by a person in the nebourwood of Birmingham before I was acquainted with him my charactor was undeneable as I never was guilty of nothing of the Kind before

The Honorable Baron Knight Wood inform'd me that Throught your Honors recomdetion my life was saved therefore I am willing to give you every information that there is in power if your Honors will think proper to order your solicitor to come forward to me I shall give him such information that will give your honors a great satisfaction and sooner is the Beter it may easy put an end to it with very little atention he has agreed with a paper maker to make him for this present year 9600 Blanks for the Bank of England with the water in. He has by him upwards of Thirty Plates beside Dice for Different Coins the Engreaver works for many beside him in Birmingham he tould me that he gain Three Thousand pounds by the Bank of England last year and will gain more this year as he found out where to get the paper with the watter mark in therefore I have considered it to be my Duty to give every informetion and Lickwise the goverment of the mint Therefor I humbly beg leave to represent that I am with sorrow most sencibly affected for my past Fault on mater reflection That I have been the unhappy Instrument of bringin my self into Such unhappy circumstances and most humbly implore your Honors pardon and forgiveness and that it may be your good pleasure and candor to mingle mercy with justice to medicate my Sentance Solemnly Promising that no future time shall find me wanting in assisting your Honors in every respect and shall be in Duty bound will ever pray

I am your Honors most Dutifull and faithfull Servant Hugh Pierce

601. *[F25/10/52] Richard France,* Portland *hulk, Langstone harbour, Portsmouth, 30 June 1811*

Gentlemen, I humbly Beg pardon for useing this Liberty I have now taken of writing to you But my Distressed situation oblidges Me to state my unfortunate Sircumstance to you Gentlemen hopeing that you Will not Contemn what I am going to State as you are Mercifull and Wishes not the punishment of the Inocent. Was my punishment Inflicted on me Justly or had I been Guilty of What I am Convicted for I would Not Repine, but Certainly my Inocence Will Call for Vengence on the perjured prosecutor if his Direfull Carrecter Was Enquired Into such as the Neighbourhood Could testify at Large the Laws of England would not suffer any to be Convicted on his Evidence

This Note for Which I was Convicted was a £5 – I had the same In payment of a sum of Money that I Lent I not Being any Judge of Notes – and the said Note being New I took No further Notice but Laid it up in my Bearow at the End of one Month I had Occasion to Lay it out and took it from hence But observing that it Grew pale in the plate and the Paper seemed Very Much Dimed I harboured a suspicion in my own Breast that it was forged I then carried it to one whome I took to be a Judge of Notes And also a Man of Aimable Caracter he told me to see The person I Rec'd it off and have it Changed I sent for the Person Imadiately I had it off and asked him if he Knew he said he Did I then Demanded the Exchange of it but he Not having as Much as amounted to the Sum Contained in the Note he Gave me What he had and bad me Keep the Note till he Could Get the Remainder for me

this transaction was known to Whitehead My prosecutor (for so Is he Called) and he being an acquaintance I told him freely how it was – he asked me then to Let him see this note which I made no scruple in Doing Upon seeing it he Instantly offered me £2 for it I told him Not it was not my property observing at the same time that there was only 25 shillings Coming to Me and When I was pd. I would Return it to the man I had it off. But When he found I would not sell it he attempt to Steal it or pick my pocket of it I told him I supposed he wanted to some money by it – if you had got it out of my pocket I Replied I suppose you meant to swear I sold it you

At this Expression he Got Enraged and Ran out called the Constables and acctually swore I offered the same note for sale. Now Gentlemen I beg your atention to what I have stated but I Will yet make one observation – that maney wanted me to pled Guilty to Which I Replied I never would Wrong my own honor to plead Guilty to What I was not Guilty off should I suffer the Most Ignimonious Death that Could be Inflicted on Mankind I beg to be Excused In takeing up so much of your time but I trust in God as you are Gentlemen touched with humanity & Lives in a Nation Who fears that God Who is the Justifier of all who suffer wrong. I trust you Will Look Into this Matter of Extremity My family is Driven to Sore Disolation and I am My selfe an Old Man and since my Confinement My health is much Impaired – and for me to Goe now in my old age to a Warm Climate and by all accounts to a Land of Barbarity to be torn from My Native Country and friends and Leaving a Distressed family behind is worse to me than Death

Gentlemen I have stated my Miserable Condition to you and if you Deny me your Benevolence tis all in vain for me to make any further progress – but if your Generous feelings will Sympathize With my unfortunate Down-fall I will Encourage my selfe by Expecting some Enlargement as I trust none of the Governors of the Bank of England wish any to suffer in the Wrong

if my State is taken into Consideration by you Gentlemen as I hope you Will take pleashure in Doing Justice you will have the Goodness to send a few Lines for Capt^{t} Blackman comanding the Portland Langston Harbour and then I shall proceed but if My humble suit meets your frown I must for Ever Desist

I beg Pardon for taking up so much of your time on this subject and Beg leave to subscribe myselfe Your Most Obd^{t} and Humble Servt Yet the unfortunate Richd France

NB I have had the sentence of 14 years passed on me by Judge Chambers on the 10th September 1810

602. *[F25/10/53] John Gilbert,* Zealand *hulk, Sheerness, 22 November 1810*
Honored Sir Under the Infliction of a very lingering Punishment, I humbly hope I shall be excused for the Liberty of sending this Address that is designed to ask you (in Answer) whether there might be a Probability of gaining any Mitigation of my Sentence which is for Fourteen years under the following Circumstances, that perhaps a Recital of may strike your Memory, you being, Sir, I believe, present on my Trial. I was convicted at Norwich Assizes in August 1808 before the Honble Judge Heath of tendering in Payment a false or forged Note for One Pound, purporting to be a Note of the Bank of England knowing the same to be false or forged and received Judgement as above. I beg to remark, which I humbly persuade myself will be somewhat taken in Extenuation of my Error, that it was apparent in several Parts of my Trial, that I was made (by the really guilty Party now with me) a deluded Person, and that thro' great Chicanary had become a devoted victim to offend Justice and, Sir, permit me to say further, it would seem as tho' this was quite manifest, when after receiving the Money for the aforesaid Note, I returned it immediately on Request and that the said Note was kept and detained from me as being surrendered a bad One, for more than a Month after that I had endeavored so to exchange it, yet so little Apprehension had I of Mischief arising to me that I never offered to go out of the Way, or leave my usual Abode, for the best of Reasons that I thought no Wrong. There, Sir, are the principal of the Circumstances I wish to signify in my Behalf, except that I have faithfully served my Country and King in a military capacity (in the 58th Regiment of Foot) for a Length of Time. I was in the Three chief Engagements, Viz: the 8th, 13th and 21st of March 1801, with the French Army in Egypt, and present in that Battle where the much lamented Abercrombie received his lifeless Wound. I fought hard in those Battles for England's Cause, suffered, without repining, very severe Duty and Hardship, and in other Places Abroad also shewed myself a worthy and loyal subject; but which I unfortunately cannot get Testimonials of, my officers being dispersed – some dead and Others not known where to be heard of, and I am precluded any possibility of enquiring about them, because I have not a single Friend to help me in any Respect. Thus situated, Honored Sir, allow me without exciting Umbrage, to throw myself on your Humanity, by Intreating your Endeavours to disentangle me <u>in</u> <u>some</u> <u>Means</u> from my present grievous sufference, that bears extremely hard on me and if, Sir, it should happen as tho' no Pardon of the Royal Clemency could be granted to me, I would consider it with Heartfelt grateful Feelings that your Benevolence (for such it would truly be) would obtain me the <u>Mercy</u> of being sent from this suffering Receptacle Abroad by the <u>first</u> Conveyance of Prisoners thither John Gilbert, Late of HM Cambridgeshire Militia

603. *[F25/10/54] Michael Gearing,* Zealand *hulk, Sheerness, 13 August 1810*
Gentlemen, I humbly beg leave to submit my deplorable situation to your merciful consideration & trust after reflecting on the deep and Melancholy

state into which I am plunged that your Clemency and compassion will prompt you to have the goodness to render me some Assistance for which I shall be ever grateful, and as my Grey hairs are likely to come with sorrow to the Grave and feeling that soon, I hope your Merciful Clemency and generous Benefactor will not be witheld from your truly penitent supplicator who has not a Friend in the World to assist him, he therefore most implores your Assistance in such a way as may seem most pleasing to you, and should this application be fortunately crowned with success I shall ever think myself in Duty & Gratitude bound to pray, Honr[d] Gentlemen, with due respect Your most obedient & very Humble Ser[t] Michael Garing
[*BECLS: 7 Aug. 1810, request rejected.*]

604. *[F25/10/59] Michael Gearing,* Discovery *hospital ship, Sheerness, 9 June 1812*
Hon[d] Sirs, With all submission I beg leave to lay my afflicted Case before your Hon[rs] benovolence – I am Hon[d] Sirs the unfortunate Man Michael Gearing who was tryed at the Old Bailey Sess[ns] Jan[y] 1810 and Convicted for 14 years Transportation – Yours Hon[rs] great goodness and Compassion on my old Age – viz. 65 years alowed me 5[s] per week in Newgate which was of infinate service to me having no friends to give me the least assistance now I am onboard the Discovery Hospital Hulk at Sheerness I humbly pray your Hon[rs] Charity for a small portion of your Hon[rs] well know feeling for the distressed – I am with all Hble submission your Hble Serv[t] Michael Gearing
[*BECLS: 10 June 1812, request refused.*]

605. *[F25/10/55–7] Richard Bricker, Devizes gaol, undated in January 1811*
Bricker, 60 years old, butcher and tything man of North Bradley, Wilts., sentenced to twelve months' imprisonment for letting Bank suspect, James Windle, escape, petitions Bank to obtain release; petition signed by high sheriff of Wilts., magistrates, vicar, churchwardens, overseers and sixteen inhabitants of North Bradley. Petition covered by letter, 7 Jan. 1811, from John Pinehard, solicitor, Taunton, deploring severity of sentence, describing him as an old man with young family; 9 Jan. 1811 Bank refuse interference.

606. *[F25/10/58] William Stewart,* Zealand *hulk, Sheerness, 28 July 1812*
Gentlemen By a letter from my Wife, I have rece[d] your answer and descisione to my last application. I am extremely sorry to observe, that it is an alternative repleat with more Misery than the one I am at present in, one condition excepted, Viz. the priviledge of entering into any other Regiment but a Condemned one to which I am given to understand all persons of my discipline are in general sent. I am not so hardened or Contaminated as to wish to join such a body of Men
Gentlemen, after permitting me to plead Guilty to the minor offence, I should not have presumed to apply to you for any further Mercy, but out of

a feeling consideration for my Wife and Children, I have taken the liberty to request that you will have the goodness to look at them; who will presume to present this, I make not a moments doubt, but you are parents yourselves, if so put your hands on your Hearts and ask them faithful monitors if it would not be the height of inhumanity to deprive such Children at so early an age off their Natural Protector and have them exposed to a Merciless World:- Gentlemen you will thus see, that it is only out of Consideration of them, that I refuse your generous and Humane Offer held forthe to me, had I been a single Man I should with Gratitude have accepted it, and gladly have spent the remainder of my Life in the service of my Country

Gentlemen, permit me once more most earnestly to implore you will have the goodness to reconsider the Circumstances of my unhappy Case and condescend to grant me a Mitigation of Sentence I might then have an Opportunity of being serviceable to my Children as I am by trade a Shoe maker, was several years in the Employ of Mr. Macnortore in Berkley Square; and did all the Work for HRH the Duke of York, and am Confident I am able to do my Work with any Man in England, Industry is particularly encouraged in this Hulk I am confident my Masters in Sheerness would readly give me Work to imploy my leisure time. I would think late and early and suffer any privations for the support of my Family, and I am well assured my earnings would be sufficient to make them a Little Comfortable added to by their own endeavours, let me humbly beg Gentlemen you will have the humanity to grant my Request, no conduct of mine shall ever Give you reason to repent, and my Children shall be teached to remember your Goodness to the last moment of their Existances

If Gentlemen you cannot Acquiesce with the above request, permit me to hope you will not refuse to let my Wife go with me to N, S, Wales, and my Children I must commit to the Care of their Grandmother, I am Gentlemen with every Submition & Gratitude your Obedient Humble St W. Stewart

607. *[F25/10/60] William Stewart, Zealand hulk, Sheerness, 28 July 1812, second letter to Mr Weston* [*?Westwood*], *Bank solicitors' clerk thanking him for assistance with his requests to solicitors, explaining that life in the army is not an acceptable alternative sentence, and asking him to use his influence to get him shoemaking work.*

608. *[F25/10/62] William Simpson Henningham,* Zealand *hulk, Sheerness, 17 May 1812*

I humbly hope will take my unfortunate case into their consideration that they will be generiously pleased to sign my petition that I may be restored to my family and in case of noncompliance with that Request that they will use their Interest at the Secretary of State's Office to send me and my wife and children out of the Country in the first Ship that goes to New South Wales with a recommendation that I may be able to support my Family by Honesty and Industry I humbly beg that the Right Honble Company will continue the Allowance granted to me the last six weeks I was in Newgate as long as I remain in the Country and I can Justly assure the R^t^ Honble

Company that it is more requesite here than in Newgate without my makeing my remarks on my or my fellow sufferers sufferings. My wife will call upon Mr Westwood for an answer.
With all due respect The R^{t} Honble Companys Very Humble Servant Wm Simpson Henningham
PS Since writing the aforesaid I have heard from my wife that she is going in the Country Therefore the favour of an answer from Mr Westwood by Post will be a Particular favor
Annotated: Rejected

609. *[F25/10/163] Isaac Newland,* Zealand *hulk, Sheerness, 31 August 1812*
Mr. Westwood, Honoured Sir I do most humbly intreat your Goodness and Humanity to excuse this Intrusion, in reminding you of my unfortunate situation, and my most sincere Sorrow and Contrition for the Offence which I had so unjustly committed. 'Till this my fatal Error I had ever been in the Habit of earning my Bread by the most honest and industrious Means, which several Merchants and Others are ready to certify, and that my Conduct altogether was free from Stain or Reproach.
Under these Circumstances I humbly implore your Humanity in my Behalf, by signing a Petition in my Favor praying for a Mitigation of Sentence or for Leave to Serve His Majesty either by Sea or Land and in any part of the World it may be pleased to send me; this is all I can possibly crave or expect, and this I do most earnestly intreat (in either case as you think best and most provident), your Intercession and Humanity in the Endeavours to gain me; And I do most faithfully and solemnly assure you that as far as it can possibly lay in my humble power I will gratefully acknowledge the same by my future conduct to the end of my Days. I have no Friends to relieve or comfort me, a Interest to obtain any Remission of Punishment, I must therefore humbly leave myself to your Consideration and Mercy; hoping there may prove to be some trifling Circumstances in my Case, which may so far induce you to shew your Humanity to One, who as now situated, is labouring under the most severe and distressing Anxiety of Mind at his awful situation, which Deprives him of all the Enjoyments and Comforts of his Life, as all the best Days of his Existance will be lost without Benefit to him or Society
Most humbly leaving myself therefore to your most merciful Consideration, I beg leave to subscribe myself Your most humble and most ob^{t} though unfortunate Servant Isaac Newland his Mark
[*In different hand*] NB Sir Should you think proper to come down here or send some person to me I could Communicate Matter to that would lead to a great Discovery Concerning the Manufacturing or forging Bank of England Notes which is very Busy at this time but hope no persons would come here that Belongs to any Police Office as they would be known here which w^{d} not serve me if I was seen talking to any of them I was so fool hardy I was quite led a stray with respect of making this Confession in due time but it is better late than never, I hope

The writer of the first part of this letter I w[d] not Communicate this subject to nor to no person on Board but to the writer of the last part of this. Any Person that may come may Enquire for me and then I Can go along Side.

610. *[F25/10/64] Isaac Newland,* Zealand *hulk, Sheerness, 22 September 1812*
Writes again believing his letter of 31 Aug. not received; omits request about military service and does not offer information since, he says, time is short, the ship for the Bay *is due to arrive and he must go on board.*

611. *[F25/10/65] Dennis O'Connor,* Zealand *hulk, Sheerness, 21 July 1812*
Counterfeit dollar maker, sentenced to seven yrs' trspn, offers to help Bank if they will protect his wife, known to gangs of forgers who suspect she will inform on them.

612. *[F25/10/66] D. Townsend, Fisherton gaol, Salisbury, 20 April 1813*
A bankrupt and his son write to Bank, who had agreed to assure their discharge under commission of bankruptcy, to assist in obtaining their release: they have been in prison four months.

613. *[F25/10/67] Isaac Newland,* Fortune *transport ship, Spithead, 19 November 1812*
Honour[d] Sirs, As I have before experienc[d] your lenity, I humbly trust you will not consider this liberty impertinent or inpassive, when I assure you, Gentlemen, nothing but the abject Misery I am in, would induce me to trouble you, I have been totally abandon[d] by my friends since I was convicted, in consequence of false reports from what was surmis[d] in consequence of Mr Westwood coming to see me to prison, And it was James Wheeles that put forth them reports to my prejudice – together with reports of A similar nature brought by Red bills woman to the hulks, I would have let you know these Matters before but I had no opportunity as Unfortunately I cannot write myself
As I am totally Destitute of every necessary and going friendless to a strange country I humbly trust, Gentlemen you will consider my distressed situation – Honour[d] Sirs I Remain with respect your very Hum[le] Sert unfortunate Isaac Newland on board the Ship fortune Capt[n] Walker lying at Spithead – bound to new South Wales

614. *[F25/10/68] Thomas Dardis,* Portland *hulk, Langstone harbour, 30 September 1812*
Honored Sir, Being at this time in very great distress, and having no one to afford me the least assistance, I hope you will be kind enough to let me have the Money that was taken from me before my trial according to your promise while I was in Newgate. The Sum is £4-3-0 and it will be of essential service to me in this unfortunate situation. By so doing you will confer a lasting obligation on your humble Servant Thomas Dardis

615. *[F25/10/69] Thomas Dardis,* Portland *hulk, Langstone harbour, Portsmouth, 7 February 1813*
Gentlemen Whereas there is much Distress Arising to me from pecuniary Circumstances I am oblidge to Make application to you and I hope M[r] Westwood Solicitor will represent my Case in as favourable a Light as it will Admit of as he has a knowledge that I was Apprehended on a Charge of uttering a forged Note for which I Was Convicted and sentenced to be transported for the term of 14 years when I was taken into Custody there Was property to the Amount of £4–3[s]-0[d] in Silver and Copper taken out of a Box Lodged in the House of John M[c]Cormick below Kingstreet Which property belong to me and I trust and hope Gentlemen that you Will Remit the same to me as my unfortunate situation at present much Requires it Tho[s] Dardis
Annotated: Rejected

616. *[F25/11/2] John Chave,* Portland *hulk, Langstone harbour, 18 April 1813*
Hon[d] Sir I must beg to trouble you in Respect of that Money that is in your Hands which Sir, you might rely ont is ours every farthing of it and further that Ruff [*Bow Street police officer*] will never Never Offer to Claim it our Sufferings is Great. Mean not Sir, to Imply Unjustly My Distress on my familys Account with whom as Tradesman in this Metropolis has Lived in greater Love & Comfort. But i Cherefully Resign to the will of God whom is Working every thing for the Best I hope & trust that you will have the Humane Consideration to give the Bearer the Money, which is my Wife, you will realieve the Distress of an industrious and affectionate woman and Likewise of your very Much Obig[d] Serv[t] John Chave

617. *[F25/11/1] John Chave,* Portland *hulk, Langstone harbour, 7 August 1813*
Hon[d] Sir I hope you will Pardon the Liberty of my troubling you Once More to Solicit your Mercifull Aid to Alleviate my Present Burthen which rends my heart a sunder to think of Leaving my Native land – a poor Distressed Infirm Aged parent to whom for y[rs] i have been the Chief support by my Industry & Sobriety i have kept my much Honourd & rever'd Mother from a Workhouse My self & family i have kept in Credit, & Sir you would most assuredly find by a Minutely Prying in to my Moral Conduct that it was such as Constituted a Good Member of Community, untill that hypocrite & Delusive Wretch, Bogg [*sentenced to fourteen yrs trspn, OB Feb. 1813*], came & told me of his Great Benefits i yielded to the temptation i am not the only one that is suffering through having a knowledge of that execrable wretch i was self Convicted from the first Moment i ever had one & i Declare that i shoud never have Entertained him nor any other Person connected with any dishonest profession, after i had bought myself a new coat that which was my Intention after he made the Inducement, to have got them two Articles easy, no person i thought woud be the Wiser, it was not a Vicious or Depraved heart it might be more Justly

Alluded Sir, to a Proud Spirit in not having Patience to Wait to gain it by my former Custom Industry
Pray Sir do Compassionate the Sufferings of a fellow Creature
By which Intercession i trust i shall have my sentence lessened that i may once more have an Idea of Surviving this Dreadfull Dilemma which is the dire effects of being easily Persuaded and Sir with a heart full of gratitude i shall never cease to Pray – I Beg to Subscribe Myself y^{r} Most Obedient Humble Servt John Chave

618. *[F25/11/3] Joseph Jennings,* Laurel *hulk, Portsmouth harbour, 7 August 1813*
Gent^{n} Having been unfortunately convicted at the last Lent Assizes at Warwick for having in my possession forged Blank Bank of England Notes and Sentenced to Fourteen years transportation I have most humbly presumed to request you will recommend my Case to the Governors & Directors of the Bank of England as the whole of my Small Property was wasted and Sold in Consequence of my Misfortunes and being now much reduced respectfully solicit those gentlemen will condescend (as there is no doubt of my immediately leav^{g} this Country) to extend to me the same benefit which has lately been afforded to other unfortunate objects of their Prosec^{n} as in my present distressed situation the most trifling Sum will be very acceptable & remain Sirs Your most obed^{t} hum^{ble} Servt Joseph Jennings

619. *[F25/11/4] Isaac Wise,* General Hewitt *transport ship, Gosport, August 1813, formal petition*
Your petitioner, being fully contious of his Guilt pleaded Guilty to the Minor Offence of haveing forged Notes in his possession, in October Sessions last past at the Sessions House in the Old Baily, and received Sentance of transportation for the term of fourteen years
That petitioner returns his most Sincere thanks for the Humanity he has already experienced, that the long Confinement he has underwent has expended all his money that he has not had it in his power to Lay in any sort of Sea Stock, to preserve Health or Sustain nature during so long a Voyage, And that he has no freinds to enable him so to do.
Therefore your petitioner most humbly Implores your Honour to take his Case Into consideration And Grant him some temporary Aid for the Above Purpose And Petitioner in Duty bound will ever pray &c &c &c Isaac Wise his mark

620. *[F25/11/5–6] John Davis, State Side, Newgate, 13 April 1813*
Gentleman, With the utmost Contrition & Sorrow for my past folley & faults I do most Earnestly beg Your Pardon, Permit me therefore Honnerd Sirs in behalf of my self & Family once more to implore your Mercy & Clamency towards me, and by which means I may be Enabled to render you All the Assistance in my power and I do hereby solemnly pleg^{d} myself and likewise sevral of my Nearst friends, Constantly to be owed Study henceford to render you every Assistance, as soon you will pleace to put

me in that situation to convince you therof: untill then Gentlemen I offer my Friends to be Security for me in Two hundred Pounds:- I am respectfully Gentlemen your most ob[t] humble Ser[t] John Davis
Attached: covering letter from Davis.

621. *[F25/11/8] Thomas Davis, brother of John Davis* [**620**], *21 April 1813*
Sirs, The very distressed and unfortunate Situation of my Brother John, and my natural feelings for him as a Brother will I presume apologise for this address, and I beg to assure you I have no interested Motives in contemplation while I am endeavouring to serve you but the amelioration of my Brother's Sufferings; and allow me to represent to you that if he should be sent to the Hulks his Life will be endangered from the discoveries I have made by the persons who have been the Objects of my Information; and others who are also in confinement for the same offence; and it is to him you are alone indebted for the discoveries that have been made as I had no means whatever from my own Knowledge of distinguishing who the parties were that have been pursuing the nefarious practices of passing counterfeited Notes without having had them first pointed out by him, and even now confined in Newgate he is afraid to attend the Church lest some personal Violence should be offered him by those persons in confinement on the Felons Side and from this he can form an Idea What would be the result if subjected to the Imprisonment aboard with those persons. I therefore most respectfully & humbly entreat as a remuneration for my services that you will be pleased to prevent it & extend to him your gracious Mercy & pardon; or any fine that you may think fit – and should you be disposed to grant him any Indulgences or mitigation Permit me to inform you that he is in hourly expectation of a removal and that no time ought to be lost to prevent it – any Communication you may have to make now upon the Subject the Bearer of this will be happy to take it as he is in waiting
I am Sirs; Your most obed[t] servant Thomas Davis Prujean Square, Old Bailey
John informs me he can give further information from two different quarters which I will inform you with Thomas Davis his mark

622. *[F25/11/9] John Davis,* Laurel *hulk, Gosport, date obscured by water damage, formal petition*
Your Pertitioner most Humbly begs that your Honors will extend your Mercy towards him and Grant him a Medigation of his sentence having given Information before his last Examination that he bought them of a Man of the name of Tavenor [*sentenced to fourteen yrs trspn, OB, Apr. 1819*] & M[r] Westwood your Solisctors managing Clerk said all he could Promiss him was that the Capital should be taken off
Your Pertitioner at a expence has done all in his Power like wise his frinds, to Detect, Tavenor but unfortunately, has not secoseaded
Your Petitioner begs farther to state while he was at the house of Correction in Cold Bath fields in the Sells he got acquainted with a man of the name of Palmer and when they where Committed to his Majestys Goal of Newgate with the consent of M[r] Westwood on purpose for your Honours;

Information had frequent interviews with him & other Prisoners in the Vine room pretending he wanted to buy some Notes being short of Money & could git them passed Palmer gave him a Letter to a man of the name of Able & he sent his wife with it to M[r] Westwood and implied his brother to buy some Notes & he bought two five Pound Notes N[o] 9170825 N[o] 91730 dated Augst 7th 1812 and he sent his Wife with them to M[r] Westwood. My brother after wards bought of him which led to his Detection and Conviction. Your Petitioner also got a nother Letter to a man of the name of Wood this with every other information he gave to M[r] Westwood thear fore most humbly begs that your Honnors will take his case into farther Consideration and assist him in procuring a Medigation of his sentance

623. *[F25/11/7] Ann Davis, wife of John Davis, petition for mitigation for her husband, undated, in same hand as* **622,** *making same points. She writes from Church Lane, St. Georges East, County of Middlesex.*

624. *[F25/11/10–12] John Davis,* Laurel *hulk, Portsmouth, 10 June 1813*
Mr Westwood Sir I have taken the Liberty of informing you that I have sent a Letter; penitant Letter to the Governor & C[o] of the Bank of England requesting their kind interference in my behalf for a Mitigation of Sentence or to procure me a grant either to go into the Army or Navy and hope you will be so kind as to assist me with your kind interference as you promis[d] me and if possible to get me permission to serve in the Army or Navy as you are well aware I did everything in my Power to serve them by giving every information in my power and hope you will please to take my very Unfortunate Situation into your Consideration & use your utmost efforts for me with the Gentlemen of the Bank of England to obtain for me a Mitigation or a grant to serve in the Army or Navy which ever your Wise advice might think proper. I am extremely sorry for the Offence and I through myself upon your kind Benevolence & Humanity so Conspicuous to your Hon[e] Character and Profession I have made every Contrition in my power by Strict Conformity to penitence and good morals for the Offence done Contrary to Law and in Violation of Justice and hope I shall be permitted to go into the Army or Navy
and I remain your Most Obed[t] & Humble Servant John Davis
Attached: further letter from John Davis to Bank governor, repeating **624**; *copy reply from Bank solicitors, 17 June 1813, stating Bank decline to comply with his request.*

625. *[F25/11/13] John Davis,* Surrey *transport ship, Portsmouth, 19 January 1814*
Honored Sir Pardon me for this intrusion on a Person of your Rank & Character; Be Pleased to understand I am now on Board the Surry East Indiaman bound to New South Wales. I left the Laurel Convict Ship Three Days since, & am now Placed in a very disagreeable & wretched situation; I have ever looked forward that your honor would stretch out your aid to deliver me from this unfortunate situation; but as that most likely has not been in your Power; I hope you will by no means with hold some Pecuniary

Assistance to alleviate my distress, on your superior Judgement on such a case I relie every fear with your means of Protection ever be unneccesary. I beg to state that I were hurried away 'ere I could dispose of the little Tenement I were Master of & now expect to sail from this Port in or about 8 Days to the Most distant Period. I need not I hope enumerate any thing which were mentioned at a distant Period – I am well aware that your Powerful Interests can Procure me a Mitigation of my Sentence it being only that which were held out during the time I were in Newgate, rest assured Sir, I have never in the instance misled you & every thing has been done to giving you satisfaction, otherwise I would not by any means have been thus explicit You cannot by no means think me I hope trouble since it being the first time I ever craved your aid, I can assure your honor I have at various times expended a great deal of money & humbly hope that some assistance will be given me to soothe the anguish which I at Present endure – should this meet with the approbation of your honor so as to comply with my request have the goodness to forward it to me on Board the Surry East Indiaman at Portsmouth [*three illegible words*] At the same time have the goodness to make mention if your honour received a Note from my Wife that I sent her from the Laurel about 3 Weeks since; it were of Importance. I said that you are aware how assidious I have been to give satisfaction therefore I hope shall expect a Proof of your honors Humanity I beg leave to subscribe myself kind Sir Y[r] Most Ob[bt] Serv[t] John Davis
PS I hope every attention will be paid to my request

626. *[F25/11/14] John George Hearson, Thomas Slater, James Ashton, Henry Rodgers,* Earl Spencer *transport ship, Portsmouth, 28 April 1813, formal petition*
That your Petitioners were ever truly contious & sensible of the truth of the charges for which they are transported: that your Petitioners return their most sincere thanks for the Mercy & favors they have received already.
That your Petitioners most humbly beg leave to observe that they have it not in their power to provide any sort of Sea Stock for the voyage to New South Wales all their money & friends being exhausted; leaving them no other resource but applying to your Honors. May it therefore please Your Honours to take the Petitioners case into your humane Consideration (and through your Honors accustomed goodness) be pleased to grant them such Pecuniary aid as in your Wisdom & judgement seems fit & your Petitioners as in duty bound shall ever pray &c, &c
J. G. Hearson [*letter in his hand*], Thomas Slater, James Ashton, Henry Rodgers

627. *[F25/11/15–16] Thomas Slater,* Earl Spencer *transport ship, Spithead, 8 May 1813*
Sir Excuse the Presumption of an unfortunate man Convicted for Passing forged notes being so very much distrest and having no one to asist and my Wife in Prison waitting to follow me without one shilling to asist us and having aplyed to the Hon[ble] Companys solisitors and cant get any releif I make bold to Informe you that I am not an old ofender but that I did give to

Mr Westwood all the Information I could and would have done more If i could and after all the Oldest offenders you have are aloud 7^s/6^d Per Week and have got Hundreds of Pounds by them Meaning Isacks Wise Wife [*Cathrine Watson*] and George Hearson Wife [*Hannah*] and I have not got a shilling to keep me am going to Leave my Contry distitute of one to Leave her that wish to follow me Excuse me sir for thus intruding on you as I have no other way to make my Case know and If your Honnour Should in your Judgement think by Enquiring my Character of Mr Westwood Worthy of a little releife you will be so good if the ship is sail'd to alow it to my wife Elizabeth Morris in Newgate I shall with fervency Ever Pray Your unfortunate obedient Humble Servt Thos Slater
Addressed to Henry Hase, Bank chief cashier
Attached: copy note from Bank solicitors stating that governors decline to comply with his request, or requests of Hearson, Ashton and Rodgers [**626**].

628. *[F25/11/17] Martha Pedley, Sarah Ashwell, Sarah Startin,* Wanstead *transport ship, Deptford, 4 July 1813*
Mr Kay, Sir, I hope you will Pardon the Leberty I have takein in writen to you But it is nessety for I have Been taken up Ever sence the 30th of October and A small famley and have Been fost to sell all my things to Live on and I am very much Distrest and if you will have The Goodness as to give me A trifle it will be very thankfully Received By me martha Pedley as I have A Child with me and I have no money to Purcehs any thing But the alounce and there is 2 moor women that was Convected at Warwick the same time as my Salfe and very much Disstrest in Deed the Be Honnerd Sir I hope you will atend to the Above and your humble Pektichners is in Duty Bound and will for Ever Pray for you, Martha Pedley, Sarah Aswell, Sarah Startin

629. *[F25/11/18] Mary Best,* Wanstead *transport ship, Deptford, 5 July 1813*
Honnerd Sir I hope you will Pardon me with the Leberty of Riting to you But it is nessety that oblidges me to it and I hope your Goodness will Conceder my Long Confinement and my family to Be Suported as oblidge me to part with all I ad, and now I am Going to Leve my naterve Countrey and I am very much Desstrest in Deed. Honnerd Sir I Rely on your goodness and I hope you will atend to the Above and your humble Pertichner will Be in Duty Bound and will ever Pray Mary Best

630. *[F25/11/19] Eleanor Thorpe,* Wanstead *transport ship, Deptford, 8 July 1813*
Worthey Sir I have to inform you that I am now on board of the Ship a Going to Botaney Bay for 14 years and I have not troubled you before I hope you Goodness will kind enough to think of me now I am very much Distress for Cloaths indeed and leaving 4 Small Children behind me and not a friend to assist me in the Least thing in the world I was taken at Worrington with 12 two pound notes in my Charge and was tried at

Lancaster Last august assizes and pleeded so I hope your goodness will not forget me I am Sir your Most Humble Servent Elenor Thorpe

631. *[F25/11/20] Martha Hughes,* Wanstead *transport ship, Deptford, 8 July 1813*
Worthey Sir I have to inform you that I am now on board of the Ship Going to Botaney Bay and I have not trouble you yet so I hope your Goodness will be kind enough to think of me now I shall be humbly oblidge to you as I have 5 small Children to Leave behind me and myself very much distressed for Cloaths indeed I was taken at Manchester and tryed at Lancaster Likewise Last March assizes and not any thing of bad notes found on me so I hope your Goodness will not forget me I am Sir your Most Humble Servant Martha Hughes

632. *[F25/11/21] Phoebe Chandler,* Wanstead *transport ship, Deptford, 8 July 1813*
Worthey Sir This is to inform you that I am now on board of this Ship Goeing to Botaney Bay and have not troubled you before if your Goodness would be kind enough to think of me how I was appehanded at Bristol with and onley 1£ in my Care and was tryed the 12 April at Bristol and I am Goeing for 14 years and Leveing 5 small Children behind me and not a friend to assist me in the Least thing in the World and am very much distress for Cloaths indeed so I hope you Goodness will not forget
I am Sir your Most Humble Servant Phebee Chandler

633. *[F25/11/22] Elizabeth Dewhurst,* Wanstead *transport ship, Deptford, 8 July 1813*
Worthey Sir this is to inform you that I am now on board of the Ship a going to Botoney and I have not troubled you before so I hope your Goodness would be kind enough to think of me now as I have two small Children to Leave Behind me and very much distress for Cloaths and not a friend to assist me in anything I was taken in Leeds in Yorkshire[7] and not any found on me I was tried at Lancaster in March Last so I hope your Goodness will not forget me I am Sir your Most Humble Servant Eliz[th] Duert

634. *[F25/11/23] Elizabeth Chedlow,* Wanstead *transport ship, Deptford, 8 July 1813*
Honnerd Gentlemen I hope you will Pardon the Liberty I have takeing in Riteing to you But it is nesseaty that oblidges me to it for I am in Grate Distress and as you have Been so Good as to give the other Poor unfortunate Women a little as I was Conveceted at Stafford with M[r] Booths [*cap. con., summer 1812*] and Mrs Booth as Baveid very Ill to me and I am very much in want of nessarys and I hope your Goodness will think of me and

7. Elizabeth Dewhurst here refers to an earlier case against her in Yorks. where she was found not guilty; a second case against her was in Lancs. for which she was sentenced to trspn.

your humble Pertichner is in Duty Bound and will for Ever pray for you Elizabeth Chedlow

635. *[F25/11/24] Hannah Hearson,* Wanstead *transport ship, Spithead, 23 July 1813*
Hounered Sir I hope that you will excuse my taking the liberty of Writing to you but Necesity Drives me to it but I hear that all the other woman is rote for A little Adition for A few necesaries for the long voyge that we are A going to take I hope Gentlemen that you will excuse the liberty that I have taken if you please to Direct Your Humble Servant Hannah Hewson on board off the Wansted Womens Convict Ship Spithead or elsewhere Hannah Hewson

636. *[F25/11/25] Eight female prisoners,* Wanstead *transport ship, Spithead, 23 July 1813*
Honerd Gentlemen Wee humble thank you for the favour wee have Recevid from your hands and as wee are Likeley to have a Long Voyege and most of us as Childrin and wat you have Been so Good as to give us all moust Expinded with By in a few things as we wanted very Bad and if you Goodness will Remit us a trifle moar it will Be thankfully Receveid By your humble Pertichner and wee shall Be in Duty Bound and will for Ever Pray Sarah Startin, Sarah Ashwell, Martha Pedley, Elizabeth Chedlow, Elizabeth Jones, Catherine Watson, Mary Best, Jane Smith

637. *[F25/11/26] Martha Pedley,* Wanstead *transport ship, Spithead, 4 August 1813*
Honoured Gentlemen Relying on your goodness I take the Leberty of trubling you with thes few Liens for wich I hope your Honour will Pardon me for and since I Recevied your kind Present I have Been very ill and wee have neather tea nor Suger allowed till wee get out to sea and I wented a few od things that I could not well do with out such as Shoes and Stockings for me and my Child and other Little Necessarys as is not allowed hear and I have Layd out my Last Shillings so if your Honour Can Stand my ferind with sending me a trifle moor if it is Ever so Little it will Be thankfully Recevied and your humble Pertishnor is in Duty Bound and will for Ever Pray for you Martha Pedley

638. *[F25/11/27] Jane Smith and Elizabeth Jones,* Wanstead *transport ship, Spithead, 5 August 1813*
Honrd Gentlemen Your Goodness will I hope Pardon the Liberty of your unfortunate Pertitioner who is After a Long Confinement in such Distress having no Freinds to Assist Render them compleaty misra misrabl if Gentlemen this should merit Your Aprobation and you should think it Proper to Remit us A trifl to inable us to Procure A few Nessary thing as are not Alowed
We shall be in Duty Bound to Pray We are Honrd Gentlemen your Hum^{le} Ser^{ts} Eliz^{h} Jones Jane Smith

639. *[F25/11/29] Eleanor Tomlinson, Newgate, 24 June 1813*
Hon[ble] Gentlemen Your goodness will I hope pardon every liberty I take in sending to you But having never had anything of assistance from you hope you will dewly take into consideration and advance me some money to Enable me to get a few Nessesary Articles for Myself and 3 Children leaving and to be Banish from this Country for 14 years is a very distressing thing to think of. Therefore I hope I May be so fortunate as many more in the Prison for the like offence have Received at your hands that will Render them comfortable and I hope I may Become of them Being the first and certainly will Be the last having Been a prisoner now 6 months I can Assure you was I not Much Distress I would not trouble you I once mor reepeat Gentlemen that I also hope you will consider my case
I am Hon[le] Gentlemen with every dew respect Y[r] very Obt Hum[ble] Ser[t]
Elenoria Tomlinson
PS the Ship goes on Monday and we are Desired to Be on Board on Morning Early

640. *[F25/11/28] Eleanor Tomlinson, Newgate, 28 June 1813*
Hon[ble] Gentlemen I was in great hopes by this time I should have had the pleasure of hearing form you having trouble you with a letter to request the favour that you would kindly Consider My Distress[d] Situation My Husband is out of Employmend and having 3 Children and Being long confind has truly Much Bereaft me of My Cloaths having being oblidge to pledge nearly all my Cloaths for suport therefore hope Gentlemen that you will Consider My case as I can Assure you It would be truly Exceptable and thankfully received by Your Humble Pertitioner Believe me was I not realy distress I would not trouble you hope you will have compassion on me and pardon the liberty my writing to you
I am Hon[ble] Gentlemen with every dew Respect Y[r] very Obt Hum[ble] Ser[t]
Elenoria Tomlinson
PS Gentlemen I hope you will give the Bearer a favourable Answer and shal ever Be in duty Bound to Pray

641. *[F25/11/30] Eleanor Tomlinson,* Wanstead *transport ship, Spithead, 23 July 1813*
Honoured Sir I hope that you will excuse me taking the Liberty I have takeing in riting to you but I hear that the other Women has rote for a little addition for to by A few nescery Articals to take for the Long Voyge that I am A going to take I hope you will pardon the Liberty I have taking Your Humble Servant if you please to direct to Elenor Tomlinson

642. *[F25/11/31–2] Margaret Palmer,* Wanstead *transport ship, Spithead, 23 July 1813, with three children; widow of James Brown, hanged August 1812 at Hertford for uttering in St Albans, requests money for voyage to NSW; attached letter, 22 Apr. 1813, in which she calls herself Eliza Palmer, asking for money while in prison. Not convicted for offence against Bank.*

643. *[F25/11/33] Joseph Barresley, Lancaster castle, 11 September 1813*
A bankrupt petitions Bank for clemency on his debts.

644. *[F25/11/34] John Carr, York castle, 3 June 1813*
A debtor for £50, sends account of expenses while in gaol; since he helped Bank achieve arrest of many forgers, he asks them to pay him and expresses concern about his family; Bank refuse.

645. *[F25/11/35–6] John Carr, York castle, 9 July 1813*
Further request for help; Bank still refuse to pay expenses but say they will put up £20 to get him out of gaol.

646. *[25/11/37] Dennis O' Connor,* Zealand *hulk, 25 September 1813*
Counterfeiter of dollars sends list of information about forgers.

647. *[F25/11/38–46] Henry Moore, Stafford gaol, 26 March, 1, 6, 15, 21 & 22 April 1814 offers information on master-forgers in return for release when he proposes to work for Bank; three copy notes of response from Bank show interest, but they will neither visit him in gaol nor allow him to travel to London to see them; he must put all evidence in writing; they will contact under-sheriff to request that none of his letters to them be opened. No trace of Bank prosecuting Moore.*

648. *[F25/11/47] Thomas Smith,* Captivity *hulk, Portsmouth harbour, 2 June 1814*
Honor'd Sir, My unfortunate situation will, I hope, plead in my favour for thus troubling You. I was tried in February last, at the Old Bailey Sessions with a man of the name of Tho[s] [*John*] Borham [*sentenced to fourteen yrs trspn, OB, Feb. 1814*] for uttering Forged Notes on the Bank of England and being convicted was sent to this Ship 'til another is ready to convey me to Botany Bay which is expected shortly – as I know not the regular mode of making application most humbly throw myself on Your Goodness, trusting that You will interfere and render me some little assistance. Previous to my leaving the Country; as I am in the greatest distress and have not a Friend on Earth who can in any way relieve me and for such goodness I shall with the utmost gratitude for ever Pray
With every respect I am Sir Your most Obedt and very humble Servant
Tho[s] Smith
Letter addressed to Henry Hase, Bank chief cashier.

649. *[F25/11/48] Thomas Smith,* Captivity *hulk, Portsmouth Harbour, 14 June 1814*
Not having received reply to earlier letter, Smith writes almost identical letter to Mr Lees, Bank investigator.

650. *[F25/11/49] Thomas Smith,* Captivity *hulk, Portsmouth harbour, 15 July 1814*
Gentlemen, I have most humbly to intreat Your Pardon for thus intruding; but when I make you acquainted with my distressed and miserable circumstances; I trust and hope Your humanity and Generosity will need no other apology; I was in February Sessions last, at the Old Bailey convicted in the company of a Man of the Name of John Boreham [*see* **648**] for having in our possession a Quantity of Forged Bank of England Notes; and received the sentence of Fourteen Years Transportation.
I am now on Board the above Ship, awaiting the arrival of a Ship that is to convey convicts, from this Country, to Botany Bay, and which is daily expected to arrive
I have most earnestly to implore Your commiseration; and trust that You Gentlemen, will, so represent, my situation that I may be, in some measure assisted by some Pecuniary Relief; having no Friends living, who can; in any Way assist me; I am totally at a loss to whom to apply but hope that in case it does not remain with You to grant me any Relief You will be Pleased to inform me to whom and in what manner I am to apply and such information will be most thankfully received and acknowledged by an unfortunate Man who with the utmost contrition for his Offence begs leave most Humbly to Subscribe himself, Gentlemen, Your most obedient and very Humble Servant Tho[s] Smith
Annotated: Rejected

651. *[F25/11/50] William Allen,* Portland *hulk, Portsmouth harbour, 16 June 1814*
Sir, Having been convicted at the Assizes held at Lancaster (Sept[r] 1811) before Sir Allan Chambre Kn[t] one of the Judges for the Court of Common Pleas on a Charge of Uttering Notes with intent to defraud the Governor and C[o] of the Bank of England and received Sentence of transportation for the term of fourteen years
I am still suffering the said sentence on board the Portland (Hulk) on the Portsmouth Station; having made application to Lord V Sidmouth; to Sir Allan Chambre and to the Captains of the respective Hulks to carry the said sentence into execution (by sending me out of the Country) without effect, as five different Ships have sailed with Convicts from Portsmouth for New South Wales since my conviction and I continue to be detained
As the state of my health; owing to my Age [*space in brackets blank*] and infirmities of Body are such that continuing me in Confinement at the Hulks would be certain death to me being unable to bear the severity of the Climate, I take this liberty to humbly implore you will be pleased to take compassion on my present unhappy Situation and interest yourself on my behalf, to procure and order for my being sent away to a Warmer climate where I hope to have an opportunity to pass the remainder of my Existence in repentance and preparations for another and a better life –
My present debility of body will I hope plead my Applogy for this Intrusion and hoping you will be pleased to seriously consider my situation & alieveate my sufferings in obtaining my ernest request

With the greatest Submission I beg permission to Remain Sir Your Ob[dt] h'ble Serv[t] William Allen

652. *[F25/11/51–4] J. Beckett, home office, Whitehall, 20 October 1813 re: Ann Harris (alias Fleming) held in Worcester gaol, awaiting trspn. Lord Sidmouth requires him to pass Harris's petition for mitigation to Bank governors and directors; they must let him know outcome of their discussion. Copy reply from Bank solicitors, 29 Oct. 1813, to Beckett stating Bank will not interfere but if Lord Sidmouth requires, they will explain the case against Harris. Further letter from Beckett to Bank, 2 Nov. 1813, stating that Lord Sidmouth requires these facts; also attached is much reworked draft reply from Bank, same date, explaining Harris's significant uttering of high value notes, and her (and husband's) previous trspn for similar offences.*

653. [*F25/11/55*] *Thomas Roberts and John McCann,* Baring *transport ship, Spithead, 24 March 1815*
Sir we the Two unfortunate men under Mentioned take this liberty of addressing your Honour to Solicit your Friendship and hoping you will be so good as to forward us the Bounty which is allowed by Govrment for unfortunate men in our Situation we was tried at Lancaster Assizes August 31st in 1814 and Transported for Life and in so doing we Shall be bound for your Honour ever to Pray Thomas Roberts, John McCann
Sir, we are now on Board of the Bay Ship therefore we humbly solicit your Answer
[*BECLS: 30 Mar. 1815, rejected request.*]

654. *[F25/11/56] William Allen,* Portland *hulk, Portsmouth harbour, 4 February 1815*
Reiterates letter of 16 June 1814 [**651**], *adding he would like remission of sentence.*

655. *[F25/11/57–8] Commander S. Owen of* Portland *hulk, Langstone harbour, 23 August 1815, gives information about forgers and sellers of notes; attached copy note of thanks to him from Bank, 25 Aug. 1815.*

656. *[F25/11/59–61] Mark Brown,* Portland *hulk, Langstone harbour, 21 August 1815*
Hon[d] Sir I humbly implore your pardon for this liberty but being unfortunately now on the eve of departing from this Country under the deplorable sentence of fourteen years transportation (which sentence I received at the Sessions held at the Old Bailey in February last on pleading guilty to a charge of Feloniously uttering Bank Notes (forged) with intent to defraud the Governor & C[o] of the Bank of England) I humbly entreat permission to submit the following statement for your Consideration
I was unfortunately in Company with Stalard and Giles [**661**] at the time that they uttered the Notes but without my knowledge of their Business or connection with them, neither did I know anything thereof untill my

apprehension but having unfortunately only having left the Hulk at Woolwich a short time previous, my Character was suspected, and caused me, at the persuation of my friends to plead guilty, altho' I most solemnly assure you Hon[d] Sir of my entire ignorance of the Business
The above Hon[d] Sir is a true statement of the unhappy Business, for which I am now innocently suffering and myself involved a second time into the lowest abyess of human misery with a distressed and unhappy Wife who by my Separation from her is reduced to the greatest distress
I therefore under these deplorable Circumstances most humbly implore your Compassion for my unfortunate situation, and your humane intercession on my behalf with Lord Sidmouth to induce his Lordship to take my unhappy case into his consideration and grant me a remission or mitigation of Sentence, thereby enabling me to return and by honest and laudable industry to become an useful member of Society
Entreating your Pardon for this Intrusion and most humbly imploring your humane compassion for my distressed situation and your intercession to procure me an alieviation, most respectfully I beg permission to remain Hon[d] Sir Your obliged & very hble serv[t] Mark Brown
Annotated: Rejected
Attached: copy note from Bank solicitors noting refusal to comply; letter from Maria Brown, lawfull wife *of Mark Brown, thanking Bank for allowing his life to be saved, asking them to support petition to Lord Sidmouth to allow her to accompany him since they both are young, in good health, of honest character and she can get a grant to get their clothes out of pawn.*

657. *[F25/11/62–72] Edmund (or Edward) Bamford,* Captivity *hulk, Portsmouth, 24 May 1815 sentenced to seven yrs trspn for stealing cotton goods, writes several letters hoping to get mitigation of sentence by providing information about forgers, paper makers and utterers in Birmingham; Bank say investigator, Glover, will visit him; after Glover's visit, Bamford sends information, 31 May, 1 & 12 June 1815; Bank pass this to Nadin, deputy constable of Birmingham. Bamford, 10 Sept. 1815, requests employment as Bank investigator; Bank refuse,15 Sept. 1815, but say if he presents petition they will mention help he has given.* [*Further contact made 21 Feb. 1818,* **704.**]

658. *[F25/11/73] William Sharples,* Captivity *hulk, Portsmouth, 5 June 1815*
Sir, I trust you will pardon me troubling you but having been convicted at Lancaster Assizes in March last for Bank of England Notes and Transported for 14 years and now going to leave the Country totally penniless and leaving behind me An Affectionate Wife and four Children and I understand through your kind Interference unfortunate men in my situation get a Trifle of Money allowed if that his the case I request you will be kind enough in making the necessary application for that purpose. But I have to request another favour for my Wife and Family to come to Botany Bay in the next Ship after me and I most sincerely hope that I shall be favoured

with your answer and advice on how My Wife and Family should proceed to follow me, Being destitute of friends to take the trouble of making application for my Wife and family; and I most sincerely trust you will be kind enough to stand my friend I remain Sir with the greatest submission Your much obliged and very humble servant Wm Sharples
Hear his another hand of the name of Samuel Jackson convicted for the same offence and he trusts for your kind Interference in case any allowance his granted

659. *[F25/11/74] William Spurrier, solicitor acting for Bank in Stafford, 16 September 1814, having visited Henry Moore in Stafford gaol* [**647**] *reports what was done with information gained from him.*

660. *[F25/11/75–6] E. Griffith, chaplain, Shrewsbury gaol, 23 August 1815, re Hannah Shone*
Gent. On my appointment to the Chaplaincy of the County Gaol last Xtmas, my Predecessor Mr Poulett recommended strongly to my notice a prisoner of the name of Hannah Shone under sentence of transportation for 14 years for having in her possession forged Notes of the Bank of England. She had been strongly recommended to V The Hon. Henry Grey Bennett one of the Members for this Borough, who promised to procure some mitigation of her punishment: but as yet I do not learn that any attempt has been made for that purpose. She was tried in March Assizes 1810 with her Son, who was transported and soon afterwards went out of the Country. The report is, and as far as I am able to learn is true that her son was connected with a party at Peterborough or in Birmingham in forging and uttering forged notes of the Bank of England and one of these forged notes of 1L he paid to his mother and she passed it again without being conscious that it was a forged note; and this report gains credit from her general character thro' life. Her husband was a respectable Farmer and they lived at the Vicarage of Stanton for considerable time in the neighbourhood of Wem. I have now in my possession a Letter from the Rev$^{d.}$ G. Dicken, a most respectable Clergyman at Wem, who says 'In reply to your letter, Hannah Shone the person You allude to lived at the Vicarage about twenty two years, during which period she behaved herself honestly & correctly as far as my observation extended'. She is now in her 67th year of her age & her health after a confinement of 5 years is as she says much impaired. Her conduct, since she has been in Gaol, Mr Cartwright the Gaoler informs me has been in every way correct. Her Son and I believe some of the party with whom he was connected have been transported and the Bank I should note, cannot entertain any fears of being further injured by the liberation of this poor woman. My object in writing this letter is to request your permission for her to address a letter to the prince Regent to shorten the time of her sentence. If any opinion can be formed from her fragile appearance, she is not likely to live to the expiration of her sentence whether she be confined or not at liberty.
I am Gent. Your Obd^{t} Servant E. Griffith

On outside of folded paper: I am informed that her confinement or release depends much upon yourselves – if that be the case, I am strongly of opinion that it cannot be exercised towards a more worthy object than the prisoner in whose favor I make this application.
Attached: copy letter to Griffith from Bank solicitors stating directors fully considered Shone's case before and after they prosecuted; there were no circumstances to warrant their interference as her conduct was that of a person very familiar with the Traffick in forged Bank Notes.

661. *[F25/11/77] Six male convicts on* Fame *or* Sir William Bensley *transport ships, Spithead, 20 September 1816*
Gentlemen The undersigned humbly request that they may be favoured with the usual allowance granted to such as are convicted at your suit; on their quitting England, and as they are totally destitute of Money humbly beg that your benevolent donation may be extended to them
Josiah Allen, 1816 March Ass. Lancaster; Tho[s] Erstwaite, 1815 Dec. Old Bailey; Thomas Giles, 1816 March Ass. Stafford [*on Fame*]
Robert Henry Dye, Henry Dye, Archibald Small, 1816 May, Old Bailey [*on Sir William Bensley*]

662. *[F25/11/78] Anthony Halliwell,* Sir William Bensley *transport ship, Spithead, 18 September 1816*
M[r] Hase, Sir, I took the liberty of addressing you from the Retribution Hulk Sheerness intimating the cause of my troubling you; I find I am still equally unpleasantly situated as to ignorance in regard to your silence. I before apprised you of the time of my being arraigned & pleading Guilty to the indictment of having paid forged Notes purporting to be Bank of England ones – by my thus pleading Guilty the Bank of England is gracious pleased to allow the Sum of £5 – which I intreat you will condescend to have forwarded to me prior to my leaving this Country, which will take place in the course of a few days, being already on Board of the Bay Ship & proceeded thus far. Fearful of any mistake again occurring, I will specify the Date of my being arraigned which took place on the 26th day of March 1816 at Lancaster Castle in the County of Lancaster, as Witness my Hand at the foot here. Any inaccuracy that I may commit thru the medium of this application, I humbly beg leave to apologize for, & trust it may be imputed to its proper cause; ignorance as to the proper mode of application – Relying upon the favor of an early ans[r] I beg leave with due diffidence to subscribe myself – Sir Your most ob[t] & humble serv[t] Anthony Halliwell [*own signature*]
Witness to the signing before Wm Fisher [*Bank offender, Lancs spring ass. 1814*], John Robinson, W Leagh [*Bank offender, Lancs summer ass. 1814*].

663. *[F25/11/79–80] James Quin and John Bell,* Elizabeth *transport ship, Spithead, 15 May 1816*
Sir This is to inform you We are tow of the unfortunate Men that Was Convicted at the Last Lancaster Assises for Paying bad Banck of England Notes to Wich We both of us Peaded Guilty and Was Transported for 14

Years Now Sir as there is five Pounds Allowed by Goverment for each of us Shall be for ever in Duty Bound to Pray for you if you Will Please to give us that Indulgence to Procure a few Nessarys on our Voyage and as the Ship is Laying at Spithead there is not much time to be Lost in So Complying We shall be ever in Duty Bound to Pray From your Obedinent unfortunate James Quin John Bell

Please to Directt as follows on Board of the Elizebeth Spithead Portsmouth Bound to New South Wales Cptain Osten

Attached: copy letter from Bank solicitors, 18 May 1816: I have received your Letter, & I can only inform you that you are mistaken in supposing that there is five Pounds or any other allowance made by Government to Convicts in your situation. In some cases of female Convicts the Bank has as a matter of Charity given them £5 each to provide them with necessaries, but this has never been extended to Male Convicts

664. *[F25/11/81] Benjamin Dicken/Oliver,* Morley *transport ship, 'Downs or elsewhere', 17 December 1816*

Hon^rd^ Sirs, In the most reduced state of Mental affliction I most humbly beg pardon for daring to intrude upon Your important time But beg leave to state, that I was convicted in the Name of Benjn Oliver before Lord Chief Barron Wood, at the last Lancaster Assizes, for having forged Notes in possession and was then Sentenced to 14 Years transportation.

It is no Doubt within your exalted knowledge that at the time I was committed, I had only rec'd a pardon from transportation the short period of 3 weeks from the Retribution Sheerness (Cap^n^ Meers) on account of good behaviour after serving 4 years as captains Joiner in my own Name Viz- Benjn Dicken, I therefore most humbly beg leave to state that I have a tender Wife together with a darling child 5 years Old, who on account of our long seperation, implores Me to represent the truely distressing and unfortunate case to your benevolent feelings, that She is earnestly joining with Me in fervant and affectionate prayers, that You will be pleased to view her destitute and deplorable situation, being entirely bereft, of every friend or Protector, at the same time is subject to the cruel ubbraiding of those who where once Most Dear; on account I am sorry to say that herself as well as Me being once unfortunate

I beg leave to state that my character will bare any enquiry with respect to sobriety and industry, even from the officers of the Retribution who advised Me to Make this Solicitation, and will I persuade Myself convince the Secretary of State that I am fully competent to Maintain a Wife and family – and I am given to understand that these are strong objections the Secretary of State as of granting orders for Wifes to be sent

I most humbly and devoutly crave you will condescent to recommend a complyance to the Hon^le^ Lord Sidmouth, that My Wife togeather with her Child May be sent in the first Womens Ship to the Colony, Should My Solicitations Meet your favourable consideration, I May then timerously expect to be again united to a distress'd and disconsolate Wife, which will cause Your humble supplicant to pray while I have life with devout

fervency and in Such Sweet hope, I beg to subscribe Myself Your Most Obediant Very Sorriful Servant Benj[n] Oliver
PS I am sorry to say My Wife is deprived of Making personal application on account of her humble finances, and residing in Birmingham. She is therefore waiting in the Most painful anxiety for an answer from you and be pleased to address for Ann Dicken at Sarah Dickens 33 Old Inkleys Birmingham

665. *[F25/11/82 & 85] William Doyle,* Morley *transport ship, Sheerness, 22 November 1816*
Hon Gent[n] I humbly entreat your pardon for presuming to address you which nothing but a due sense of your humanity and benevolence could have induced me to take. I am indicted at the Last Assizes held at Lancaster on a charge of having in my possession certain forged Notes purporting to be Bank Notes of the Governor and Company of the Bank of England, to such indictment I pleaded Guilty, and for such offence I am now on board this Ship under sentence of Transportation for Fourteen Years, and am in hourly expectation of leaving this place – I beg leave therefore with the deepest humiliation to state to you that I am in very great distress at present for necessaries and as I am given to understand there is a certain sum allowed me for the purpose of releif on my passage to my place of Exile, on account of my pleading Guilty to the Indictment, I have therefore to request you will be pleased to take my distressed Situation into immediate Consideration – and cause the same to be remitted me as early as possible Your Compliance will ever be esteemed a particular favour conferred on Hon[d] Gent[n] With the highest respect Your most obedient humble Servant William Doyle.
Direct for me Morley bound to New South Wales Sheerness or Elsewhere
Attached: copy reply, 25 Nov. 1816, from Bank solicitors stating governor and directors decline complying.

666. *[F25/11/83–6] John Nield, Thomas Kershaw and John Taylor,* Morley *transport ship, Sheerness, 22 November 1816*
Hon[d] Gent[n] We trust you will not deem us unpardonably intrusive if we again solicit the favor of your causing an answer to be sent us in reply to our Letter to you of the 14th November, as we are now on board this Ship destined to our place of Exile and ever in hourly expectation of leaving this place, we before informed you of our helpless Situation, and once more beg leave to request you will cause our unfortunate and lamentable Situation to be taken into your humane Consideration and send us an answer as early as convenient Your Compliance will ever confer a lasting obligation on Hon[d] Gent[n] With the highest respect & esteem Your Obed[t] humble Servants John Neilde. Tho[s] Kershaw, John Taylor
Annotated: Rejected
Attached: letter from same three men, 14 Nov. 1816, on Bellerophon *hulk, with same facts and request; copy replies from Bank solicitors stating Bank decline to comply with requests.*

667. *[F25/11/87] George Young,* Captivity *hulk, Portsmouth, 3 November 1816*

Sirs I trust that you will pardon this trespass on your attention which I presume to make in the confident expectation that you will regard this appeal with the feelings of compassion made to you from one who sincerely repents the Commission of that Act which had doomed him to his present state of sufferings. In addressing you Sir I consider that I address a Gentleman in who the noblest feelings of the Heart are blended and consequently Mercy that noblest feeling of the noble Heart there reign predominant

Although to answer the designs of Justice you were become an instrument to execute its Sentence on me for a Criminal offence, yet I presume to submit to your sincer feelings that the nature of the Offence as also the Character of the Offender should afterwards influence the instrument of the Law to weigh well the merits and demerits of such and as they may appear deserving to extend to them such alleviation as may be equally consistent to Justice as to Mercy. On this plea I presume to offer myself an Object for your Commiseration.

I confess myself but little Conversant with the refined feelings of Study, but the little store of Knowledge which Nature has endowed me with has led me to consider that, as there are various offences, so there are various degrees of them and that though the sentence of the Law may necessarily be denounced against every offender, yet that the punishment of such should be ever regulated by the general Character which the Criminal has supported in Life.

A Man, who in the years of his Life for which he is accountable, supports an uniformity of integrity and sustains an Honourable Character, who, from the sudden impulse of an unguarded moment, commits an Act of Fraud which on serious reflection he recoils at such a one surely may not be deserving an equal share of punishment with a man who by being accustomed to violate the laws of his Country becomes dead to all sense of feeling, and a Hardened and depraved Character.

My Sentence has doomed me to Banishment from my Native Country, and I feel less regret leaving it than I otherwise should because that (excepting an Aged Mother) I have no friend to visit me, and consequently none to lament Me leaving, moreover that in England after the forfeiture of my Character I could not be able to obtain any employ

I am sorry that my improper Conduct has barr'd me from obtaining a recommendation to the Governor of New South Wales, but I trust (and rest my sole hope in the resolution I have formed) that in future by treading on and persevering in the paths of rectitude and in uprightness of Conduct, I shall be able to obliterate all recollection of my past errors and also to gain the Confidence and friendship of my Superiors and of those around me.

Trusting that you will oblige me with an answer I subscribe myself your Obedient Humble Servant Geo[e] Young

668. *[F25/11/88–9] George Morris,* Bellerophon *hulk, Sheerness, 28 October 1816*
Hon[rd] Sir I hope You will excuse the Freedom I take in addressing a letter to you, the purport of which is I was Convicted at last Assizes for Warwick for Disposing of Forged Bank of England notes and sentenced to transportation for life, by name of George Morris, I have a wife and three Children residing in London, Which I hope and trust the Bank will comply with My request in permeting them to acompany Me to my destiney in the same Ship, the object of My asking the favor of them going in the same ship is to prevent Her plungeing herself into the same Delima that has happend Myself, I should be very sorry to have a Recurrence of this nature, but if Distress should oblige her, which I am Certain would be the case provided I was to leave her behind me as I was the Chief support of the Family Consequently that would happen very soon; As her Finances would soon be exhausted
Sir, had not the Evidence George Robinson taken from my Wife twenty Pound under a pretence, I should in a great measure have had it in my power to have taken her passage but now it is a moral impossible, as it has depriv'd Me of the means, I now throw Myself and Family On the Benevolence of the Bank, hoping they will grant Me my request, and in return I will give them all the satisfaction that Lies in my power George Morris
PS Sir If You should think proper I will send My Wife and Family to You
Attached: copy reply from Bank solicitors, 29 Oct. 1816, stating it was not in their power to give permission for wife and children to accompany him, but advising that if his wife comes to see them, and he gives them information, they will explain to her how to apply to sec./state for permission.

669. *[F25/11/90–3] George Morris,* Bellerophon *hulk, Sheerness, 31 October 1816*
Sir, I Rec[d] Your letter and am willing to do what You Propos'd, upon consideration of You granting Me the favor I ask that is of My Wife & family going with me in the same ship, it being her wish to go with Me. I should not consider it a great favour to grant her a passage in the Womens Ship, upon the account of her being subject to many Abuses as she is a Woman that would like to keep Herself very reserve, Sir I must be convinced of your favour before I can do any good for You, there is not the smallest doubt of Your getting it acomplish'd if you think proper, I must beg of you not to mention any thing to my Wife as I shall send her to You from your Obedient Humble Servant George Morris
Attached: copy reply from Bank solicitors, 5 Nov. 1816, stating his wife came to see them that morning; they would not assist her unless Morris gave information; they would send someone suitable to see him; note from J. Beckett, home office, to Bank, 7 Nov. 1816: The bearer Eliz[h] Morris his the person you desired me to send to your office; *and sheets of information obtained from George Morris 16 Nov. 1816, written by Bank investigator.*

670. *[F25/11/94] A prisoner, Maidstone gaol, 19 September 1816* [*illegible signature, surname probably Smith*] *writes to* Mr Foy at the Vestigation Office Bank of England *offering information on forgers and utterers if he is allowed out of prison to assist; not prosecuted by Bank.*

671. *[F25/11/95–9] J M Wallis, Maidstone gaol, 17 December 1816, to solicitor Frankling Esq., 10 New Square, Lincoln's Inn; says he received message via his wife that written information on forgery welcomed; he would like to assist; this is his second letter so assumes previous letter did not get through; since letters in and out of gaol are read, he requires secrecy. Copy note from Bank solicitors, 23 Dec. 1816, to Mr Cuthbert, keeper of Maidstone gaol, requiring correspondence between them and Wallis to be delivered unopened. Wallis sends Bank solicitors extensive information, 31 Dec. 1816, asking them to pay for his discharge so he can better assist; Bank solicitors 2 Jan. 1817, refuse but suggest paying for information; further letter from Wallis, 10 Jan. 1817, saying he cannot help unless liberated. Unknown for what crime Wallis held; not prosecuted by Bank.*

672. *[F25/11/100–1] James McLean Boyd, Lancaster castle, 20 September 1816*
Sir I hop you will Pardon My freedom of thus Adrising you as I ham now confined Ja[s] Mc Lean Boyd now hunder sentenes of Death in L Castle And Saterday week his the Day that I am to Peaye the Deabt of Nattuer if no help comes an it is in yourer Power to Do A Deall in My Beihaf and from My Lord Milne when I was first teaken at Liverpoall I gave John Miller all the Infamatian that I Could think ov at that Time And I Also Sent A Letter wich will Do A Deall of Good in Manchester Mr Joseph Neadon [*Nadin, deputy constable of Manchester*] and After I came thear And Settelled I Sent A full Acceaunt to your Honnour Mr Neadon & Mr Higgins My Governor heare to I Could think on only I Negleted puting Dowen the Neames of the Partyes wich I Exepted the Scelator would Called for but I will never Subscibe them And if the will Not Do Me any Good it will Passabily do good to some that I have [*illegible word*] Bealieved Me and the only one thing Needful at Present for me to Dwell on his to implore your Mercy so far has to Save my Life and I will As in Duty Bound Ever Pray But if the [*illegible word*] of my Life was as well known to the Gentlemen of the Bank As I know the Good that I could do & would do My Life would soon be Reprieved and I would be very heapy if my Life depended on my Performing all that I [*illegible word*] that his to Put you in the Compleance of the deall of Forged Notes that his Cased so many unfortunate Men & Women to saves there lives and Libertyes But it could not be Don all at first it would teake some time and all that I would ask would two 2 Bow Street Officis that was not known and I would Marke the Bales and they could shut them You Need not be Afread or think that I am holding this out to selef Interastes now only to Seave my Life but you Mey be well Ashured that what I seay his [*illegible word*] A [*illegible word*] and [*two illegible words*] theat in sorrow for what I heave Don And whitever this be the

Means of Seaving My Life or not I Sheall Give it for the Good of Secietiy and the Contry at Large so no Mor from your Humbill Pittioner and I am with Due respet your very obedent &c Hubl Sev Ja[s] Mc Boyd
Now Gentelmen You Mey think What I am Going to Seay but I ashuer you As a Deaying Man that the first Bad Note I heaver plazed My heand on to the Beast of My Knowledge was in Sept the 8 1815 and All the times that I was at Birmingham that Sead Bussnes was 3 this would Aper not so but it is Truth As I Except for [*two illegible words*] Let Me As a Man theat Except to Suffer recommend you to feach Some one that his an offender As you Never can come at the right Parteyes in no other waye and it will not do to let them Do it them selves ther Mus be one in front
Exceuse My Power had
Attached: list of names.

673. *[25/11/102–3] Peter Hughes, Lancaster castle, 20 September 1816*
Gentlemen, From the awfull situation in which I am now placed (being under sentence of Death for uttering Forged Bank of England Notes) I am disposed to give you material information relative to the Traffic in forged Notes upon condition that you will promise to cause my Life to be saved, an early reply will oblige Your Humble Servant the Unfortunate Peter Hughes
Attached: copy letter from Bank solicitors to John Higgins, governor of Lancaster castle, 23 Sept. 1816, asking him to tell Peter Hughes and James McLean Boyd that Bank decline to interfere to save them; if they want voluntarily to give information Higgins should ensure it is put into writing and sent to Bank.

674. *[25/11/104–5] Samuel Gilbert, unspecified prison or ship, 10 January 1816, formal petition*
That Your Petitioner was Indicted the last June Sessions at Justice Hall in Old Bailey for selling Twenty forged Notes of one Pounds each purporting to be Notes of the Bank of England to which Indictment Your Petitioner Pleaded Guilty & was Sentence to be Transported for the Term of Fourteen Years. That Your Petitioner is by Trade an Engine Weaver & worked in the employ of the Honble East India Company for fourteen years with unblemished Character till in anfortunate hour he became acquainted a man Name George Morris [**668/9**] who by the artful allurement of a reward prevailed on Your Petitioner to Convey the said forged Notes to one of his acquaintances named Aikens for eight Pounds which your Petitioner through Inexperience not knowing the fatal tendency of his Mission complied with. When Aikens informed against your Petitioner on which he was apprehended, tried and Convicted in order to atone as far as lay in his power for so flagrant breach of the Law Your Petitioner sent his wife to M[r] Westwood to inform him of every Transaction he knew of Morris both in respect of the forged Notes and the making the three Shillings pieces for which the said George Morris is sentenced to three months Imprisonment in the House of Correction. That Your Petitioner has a wife and four Infant Children entirely dependant on his for support but his being upwards of Six

Months confined they now descend to the lowest ebb of misery and distress having been obliged to part with every saleable Article they have for subsistence she is now using her utmost endeavours to obtain permission to take herself & family to New South Wales the place of his Destination which she has hopes to obtain

Your Petitioner therefore most humbly prays that your Honours would be pleased to take his familys most unfortunate situation into your humane consideration to grant them some present relief as to your Honours Wisdom & Humanity may seem meet

And your Honours Petitioner as in gratitude &c Duty Bound shall ever pray Sir Samuel Gilbert

Annotated: Rejected

Attached: petition of Mary Gilbert, Samuel's wife asking help to get work to support her children.

[*BECLS: 29 Feb. 1816, agree to send her £25.*]

675. *[25/11/108] George Blaker, Newgate, undated in 1816*

Sir I am sorry to be thus troublesome to you but owing to me and my wife being so long Confined we are reduced to the Greatest distress and at the time I was taken into Custody Mr Reed the officer took from me 2£ in Notes and some silver, I have applied to him Several times for it and he always put the person I sent to him Off with Evasive answers. Till Absolute Necessity Obliged me to Apply to the Magistrates for it, when Reed informed him he had given the money to a Turnkey belonging to this place, but he has since been with me and says he has given the 2£ to you. If that is the Case, I hope you will Take my distressed situation into your Consideration and Let me have it, as I assure you I have no means to procure any necessarys without it &c

I am Sir your Obedient Servant George Blaker

676. *[25/11/111] Female prisoner* [*undoubtedly Grace Blaker*], *Newgate, undated in 1816*

Honored Sir With Humble submission I beg leave to Address you relying on your Well Known goodness to Excuse this presumption but as you have extended your Benevolence to my fellow prisoners and hope You will not Exclude me I have been a long time in prison without a friend to render me any Relief which is mostly the case with those who depart from on Rectitude which I Unfortunately Experiance[d] and I humbly hope you will Extend Your Charity for I am in the greatest Distress there is 2£ 12 shillings which the officers took from My Husband which we never have had

I am Sir with the greatest Respect your Humble Petetioner

677. *[25/11/109] George and Grace Blaker, Newgate, undated*

Hon Sir the Nam that I Menshont in the Letter was Rong I was Thomas Larence [*sentenced to fourteen yrs trspn, OB, Jan. 1818*] and the Names of the Maker of they Notes Is Jo[n] Lowes and the Other Jacakeps and thay have Both in wone [*illegible word*] and thay Live in Bromigham and Were near the Ship Pubelick Hous and is all the Intiglenes that I Can Give at Preasant but you May Depend that I Will Give you all the Informashon that I Can for I hav mor Shall think My Self in Dutey Bound to Sarve your Gudnes We Remane Hon^{d} Sir you Humbol and Trueley Sarvents George and Grace Blaker

678. *[25/11/106] George and Grace Blaker, Newgate, undated in 1817*
Your well known Humanity to the unfortunate induces me to trouble you, with thes few lines, as I flatter myself you can render me, and my unfortunate wife, happy, in our truly Wretched Situation, we are both Convicted by the laws Our Country and are to be Transported for 14 Years, if through your goodness you Could make interest, for us to go together, We will as in duty bound for ever pray. I trust Sir if you could take the trouble to enquire the Behavior of me and my Wife Since our Unfortunate Confinement, hope you will find we shall not disgrace your kindness
We remain Hon^{d} Sir Your most Obedient and Truly Humble Servants George and Grace Blaker

679. *[25/11/107] Grace Blaker, Newgate, 4 November 1816*
Sir With due respect I humbly beg leave to Solicet your well known benevelence to the unfortunate Give me leave Sir most respectfuly to inform you my Husband is gon on Board redy for his Voyge and I am left in the greatest Distress haveing no Friend now he is gon and nothing but the alowence of the Prison to live on his Relations haveing done all in their power Since our Confindment I therefore have Presume to write to you trusting to your goodness to Excuse this Liberty if Sir you will Pleas to assist me in this my distress it Shall be Ever Greatfully acknoledged by Sir your much distresed humble Sevant Grace Blaker

680. *[25/11/110] Sarah Gardener, Newgate, 17 January 1817*
Sir I hope you will excuse the Liberty I am takeing in asking for the money that was taken from me as Mr Gardener is not able to do any thing for me and I am in great distress being oblidged to part with all my few things and have nothing but the Prison alowance these few lines I humbly submit to your kind consideration and Remain your Obe^{t} Humble Ser^{t}
S. Gardener

681. *[25/11/112] Robert Waples,* Bellerophon *hulk, Sheerness, 11 September 1816*
James Westwood, Esq, Sir Understanding that the Attachmment lodged against the forty Pounds which you had in your Hands by Virtue of the Authority delegated to you from the Bank of England has been withdrawn, and being at present in a very reduced and necessitous State, not a little encircled by my sudden and unexpected Removal here, I take the liberty of addressing you, humbly entreating your Kindness in asking the Restitution of the same to the bearer hereof, in conformity with your express Promise made at the Time of my Confinement in Cold Bath fields House of Correction. During my Imprisonment I have been compelled to dispose of those few Articles of Sustenance which I had been possessed of for immediate

support, thus am at this moment literally penniless, destitute of even a shilling to soften the hardship of my distressed Situation or purchase the most common Articles which may be necessary on Arrival at Botany Bay
Should the Case of my Right to the Sum in Question remain yet Undecided, your well known Humanity and Liberality of Character will doubtless induce your making all possible Expedition in the Procedings or give such Instruction to the Bearer hereof as may lead to her being speedily put in possession of the same
Dwelling however on your Promise and referring to the same with every Certainty if an honourable fullfillment thereof I make no Doubt of being speedily put in possession of my Claim and under this Conviction have empowered the Bearer hereof to give every necessary Receipt and Acknowledgement for the same.
With every sentiment of Respect and humbly requesting a speedy reply.
I have the Honour to be Sir Your most Obedient and humble Ser[t] Robert Waples

682. *[25/11/113] Robert Waples,* Bellerophon *hulk, Sheerness, 25 September 1816*
Hon[d] Sir, Your goodness I hope will Pardon me troubling you so often – nothing but distress shou'd induce me – my Present situation is truly awful – myself wanting some trifling assistance – and my Poor distressed Wife Parting with her Firniture for subsistence may I presume to solicit your humanity in advancing Me some Part of the money now in your hands, any such part as you may be Kind enough to advance, this acknowledgement I hope will be sufficient –
Shou'd you not be able to grant my request, will you do me the Honor to name the time, when the Final arrangement will take Place – as I am likely to leave this Country very shortly – your Compliance will Confer an everlasting obligation on D[r] Sir Your ob[t] Very Hum[ble] Servant Rob[t] Waples

683. *[25/11/115] Robert Waples,* Bellerophon *hulk, Sheerness, 17 October 1816*
Sir I beg to return you my sincere thanks for the Kind answer you gave my Wife, respecting the settlement of the Cash in your hands. She informed me it was to take Place in three Weeks from that time – that time having elapsed I once more intrude on your goodness to forward it as much as Possable – as the distress of my Wife and Self is great – In fact I am deprived of the Pleasure of seeing her – for the want of the Means – the Business as now been in hand five Months – and I looking for a Settlement almost every day – I beg to Conclude, with hopeing you will excuse the repeated Visits of a forlorn Woman –
Sir Your Ob[t] Very Humble Servant Rob[t] Waples

684. *[25/11/114] Robert Waples,* Retribution *hulk, Sheerness, 5 November 1816*
Sir, I am given to understand by my Wife that all hopes are given up, of a settlement of my Business – untill the latter Part of the Sessions – and then

by the Recorder – what he can have to do with it, I am at a lost to guess I think it must be a Mistake of hers – Your answer in writing will much oblige Sir, Your Ob[t] Ser[t] Rob[t] Waples

685. *[25/11/116] Robert Waples,* Morley *transport ship, Sheerness, 18 November 1816*
Sir, I Cannot but Express my astonishment at not having my Business arranged – now in your hands – I have greatly depended on you (knowing you to be a Prisoners Friend) I thought you would have got me my Money – before I left England. I am now on Board the Morley on the Point of Sailing for New South Wales – may I once more solicit your kindness in Paying over to my Wife the Money you have in hand – you will Ever receive the thanks of an unfortunate Man Your Ob[t] Ser[t] Rob[t] Waples

686. *[25/11/117] Robert Waples,* Morley *transport ship, Sheerness, 29 November 1816*
Sir I have beged leave to remit you a Receipt as desired by my Wife – Witnessed by Capt[n] Brown – hope it will be a sufficient acknowledgement for the money – for which I beg leave to return you my Heartfelt Thanks – and assure you it will be the means of my administering many Comforts to my Wife – as well to myself, for which I shall feel myself under many obligations to you for Your Ob[t] Ser[t] Rob[t] Waples

687. *[25/11/118–22] Robert Waples,* Morley *transport ship, Deal, 6 December 1816*
Sir I have this moment received a letter from my Wife, informing me of her Visit to you, and M[r] Miller [*keeper of a public house*] and the subject of Conversation – of which I declare to be false. I must again solicit your goodness in Paying her the Allowance, after deducting the £6 – for which she as a Receipt. Nothing but the greatest distress would induce me, to so repeatedly trouble you. I am now on the Point of leaving my Native Country for Ever – and shall, with Heartfelt gratitude – speak of your Name as it deserves with knowing, I owe my Life to you – in hopes you will grant me this last favour – allow me to subscribe myself Hon[d] Sir Your ob[t] Ser[t] Rob[t] Waples
Attached: copy letter from Bank solicitors, 6 Dec. 1816, to Mr Callaway, town clerk of Portsmouth, enclosing £36 for Robert Waples on ship which that evening or next morning would call at Portsmouth; they had taken £4 of his money to pay back the Person *who was deceived by his forged notes; should ship not pass Portsmouth, Callaway should take his expenses and return rest to them. Letter, 11 Dec. 1816, from Waples on* Morley *at The Downs* [*off Deal*] *to Mr Callaway, stating he had received letter from Mr Westwood of Bank solicitors about his money, but the ship was not going to call at Portsmouth; he requests Callaway to post his money to him by return; note from Callaway's clerk, Archibald Law, 13 Dec. 1816, covering return of £36 to Bank with copy of Waples' letter of 11 Dec.; copy receipt from Bank solicitors to Callaway, 14 Dec. 1816.*

688. *[25/11/123–5] Robert Waples,* Morley *transport ship, The Downs* [*off Deal*], *17 December 1816*
Sir I beg to acknowledge the receipt of your favour of thus informing me of your having remitted the Cash to Portsmouth – the Ship Morley not intending to touch there I on the 10th wrote to Portsmouth, beging that Gentleman to remit it by return of Post to me here – Since which I have recd no answer – and 7 Days having Elapsed I am at a loss to Conjecture. Your reply remiting the cash will be in time Sir your Obt Sert Robt Waples
Attached: undated pages of notes, probably related to events mentioned in **687,** *by Bank investigator made after two days' following Waples' wife to public houses and wine vaults in East Smithfield, the Borough, and to Horsemonger Lane gaol.*

689. *[F25/12/1–3] John Ashworth, Lancaster castle, 10 September 1817, formal petition*
That your Petitioner Now confined in His Majestys Goal the Castle of Lancaster and under the Dreadfull sentance of Death humbly presumes thus to implore the Honble Gentlemen the Governor & Directors of the Bank of England at Whose Mercy your Unhappy petitioner now lies and most humbly hopes that you will spare his life. And by your Honble Clemency you will cause him to be sent to any part of the World. And he humbly hopes you will in pity look upon him in this his Miserable Situation
Your unhappy petitioner that thus humbly implores your forgiveness and Mercy to spare his Life has for Several Years past followed the profession of a farmer in this County and never before this Unhappy Interval fell into any disgrace or had any Unlawful dealings. But always before this misfortune did by care and Honest Industry maintain and support his now perishing and Unhappy family and was by Unforeseen Accident drawn into this Unhappy misfortune
Your Unhappy petitioner being fully confident of the Erors that he has comited and being truly senceable of his Unhappy and Deplorable Situation still prays for the Welfare of that Honourable Society, that influenced by right and just motives, that have thus justly prosecuted him. But humbly hopes that they will yet spare his Life that altho' thus unhappily situated he humbly deploring and Begging Mercy of so Honourable Society as he now presumes to Address he humbly trusting and praying that their goodness will yet Spare his Life and send him to such part of the World, as he may still be of service to the Community at Large and be inabled to render asistance to his Now unhappy and perishing family Your unhappy petitioner must unless happily released by your Honourable pardon suffer Death in a few days and hopes that the Honble Society of whom he earnestly implores his Life will in pity Look upon his most deplorable situation and spare his Life and your petitioner will in Duty Bound ever pray for the good and welfare of these Honble Gentlemen of whom he now so earnestly Begs forgiveness and Mercy
And Should your Honble Society not think proper to spare his Life, he still will most Devoutly pray for the good and Welfare of so Honble Society

Your petitioner here humbly begs to Asign his Name and humbly hopes your Honble Society, the Honble the Govenor & Directors of the Bank of England will in pity look upon his now Deplorable and Unhappy Situation And is with due Respect Your Honours Most Devoted Humble Obed^{t} Servt John Ashworth

Attached: covering letter, 15 Sept. 1817, at direction of John Higgins, governor of Lancaster castle; response from Bank on same date to Higgins stating they cannot interfere, asking that this be communicated to Ashworth.

690. *[F25/12/4] Henry Smith, Guernsey, 20 September 1817, discharged Bank debtor, informs Bank that his wife, whom he sent to England to be with friends, had eloped with a* tall, stout man of 50 *whom she met on the boat; this man, he states, is an importer of forged notes from France into Guernsey.*

691. *[25/12/5–6] Hugh McMahon, Lancaster castle, 22 September 1817*
Honoured Gent^{n} It is with the greatest humiliation possible that I thus presume to lay before you my Melancholy and deplorable situation. Most humbly Craving you will pardon my Presumption
My habit and Course of Life had been for the last 12 years in trading in the Character of a Licensed Hawker, which I have regularly taken out a licence for that purpose And have travelled with Unwaried steps from town to town to Enable me to support myself and my dearly beloved Children, which it was their misfortune to be deprived of one of the best of Mothers when they was very young. And with all the tender feelings of Sencation I have laboured to support them as a tender Parant, Wishing to have them Educated And brought up in a Christian like manner. It was my greatest desire to have my little Innocent and innofensive offspring instructed in the Pathes of Religion and Virtue. But alass all my Expectations are blasted and done away. For unfortunately having in my possession some forged Bank of England Notes, for which I have been sentenced to 14 years Exile from my native country thus my Poor and Imploring Children are left as orphans without father or mother or any friend in the world to take the least care of them, or to provide the common necessaries of life for them. I must solicit and entreat your commiseration in this humble manner in behalf of my unhappy and imploring Children – Please to favour me with a few lines stating how or in what manner I am to give to those who are in the Care of them for there future support. Have the goodness to write immediately as my time of staying here is very uncertain. I may be removed all most any day for any thing that I know – you understand me. I was wishful to know if there is any Provision made by the laws of our Country for the support of Poor ones that are left in this deplorable and unhappy manner – from what I have said upon the subject you'l perceive my meaning and I most Certainly shall Esteem it a particular favour if you will Write to me as soon as convenient, in hopes of your compliance I Remain your Ob^{t} Hum^{e} Ser^{t} with all submission Hugh McMahon

Attached: copy response from Bank solicitors, stating they cannot interfere on behalf of his family: You ought to have considered the destitute situation they would in left in before you engaged in the Criminal pursuits that have placed you in the unfortunate situation. *They advise that only the Poor Law deals with the destitute.*

692. *[F25/12/7] Ann Agnew, not Bank prisoner, Lancaster castle, 31 August 1817, asks to speak to Mr* 'Frishfield'*, Bank Solicitor; see* **714.**

693. *[F25/12/7 double numbered] Stephen Bryant, Maidstone gaol, undated in September 1817, informs Bank his arrest was a mistake; he was employed as agent to sell horses for men called Smith and Newman, had witnessed selling of forged notes and was advised to take some of the notes to Bank; he never meant to offend. No trace of prosecution of Bryant.*

694. *[F25/12/8] William Hammond Crampton and Robert Grey,* Retribution *hulk, Sheerness, 6 July 1817*
Sir We Most Humbly Beg pardon in troubling You. But having sent Once to the Company of Bank of England Concerning Getting the £5 Which His Costomary to be paid after Receiving Sentence. And has we have Received no Answer We Are Informed to Make Our Application to You Which we humbly Beg You will be pleased to Look Into Has we are now in the Greatest Distress And should You butt Condecend to Answer this Letter We Should Be Extremely thankfull. We was try'd at Last York Assizes 11th March 1817
And has we going out of the Country for Life the Money if Could be Gott would be of the Greatest Service and we should have butt Little Doubt of Success if You would Kind Sir Butt Intercede In Our Behalf
We remain Your Most H Sts W Hammond Crampton & Robert Grey

695. *[F25/12/9–11] Johanna McCarthy, Bristol bridewell, 12 May 1817*
Gentlemen I most humbly take the Liberty of acquainting you that I was tried last month at the Assizes in this City before Sir Vickery Gibbs, and was sentenced fourteen years transportation, for uttering forged Notes purporting to be Bank of England. Having some conversation with Mr Evans, Keeper of the Bridewell, respecting the Man that I got the said Notes from, he informed me that if I would tell where the Man was to be found, and taken into custody that I got the Notes that thro' your interference, that my punishment might be altered from transportation to imprisonment. If you should wish for such information, you will please to send a proper Person to treat with me on the subject. In case that there is any thing that can be done for me, respecting my punishment being altered I can assure you that I can so put you in the way of bring him to justice, and come forward to prosecute. There is a number of his Notes at present in circulation, and many people striving to pass them in different parts of the Kingdom. I leave to your better judgement, what is to be done in this business. If you should have occasion to write, you will please to direct to the Care of Mr T Evans, Bridewell.

I am, Gentlemen, Your Humble Servant, Johana McCarthy
Attached: copy letter from Bank solicitors to Mr Evans, keeper of Bristol bridewell, 16 May 1817, asking him to take McCarthy's evidence in writing and submit it to them, emphasising that they can make no promises; letter from Evans to Bank, 25 May 1817, informing them that McCarthy refuses to give evidence without promise of mitigation of sentence.

696. *[F25/12/12] Robert Howes, White Horse Alley, Queens Place, Portsea, undated in March 1810, a discharged prisoner* [*not Bank offence*] *who served six years on* Captivity *hulk, writes confused letter to Bank avowing abhorrence of forgery, his extremely respectable family history, his elevated connections, asking Bank solicitors to tell Mr Capper, superintendent of hulks, home office, that Bank will give him* some hackney writing to copy.

697. *[F25/12/13] William Bagnell, sr,* [**222**] *unspecified hulk, probably* Portland, *Langstone harbour, 17 September 1816, sentenced for counterfeiting silver dollars, thanks Bank for mercy to his two sons who have been pardoned and asks them to support his petition for pardon which is with Mr Capper, home office; he is old, in bad health, and will not be able to stand more years on hulks or in NSW.*

698. *[F25/12/14–15] James Walker,* Bellerophon *hulk, Sheerness, 15 June 1818*
Gentlemen Being sentenced in March last for uttering Bank of England Notes (tried at Lancaster) to 14 years Transportation, I am very desirous of obtaining a passage for my Wife and I am more particularly anxious knowing that she has nothing to subsist upon, and may be led from dire necessity to adopt the same evil practices for which I am found guilty – And if you will have the goodness to solicit the Governors and Directors of the Bank to obtain such favour from Government I shall gratefully make such discoveries – that will prove of the utmost importance and render my Services accordingly
I am Gentlemen your Most Obedient very Humble Servt James Walker
Attached: copy reply from Bank solicitors, 19 June 1818, advising him to apply to sec./state.

699. *[F25/12/16–17] John Whitehead,* Bellerophon *hulk, Sheerness, 14 June 1818*
Gent^{n} I most humbly beg your Pardon in thus Persuming to address you. I Cannot forbear thinking my situation very deplorable when I reflect how, or in the manner in which I was betrayed and persuaded to fetch the notes, for which I have brought myself into such an awful and distressing state, deprived of everything that is dear to me in this world, with no hopes or expectations of ever being restored to my poor unhappy and disconsolate Wife and imploring Children and myself far advanced in years and am in daily expectation of being sent in Ignominious exile from my native

Country in all probabily must never return – and to add to my distress have scarcely a penny in the world. Now if Either you or the Country would have gain'd anything or would have been benifited by using me in this way I must then have thought it would have been nothing but what I should have deserved. But I utterly deny ever being in the habit of making use of the bad Notes. And you may rest assured that it was for no other purpose than what is generally Call'd blood money. I must acknowledge I have committed a very Great Error in not Causing the parties to be brought to justice at the time I first knew anything about them. However I think the information that I have given you both through the Channel of Mr Higgins of Lancaster, and likewise our worthy Captain Mr Owens will be more in your favour than any injury that ever I did in the Notes in all my life. (I absolutely think that it is not lawful to persuade People to commit such Crimes.) Now if no medigation can be effected Either now; or at any future Period, you'l surely have no objection in granting me the favour of my Wife and Children following me as I suppose they cannot go along with me. In Hopes and Expectation of your using your interest in my favour. I remain yours in all due respect John Whitehead

N.B. Please to write to me by the next Post

Annotated: Convicted Spring Assizes 1817

Attached: copy letter from Bank solicitors, 19 June 1818, advising him to apply to sec./state for permission for wife and family to accompany or follow him as Bank have no power to grant this.

700. *[F25/12/18] George Farney,* Bellerophon *hulk, Sheerness, 26 February 1818, not Bank prisoner, offers information about forgers on board hulk with him; he gave Bank information while in Newgate and has now learned more; his wife will attend the solicitors if they wish.*

701. *[F25/12/19–20] Hugh McMahon,* Bellerophon *hulk, Sheerness, 5 January 1818*

Gentlemen I Humbly Take the Liberty of Informing you that it is in my Power to be of Great Service to you to Endeavour to put a stop to the abominable scheme of forgery on your Bank by which so Many Looses their Lives and Liberty of which I am Now Suffering under the Sentence of Transportation to be Banished from my native Country and Leaveing two orphan Children Behind without friends or relations in My absence to be Tortured among strangers which is a Second Death to me in my Present unhappy Situation. I am Particularly well acquainted with the Makers in Birmingham whose names are as follows Mr Lowe Mr Hope Mr Pauls Benjamin Patrick and Mr Shanton that is Liveing in the Neighbourhood of Worcester since his Exit from Birmingham at the time that Joseph Jenings was sent to the [*sic*] [*sentenced to fourteen yrs trspn, Warws. spring ass. 1813*] I also Can Point out to you a press that is Erected in the Neighbourhood of Liverpool for the purpose of Counterfitting the New Gold Coin when put into Circulation. I Further Inform you that I am Particularly acquainted with the Principal Dealers in Notes that Travels to Scotland and Ireland and the towns Frequent which is Edinburgh, Glasgow & Greenock

in Scotland Belfast Dublin and Cork in Ireland since the Bank of England Notes Became a Legal Tender, it is in Power to put a Stop to their Career in which I have seen the Madness and Folly that attends such a Practice by bringing So Many men to shame and Disgrace Sirs, your answer will much oblige your most Ob[t] and Humble Serv[t] Hugh M[c]Mahon
NB Please to Direct for me on Board his Majesties Ship the Belerophon lying at Sheerness Harbour
Attached: investigator's notes listing names and addresses provided by McMahon.

702. *[F25/12/21] Joseph Armstrong and James Jones,* Retribution *hulk, Sheerness, 24 November 1817*
We J[s] Jones and J[h] Armstrong Jointley agree to solicit Your Honourable Com[py] for what we are given to Understand you allow to those persons who accept the privelige Your humanity induces You to offer we mean that of pleading, we are Informed that upon leaving the Country You allow a certain Sum which we trust Your Justness and Generosity will not withold from Us we further trust that You will favour Us with an answer and if we have acted imprudently by asking what Your Bounty allows or have been misinformed that your Honourable Company will overlook & Pardon the liberty we have taken we here Subscribe Ourselves Your petitioners Jos[h] Armstrong James Jones
Annotated: £3–19–0 Wrigglesworth & Thorpe Oct 1813

703. *[F25/12/23–6] John Oseland,* Laurel *hulk, Gosport, 10 November 1817, not Bank prisoner, offers information on forgers. Bank solicitors write, 22 Nov. 1817, to town clerk of Portsmouth, Mr Callaway, requesting him to obtain statement even though unlikely Oseland has anything useful to say. Callaway sends, 24 Nov. 1817, long statement from Oseland, advising that if Bank want to interview him they need permission from home office to detain him from boarding transport ship which he is due to do that day. Bank solicitors thank Callaway, 25 Nov. 1817, but say information given is useless.*

704. *[F25/12/27] Edward Bamford,* Leviathan *hulk, Portsmouth, 21 February 1818, not Bank prisoner, asks Bank solicitors to request Captain Steadman of the* Leviathan *to release him; he has been in* fetter'd bondage *for three years; they should also apply to Mr Capper, home office, to explain that he has assisted them to catch forgers and will be of future help.*

705. *[F25/12/28–32] W. H. Brown, keeper of Newgate, 11 February 1818 says he has received letter from prisoner, Lazarus Levy [sentenced for simple grand larceny Jan. 1818], just transferred from Newgate to* Leviathan *hulk, Portsmouth, who wishes to inform on forgers and asks solicitor to come to Portsmouth. Bank solicitors send Levy's letter to Callaway, town clerk of Portsmouth, 13 Feb. 1818, asking him to take statement from Levy but promise no favours. Callaway replies, 15 & 17 Feb., sending Levy's statement [missing from archive], saying since he* *has been transported before he knows he will not be favoured but wants to save others' suffering.*

706. *[F25/12/33] William Shaw,* Batavia *hospital ship, Sheerness, 16 October 1817*
Sir I William Shaw was trid for uteren forged Notes which I pleaded Guiltey to the Same and I understand their is five pounds Given to Each Convict for pleading Guilty for Forgrey and I should be Glad if you will Send the Same if it be Given I ham on Board the Battavy Now lying at the nower Sheirness I ham your humble Servant Wm Shaw
Annotated: Convicted Minor Offence Spring Assizes Lancashire
[*BECLS: 23 Oct. 1817, request refused.*]

707. *[F25/12/34] William Wolstencraft,* Batavia *hospital ship, Sheerness, 16 October 1817 Identical letter to* **706**, *written in same hand, same spelling, Wolstencraft's name in place of Shaw's. Annotated similarly.*
[*BECLS: 23 Oct. 1817, request refused.*]

708. *[F25/12/35] John Outridge, Bedford county gaol, 20 April 1818*
Sir The Declaration of John Outridge who is now a prisoner in the County Gaol at Bedford, under sentence of transportation for 14 Yrs for uttering forg'd notes of the Bank of England; being unhappy in his mind for his past unlawful conduct in the instance for which he was prosecuted and anxiously wishes that the crime so injurious to community for which he suffers, and which he knows is so frequently committed, he conscientiously makes this Declaration, in the hope that he may hereby be instrumental in diminishing and checking that hurtful evil; and may also prevent many persons being drawn into the connection of those men, who ensnare the unwary, by engaging them in various ways to distribute their notes. As he was thus ensnared by the men, who he now herein exposes and discovers, he hopes that it may save many others from falling into their hands.
The men whose names he now discovers, are chief and principal offenders in this unlawful traffick, and who engage others under them to go about the Country at the hazard of their lives and liberty whilst they stay at home, and are enriched by the labour and suffering of them. The first and chief person, whom he discovers is William Taviner No 23 of Hatfield Street, Goswell Street, a young man with a wooden Leg, about 23 or 24 yrs of age discharged from St Thomas's hospital about 9 months ago, where his leg was amputated: a stout made man, about 5 foot, 8 inches high – dark brown hair; this man distributes many forged notes and scarcely a day passes without persons going to receive them of him. The mother ... Taviner [*sentenced to fourteen yrs trspn, OB, Apr. 1818*] of the above man who lives with him, pretends to fetch the notes for the persons who go for them, and she is gone about five or six minutes, and those who apply for the notes pay 10^{s} for a 1£ note; and if they are able to purchase 20, they pay 8£. His mother is about 50 Y^{rs} of age, of the middle size. John Outridge look after Wm Taviner's horse; and when he sent another person to sell the horse at

Smithfield, he then sent Outridge to Biggleswade fair to buy him another, and gave him the forged notes which were found upon him; John Outridge say's that if the above persons have any notes by them, they are kept in a backroom where the mother sleeps.
Another person is Phil Smith [*sentenced to fourteen yrs trspn, Kent summer ass., 1818*], of French Alley, a Corner house, near Hatfield Street, his horses stand at the Black horse Yard, Aldersgate Street, where he may always be heard of, and often seen, at least once a day. This man frequently goes into the Country and takes two or three men with him. He carries the notes, and when they are about twenty miles from London, he gives his men one or two of the notes at a time to purchase articles of various sorts, and they give him the change. The way by which Outridge came to the knowledge of this man was, by his applying to Outridge, and wishing to engage him to travel with him into the Country but Outridge did not agree to his proposals. Phil Smith has his notes from Taviner, the man mention'd before, and whose horse Outridge looked after. John Outridge says that the above men and several others on the same business are always at Smithfield on fridays at the horse market, and go to a public house near they greyhound
Declared by me the mark of John Outridge Witness Henry Goode

709. *[F25/12/36] Bank investigator's notes, 31 March 1818, from interviews with Thomas Atkins and Sarah Orton in Leicester gaol, Atkins under sentence of death, Orton awaiting trspn; they give information on forgers.*

710. *[F25/12/37 9] W. Coles, Oxford Castle gaol, 16 November 1817, debtor, offers information about a horse dealer in prison with him who has forged notes; his letter forwarded to Bank solicitors by governor of gaol, W. Shrubsole, 17 Nov. 1817; 18 Nov. 1817, Bank solicitors ask Henry Taunton, solicitor in Oxford, to interview Coles.*

711. *[F25/12/40] Hugh McMahon, Lancaster castle, 1 October 1817*
Honoured Gent^n^ This is the second time I have to you wrote. [*this letter written between* **691,** *22 Sept. 1817, and* **701** *5 Jan. 1818*] I most humbly desired you to write to me by return of Post. I have waited with the greatest Anxity for some time for an answer, but to no purpose. It is with the greatest humiliation that I thus Presume to address you in behalf of my helpless and imploring Children they are now left Orphaned and destitute of any friends in the World to support them. You must know my time of Staying here is very uncertain. I may be Called away almost any day. And what would become of my poor little ones? I cannot form any idea whatever. My heart is almost burst within me when I reflect upon the awfulness of their Unhappy and distressed Situation. I have as I mentioned in my last been in the habit of Traveling from Town to Town in the Character of a Licenced Hawker, And have done all in my power to support Myself and Children in a just and an honest way. And though I say it no one ever Paid more regard to true honour and discharged their account with more Puntuality than I have done.

Impressed with the tender feelings of a Parent induced me thus to write to you. Not doubting but your honour will Pardon my Presumption in thus soliciting your Consideration.
If their is any Provition made in our Wise and humane Lawes for the support and mentenance of poor helpless and distressed Children left in the manner mine are Please to Condescend so far as to write to me as soon as Convenient Pointing out to me were I am to apply to in behalf of their Succour. In hopes of your compliance to this my request I Remain your most Obedient Servt with all submission Hugh McMahon
Annotated: Com^ee for Law Suits, 25 Septr 1817 Mr Kaye was Directed to write to Hugh MacMahon and state that the Bank will not interfere

712. *[F25/12/41–2] William Stewart, Robert Wardlow and Thomas Currey, Lancaster castle, 8 April 1818*
Humbly implore your Honble Company to take into your Most Serious consideration our Dreadful Condition and humbly Beg you will in your Goodness Spare our Lives, in hopes we might become useful Members of Society in a Foreign Country As we are Doubtful of our unprepared State for Eternity
We beg leave to Observe to Your Honble Company that there are three Men and One Woman that have their Lives Spared for the like offence at the present Assizes
We therefore Humbly beg you will intercede with his Royal Highness the Prince Regent to extend to us the Royal Clemency and your Petitioners as in duty bound will ever Pray
Wm Stewart's mark; Robt Wardlow and Thos Currey
Attached: covering letter from John Higgins, governor of Lancaster castle, 8 Apr. 1818, forwarding petition to Bank, adding that Stewart declared that he was never previously involved in uttering, that he was induced to do so and is extremely distressed; Higgins hopes his case will be considered compassionately.
[*BECLS: same date, petition rejected.*]

713. *[F25/12/43] Alice Willcock, Betty Healey, Catherine Hardacre, and Elizabeth Stott, Lancaster castle gaol, 30 January 1818, to Mr Glover, Bank investigator*
Honoured Sir, I hope you Will Excuse the Liberty We unfortunate Wemen take in addressing you Relating to a little Subsistory Money We understand the Governers of the Bank alows to us unfortunate Wemen Which if you will have the goodness to Intercede with the Governers of the Bank of England We unfortunate Wemen Will for Ever be Bound to Pray for you by so Doing the undersighned Will for Ever Pray for you Alice Willcock, Betty Healey, Catherine Hardacre, Elizabeth Stott

714. *[F25/12/44] Ann Agnew, Lancaster castle, 25 November 1817, writes further letter* [*see* **692**], *fearful that, as she has given evidence in Bank cases, she will be subject to revenge attacks in NSW when she is* *transported* [*seven yrs for another offence*]*; she asks Bank solicitors to get her to* this nue pleas in London, [*presumably Millbank penitentiary*].

715. *[F25/12/45–6] Ann Lord, Lancaster castle, 28 November 1817*
Sirs I have taken the liberty to write this to you, hoping you will excuse the freedom I have taken. I have got a petetion to Lord Sidmouth Secretary of State, signed by all the respectable Inhabitants in and about Newchurch, my native place, the purport and prayer of my petition is that my sentence of transportation for life may be commuted into, and that I may be allowed to be admitted to the Penitentary at Millbank established for the reception of Convicted offenders. I have given you all the information I can respecting forged Bank of england Notes, and shuld any further information come to my knowlidge, rest assured it shall be communicated to you, Sickness and death are light afflictions, nay are blessings when compared to the anguish of the heart, under a sense of being far separated from any communication with my three dear Children, I therfore humbly beg and pray that you will be so kind as assist in forwarding my views and use your Interest in my behalf, with the Bank of england to procure its signature to the Petition (which send herewith directed to them) and forward same to his Lordship and I am sirs your very humble servant Ann Lord
Attached: copy letter from Bank solicitors to Lord, 5 Dec. 1817, saying her petition submitted to governors but, consistent with their duty to public, they will not interfere on her behalf any more than they have already done, but will hand petition to anyone whom she directs to apply for it.

716. *[F25/12/47] Isaac White, Winchester county gaol, 12 January 1818, to James King Esq., Banbury Oxon. (fowarded by a Mr Haynes to Bank solicitors)*
Sir From Your known Benevolence I am induced under my present unfortunate Situation, considering the future happiness of my Wife and Children totally depending on my immediate exertions, to solicit your support, and to point out for your consideration wherein I now consider it in my power to render my Country a piece of essential Service and bring to Justice a Villain by whose artifices numbers of unfortunate Men have been brought into disgraceful punishment. And by due representation of these facts – a Gentleman in your Situation (should you be pleased to support my endeavours) I doubt not, but will convince the Public, that I am not a Man totally lost to the feelings of humanity, and may in a great Measure be a means of Attonement for my past Error in life. My unfortunate and distresfull situation was brought on at an unguarded moment by the Villanous persuasion of a person of Banbury who is a wholesale dealer of Forgeries, and base Coin, and who is daily and hourly in the Vilest practices of seducing great numbers of Young Men to enter into illicit Transactions in defrauding the Public. While I was at Devizes Prison a Young Man was brought there for passing a forged Bank of England Note (Committed for Salisbury Assizes) I asked the Young Man (Taylor his Name) where he took the Note, he told me he had it of his Brother a Horse Dealer, and he purchased them of S___s of Banbury who he said intended to visit the Fairs in Kent and the adjacent

counties this Winter. Were you kind Sir benevolently pleased to represent the case to the Solicitor of the Bank of England perhaps I might be permitted to bring convincing proofs that must convict him in his abominable practices. To this Man only have I cause to appeal to a Just God to bring him to that just punishment he richly deserves. You will be pleased Sir no doubt to understand the purpose of my addressing you on this Subject. And intreat you will also be pleased to advise me on the probability of the business being brought forward, and whether you would imagine it would render me any Service in my deplorable situation I am Sir Respectfully Your most Obed[t] Serv[t] Isaac White
Bottom of letter annotated by its forwarder, Mr Haynes, stating that original recipient wishes it to be sent to Bank.

717. *[F25/12/48–50] David Morgan, keeper of Carmarthen borough gaol, applies first to Mr Bloome of Messrs Biddulph and Cox, bankers of Charing Cross, 4 April 1818, and then, 18 April 1818, to Charles Kaye of Bank solicitors for premium or reward he believes due to him for his exertions in arrests of four Bank offenders. Charles Kaye responds, 30 April 1818, to say he has already been paid two guineas by the mayor, who was in a better position than he to judge what was appropriate; he believes it ample remuneration but will send Biddulph £1 11s 6d to add to the amount already sent.*

718. *[F25/12/51] William Hodge, Bodmin prison, 10 June 1818, utterer of base coin, offers information about six people dealing in forged Bank notes. See* **729**.

719. *[F25/12/52] George Eaststaff, keeper of Reading county gaol, 23 March 1820 to Mr Salmon, Bow Street officer, informing him that prisoner in his gaol has given information on Mdx dealers in forged Bank notes who were waiting for a new design of notes to be issued by Bank as they are ready to copy and issue them.*

720. *[F25/12/53–4] Mary Ann Bradney, Elizabeth Bamford, Rebecca Bamford, Amelia Hines, and Frances Hitchens, Warwick County gaol, 28 July 1818*
Gentlemen, We the undersigned prisoners Confin[d] in the County Gaol of Warwick and Convict[d] at the last March Assizes of uttering Notes purporting to be of the Bank of England for Which We receiv[d] Mercy by being allow[d] to plead Guilty – haveing been in Confinement Seven Months and seeing No prospect of being sent out of the Country (upon Which We are Anxious) – Most Humbly pray to be allow[d] to Expeirance that Bounty Which the Bank as been Know to allow to persons under Circumstance Similar to Our Own – as by Long Imprisonment Our Means of support is Entirely Exhaust[d] and We are Individualy reduc'd to the Bare allowance of the Gaol – Could We be allow[d] the small weekly sum We Shall be for Ever thankfull – Otherwise We pray to be Number[d] With the First Women who are sent out of the Country

We remain Your Very Humble and Grateful Petitioners Mary Ann Bradney [*own signature; she also wrote letter*], Elizabeth Bamford, Rebecca Bamford, Amelia Hinans, Frances Hitchens [*these four names written by Bradney, and signed by mark*].
Attached: copy letter from Bank solicitors to Mr Tatnall, gaoler at Warwick, 3 July 1818, informing him that these women are not fit objects for allowance; date of departure is entirely down to sec./state.

721. *[F25/12/55] William Dowding, gaoler of Fisherton gaol, Salisbury, 19 November 1818, reports to Bank that William Sherwood, apprehended at Kingswood for uttering, who escaped from his prison in Mar. 1817, had been gaoled again, in Brecon, for horse stealing.*

722. *[F25/12/56] James Cannings, keeper of Devizes gaol, 7 December 1818, reports to Bank removal of three Bank prisoners, Isaac White* [**716**], *John Burton* [*cap. con. Winchester spring ass. 1819*], *Henry Manners from his gaol to Winchester gaol to await assizes.*

723. *[F25/12/63–4] James Jelly,* Bellerophon *hulk, Sheerness, 14 May 1818*
Honourable Gentlemen I take the liberty of addressing You in hopes Your honourable company will take it into Your most serious consideration the distressed situation I am now placed in leaving my Wife and family destitute of money and friends; And if Your Goodness would interfere in her going with me as She is anxious to go; And I am doubtful that if I could not be allowed to get her to go with me that poverty would cause her to be guilty of Some Such like crime as mine; And be the means of leaving Six Small children in A Distressed Situation as neither of us has any friends to look after them if She would happen any misfortune which I am Doubtful that by being reduced to poverty as She now is may be the case hir Knowing them that are concerned in Such like as I am hire for I hope that Your Honourable company will consider what I have formerly made Known to you or be the means of sending my wife with me and also that I might gain the liberty of the Island when I reach New South Wales And I and desirous to leave this place as soon as it will be convenient for You to Send me away as I am not of ability to undertake the hardships I have to undergo here
So Honourable company if your Goodness will be pleased to inform me as Soon as possable if I may expect Your Goodness doing any thing in regard of the above mentioned and to be pleased to answer this by return of post and it will greatly oblige Your[s] &c James Jelley
Attached: copy letter from Bank solicitors to Jelly, 15 May 1818, stating governors and directors did not have power to comply with his request, but if his wife would come to London [*from Manchester*] *to petition sec./state, they will recommend her application.*

724. *[F25/12/57–8] James Jelly,* Bellerophon *hulk, Sheerness, 4 June 1818*
Honourable Company By the encouragement You gave me in your letter inabled me to write to my wife to come; Which now She came here to me; and from here She is going to London Where She will call on Your Honourable Company; And I hope Your Goodness will be pleased to consider what I have done for you and both Her and I are ready any time to lead to Your Knowledge whatever we Know and will be pleased to get her liberty to go with me and that if possible in the Same Ship; And assist and inform her how She Should proceed And by the doing it will Greatly Oblige Your M[o] Obed[t] Serv[t] James Jelly
Attached: copy letter from Bank solicitors to Mr Capper, home office, 5 June 1818, saying it is delivered by Mrs Jelly who wants to accompany her husband; they have reason to believe she was involved in Bank note crime and would continue if left behind, thus Bank support her request.

725. *[F25/12/59] William Furman, unidentified prison, 1 August 1818, writes to friend, Mrs Knotts of St George's Street, Boston, Lincs., asking her to visit him and bring some of his clothes; he finds it hard to live on bread alone* in this hot weather; *he hopes to be released in seven or eight months. No trace of this man in Bank records.*

726. *[F25/12/60–2] Thomas Dale,* Batavia *hospital ship, Sheerness, November 1819*
Dale, barber on Batavia, *says that prisoner, Thomas Grey, head nurse on ship, has connections with makers of false notes and coin; the two of them would like an interview with someone from Bank. Grey writes to corroborate this. As no reply received, George Farney* [**700**] *writes, 24 Dec. 1819, to Thomas Atkins* [*Adkins?*], *Bow Street police office, with similar information*

727. *[F25/12/65] John Moore,* Bellerophon *hulk, Sheerness, 23 December 1819, formal petition*
That Your Petitioner is now a Prisoner on Board His Majestys Hulk Bellerophon Sheerness, having been Sentenced to transportation for the term of Fourteen Years.
That Your Petitioner has a Wife and Four Children, three of them Your Petitioner is induced to believe will be provided for by the humanity of Your Petitioners relatives; the Youngest of them, with its Mother are totally destitute, and without the least prospect of a Provision being made for them
That Your Petitioners Wife is in possession of a recommendatory Letter from Sir John Jackson M.P. to Lord Sidmouth soliciting his Lordship to send her to New South Wales on Your Petitioners arrival there, but Your Petitioner being aware of the great lapse of time that must necessarily intervene before that event takes place, is anxious that She may be allowed a Passage in the earliest Female Convicts Ship that leave this Country
Your Petitioner has therefore to Pray You will be pleased to aid with Your influence with Lord Sidmouth her being permitted to do so; whereby a

recurrence to crime may be prevented, which her helpless and unprotected state might otherwise urge her to the commission of
And Your Petitioner will ever Pray
[*BECLS: 30 Dec. 1819, refuse to support petition.*]

728. *[F25/12/66–71] Henry Hobhouse, superintendent of convicts, home office, 28 December 1819, sends extract, at request of sec./state, from letter from master of* Retribution *hulk who has heard about forging activities through prisoners on board, Leeson and Ferguson. Home office authorise Bank to deal with this as they wish and will give support. The master's letter, 27 Dec., gives details of forger, Ellis, and his agents in Birmingham and London. Bank solicitors reply, 3 Jan. 1820, that they have engaged a prisoner, John Wales, lately discharged from hulks, to assist in detection; they require a forged letter purporting to come from Leeson to introduce Wales to Ellis; they ask Hobhouse to organise this, and to ensure that Ellis does not know that Wales has been a prisoner. W. H. Capper's clerk in home office writes to Bank, 31 Jan. 1820, sending first attempt at forged letter, 2 Feb. 1820, which was turned down by Bank solicitors; second attempt sent, 25 Feb. 1820.*

729. *[F25/12/72–3] James Chapple, gaoler of Bodmin gaol, 20 May 1818, sends statement made by prisoner, William Hodge,* **[718]** *about counterfeiters of coin; Bank solicitors forward this, 26 May 1818, to Messrs Vernon and Franklin of Lincoln's Inn, solicitors for royal mint.*

730. *[F25/12/74–5] Thomas Cole, Chelmsford gaol, 17 January 1820 to Mr Archer, clerk to magistrates at Chelmsford*
Sir I have taken the liberty of wrighting theas few lines to you hoping thay will find in a good state of helth as it leves me at presant thank god for it and Sir if you pleas i will turn everdens of the Bank of Forged knotes I Thomas Coal is in Confinement in Chelmsford Goal now and if you will Com down to me I will tell you ware the place is to get them and how i was let in to the like of them and how is Consarned in them for I my self can nather reed nor wright so i hope you will come to me your Self for I dont like to trust to mouch to other pepul for i think it the bes way to aquaint you of it so i hope if you dont Com you will send me a letter and let me know ware you will Com or know so no more at presant from your Humble Sarvant Thomas Coal
Attached: copy letter, 20 Jan. 1820, from Bank solicitors to Mr Archer, asking him to see Cole and take down in writing his information.

731. *[F25/12/76–9] John Yates, Coventry gaol, 5 May 1818, held for possessing sixty-one counterfeit shillings, claims they date from time he was employed by Bank to detect dealers in forged note and coin and requests their help in getting released. Bank solicitors reply, 7 May 1820, that they will not interfere as they understood he had given up to the constables all counterfeit money he collected. Yates asks, 20 May 1820, for compensation for his efforts for them and his expenses. Bank reply, 22 May*

1820, that they will consider his request after his trial provided he is acquitted and can show he is going to earn an honest living.

732. *[F25/12/80–1] Charles Boutcher, keeper of Devon county gaol, February 1820, sends copy of arrest warrants for Samuel Johns and James Bennett, jr., to be brought to London for trial.*

733. *[F25/12/82] Thomas Dudley, Horsham gaol, 1 October 1819, not Bank prisoner, provides formal statement about activities of Benjamin Patrick, die sinker, Handsworth, Birmingham.*

734. *[F25/12/83–6] J. Velton, high constable of Bray, Maidenhead gaol, 8 March 1820, to Henry Hase, chief cashier of Bank, telling him of suicide in the gaol that morning of a young man, James Baxter, held on suspicion of dealing in forged Bank notes. He draws attention to words written in chalk in his cell:* Pray let my dear Wife have the Money the man has got – Mary Baxter, 24 Bryanston Street, Portman Square and My Clothes. *Velton suggests that Mary Baxter be investigated. Further letters, 9 & 10 Mar. 1820, from Stephen Westbrook, Baxter's victim, who had him charged, who says he recovered a piece of torn paper when Baxter was apprehended, containing names and addresses which Bank might find useful. Bank solicitors respond to Westbrook, 10 Mar. 1820, advising they will pay for information if he finds someone to work on the case; they call the deceased Henry Paxton, formerly a gentleman's servant. No trace otherwise of Baxter/Paxton in BECLS records.*

735. *[F25/12/87] James Grime sr, James Grime jr, and Soloman Mather, Lancaster castle, 21 February 1819*
Honoured Sir We they undernamed, do most Humbly Solicit you, to let us have some Money that was taken from us on the 13th day of September last, we was apprehended for Passing Notes, which we understand You Know about, it was taken from us by they Constables of Bolton, who refuses to Deliver it to us their names is Thomas Barrett and others, and we having no other means of Making our Defence but by getting this money makes us take the liberty of writing to you, hoping that you will have the goodness to give us an Order to get it and by so doing You will Entirely Oblige Sir your obedient James Grimes, James Grimes, Soloman Mather
N.B. the Money they took from us is Viz. Old Grime £12 – 0 – 0 Young Grime £1 – 13 – 0 Soloman Mather £2 – 4 – 0
[*BECLS: 25 Feb. 1819, decision not to interfere.*]

736. *[F25/13/1] Alexander Sinclair, Boulogne gaol (France), 10 March 1819, offers information, but says Bank will have to act quickly as he is about to be moved into the* interior of the country. *No information given as to why he is in prison.*

737. *[F25/13/2] James Moxham,* Retribution *hulk, Sheerness, 12 August 1819*
That I the above mentioned is transported for the space of Fourteen years for utering Forged Notes which was Denominated to Be of the Bank of England Has been Informed of the humanity that many individuals have received from the bank after thair conviction in Respect of haveing Remited to them a small premium to render them some thing extry to Subsist on when being convei'd to New South Wales and I petitioner most Humbly prays that if this assertion be a Fact and would return many Sincere Thanks for a trifle of money What you would be pleased to consider nesesary to render me some assistance on my passage as I am destitute of all friends Whatever except my wife which I have Left to lament my unfortunate situation
I am your Most Obedient and humble petitioner as I Duty Bound Does Ever pray James Moxham

738. *[F25/13/3–4] John Fear,* Retribution *hulk, Sheerness, 14 January 1819, formal petition*
That your Petitioner was (on his own confession) convicted at the Old Bailey in June Sessions last, for having a forged one Bank Note in his possession without lawful excuse & was sentenced to fourteen Years transportation for the same
That your petitioner begs leave most respectfully to state, that he has a Wife & 3 small Children dependent on him for support and which by his conviction are reduced to great distress
Your Petitioner therefore most earnestly intreats Your Honors will be pleased to take his situation into consideration, and recommend his case to Lord Sidmouth as deserving of his Lordships interposition with His Royal Highness the Prince Regent for a mitigation of his present Sentence
And your Petitioner will ever pray &c John Fear
Attached: copy letter, 15 Jan 1819, from Bank solicitors to Henry Hobhouse, home office, advising that Fear wishes to petition for remission of sentence which governors and directors of Bank recommend as his wife was principal means of bringing William Weller and George Cashman, notorious dealers, to justice [*both cap. con., OB, Sept. 1818*]; *Bank had enquired into Mrs Fears' character, then employed her under supervision to purchase notes from Weller. Further note on separate paper, in more modern script, undated,* Request for financial assistance £5 given. ref F1/38A, *which is likely to relate to payment made following* **739.**

739. *[F25/13/5–6] John Fear, transport ship* Grenada, *Sheerness, 30 April 1819*
Gen[tn] I hope you will excuse the Liberty I have taking troubling you with Letter but if you will take my unfortunate case into your consideration I am sure you will do all you can for me, I think it very hard that I should now be sent out of my countrey after serving Twelve Months of my time at the Hulks Now I am going away and have not one Shilling to help myself with and what is Wores than all my Wife and family is in the greatest distress

and totely out of there Power to assist me therefore I hope you will supply me with a little Money to obtain me a little Sea Stores and if you would give me a Letter of Recommendation to Some Gentlemen in the Countrey I am going to I shall ever be in duty bound to Pray John Fear

Attached: copy letter, 6 May 1819, from Bank solicitors to Mr W. Bentham, solicitor in Sheerness, asking him to pay enclosed £5 to Fear on Grenada *and tell him his letter of 30 Apr. received but governor and directors can do no more for him; they request advice of payment; letter from Bentham to Bank advising payment made and message delivered.*

740. *[F25/13/7–9] Thomas Porter,* Retribution *hulk, Sheerness, 13 July 1819*

Sirs I hope you Will Pardon me taking the Liberty of Writing to you these few lines to You as my situation his Realy Distressing as I Expect Every Day to be Sent to Botany Bay and if you Will be so Good as to Send me a Trifle of Money to Enable me to Get my Self a few Nessary things for me take With me as I am Very Bad of haveing no one to Give me any Thing in the World but Depending on Your Goodness I am in Duty Bound Will Ever Pray Thomas Porter

Annotated: £5 to Jn^{n} Fear 5 May 1819. 23^{d} July 1819 £5 Sent to Mr Bentham Sol^{r} Sheerness for Thos Porter by Order of Law Commee. Thomas Porter has already given much Information, & has ever since his Conviction evinced a strong desire to be serviceable to the Bank JR

Added to letter, undated, not in same hand, possibly Porter's own: Sir Enny informasion i can give you i will beg a few lines to me be for i go – if Common garden market is Atended on Saterday morning you may be sur to see sum of them i told you pleas to go it mund the Cuntrymen as thay go thair Names Jack Peacock Bib Sammon and Olds Wells besides 6 or 7 woman Sir if you dont send me A penny i will tell you all the same

Further annotated: 23 July £5 sent to Mr Bentham Sol^{r} Sheerness for Thos Porter by order of Law Committee *and note that Thomas Porter had given much help and wanted to be serviceable in future to Bank*

Attached: copy letter letter from Bank solicitors to Mr Bentham, solicitor, Sheerness, 23 July 1819, requesting him to take enclosed £5 to Porter and tell him that his letter of 13 July received; letter from Bentham to Bank, 24 July 1819, reporting he had done as requested.

741. *[F25/13/10] David Crawley,* Retribution *hulk, Sheerness, 14 January 1819*

Honrd Gentlemen With Submission I humbly Petition your Clemency stating my Destress^{d} & Deplorable situation having a Poor Wife and a helpless Charge of Two Children being compell^{d} During my Imprisonment in Newgate to Dispose of every useful necessary even my Wearing Apparel to supply the cravings of Nature & prolong a Burthensome Existance in Keen Distress. Now I Can Learn your honours are Impartially kind to allow the unhappy Convicts who are under a Similar Conviction to myself a trifle to buy some necessaries on the Long passage, and my being Destitute of friends to help my Distress or yield the least Consolation to my

poor Wife and family, which induceth me to write these lines hoping your Hon[rs] Clemencies will Grant to me the same Indulgence, my Prayers shall be to the Celestial Deity for your honours Eternal Felicity
Your Hum[le] Pet[nr] in Duty bound shall ever pray David Crawley

742. *[F25/13/11–12] John Jackson,* Leviathan *hulk, Portsmouth, 21 March 1819*
Sir I hope you will excuse the liberty I have taken in writing to you, but I should not think I did my Duty to my family if I was to leave the Country without disclosing something to you, which will be of great service to the Bank of England, and as I hope and trust I shall go very shortly, if you think it worth while to send some Person down to me I will upon Conditions, disclose to him particulars affecting the Bank which will be of infinite service to it, and the Publick in general, the Condition I do not wish to affect my own releasement, as it is my particular wish to go to the Bay by the first conveyance.
I am Sir Your obedient Servant John Jackson
PS I was prosecuted by you last Sessions at the Old Bailey
Attached: copy letter from Bank solicitors to T. C. Callaway, town clerk, Portsmouth, sending copy of Jackson's letter, asking him to receive communication from him, but not to discuss conditions; they also say that a material Bank witness for prosecution pending at next Surrey ass., has removed herself to Portsmouth, so they wish Callaway to locate and interview her.

743. *[F25/13/13–14] John Jackson,* Leviathan *hulk, Portsmouth, undated in March 1819*
The communication which I stated in my Letter of the 21st instant, is simply this, to inform the Bank, the name of the Person who supplied me with the Notes, his name is Henry Dart [*sentenced to fourteen yrs trspn, OB, Apr. 1819*] who is supplied by a person of the name of Crowder, who lives, I think, at No 9 Pear Tree St Goswell Street Road. Henry Dart is a young Man who did use the Coach and Horses, in Fann St Goswell St but, I believe he now uses a house a few doors one way or other from Fann St. I mean a Public House, Crowder is a Person who has before been transported, but the other is not.
The Conditions that I named are simply these, that I may be sent in the first Ship that goes to the Bay, and that as soon as I get over and write back, my Wife may be sent over to me, and any trifling sum, by way of an outfit you may think proper, but my principal object is to go as soon as I can to the Bay the above is the whole of what I have to say, as to the main facts
I have the honour to be Gentlemen Your obedient Serv[t] John Jackson alias Tarbox
P.S. Henry Dart has a Brother of the name of John, who gets his living by uttering and there is another Person of the name of James Bentley who is always with him for the same purposes. I hope this will be kept a profound secret, as any thing said would be the occasion of very serious consequences

Henry Dart is a thin young man, about 23 years old, and Chas Crowder is a very stout man about 35. Any pecuniary Sum you may think I deserve I would be glad if you would transmit the same to me here
Attached: copy letter, 27 Mar. 1819, from Bank solicitors to Mr Callaway, town clerk, Portsmouth, who forwarded above letter to Bank, saying information given already known to Bank; Jackson well-known to them and he only wanted money; should he contact Callaway again, he should be ignored; they thank him for locating the witness for Surr. ass. [*see above*].

744. *[F25/13/15] John Jackson,* Leviathan *hulk, Portsmouth, 31 March 1819*
Sir, Since writing my first Letter of the 14th instant, a Gentleman has been here to me, but was not empowered on the part of the Bank to offer, as he said, any conditions to me, neither did I expect he would, but I have been waiting, with some anxiety, since Tuesday week last, the day on which Mr Law [*Callaways's clerk*] called on me, for an answer to the Letter, which I then sent to you, but without success, which I am very sorry for, as I should like to have some kind of an understanding previous to my leaving England, which may be in a few Days, indeed it is a thing expected and I should like to know if I have any chance of my Wife coming to me, which would be done, by a mere recommendatory Letter, as I am told, from you to the Secretary of State, after I am over at the Bay, and am settled there, which I hope will not be long first, and as I have no children the expence would be trifling
Sir, I should be extremely glad if it meets the approbation of the Gentlemen of the Bank, if they would, as I am very poor, make me a present of any sum of money if they think I deserve any, for the information I have given you, by way of an outfit, before I go to sea, as I have no means of getting a Shilling, without getting it from my Wife, who cannot spare it, but who will endeavour, by her industry to keep from the Parish, 'till I get her over to me, I am a good mechanic myself, and shall do well there I have no doubt trusting to the well known generosity of the Gentlemen of the Bank
I am, Sir, Your very obedient humble Servt John Jackson, alias Jos^{h} Tarbox
P. S. I might have named two or three who go out regularly with John Dart, & Bentley, there are two more who do go the name of one is George Mason, the other is --- Branch [*Josiah Branch, sentenced to fourteen yrs trspn, OB, Apr. 1819*], a man who hops with one leg; Henry Dart also supplies a great many with notes, to go to him for that purpose I should like to have a speedy answer and please to pay the Post, as I have no money myself

745. *[F25/13/16] John Jackson,* Leviathan *hulk, Portsmouth, 14 April 1819 demands reply from Bank, still wanting to organize his future, requesting money to do so.*

746. *[F25/13/17] John Jackson,* John Barry *transport ship, Spithead, 23 April 1819*
Gentlemen, It is with reluctance that I have taken up pen to write to you again, but it appears to me so very extraordinary that I should not be able to get an answer of any description from you that I am induced to send this my fourth letter to you, requesting an immediate answer to my former Letters, as I am now on board the John Barrey, of Whitby, Capt[n] Ellerby, at present lying at Spithead, but in a few days shall, no doubt, put to sea for the Bay;
Gentlemen, I think you have used me extremely ill in not sending before, you had better direct to me, on board the Leviathan, where we came from as I shall be able to get it better, and please pay the Postage
I am, Gentlemen your very humble Servant John Jackson, alias Tarbox

747. *[F25/13/18–19] John Clark, Lancaster castle, 1 April 1819*
Gentleman of the Bank I have receved a Letter from the Bank stating that the Enformation that I have given is of no kind of use to you But I hope that the Enformation that I have given to the Bank and likewise to M[r] Naden the pelece offeser in Manchester of people that he never nowed on and Likewise I have Informed you the Maker of them which I Could do at aney time for he will mete me at aney distenss with aney number of notes. Besides I have the opertuney of nowen always when he goes to make them being as I slepe in the house with him and if he had no dowen of me I mite now where the plase was that they maid them at But-if had any dowen of me it would onley Be for a week or two so I am shure I Could dow him and them when they were at work Besides I could do M[rs] Smith at aney time and doing hir will Be Better then dowing aney of the makers Because She Serves the whole of the wholesale delers in England and if you Could relese me to do them I would be willing to do aney thing to save my Life and I would do aney wholesale delers in England that you wished and I would be honerable in Everey respect in doing them as fare as lay in my poer which there is not one man in England has the opertunety of dowing them as well as I with the Correspondence that I have had with them and being as I was not allowed to plead Guilty I hope you will consider and spare my Life and Banesh me into another Country where I may hide my Fase and mite take my Famely with me which I hope you will Be merciful to me through my Wife and Children Being as I will Leve a wife and Seven Children that is quite helpless in the world which I hope you will spare my life through taken pitey of them as otherwise I am not worthy of pardon From your hands although I have given you Everey Enformation that Lay in my poer Likewise to the pelese which I Could do aney thing that I propose if I was at my Liberty which you can Liberate me on account of the 20£ note being marked with Red Ink as for me it was as my Witness swore if you think I Can be of aney kind of use to the Bank I hope you will spare my Life as I was not allowed to plead guilty being as there was onley the note against me for payeing which I may be Come a good man and Be baneshed into another country and repent at my Former doings and there is not aney of the priseners that nowes aney thing of me Given you aney

Enformation concerning aney people that is in the note way which cannot give you any more information onley on traveling people and I now that is of no kind of use to the Bank and as I do not mene to say aney more then I am shure to preform Because it is of no kind of use me mention things that now Can not Be of use But if you spare my Life and Banesh me I shall pray for you untill my dying day and Reflect on my former ways which I hope You will be merseful to me a siner John Clark Your humble prisener Lancaster Castle
Attached: copy letter from Bank solicitors, 5 Apr. 1819, to Clark saying they cannot interfere.

748. *[F25/13/20–4] Thomas Le Breton, keeper of Cardiff gaol, 16 April 1819, sends covering letter to rambling statements giving information about dealers making a fortune, from prisoner, Morris Morgan, sentenced to death* [*for uttering, Glam. spring ass. 1819, resp. to life trspn*]*; Le Breton was sure Morgan would not be executed as judge told him, before leaving Cardiff, that there would be no executions in his area. Le Breton states that Morgan is not an old offender and did not warrant severe punishment.*

749. *[F25/13/25–6] Mr Bridle, keeper of Ilchester gaol, 12 May 1820, gives information passed to him by prisoner in his gaol about George Philips, major note dealer in Birmingham. Bank solicitors pass letter to Spurrier and Ingelby, solicitors in Birmingham, 18 May 1820, requesting them to pass this information to police.*

750. *[F25/13/27–8] Edward Hunt, keeper of Portsmouth gaol, 2 May 1820, gives information about David Cunningham, apprehended in Lymington for uttering, but discharged; Cunningham had been re-apprehended and was in Portsmouth gaol; he attaches statement from witness.*

751. *[F25/13/30–3] William Howard, Newgate, 19 October 1820*
Hon[d] Sirs relying on your generosity and Goodness to Pardon this liberty I have taken in Intruding myself upon your notice – I expect we are going away this night and I should not wish to leave this Country before I have fully satisfied you what I know on those very people that brought my wife [*Mary Howard*] in it are the very people that deserve to be punished also I can inform you of our Master Tradesmen that have long been paying this man with them and was so daring to pay them in a Banking House and they will soon know it there If you will Condescend to Call on me or send any Gentleman to me I will inform you of everything I am in Possession of these People's Names where they Live and when they have Passed them as I should be very sorry to Leave this Country before I have Disclosed the whole I have already given one Gent[n] Information of the person who Pass'd a note at his house
I am sir Your most Ob[t] Ser W Howard
Attached: copy letter, 20 Oct. 1820, from Bank solicitors to Mr Callaway, town clerk, Portsmouth, sending copy of Howard's letter as he had left

Newgate and was on Leviathan *hulk where they wished Callaway to interview him; letter from Callaway to Bank, 24 Oct. 1820 with statement from Howard, adding that Howard was now lame from two paralytic attacks; he claimed innocence, induced to plead guilty to accompany his convicted wife to NSW.*

752. *[F25/13/34–7] John Gregg,* Leviathan *hulk, Portsmouth harbour, 8 October 1820, to Mr Ruff, Bow Street officer (forward by him to Bank)*
Sir I have taken the Liberty of writing to You Wich I hope you will excuse me in so doing I am Sir now on Board a prison ship att Portsmouth Wich my sentence is for 14 Years for having In my Preshion forged Notes wich Sir I should Be very much obliged to you if you Could But make itt aney way convenite In comming down to portsmouth as I have Some thing to relate to you wich I cant In Letter, of great consequence, I was tried at the Warrick March Assises wich I hope Sir You wont fail in cooming Down if You Please
I Remain Your Most Humble & Obedient Servant John Gregg
Attached: copy letter, 10 Oct. 1820, from Bank solicitors to Mr Callaway, town clerk, Portsmouth, sending copy of Gregg's letter, asking Callaway to interview him; Callaway responds, 16 Oct. 1820, with statement from Gregg, detailing people and places, taken down by Callaway's Clerk, Mr Blyth.

753. *[F25/13/38–40] J. H. Capper, home office, 17 July 1820, forwards information sent to him, 16 July 1820, by Mr Briant, Master of* Leviathan *hulk, obtained from Bank prisoner, Samuel Lester, via another prisoner, Lester, convicted of possession at Bury St Edmunds, Mar. 1820, provides information that £1 notes can be obtained from William Bullock at the Coach and Horses, Drury Lane, London at 7s. a note.*

754. *[F25/13/41] Abraham Wade, Lancaster castle, 10 April 1821, formal petition*
That Your Petitioner was tried and convicted here of uttering forged Bank of England Notes last Lent Assizes. That Your Petitioner received the sentence of death and is now waiting the time appointed for his execution, which is the 21st of this month. Your Petitioner acknowledges the Justness of his sentence, but having had the plea of Guilt offered him, and not being aware of the Consequence of not accepting it humbly implores your clemency – Your Petitioner is 67 Years of age; has a Wife and four Children who with Your Petitioner humbly beg for a mitigation of the awful sentence to banishment for life
Oh, save then the life of Your unhappy Petitioner – and Your Petitioner will to the remotest period of his existence, for your extending mercy – offer up his prayers for your eternal and everlasting happiness as in duty bound ever pray Abraham Wade his mark

755. *[F25/13/43] Letter, 17 April 1821, to prisoner Jemima Burton, held in Ilchester Castle gaol, from T. Holyland, police officer, Bow Street,*

London, in which he asserts that Burton, used as a witness in Bank case in Bristol, in which he had been an investigator and witness, had given false or incomplete evidence, the case had failed, and he had been ridiculed under cross-examination; he is indignant that she led him into error and harmed his character as an experienced police officer; he cannot understand her motives.

756. *[F25/13/42] Jemima Burton, Ilchester castle gaol, 19 April 1821*
Sir, If the Bank of England will give me my Liberty I will Engage to put Robinson once more in their hands, before the Comeing assize and to do it without their assistance so Effectually that the ends of Justice shall be answered I am Sir your Hu[ble] Ser[t] J Burton

757. *[F25/13/44] Jemima Burton, Ilchester castle gaol, 9 May 1821*
Sir, Long have I hesitated fearing to give offence but at last have ventured to address you, feeling that the Law of Nature allows to every human Being, however their Situation, the priviledge of Justifying themselves when they are wrongfully accused, not for the purpose of endeavouring to Intreat anyone with Respect to my Liberty do I write but merely to vindicate myself from the aspersions Mr Holyland [*Bow Street police officer*] in the enclosed [*see* **755**] hath Cast upon me, that Waldon [*discharged*] knew of Thornleys [*illegible word*] I was aware otherways he could not possibly have engaged to detect them, but that he or his wife was connected with him in the way that Mr Holyland seemed to express I am quite Ignorant of, nor can I ever be persuaded that Waldon deserved the odure thrown on him, I consider myself Bound by every tie of gratitude for the part he took in the Late transaction, nor have I doubt that the plan would fail of success, and that it did, shall ever attribute to mismanagement, as to the Expence that Mr Holyland speaks of I proposed to a Gentleman in the presence of the Governor that Waldon should have of me what money was wanting on the occasion, therefore it cannot appear that I wished to Impose on the Bank of England by engaging them, in a needless pursuit, on Mr Holylands Discernment, that I am obtrudeing on your time I know but Believe me Sir it will be a meritorious act to hear the justification of an unfortunate (and so far as Regards Mr Holylands letter) an Injured Woman, from my Situation my Veracity may be doubted but I can appeal to the Searcher of hearts that I have made use of no Deception in any Information I have given concerning myself Waldon or Thornley [*acquitted on cap. ch., Bristol ass., spring 1821*] and if the Bank Directors will trouble themselves to Consider the Confession I made before trial they Cannot for a Moment Conceive that I substituted falshood for truth as the statement I made must operate much to my disadvantage, but I pay as great a Regard to truth as Mr Holyland and Consider however fallen above the pitty of those that entertain so foul an opinion of me, as to my Conduct since here Mr Bridle [*gaol keeper*] will do me justice I know, I was told that on the Commencement of the plan respecting Thornley a Request was made for me not to be sent off if I am Rightly Informed and Such a Request was made to the Secretary of State I must particularly desire that the [*illegible word*] may be Removed, to keep

me longer here will [*illegible word*] me into the Lowest Abyss of misery tho I am not far Removed from that at present, allow me to present to your Imagination four fatherless Children their mother Situated as I am the little property that I had nearly exhausted from Impositions practised on me since my Confinement, every passing hour teeming with the fate perhaps of one or other of my Children the Recollection of whom drives me to Madness, to desperation, to discribe my feelings Language falls Short, in mercy hear my prayer may I be sent with my family to my place of Destination by the first ship that sails is now my most ardent wish, mine are fine healthy children my own health good – there comes circumstances in human Life by which Individuals however situated are Constrained to pass by the formalities of custom and assume a tone that may appear too familiar or wanting in Respect, this is the predicament in which I now stand and I have no Excuse to offer but my situation and a wish to clear myself of Mr Holylands Accusations. I should be most thankful for it to be known to those who are now the arbitrators of my destiny that its my particular wish for the Sentence awarded me to be Carried into Immediate Effect and for the priviledge of takeing my Children (for from them I cannot be separated) I will devote the Remainder of my Life to Government I care not how hard I work Nothing will be a Hardship to me if permitted to be with my little helpless family with every respect
I Remain Sir Your Hum^le^ Sert J Burton [*letter written in own hand*]

758. *[F25/13/45–9] Robert Wood, Chelmsford gaol, 26 July 1821*
Formal petition requesting to plead to minor offence. Bank had already taken decision, 25 Apr. 1821. Attached: sub poenas for witnesses for Bank in this case, demands from one witness for reimbursement of her significant expenses, and local solicitor's requests for more witness money.

759. *[F25/13/50] Simon Evans,* Leviathan *hulk, Portsmouth, 2 February 1821, to Charles Pole, governor of Bank*
Sir, Pardon the Leberty I have Takon in writing to you to enform that I have been the Dupe of A Hartfull villan woo Was a Compnion of james Gardnor [*cap. con., OB, May 1820*] woo sufferd the Last May for Selling Thes distructive Bad Notes but he Never Could bee Pervaled on me Till that unfortnight Munday Night wich he gave me the Bad Ten pound Note & shood me the Brothell ware him and wife had Been the Sunday Night beefore and gave a Bad five Pound Note an if I would go with the Ten I Should have the Half of it I Bee Came Akuented with these Men throw Living in a Publick House ware thay Both used and I Lodged in the Same to my Misfortune His nam is John Frier and thare is a Nother deler in this wicked Prectis with im the Name James Seath Who Lives in Vine Street Shandos S^t^ and A Cusen of the Same Name in Chaple St N° 8 Oxford Rode and Maney Others of thare Akwentans wich I now suffer for and Labor under Rumatick Panes in my Limbes and very Sory to hear that my Aged Mother 80 years old Lies very ill as I ham the youngest Son and the first that ever disgrast the famley and am now 40 years of Age and Can Prove at the furst Boot Makers Shops in London to the very Hour that I holwas

folwed my Employment for my Living I have Worked Last for Mr McNoughtion Mount St Mr Hoby St jamess St and Mr Ladlow Coventrey St and Mr Burn Pickdilley wich will ancor for my Carector Ever Sence I have been in London and the man that as been My Roun as Lived in this wicked Pracktis this 3 years as is wife as 2 Women that goos with him [*several words illegible under ink blots*] Pasing thes Bad Noats Beiong Furneter to furnich a House for to make into it A Brothell and he Lives in Marabone ner the New Roode and goos to the [*illegible word*] Ship in Wardor St [*illegible word*] and Cooles him Self York Shire jack Pardon this Liberty I have Takeon your humbell Servent Simon Evans

760. *[F25/13/51–2] James Holman, Maidstone gaol, 24 February 1821*
Mr Glover, Sir, Pardon the liberty I have taken for soliciting your interference in my behalf – I am one of the unfortunate individuals who was taken in custody at Greenwich for uttering forged Notes.
My present awful situation I feel with all its force and am truly Repentant for having offended against the Laws of my Country and wish to make every reparation within my power, so that in return the Gentn of your establishment may extend their mercy towards me.
Should the Honble Governor and Company of the Bank of England think proper for you to wait on me I feel confident my information will ensure their most gracious indulgence, and Protection, and that the Country at large will be most essentially benefitted – Your representation of the above statement to the said Honble Company will be for ever imprinted upon my grateful heart and acknowledged by myself and unfortunate Wife I remain My dear Sir Your most Obt Humble Servant James Holman
Attached: copy letter from Bank solicitors to Burr Horn & Burr, solicitors, Maidstone, requesting they visit Holman and take down his evidence, making no promises to him.

761. *[F25/13/53] James Holman, Maidstone gaol, 14 March 1821*
Gentlemen Since my last letter to you I have been considering the great advantage that would be derived (not only the Bank of England but the Publick in general) by having communication with a person who has a Knowledge of the Agressors of crimes particularly those which I have Related in my former correspondence and what I herein state. Viz Manufacturers of Base Coin, Forged Stamps &c &c I make no doubt but this information as well as the former can be accomplished, it therefore remains with you – and the Honble Governor & Company of the Bank of England wether dependancy can be placed in such individuals I Remain Gentlemen Your very Obt Humble Servt James Holman

762. *[F25/13/54] James Holman, Maidstone gaol, undated between February and March 1821, formal petition*
That Your Petitioner was born of respectable parents, who education your petitioner, and brought him up with the prospect of his becoming a worthy and useful member of Society by placing him with Mr Hebb of the Borough aforesaid Tobacconist as a Shopman, and upon Mr Hebb retiring

from Business, your petitioner commenced the Business of a Tobacconist for himself at Saint Margarets Hill in the Borough aforesaid
That your petitioner was unsuccessful in Business owing to his having connected himself with persons whose circumstances afforded them an opportunity of living in a Superior Stile to your petitioner, and your petitioner therefore became involved and was at length compelled to quit his Business which had been the Total Ruin of him and led him to the Commission of the Crime with which he stands charged
That your petitioner was committed early in the month of February to take his Trial at the approaching Maidstone Assizes for uttering forged & counterfeited Bank Notes a Crime for which the Laws of this Country punish with Death which your Petitioner is anxious (not only on account of himself but for the sake of the reputation of an affectionate and virtuous Wife) to Avert
And therefore most humbly prays that the Governors & directors of the Bank of England aforesaid will be pleased to seriously consider his Case and permit him to plead Guilty to the Minor Offence, and prevent the forfeiture of Your Petitioners Life, so that he may yet live to make reparation for his offences
And your petitioner will as in Duty bound ever pray &c James Holman
Attached: page of twenty-nine signatures, names and addresses of inhabitants and housekeepers of the Borough in support of petition.
[*BECLS; 31 Jan. 1821, lesser charge to be put.*]

763. *[F25/13/55–7] Edward Johnson, keeper of Norwich castle gaol, 8 March 1821, informs Bank that George Fryer, Bank prisoner, also head of gang of dangerous housebreakers, escaped from gaol the previous day but had been recaptured* [*sentenced to fourteen yrs trspn, Norfolk summer ass., 1821*]*; another Bank prisoner, John Upcroft, was still at large. Copy of printed notice for Upcroft's recapture under reward enclosed with letter. Both men heavily ironed and desperate; Johnson feels that Bank prisoners should not be held at castle prior to trial but in county gaol. Bank solicitors write to John Skipper, Norwich under-sheriff, 14 Mar., informing him that they have many cases coming up all over country and do not have capacity to move prisoners in Norwich castle to county gaol. When current cases are over, they will obtain writs of* habeas corpus *to move prisoners.*

764. *[F25/13/58–9] J. E. Hudson, keeper of Chester castle gaol, 28 February 1821, writes to John Lloyd, solicitor, Stockport, informing him that a prisoner can tell where to find a cache of printing plates for notes, and £4,000 worth of notes already made; a reward required. Lloyd forwards his letter to Bank; Bank solicitors, 5 Mar. 1821, thank Lloyd and approve letter he wrote to Hudson.*

765. *[F25/13/60–1] Eli Mills, 'Robinhood & Little John', Broad Street, Portsmouth, 13 March 1821, sends copy of threatening letter from J. A. Johnson, attorney, held in Winchester gaol for debt, but carrying on business there. Johnson acts for Bank prisoner, James Stilbee, in same gaol.*

Mills holds, at Bank's request, a forged Southampton Bank £5 note taken from Stilbee; Johnson demands its return to his client otherwise Mills may meet with injury. Mills says note is of no value, asks Bank what to do, adding that the £2 they have already paid him for work on their behalf is not enough. Bank solicitors, 14 Mar. 1821, tell Mills, since note is of no value, to return it to Stilbee to avoid further trouble. When hearings are over they will report to governors and directors who may authorise payment to him. [*Stilbee acquitted, Southampton spring ass. 1821.*]

766. *[F25/13/62] Joseph Franks, Winchester gaol, 10 March 1821*
Gentlemen I most humbly entreat that you will be pleased to communicate to the Governor and Company of the Bank of England, that I am most gratefully obliged to them for having excercised their Mercy towards me on my recent conviction – I beg to assure them as well as yourselves, that I feel that I am indebted to them and you, for a Life which has been generously spared – I hope my future Conduct will prove that the Contrition I feel, is such as will lead to sincere Repentance and Atonement
I am an Old Sickly Man, and from having a severe rupture, cannot endure the Miseries of Confinement equal to others who are free from Infirmities; for which reason (if it is consistent with propriety) I shall feel an additional Mercy confered on me, if I could be removed to the Hulks at Portsmouth, where my Wife and Children could supply me with such trifling Assistance, as may alleviate my distress
I am Gentlemen Your very grateful humble servant Joseph Franks

767. *[F25/13/63] A 'stray' letter, written 30 November 1840 by William Styles,* Duncan *hulk, Sheerness, informing Bank of forgery activities in Birmingham and suspicious activities on board ship.*

INDEX OF PRISONER/LETTER WRITERS

(those accused/convicted of Bank note forgery offences)

Information, where known, given as follows:
Name; ref. no. of letter; age; no. of children; offence; place of apprehension; whether PB offered; court & date of trial; outcome & sentence; further judicial history (e.g. trspn, disposal to hulks or other prisons; payments received from Bank).
[Source references include dates prisoners' cases or letters discussed by BECLS; for London and Mdx convicts, OB case nos. Sources for sentencing, trspn, execution, pardon etc; are TNA: HO26, HO11, HO17, HO 77].

Letter ref. nos **in bold** where written by or on behalf of prisoner; *in italics* where prisoner referred to by another writer.

Abell, Edward [**147**, *622*] 30, sell, London, PB OB Apr. 1813, 14 yrs trspn, sailed on *Surrey*, Feb.1814 [M/313: 17 Mar., 28 Apr. 1813; OBSP: Apr. 1813, cases 405–6].

Adams, John [**440**] 25, utter, London, cap. ch., cap. con. OB Jan. 1819, executed [M5/321: 18 Dec. 1818, 5 Feb., 12 Mar. 1819; OBSP: Jan. 1819, case 201].

Allen, Josiah [**661**] forge, Liverpool, Lancs. spring ass. 1816, charge unclear, sailed on *Fame*, Sept. 1816; see wife Mary Ann, below [M5/316: 15 Feb. 1816].

Allen, Mary Ann [**235**] see husband Josiah, above, utter, Liverpool, PB Lancs. spring ass. 1816, 14 yrs trspn, £5 Aug. 1816 to sail on *Lord Melville* [M5/316–7: 15 Feb., 25 July 1816].

Allen, William (or **Thomas**) [**651, 654**] utter, Lancs., PB Lancs. summer ass. 1811, 14 yrs trspn, still on *Portland* hulk, Portsmouth, Feb. 1815 [M5/311: 19 June 1811].

Anntwistle (or **Entwistle**), **Ann** [**169–70**] utter, Little Bolton, Lancs., PB Lancs. summer ass. 1813, 14 yrs trspn, £5 Jan. 1814 to sail on *Broxbournbury* [M5/314: 15 Sept. 1813, 11 Jan. 1814].

Appleton, Sarah [**533**] utter, London, PB OB June 1821, 14 yrs trspn, £5 to sail on *Mary Ann*, Dec. 1821 [M5/325: 18 Apr., 20 June, 5 Dec. 1821; OBSP: June 1821, case 731].

Armstrong, Joseph (or **John**) [**340, 702**] 25, utter, London, PB OB Oct. 1817, 14 yrs trspn, on *Retribution* hulk, Sheerness, 1817, sailed on *Neptune,* Dec. 1817 [M5/319: 9 Oct., 6 Nov. 1817; OBSP: Oct. 1817, cases 1458/9].

Arnold, Thomas [**441–2**] 21, utter, London, PB OB Apr.1819, 14 yrs trspn; ready to sail Apr. 1819 [M5/322: 24 Mar., 5 May 1819; OBSP: Apr. 1819, cases 530/1].

Ashby, Esther [**235**] sell, Birmingham, cap. ch., cap. conv. Warws. spring ass. 1816, resp. to life trspn, £5 Aug. 1816 to sail on *Lord Melville* [M5/316–7: 15 Feb., 25 July 1816].

Ashton, James [**626**, *627*] 49, previously in Newgate as James Taylor, utter, London, PB OB Sept. 1812, 14 yrs trspn, sailed on *Earl Spencer,* June 1813 [M5/312–3: 19 Aug., 23 Sept., 18 Nov. 1812, 28 Apr. 1813; OBSP: Sept. 1812, cases 634/5].

Ashwell, Sarah [**628, 636**] sell, Surr., PB Surr. spring ass. 1813, 14 yrs trspn, £5 to sail on *Wanstead,* July 1813 [M5/313: 21 Jan., 28 Apr., 7 July 1813].

Ashworth, John [**689**] farmer, sell, Lancs., cap. ch. Lancs. summer ass. 1817, cap. conv., executed [M5/319: 3 July, 11 Sept. 1817].

Astell (or **Esden**), **Lydia** [**398**] utter, Suss., PB Suss. spring ass. 1819, 14 yrs trspn, £5 to sail on *Janus,* Oct. 1819 [M5/321–2: 18 Mar., 14 Apr., 14 Oct 1819].

Austin, David [**439**] 20, utter, London, PB OB July 1819, 14 yrs trspn, about to sail end July 1819 [M5/322: 7 July, 14 July, 29 July 1819; OBSP: July 1819, cases 948–50].

Baddeley, John [**574, 593**] utter, Stafford, PB Staffs. spring ass. 1808, 14 yrs trspn, on *Captivity* hulk, about to sail Feb. 1809 [M5/308: 10 Dec. 1807, 11 May 1808].

Bailey, Ann [**177**] 26, 3 children (one died Newgate), husband also prisoner, utter, London, PB OB, June 1814, 14 yrs trspn; despite continuing trade in notes in prison, Bank paid her 7*s*.6*d.* a week from July 1814 - Dec. 1814; £5 to sail on *Northampton*, Jan 1815 [M5/314–15: 31 May, 14 July, 22 July, 8 Dec. 1814; OBSP: June 1814, cases 580–2].

Bamber, John [**241**] 24, utter, Mdx., PB OB July 1817, 14 yrs trspn, sailed *Lady Castlereagh*, Dec. 1817 [M5/319: 26 June 1817; OBSP: July 1817, case 965].

Bamford, Elizabeth [**449, 720**] sell (with other members of family - see Rebecca below, Ann executed, Benjamin acquitted), Birmingham; refused PB Warws. summer ass. 1818, unsuccessful not guilty plea, cap. con., resp. to life trspn, continued selling in Warwick castle gaol, Bank demanded sec./state remove her to NSW, was refused payment on sailing on *Lord Wellington*, May 1819 [M5/320–2: 1 Jan., 8 Apr., 2 July 1818, 7 Apr., 19 May 1819].

Bamford, Rebecca [**449, 720**] sell (with other members of family; see Elizabeth above), Birmingham, refused PB Warws. summer ass. 1818, unsuccessful not guilty plea, sentenced to death, resp. to life trspn, continued selling in Warwick castle gaol, Bank demanded sec./state remove her to NSW, was refused payment on sailing on *Lord Wellington,* May 1819 [M5/320–1: Jan., 8 Apr., 2 July 1818, 7 Apr., 19 May 1819].

Banister, William [**64–8, 87**] 30, possess, guilty plea Cheshire spring ass. 1808, 14 yrs trspn, on *Retribution* hulk, Woolwich 1808–10, sailed on *Indian,* July 1810 [M5/308: 9 Feb., 27 Apr. 1808].

Bannister, Moses [**494**] saddle & harness maker, utter, London, PB OB Oct. 1820, 14 yrs trspn [M5/324: 1 Mar., 4 Oct., 8 Nov. 1820; OBSP: Oct 1820, cases 1253/4].

Barnard, Mary [**191**] utter, Hatfield, PB Herts. spring ass. 1814, 14 yrs trspn, £5 to sail on *Northampton*, Jan. 1815 [M5/313–15: 1 Sept. 1813, 20 Apr., 22 Nov. 1814].

Barnes, George [**111**, *149*] sell, Kingston, PB Surr. spring ass. 1813, 14 yrs trspn, on *Retribution* hulk during 1813, sailed on *General Hewett,* Aug. 1813 [M5/312–13: 28 Oct. 1812, 24 Apr. 1813].

Beavitt, Mary (*alias* **Gager**, *alias* **Beverton**) [**164, 208**, *210, 235*] 52, 5 children, utter, London, PB OB Apr.1814, 14 yrs trspn; despite continuing trade in notes in Newgate, paid 7*s*.6*d*. a week until Sept. 1816, £5 to sail with 4 children on *Lord Melville*, Sept. 1816 [M5/314 & 317: 16 Mar., 26 Apr., 24 May 1814, 18 July 1816; OBSP: Apr. 1814, cases 216/7].

Belcher, William [**322**] 18, utter, London, PB OB Jan. 1818, 14 yrs trspn, sailed on *Isabella,* Apr. 1818 [M5/319–20: 11 Dec. 1817, 22 Jan. 1818, OB: Jan. 1818, cases 204 & 262].

Bell, John [**663**] possess, Liverpool, Lancs. spring ass. 1816, 14 yrs trspn, sailed on *Elizabeth*, May 1816 [M5/317: 3 May 1816].

Bell, Matthew [**63**], pros. Newcastle ass. summer 1806 for possession, offence possibly in Scotland. No entry in BECLS; only information about him is this letter.

Bellairs, John [**69, 88–91**] utter, Romford, PB Essex summer ass. 1809, 14 yrs trspn, on *Retribution* hulk 1809–10, sailed on *Indian,* July 1810 [M5/308–9: 4 May, 31 Aug. 1809].

Bellars (*alias* **Davis**), **Amelia**, [**76–8, 81**] 3 children, 'old offender', possess (large quantity), London, OB Feb. 1810, 14 yrs trspn, paid 10*s*.6*d*. a week until Apr./May 1811, £5 to sail, on *Friends,* May 1811 [M5/309–10: 24 Jan., 12 May, 6 Nov. 1810; OBSP: Feb. 1810, case 104].

Benham, William [**373**] 70, utter, London, PB OB Jan. 1818, 14 yrs trspn, [M5/319–20: 4 Dec. 1817, 22 Jan., 7 May 1818; OBSP: Jan. 1818, cases 203 & 264].

Bennett, Richard [**314**] 23, utter, London, refused PB OB Sept. 1818, unsuccessful not guilty plea, cap. conv., no record of execution [M5/321: 3 Sept, 24 Sept. 1818; OBSP: 9 Sept. 1818, case no. 1145].

Best (*alias* **Davis**), **Mary** [**629, 636**] 34, forge & utter, London, refused PB OB May 1812, unsuccessful not guilty plea, cap. conv., resp. to life trspn, £5 to sail on *Wanstead,* July 1813 [M5/312: 22 Apr., 20 May 1812, 7 July 1813; OBSP: May 1812, case 448].

Bevan, Esther [**356**] 21, utter, London, PB OB July 1819, 14 yrs trspn, paid £5 (or £2) in Newgate (very ill), further £5 to sail on *Janus,* Oct. 1819 [M5/322–3: 30 June, 14 July, 8 Sept., 15 Sep., 14 Oct. 1819; OBSP: July 1819, cases 948–50].

Biggs, John [**598–9**] butcher, utter, Bath, PB Som. spring ass. 1811, 14 yrs trspn, *Captivity* hulk, Portsmouth, 2nd half 1811 [M5/309–11: 29 Sept. 1810, 24 Apr., 12 Oct 1811].

Blake, Susanna [**185–6**] utter, Andover, PB Hants summer ass. 1814, 14 yrs trspn, £5 to sail on *Northampton*, Jan 1815 [M5/315: 30 Mar., 7 Dec. 1814].

Blaker, George [**215, 675–8**] 32, utter, London, with wife Grace; charged with possession only, OB Sept. 1816, 14 yrs trspn; sailed Dec. 1816 on *Morley* [M5/317–18: 1 Aug., 26 Sept. 1816; OBSP: Sept. 1816, case 846].

Blaker, Grace [**262–4, 675–9**] 22, with husband George, utter, London, PB OB Sept. 1816, 14 yrs trspn, was paid £5 to redeem clothes and £5 to sail on *Friendship*, July 1817 [M5/317–18: 1 Aug., 26 Sept., 1816, 21 May 1817; OBSP: Sept 1816, case 868 (incorrectly recorded)].

Borrows (*alias* **Emery**) **John** [**181**] utter, London. Bank did not prosecute, using as witness against co-utterer, Jacob Isaacs, OB Oct. 1814. [M5/315: 6 Oct., 13 Oct., 3 Nov. 1814; OBSP: Oct.1814, cases 916–18 v. Isaacs].

Boutell, Simon (*alias* **Bailey, Joseph**) [**48, 592–3**] appr. Dec. 1806 in Ireland for altering notes in Kent, PB Kent spring ass. 1807, 14 yrs trspn, hulk at Woolwich, then *Captivity* hulk, Portsmouth, Nov. 1808, sailed on *Indispensable*, Mar. 1809 [M5/307–8: 11 Dec. 1806, 18 Feb. 1807].

Boyd, James McLean [**672,** *673*] sell, Liverpool, cap. ch. at Lancs. summer ass. 1816, cap. conv., in Lancaster castle Sept. 1816 [M5/317: 3 Aug., 19 Sept. 1816].

Bradney, Mary [**449, 452, 720**] sell, Birmingham, with husband Joseph [trsp 14 yrs], refused PB Warws. summer ass. 1818, unsuccessful not guilty plea, cap. conv., resp. to life trspn, continued selling in Warwick castle, Bank demanded sec./state remove her to NSW Apr. 1819, was refused money on sailing on *Lord Wellington*, May 1819 [M5/320 & 322: 1 Jan., 29 Jan., 8 Apr., 2 July 1818, 7 Apr., 19 May 1819].

Branley (or **Brandley** or **Bradley**), **John** [**375–6**] 42, utter, London, PB OB Sept. 1818, 14 yrs trspn [M5/322: 3 Sept, 24 Sept, 8 Oct 1818; OB: Sept 1818, cases 1125–6].

Bridge, Jane [**532**] sell, Manchester, PB Lancs. spring ass. 1821, 14 yrs trspn, £5 to sail on *Mary Ann,* Dec. 1821 [M5/324–5: 22 Nov. 1820, 9 May, 5 Dec. 1821].

Bridge, Joseph [**578**] utter, Lancs, cap. ch., cap. conv. Lancs. summer ass. 1804, resp. to life trspn, on hulks 1805, sailed on *Fortune* Jan. 1806 [M5/307: 19 June 1804].

Brooks, Elizabeth [**404–8,** *418*, **438,** *453*] 43, 5 children, (said to have been cap. conv. before under another name), utter, London, refused PB OB Sept. 1818, unsuccessful not guilty plea, cap. conv., resp. to life trspn Jan. 1819, was refused relief in prison; paid £5 to sail, and further £5 as taking 4 children on *Lord Wellington*, May 1819 [M5/320–2: 23 July, 3 & 24 Sept. 1818, 21 Jan, 5 & 12 Feb., 5 May 1819; OBSP: Sept. 1818, case 1168].

Brooks, John [**248**] 36, known as 'old offender', utter, Hammersmith, PB OB Sept. 1816, 14 yrs trspn, sailed on *Morley,* Dec. 1816 [M5/317–18: 15 Aug., 26 Sept. 1816; OBSP: Sept. 1816, case 850].

Brown, Benjamin [**240–2**] 39, utter, Mdx., PB OB July 1817, 14 yrs trspn, sailed on *Lady Castlereagh*, Dec. 1817. [M5/319: 29 May 1817; OBSP: July 1817, cases 964 & 968].

Brown (*alias* **Conner**), **Catherine** [**296–8, 324**] utter with sister Louisa Kemble, London, PB OB Jan. 1818, 14 yrs trspn, was refused allowance in prison, £5 to sail on *Maria*, May 1818 [M5/319–20: 18 Dec. 1817, 22 Jan., 5 Feb., 25 Mar. 1818; OBSP: Jan 1818, cases 200 & 261].

Brown, Elizabeth [**483, 507**] 25, utter, London, PB OB Apr. 1820, 14 yrs trspn, paid 7*s*. 6*d*. a week from July 1820 until early 1822 when Bank refused to pay any prisoners; still in Newgate Mar. 1823. May not have sailed because of influence of local clergyman's petition. [M5/323 & 326: 15 & 22 Mar., 10 May, 5 July 1820, 19 Dec. 1821, 5 Mar. 1823; OBSP: Apr. 1820, cases 436/7].

Brown, Jane [**218–20, 263–4**] 21, utter, London, PB OB Sept.1816, 14 yrs trspn; paid 5*s*. a week in Newgate Oct. 1816 to July 1817, £5 to sail on *Friendship*, July 1817. [M5/317–18: 1 Aug., 26 Sept. 1816, 29 May 1817; OBSP: Sept.1816, case 847].

Brown, Mark [**656**] said to be previously transported, utter, London, PB OB Feb. 1815, 14 yrs trspn, on *Portland* hulk, Portsmouth, until Aug. 1815 when sailed on *Ocean* [M5/314 & 316: 26 Jan., 24 Aug. 1815; OBSP: Feb. 1815, cases 366/7].

Brown Owen, Elizabeth [**387–90**] utter, Lambeth, PB Surr. spring ass. 1820, 14 yrs trspn, £5 to sail on *Morley*, May 1820 [M5/323–4: 19 Jan., 19 Apr., 26 Apr. 1820].

Bult, William (or **Ebenezer**), [**498**], utter, London, PB OB May. 1820, 14 yrs trspn [M5/323: 5 Apr., 10 May 1820].

Burbidge (*alias* **Johnson**), **Richard** [**531**] utter, London, PB OB Apr. 1821, 14 yrs trspn [M5/325: 7 Mar., 16 May 1821; OBSP: Apr. 1821, case 501].

Burn, Mary [**584–5**] utter, Croydon, PB Surr. spring ass. 1806, 14 yrs trspn, 10*s*. 6*d*. a week in prison until Jan. 1807 when sailed on *Sydney Cove* [M5/307: 4 Dec. 1805, 17 Apr., 26 June 1806].

Burton (*alias* **Champion**), **Jemima** [**532,** *755,* **756–7**] 4 children, possess, Bath (long term offender) Som. summer ass. 1820, 14 yrs trspn, offer of information followed up, used as witness while held in Ilchester castle, fluent writer, £5 to sail on *Mary Ann,* Dec. 1821 [M5/324–5: 2, 8 & 30 Aug., 20 Sept., 5 Dec. 1821].

Bush, Elizabeth [**419–21**] 24, utter, London, PB OB Apr. 1819, 14 yrs trspn, relief refused in Newgate, £5 to sail on *Janus*, Oct. 1819 [M5/321–3: 5 Mar., 9 June, 14 Oct. 1819; OB: Apr. 1819, case 530].

Butler, James [**373**] 25, utter, London, PB OB Apr.1818, 14 yrs trspn [M5/320; 19 Mar., 8 Apr., 7 May 1818; OB; Apr. 1818, cases 578 & 626].

Cadman, Josiah [**513**] royal marine, known as 'common utterer', utter, London, cap. ch., OB Sept. 1821, pleaded guilty, cap. conv., appeals rejected, executed. (Wife Ann Smith/Sarah Cadman appr. month earlier, also cap. conv. OB Sept. 1821, no trace of execution) [M5/325: 26 July, 22 & 29 Aug., 7 Nov. 1821; OBSP: Sept. 1821, case 1095; HO17/49/1/Hh2].

Carnegy, Charles [**560**] utter, London, PB OB Dec. 1820, 14 yrs trspn [M5/324–5: 22 Nov. 1820, 3 Jan. 1821; OB: Dec. 1820, cases 29/30].

Carter, Jane [*514,* **516, 533**] 25, sell, London, PB OB June 1821, 14 yrs trspn, relief refused in Newgate, regarded as notorious criminal, husband and subsequent cohabiting men executed or transported, £5 to sail on *Mary Ann*, Dec. 1821 [M5/325: 23 May, 20 June, 4 July, 8 Aug., 5 Dec. 1821; OBSP: June 1821, cases 731/2].

Carter, John [*381*] 22, utter, London, PB OB Feb. 1820, 14 yrs trspn [M5/323: 19 Jan., 1 Mar. 1820; OBSP: Feb. 1820, cases 366/7].

Carter, Sarah [**465–7, 508, 540–1,** *542*] 18, utter, London, PB OB June 1820, 14 yrs trspn, refused allowance in Newgate as childless, £5 to sail *Providence*, June 1821 [M5/323–4: 7 June, 10 May, 19 July, 11 Oct., 18 Oct., 1 Nov., 22 Nov. 1820, 2 June 1821; OBSP: June 1820, case 754/5].

Chamberlain, William [**216**] 64, utter, London, with wife Elizabeth Stubbs, PB OB Sept. 1816, 14 yrs trspn [M5/317–18: 5 & 26 Sept. 1816; OBSP: Sept. 1816, case 849].

Chandler, Phoebe [**632**] utter, Bristol, PB Bristol spring ass. 1813, 14 yrs trspn, £5 to sail on *Wanstead,* July 1813 [M5/312: 28 Oct. 1812, 28 Apr., 14 July 1813].

Chave, John [**616–7**] 36, 'old offender', tradesman, utter, London, PB OB Apr. 1813, 14 yrs trspn., on *Portland* hulk, Langstone harbour, Apr.-Aug. 1813 [M5/313: 24 Feb., 28 Apr. 1813; OBSP: Apr. 1813, cases 397–8].

Chedlow, Elizabeth [**634, 636**] utter, Stafford, PB Staffs. summer ass. 1812, 14 yrs trspn, £5 to sail on *Wanstead,* July 1813 [M5/312–13: 5 May 1812, 14 July 1813].

Chrisford, William [**110–11**] utter, Feb. 1813 (provinces) PB (?) spring ass. 1813, 14 yrs trspn, on *Retribution* hulk, Woolwich during 1813, sailed on *General Hewett,* Aug. 1813. [M5/313: 3 & 24 Feb., 28 Apr. 1813].

Clark, John [**747**] utter (£20), Manchester, cap. ch. Lancs. spring ass. 1819, death sentence [M5/321–2: 1 Jan., 14 Apr. 1819].

Clarkson, James [**47, 72**] 30, forge, London, PB OB Apr.1807, 14 yrs trspn; Newgate, then *Retribution* hulk on Thames, then back at Newgate; trspn delayed as unfit [M5/308: 18 Feb., 9 Apr. 1807; OBSP: Apr. 1807, cases 263/4].

Clowes, Sarah [**343,** *453*, **456**] possess, Surr., Sept. 1818, Surr. spring ass.1819, 14 yrs trspn, £5 to sail *Lord Wellington*, May 1819 [M5/320–1; 13 Aug. 17 Sept. 1818, 14 Apr., 5 May 1819].

Clowsley, Elizabeth, [**471**] 36, said to have been in Newgate before, utter, London, PB OB Jan. 1820, 14 yrs trspn, £5 to sail on *Providence*, June 1821 [M5/323–5: 1 Mar., 10 May 1820, 2 June 1821; OBSP: Apr. 1820, cases 436/7].

Coe, James [**22**] shopman, father butcher; held on suspicion of uttering in Surr. 1799, no Bank record of prosecution.

Cole (or **Coal**), **Thomas** [**730**] utter, Essex, PB Essex spring ass. 1820, 14 yrs trspn [M5/323–4: 2 Dec. 1819, 14 Apr. 1820].

Cooper, Charles [*129,* **145–6**] 63, utter, London, PB OB June 1813, 14 yrs trspn, died on hospital ship, Mar. 1814 [M5/313: 5 Mar., 9 June, 7 July 1813; OBSP: June 1813, cases 555/6].

Courtney, Susannah or **Susan** [**237, 249, 276**] 24, utter, London, PB OB Apr. 1817, 14 yrs trspn, paid 5/- a week from May to July 1817, £5 to sail on *Friendship,* July 1817. Returned from NSW (as Elizabeth Jones) before expiry of sentence, appr. London, Aug. 1823, cap. conv. OB Sept. 1823. (Not executed, probably re-trsp'd) [M5/318–19: 3 & 24 Apr., 29 May 1817; OBSP: Apr. 1817, cases 584 & 590, Sept. 1823, case 1042].

Coutts (or **Coote**), **Thomas** [**313**] 17, utter, London, PB OB June 1818, 14 yrs trspn [M5/320: 27 May, 26 June 1818; OBSP: June 1818, cases 914 & 927].

Crampton, Hannah [**275**] utter with husband William, Yorks., PB Yorks. spring ass. 1817, 14 yrs trspn, £5 to sail *Friendship*, July 1817 [M5/318–19: 27 Feb., 24 Apr., 29 May 1817].

Crampton, William Henry (or **Hammond**) [**694**] utter with wife Hannah, Yorks., refused PB Yorks. spring ass. 1817, cap. conv., resp. to life trspn, *Retribtution* hulk, Sheerness summer 1817 [M5/318: 27 Feb., 24 Apr. 1817].

Crawley, David [**370, 741**] utter, London, PB OB Oct. 1818, 14 yrs trspn, family to sail with him Nov. 1818, but still on *Retribution* hulk, Sheerness, early 1819 [M5/321: 22 Oct., 5 Nov. 1818; OBSP: Oct. 1818, cases 1430 & 1484].

Croft, Mary Anne [**366**] 19, said to have been in Newgate before (unspecified offence), utter, London, PB OB Oct. 1819, 14 yrs trspn, relief refused, regarded by Keeper as 'one of the worst sort', £5 to sail on *Morley*, Apr. 1820 [M5/323: 21 Oct., 11 Nov., 1819, 1 & 8 Mar., 12 Apr. 1820; OBSP: Oct. 1819, cases 1415/6].

Currey, Thomas [**712**] sell, Liverpool, cap. ch. Lancs. spring ass. 1818, cap. con., held Lancaster castle [M5/319–20: 20 Nov. 1817, 8 Apr. 1818].

Cuthbert, William [**212–3**] 23, utter, London, PB OB Dec. 1815, 14 yrs trspn [M5/317: 23 Nov. 1815, 3 May 1816; OBSP: Dec. 1815, case 11].

Dale, Henry [*129,* **152,** *153*] utter, London, OB July 1813, tried for possession only, unsuccessful not guilty plea, 14 yrs trspn, informer; (wife, Ann, given £5, Apr. 1814), sailed on *Somersetshire*, May 1814 [M5/313–14: 12 & 26 May, 21 July 1813, 20 Apr. 1814; OBSP: July 1813, case 739].

Dardis, Thomas [**614–5**] utter, London, PB OB July 1812,14 yrs trspn, *Portland* hulk, Langstone harbour, Sept. 1812, sailed on *Earl Spencer,* May 1813 [M5/312–13: 25 June, 8 & 15 July 1812, 17 Feb. 1813; OBSP: July 1812, cases 548–9].

Davies, **Prudence** [**532**] utter, Surr., PB Surr. spring ass. 1821, 14 yrs trspn, £5 to sail on *Mary Ann*, Dec. 1821 [M5/325: 14 Mar., 9 May, 17 Dec. 1821].

Davies (*alias* **Young**), **William** [**384**] 18, utter, London, PB OB Apr.1820, 14 yrs trspn [M5/323–4: 1 Mar., 10 May 1820; case not recorded in OBSP under either name].

Davis, John (1) [**593**] utter, Dorchester, PB Dorset spring ass. 1807, 14 yrs trspn, *Captivity hulk*, Portsmouth, early 1809, sailed about Mar. 1809 [M5/308: 26 Aug. 1807].

Davis, John (2) [**620–25**] utter, London, PB OB Feb. 1813, 14 yrs trspn, petition to remain in Newgate as afraid to go on hulks refused, on *Laurel* hulk, Portsmouth, Sept.-Dec. 1813, sailed on *Surrey*, Jan. 1814 [M5/313: 24 Mar. 21 Apr., 16 June, 19 May 1813; OBSP: Feb. 1813, cases 271/2].

Davis, Joseph [**386**] utter, London, discharged, evidence slight Sept. 1818; utter again, London, PB OB Oct. 1818, 14 yrs trspn [M5/321: 3 Sept., 1 Oct., 5 Nov. 1818; OBSP: Oct. 1818, case 1470].

Davis, Mary [**268**] 9 children, utter, Nottingham, refused PB Notts. spring ass. 1817, cap. conv., resp. to life trspn, £10 to sail *Friendship,* July 1817 with all her children [M5/317–19: 22 Aug., 24 Apr., 5 June 1817].

Eastwaite (or **Erstwaite**), **Thomas** [**230, 661**] 30, utter, London, PB OB Dec. 1815, 14 yrs trspn, sailed on *Fame,* Oct 1816 [M5/316: 8 Nov. 1815; OBSP: Dec. 1815, case 12].

Eastwood, John [**592–3**] utter Lancs., PB, Lancs. spring ass. 1808, 14 yrs trspn, *Captivity* hulk, Portsmouth, Nov. 1808, sailed on *Indispensable,* Mar. 1809 [M5/308: 1 Mar., 6 Apr. 1808].

Ellis, (*alias* **Latkow**), **John** (or **George**) [**517**] known as common utterer, utter, London, cap. ch. OB Sept. 1821, cap. conv., all petitions refused, executed [M5/325: 22 Aug., 26 Sept., 31 Oct. 12 1821; OBSP Sept. 1821, case 1097, HO17 Hh22].

England, Mary [**163,** *184*, **189**] 4 children, utter, London, (with husband James, whom Bank discharged), PB OB Feb.1814, 14 yrs trspn; paid 10*s.* 6*d* a week until Nov. 1814, £10 to sail on *Northampton,* Jan. 1815 with 4 children [M5/314–15: 27 Jan., 3 May 1814, 17 Nov. 1814; OBSP: Feb.1814, cases 223/4].

Evans, Ann [**235**] utter, Chester, PB Cheshire spring ass. 1816, 14 yrs trspn, £5 to sail on *Lord Melville,* Sept. 1816 [M5/316–17: 7 Mar., 25 July 1816].

Evans, Simon (or **Samuel**) [**557, 759**] boot maker, utter, London, PB OB Jan. 1821, 14 yrs trspn, on *Leviathan* hulk, Feb. 1821 [M5/324–5: 20 Dec. 1820, 12 Jan. 1821; OBSP: Jan. 1821, cases 241/2].

Farmilo, Susan [**423**] 22, utter, London (with husband whom Bank discharged), refused PB OB Oct.1818, unsuccessful not guilty plea, cap. conv., resp. to life trspn, was refused relief, [M5/321: 3 Sept., 5 Nov. 1818, 10 Mar. 1819; OBSP: Oct. 1818, case 1455].

Fear, John [**738–9,** *740*] utter, London, PB OB June 1818, 14 yrs trspn; 12 months on *Retribution* hulk, Sheerness; petition for mitigation held back by Bank as wife Ann assisting them convict two major dealers; only when both dealers executed did Bank send petition to sec./state who refused it but Bank paid him £5 for his help; sailed on *Granada*, May 1819. Ann Fear petitioned Bank, Oct. 1820 for support for 2 of their 3 children to go to a philanthropic institution; Bank referred her to Jeremiah Harman, former governor of Bank [M5/320–1, 324: 11 June, 8 Oct., 12 & 26 Nov., 18 & 24 Dec. 1818, 8 Jan., 5 May 1819, 11 Oct. 1820; OBSP, June 1818, cases 914, 126].

Fisher, Frederick George James [wife's letters **225–6**] utter, PB Surr. summer ass. 1815, 14 yrs trspn, sailed before Feb 1816; Bank paid wife £20 to enable her to go into service to support herself and child [M5/315: 29 June 1815, 11 Jan., 15 Feb. 1816].

Forbes, Jonathan [589, 593] tailor, utter, London, PB OB, Feb. 1807, 14 yrs trspn, was paid 10*s*. 6*d*. a week in Newgate presumably for information, on *Captivity* hulk, Portsmouth, early 1809, was refused further money on sailing on *Indispensable,* Feb. 1809 [M5/307: 6 Feb., 5 Mar 1807; OBSP: Feb. 1807, case 218].

Foss (*alias* **Haynes**), **Ann [35–9,** *45*] 28, born London, utter, London (with Sarah Whiley, and husband Henry Foss, mariner), cap ch. OB Mar.1804, unsuccessful not guilty plea, cap. conv.; through Bank mediation conditionally pardoned to life trspn, 27 June 1804. (Husband 44, born Devon, charged with possession, sentenced to 14 yrs trspn, on hulks June 1804 to at least Jan 1805, sailed thereafter). Ann Foss previously in prison in London 1794, one year (as Ann Gilbert) for uttering small value counterfeit coins. Bank refused relief as believed supported by husband. Sailed on *William Pitt*, July 1805 [M5/307: 28 Mar., 17 & 25 Apr. 1804; OBSP: Mar.1810, case 273].

Foss, Thomas [131–4, *149*] 32, printer employed by Bank, forgery, London; after attempting to corrupt witnesses, cap. ch. OB Sept. 1813, cap. con., executed [M/313–14: 25 Aug., 16, 22 & 29 Sept., 20 Oct. 1813: OBSP: Sept.1813, case 875].

France, Richard [601] possess, Lancaster, Lancs. summer ass. 1810, 14 yrs trspn, on *Portland* hulk, Langstone harbour, June 1811 [M5/309–10: 8 Aug., 18 Sept. 1810].

Franks, Joseph [766] utter, Portsmouth, PB Southampton spring ass. 1821, 14 yrs trspn, held Winchester gaol [M5/325: 22 Feb., 9 May 1821].

Fuller, Thomas [392] utter, Borough, PB Surr. spring ass. 1820, 14 yrs trspn [M5/323–4: 18 Aug. 1819, 19 Apr. 1820].

Games, Charles (*alias* **Garner, George**) **[158]** 'old offender', 34, utter, London, PB OB June 1813, 14 yrs trspn, on *Retribution* hulk, Woolwich rest of 1813, sailed with family (to whom Bank agreed to pay £10) on *Surrey*, Feb.1814 [M5/313–14: 12 May, 9 June 1813, 1 Dec. 1813; OBSP: June 1813, cases 548/9].

Gardener, Sarah [267, 680] 24, utter, London, PB, OB Dec. 1816, 14 yrs trspn, paid 5*s*. a week in Newgate from Dec. 1817 [M5/318: 21 Nov., 10 Dec., 19 Dec. 1816; OBSP: Dec. 1816, cases 37/38].

Gearing (or **Garing**, or **Gerain**), **Michael [603–4]** 66, possess, London, unsuccessful not guilty plea OB Jan. 1810, 14 yrs trspn: (wife Susannah, 77, cap. conv. for uttering, died in Newgate awaiting execution). He was paid 5*s*. a week in Newgate, but was refused money Aug. 1810 on going to *Zealand* hulk, Sheerness; also refused when requested from *Discovery* hospital ship, June 1812 [M5/309 & 312: 28 Dec. 1809, 24 Jan., 12 May, 17 Aug. 1810, 10 June 1812; OBSP: Jan. 1810, case 106].

Harrison, Charlotte [**238**] 18, utter, London, PB OB Feb. 1817, 14 yrs trspn, paid 5*s*. a week from 6 Mar. 1817 [M5/318: 6 & 27 Feb., 6 Mar. 1817; OBSP: Feb. 1817, case 425].

Harrison, William, [**241**], no trace of this person being prosecuted by Bank either in BECLS or OBSP.

Hartnell (or **Hartned** or **Wilson** or **Read**), **Mary** [**318, 429, 438,** *453*] 26, 2 children, utter, London, PB OB Oct. 1818, 14 yrs trspn, paid 7*s*. 6*d*. a week from Jan. to Oct. 1819, £5 to sail on *Lord Wellington*, May 1819 [M5/321–2: 24 Sept., 5 Nov. 1818, 1 Jan., 5 May 1819; OBSP: Oct. 1818, cases 1430 & 1484].

Harvey, William [**244–5**] 34, licensed navy agent, previously imprisoned for perjury, utter, London, PB OB Sept. 1817, 14 yrs trspn, sailed on *Lady Castlereagh,* Dec. 1817 [M5/319: 4 & 25 Sept. 1817; OBSP: Sept. 1817, cases 1138 & 1158].

Hatfield, Amelia [**176,** *177*] 22, 2 children, utter, London, PB OB May 1814, 14 yrs trspn. (Brothers John 29, and Thomas, 24, similarly tried/sentenced 1814; husband in prison awaiting trspn); despite continued trading in notes in Newgate, Bank paid 7*s*. 6*d*. a week from July 1814 until Jan. 1815; £5 to sail on *Northampton*, Jan. 1815 [M5/314–15: 31 May, 14 June, 22 July, 8 Dec.1814; OBSP: June 1814, cases 580–2].

Hatton, John [**582–3**] possess, Manchester, Lancs. summer ass. 1806, 14 yrs trspn, held Lancaster castle [M5/307–8: 14 Aug. 1806, 28 May 1807].

Hayselden (or **Hazelton**), **Elizabeth** [**210, 235**] 34, possess, [300 notes worth £500], Bethnal Green, unsuccessful not guilty plea OB Dec. 1815, 14 yrs trspn; continued selling in prison; all requests for relief while in Newgate refused, also refused money to sail, July 1816 on *Lord Melville*, Sept. 1816 [M5/316–17: 22 Dec. 1815, 11 & 25 July 1816; OBSP: Jan. 1816, case 202].

Healey, Betty [**333–4, 713**] sell, Lancs., PB Lancs. summer ass. 1817, 14 yrs trspn, was refused relief Feb. 1818, £5 to sail on *Maria*, May 1818 [M5/319–20: 3 July, 11 Sept. 1817, 5 Feb., 2 Apr. 1818].

Hearn, John [**373**] variously 25 and 45, utter, London, PB OB Jan. 1818, 14 yrs trspn, sailed on *Morley,* June/July 1818 [M5/319–20: 18 Dec. 1817, 7 May 1818; OBSP Jan. 1818, cases 199 & 265].

Hearson (or **Eyreson**) **Hannah** (or **Ann**) [**104–5, 141, 143,** *627,* **635**] 39, utter, London, (with husband, John) PB OB Oct. 1812, 14 yrs trspn, paid 7*s*. 6*d*. a week from Mar. 1813 in Newgate, daughter with her, £5 to sail on *Wanstead*, July 1813 [M5/312–13: 7 Oct., 4 & 18 Nov. 1812, 20 Jan., 3 Mar., 14 Apr., 30 June 1813; OBSP: Oct.1812, cases 872, 899–900].

Hearson, John George, [103–4, 626, *627*] 39, utter, London, with wife, Hannah, pros. possession only, OB Oct. 1812, 14 yrs trspn, on *Retribution* hulk, Woolwich, early 1813, sailed on *Earl Spencer,* May 1813 [M5/312–13: 7 Oct., 4 & 18 Nov., 20 Jan., 3 Mar., 28 Apr., 30 June 1813; OBSP: Oct. 1812, cases 872, 899–900].

Henningham, William Simpson [**107, 608**] 33, 'old offender', utter (£10 notes), London, PB OB Oct. 1811, 14 yrs trspn; provided information in Newgate, was paid 7*s*. a week for 6 weeks; *Zealand* hulk, Sheerness, May 1812, sailed on *Fortune*, Nov. 1812; wife was paid £5 [M5/311: 25 Sept., 6 Nov., 4 Dec. 1811, 19 Feb. 1812; OBSP: Oct.1811, cases 855–6].

Henshaw, Mary [**235**] utter, Chester, PB Cheshire spring ass. 1816, 14 yrs trspn, £5 to sail on *Lord Melville,* Sept. 1816 [M5/316–17: 7 Mar., 25 July 1816].

Herbert, Rachel [**545**] 20, utter, London, PB OB Nov. 1821, 14 yrs trspn, refused allowance in Newgate, £5 to sail on *Providence*, June 1821 [M/324–5: 27 Sept., 8 Nov., 6 Dec. 1820, 2 June 1821; OBSP: Nov. 1821, case1253].

Hewster, Sarah [**486–7,** *542,* **543**] 45, utter, London, PB,OB June 1820, 14 yrs trspn; relief refused in Newgate, £5 to sail on *Providence*, June 1821 [M5/324–5; 5 July, 19 July, 22 Nov. 1820, 2 June 1821; OBSP: June 1820, cases 754/5].

Hill, John [**303–4, 373**] 38, possess, London, OB Feb. 1818, 14 yrs trspn, was refused relief May 1818, sailed Aug. 1818 on *Mallow;* wife and children followed June 1821, bank refused their request for assistance [M5/320, 28 Jan., 26 Feb. 1818, 2 June 1821; OBSP: Feb. 1818, case 390].

Hill, William [**562**] 36, utter, London, guilty plea to cap. ch. OB Feb. 1824, executed Nov./Dec. 1824 [M5/327: 17, 23 & 24 Dec. 1823; OBSP: Feb. 1824, case 435; HO17:49/I/Hk5].

Hilton, **Catherine** [**532**] utter, Liverpool, PB Lancs. spring ass. 1821, 14 yrs trspn, £5 to sail on *Mary Ann*, Dec. 1821 [M5/324–5: 8 Aug. 1820, 9 May, 5 Dec. 1821].

Hines (or **Haines), Amelia** [**449, 720**] sell, Birmingham, refused PB Warws. summer ass. 1818, unsuccessful not guilty plea, cap. conv., resp. to life trspn, continued selling in Warwick castle, Bank demanded sec./state remove her to NSW, was refused money to sail on *Lord Wellington*, May 1819 [M5/320 & 322: 1 & 29 Jan., 8 Apr., 2 July 1818, 7 Apr., 19 May 1819].

Hitchens, Frances [**720**] sell, Birmingham, cap. ch. to which pleaded guilty, Warws. ass. spring 1818, resp. to life trspn, not listed for sailing [M5/320–1: 12 Mar., 8 Apr., 2 & 16 July1818, 7 Apr. 1819].

Hodges, Joseph [**59**] utter, Surr., PB Surr. summer ass. 1805, 14 yrs trspn, hulk at Woolwich during 1805 [M5/307: 20 Aug. 1805].

Hogan, Lydia [**364, 519–21**] 38, 5 children, utter, London, PB OB May 1819, 14 yrs trspn, paid 10*s*. 6*d* a week in Newgate from June 1819, reduced to 5*s*. a week 5 July 1819 as only 1 child then with her in prison, discontinued 14 Mar. 1821 when moved to Giltspur Street house of correction with mitigation to serve only another 2 years in prison; Bank refused request to continue payment [M5/322 & 324–5: 5 May, 2 & 16 June 1819, 5 July 1820, 14 Mar., 9 May 1821; OBSP: May 1819, cases 807/8].

Holman, James [**528–9, 760–2**] tobacconist, utter, Greenwich, PB Kent spring ass. 1821, 14 yrs trspn, on *Justitia* hulk, May 1821, sailed on *Malabar*, June 1821 [M5/324–5: 31 Jan., 9 May, 20, June 1821].

Hopgood, John [**156**] 25, said to be previously imprisoned, Newgate; utter, London, Bank changed cap. ch. to lesser ch. in view of his being witness for them in case v. William Hughes; PB OB July 1813, 14 yrs trspn, on *Retribution* hulk, Woolwich 1813, sailed on *Surrey* with his family, Feb. 1814. (Bank paid wife Mary, £5 on sailing since also witness in same case for them) [M5/313–14: 7 & 21 July, 1813, 5 Jan. 1814; OBSP: July 1813; cases 724/5, & 747 (witness)].

Hopkins, Mary [**271**] 44, utter, London, PB OB Dec. 1816, 14 yrs trspn, paid 5*s*. week in Newgate from 19 Dec. 1816; moved to general penitentiary Millbank, received general free pardon, 24 Nov. 1821, release agreed 9 Dec. 1821 on grounds of good conduct since confinement [M5/318: 21 Nov., 10 & 19 Dec. 1816; OBSP: Dec. 1816, cases 37–8; HO 17/49:Hh14].

Horne, Mary [**398**] utter, Dartford, PB, Kent summer ass. 1819, 14 yrs trspn, petition to take 6 yr-old son with her on ship refused, £5 to sail on *Janus,* Oct. 1819 [M5/321: 31 Mar., 25 Aug., 7 Oct. 1819].

Howard, Mary [**485,** *552,* **556,** *751*] 45, one child, utter, London, with husband William (see below); PB OB Sept. 1820, money refused in Newgate as child supported by friend; remained in Newgate until June 1824 when ship's surgeon refused her for sailing; since keeper of Newgate reported 'very well behaved', given free pardon. [M5/324–5: 13 July, 27 Sept. 1820, 7 Feb. 1821; OBSP Apr. 1820, cases 993/4; HO17/1/Ch37 & 17/53/2/Ik25].

Jelly, James [723–4] sell, Manchester, Bank wish him to accept guilty plea in exchange for life trspn, he refuses and offers information (Bank request aid of someone who can understand Lancs. dialect); Bank allow lesser charge, Lancs. spring ass. 1818, 14 yrs trspn, on *Bellerophon* hulk, Sheerness summer 1818; wife Catherine, also charged by Bank, acquitted; 10 children; they wish her to go with James to NSW to prevent her further involvement in forgery. [M5/319–20: 11 Dec. 1817, 15 & 29 Jan, 8 & 30 Apr. 1818].

Jenkins, George [581] utter, Manchester, cap. ch., cap. conv. Lancs. spring ass. 1807; resp. to life trspn, held Lancaster castle [M5/308: 6 Dec.1806].

Jenkinson, Mary Ann [43–5] 34, married, from Stafford, japanner, forge & utter, London, unsuccessful not guilty plea, OB Feb. 1805; cap. conv., conditional pardon, May 1805, to life trspn; sailed on *William Pitt*, July 1805. [M5/307: 3 Jan., 28 Feb. 1805; OBSP: Feb.1805, case 202].

Jennings, Joseph [618, 701] possess (98 notes buried in garden), Birmingham, PB Warws. spring ass. 1813, on *Laurel* hulk, Portsmouth, Aug. 1813 [M5/313: 11 Mar., 28 Apr. 1813].

Jervis, William [534] utter, Surr., refused PB, Surr. spring ass. 1821, cap. conv., all petitions for mercy refused, executed [M5/325: 7 Mar., 11 & 18 Apr., 9 May 1821].

Johns, Phillis [537] 39, utter, London, gave birth to boy when held in Giltspur St compter, had 2 other small children with her on arrest, £2 given; PB OB Nov. 1820, 14 yrs trspn; 7*s*. 6*d*. a week while in Newgate, £5 to sail on *Providence,* June 1821 [M5/324–5: 20 Sept., 8 & 11, Oct., 2 June 1821; OBSP: Nov. 1820, case 1253].

Johnson, Hannah [*206,* **207**] 29, with small child, deserted by husband, utter, London, PB OB Jan. 1815, 14 yrs trspn; granted 5*s*. a week until July 1815, £5 to sail on *Mary Ann*, July 1815 [M5/315: 29 Dec. 1814, 9 Feb., 29 June 1815; OBSP: Jan. 1815, case 169].

Johnson, John [592–3] utter, Staffs., PB Staffs. spring ass. 1808, 14 yrs trspn, *Captivity* hulk, Portsmouth, Nov. 1808, sailed on *Indispensable,* Mar. 1809 [M5/307–8: 10 Dec. 1807, 6 Apr., 11 May 1808].

Johnson, Robert [111] 41, utter, London, PB OB Feb. 1813, 14 yrs trspn, sailed on *General Hewett*, Aug. 1813. [M5/312–13: 3 Feb., 24 Feb. 1813; OBSP: Feb. 1813, cases 267–8].

Johnson, Sarah [*514,* **515, 533**] 22, utter, London, PB OB June 1821, 14 yrs trspn, relief refused in Newgate, £5 to sail on *Mary Ann*, Dec. 1821 [M5/325: 2 May, 20 June, 8 Aug., 5 Dec. 1821].

Jones, Elizabeth [**135–8,** *140, 148,* **636, 638**] 27, 3 children, utter, London (with servant, Jane Smith), PB OB Apr.1813, 14 yrs trspn. Previously trsp'd for possession, pardoned by governor of NSW after 2 yrs of this 14 yr sentence, on return to London, immediately committed identical offence; thus not deemed 'an object deserving relief'; £5 to sail on *Wanstead*, July. 1813 [M5/313: 3 Mar., 28 Apr., 16 June 1813; OBSP: Apr.1813, cases 407/8].

Jones, James [**702**] 27, soldier, utter, London, PB OB Oct. 1817, 14 yrs trspn, *Retribution* hulk, Sheerness, Nov. 1817, sailed on *Neptune*, Dec. 1817 [M5/319: 9 Oct., 6 Nov. 1817; OBSP: Oct. 1817, case 1457].

Jones, John [**444**] 21, soldier, utter, London, PB OB Jan. 1819, 14 yrs trspn [M5/321: 8 Jan., 2 & 5 Feb. 1819; OBSP Jan 1819, cases 190–1].

Jones, Mary [**549**] utter, London, PB OB Dec. 1820, 14 yrs trspn, to general penitentiary Millbank, Apr.1821, transferred to hulk *Heroine* during cholera epidemic, granted free pardon, Apr.1824 [M5/324: 1 Nov., 27 Dec. 1820; OBSP: Dec. 1821, cases 29/30; HO17/34/Ek28].

Jones, Richard [**592–3**] possess, Warwick, Warws. spring ass. 1808, 14 yrs trspn, on *Captivity* hulk, Portsmouth, Nov. 1808, sailed on *Indispensable*, Mar.1809 [M5/307: 5 Nov. 1807, 6 Apr. 1808].

Kain, [or **Kaine, Kane, Kean, Keen**] **Catherine** [**171**] utter, London (with husband John Kain *alias* Wright). Both tried OB Dec.1813, (John cap. ch. only, guilty, executed Dec.1813). Catherine PB, 14 yrs trspn; paid 5*s*. a week from date of husband's death, £5 to sail on *Broxbournbury,* Jan.1814 [M5/314: 24 Nov., 22 Dec. 1813, 5 Jan. 1814; OBSP: Dec.1813, cases 27/28].

Kelly, Mary [**401**] 20,' very old offender', utter, London same month, PB OB Jan. 1820, 14 yrs trspn; one child died in prison so paid £2 and then 5*s*. a week; £5 to sail on *Morley,* Apr. 1820 [M5/323: 30 Dec. 1819, 26 Jan., 23 Feb., 1 Mar., 12 Apr. 1820; OBSP Jan 1820, cases 248/9].

Kemble, Louisa (*alias* **Conner, Emma**) [**296–8, 324**] utter, London, with sister Catherine Brown, PB OB Jan. 1818, 14 yrs trspn, refused allowance in prison, sailed on *Maria*, May 1818 [M5/319–20: 18 Dec. 1817, 22 Jan., 5 Feb., 25 Mar. 1818; OBSP: Jan 1818, cases 200, 261].

Kershaw, Thomas [**666**] utter, place not recorded by Bank, May 1816, PB on trial, 14 yrs trspn, on *Bellerophon* hulk, Nov. 1816, sailed on *Morley*, Dec. 1816 [M5/317: 23 May 1816].

King, George [**558**] utter, Surr., PB Surr. spring ass. 1821, 14 yrs trspn [M5/324: 5, 8 Aug., 21 Sept. 1820].

King, Mary [**393**] utter, London, Feb. 1820, bill thrown out by grand jury (unusual for Bank cases), remained held in Newgate for uttering Surr., PB Surr. spring ass. 1820, 14 yrs trspn; £5 to sail on *Morley*, Apr. 1820 [M5/323–4: 9 Feb., 1 Mar., 19 Apr. 1820].

Kirby, Thomas [**379**] 25, utter, London, known as suspicious character, PB OB Oct. 1818, 14 yrs trspn, petition for relief refused Nov. 1818 [M5/321: 24 Sept., 1 Oct., 5 & 12 Nov. 1818; OBSP: Oct. 1818, cases 1430 & 1484].

Lambert, Mary [**548**] 17, utter, London, PB OB Nov. 1820, 14 yrs trspn, relief refused in Newgate, £5 to sail on *Providence*, June 1821 [M5/324–5: 11 Oct., 8 Nov., 20 Dec. 1820, 2 June 1821; OBSP: Nov. 1821, case 1253].

Lane, Timothy [**351**] 52, utter, London, PB OB Sept. 1818, 14 yrs trspn [M5/320–1: 27 Aug., 24 Sept. 1818; OBSP: Sept. 1818, case 1107].

Law, James [**327**] 16, utter, London, PB OB Feb. 1818,14 yrs trspn, sailed on *Morley,* July 1818. [M5/320: 2 & 26 Feb. 1818; OBSP: Feb. 1818, case 390].

Layshaw (*alias* **Wardle**) **Ann** (*alias* **Sarah)** [**565**] utter, London, and Essex, cap ch. Essex summer ass. 1822, cap. conv., resp. to life trspn, £5 to sail on *Mary Ann III,* May 1823 [M5/326: 15 Apr., 23 Oct. 1822, 30 May 1823].

Lazarus, Eleazar [**199**] possess (224 notes) Derby, unsuccessful not guilty plea to lesser charge, Derbys. spring ass. 1815, 14 yrs trspn, *Justitia* hulk Woolwich, sailed on *Ocean*, Aug. 1815 [M5/315: 16 Feb., 1 June 1815].

Leach, Elizabeth [**94–5**] 34, utter, London (with husband Thomas, 48) refused PB OB July 1811, unsuccessful not guilty plea, cap. conv., resp. to life trspn; (husband, who, 2 years earlier served sentence on hulks for another (non-Bank) offence, accepted PB, 14 yrs trspn, sailed on *Fortune*, Nov. 1812); Elizabeth too ill to sail with husband; after year in Newgate, sentence mitigated to life imprisonment in London [M5/311–12: 3 July, 21 Aug. 1811, 27 July 1812; OBSP: July 1811, case 575].

Leeson, Catherine [**400**] utter, Bath, PB Som. summer ass. 1819, 14 yrs trspn, £5 to sail on *Morley,* May 1820 [M5/321: 7 July, 7 Oct. 1819].

Lenny (or **Linney**), **Mary** [**268–9**] 6 children, lodging house keeper/school teacher, able to write; alter & utter, Winchester, PB Hants spring ass. 1817, 14 yrs trspn; £10 to sail (as taking 6 children) on *Friendship,* Aug. 1817 [M5/317–19: 6 June, 22 Aug., 17 Oct. 1816, 24 Apr., 21 & 29 May, 5 June 1817].

Leonard, Susannah [**409**] 49, utter, London (with husband John, 65) refused PB OB Oct. 1818, unsuccessful not guilty plea, cap. conv. with recommendation to mercy, resp. to life trspn, Feb. 1819 [M5/321–2: 22 Oct., 5 Nov. 1818, 18 & 25 Feb. 1819; OBSP: Oct. 1818, case 1454 jointly with husband].

Lomas, John (*alias* **Jecks, Lloyd**) [**522–4**] 19, utter large amount, high value, London, two cap. chs OB May 1822, pleaded guilty to both as believed life trspn was offered, cap. conv., petitions refused, executed June 1822 [M5/326: 6 Mar., 3 & 15 Apr., 8 May, 5 June, 4 July 1822; OBSP: May 1822, cases 758–9].

Longman, Samuel [**492**] possess, London, OB Apr. 1820, 14 yrs trspn [M5/323: 1 Mar., 10 May 1820; OBSP: Apr. 1820, cases 436/7].

Lord, Ann, [**333–4, 715**] widow, sell, with several members of family, Lancs. cap. ch., unsuccessful not guilty plea, cap. conv. Lancs. spring ass. 1817; Bank petitioned for resp. to life trspn, granted May 1817 (they wished her to come to London from time to time to give information on forgers); Bank refused to support her request for move to general penitentiary Millbank, or free pardon, Dec. 1817; £5 to sail on *Maria,* May 1818 [M5/319–20: 27 Feb., 24 Apr., 8 May, 4 Dec. 1817, 2 Apr. 1818].

Low, John Vesey [**154**], no trace of a Bank prosecution against this name in BECLS or OBSP.

Lucas, Martha [**479–80, 505,** *533*] 27, 1 child, utter, London, with husband George (PB and transported), refused PB OB Dec 1819, unsuccessful not guilty plea, cap. conv., resp. to life trspn; petitioned sec./state., Mar. 1820 for further mitigation. Bank granted £5, 12 Apr.1820 as ordered to ship, but unable to go as in poor state of health. Remained in Newgate; Bank granted 5*s*. a week from 4 Oct. 1820 until at least Jan. 1822. Worked as wardswoman. Mother petitioned sec./state, Mar. 1824. May 1824 granted conditional pardon to 14 yrs in Newgate, continuing to work there. (Report from keeper - her work as wardswoman satisfactory, 'becoming and orderly') [M5/323–5: 25 Nov., 8 Dec. 1819, 12 Apr., 4 Oct. 1820, 19 Dec. 1821; OBSP: Dec. 1819, case 51; HO17/34/Eh27 & 17/44/1/Gk22].

Macarthy, Ann [**28–31,** *45*] utter, London, cap. ch. OB Feb. 1804, unsuccessful not guilty plea, cap. conv., conditional pardon to life trspn; sailed on *William Pitt*, July 1805, having assisted Bank by informing on utterers; Bank sent £15 to ship's captain for her use. [BECLS no entry, not recorded in OBSP].

McBride, Elizabeth [**481–2**] 19, possess, London, not guilty plea OB Apr. 1820, found guilty, 14 yrs trspn, was refused money in Newgate, transferred to general penitentiary Millbank, Aug. 1820, granted free pardon as had friends to give accommodation, 1824. [M5/323: 1 Mar., 10 May, 24 May 1820; OBSP: Apr. 1820, case 487; HO17/34/Eh27].

McCann (alias **Murphy**), **John** [**653**] sell, Preston, cap. ch. Lancs. summer ass. 1814, unsuccessful not guilty plea, cap. conv., resp. to life trspn, sailed on *Baring* Mar. 1815 [M5/314–15: 18 Aug., 23 Sept. 1814, 30 Mar. 1815].

McCarthy, Johanna [**337, 695**] utter, Bristol, Mar. 1817, PB Bristol spring ass. 1817, 14 yrs trspn, held Bristol bridewell, £5 to sail on *Maria*, May 1818 [M5/318–20: 27 Mar., 24 Aug. 1817, 8 Apr. 1818].

McDermot, Thomas [**365**] 26, said to have been in Newgate before, utter, London, refused PB OB Oct. 1819, unsuccessful not guilty plea, cap. conv., rec. to mercy, petition for life trspn, in Newgate infirmary Dec. 1819 [M5/323: 14 Oct., 11 Nov., 22 Dec. 1819; OBSP: Oct. 1819, case 1439].

McMahon, Hugh [**691, 701, 711**] licensed hawker, widower, 3 children, possess Lancs., but recorded as cap. conv. Lancs. summer ass. 1817, (if so) resp. to life trspn, in Lancaster castle gaol summer 1817, *Bellerophon* hulk, Sheerness, early 1818 [M5/319–20: 26 June, 11 & 25 Sept. 1817, 8 Jan. 1818].

Maddocks, Benjamin [**592–3**] utter, Walsall, Aug. 1806, no record in BECLS of charge or trial, *Captivity* hulk, Portsmouth, Nov. 1808, sailed on *Indispensable,* Mar. 1809 [M5/307: 20 Aug. 1808].

Marr, Thomas [**363**] 20, utter, London, PB OB Apr. 1820, 14 yrs trspn, [M5/323: 1 Mar., 10 May 1820; OBSP: Apr. 1820, cases 436/7- error in OBSP numbering].

Marshall, J. [**1–2**] held Clerkenwell prison on suspicion of uttering Mar. 1796, no prosecution.

Martin, Catherine [**362, 499**] 20, utter, London, PB OB Jan. 1820, 14 yrs trspn, granted 7s. 6*d.* a week from 9 Feb. 1820, £5 to sail on *Morley*, Apr. 1820 [M5/323: 5 & 26 Jan., 9 Feb., 12 Apr. 1820; OBSP: Jan. 1820, case 234/5].

Mather, Solomon [**735**] utter, Lancs., PB Lancs. spring ass. 1819, 14 yrs trspn [M5/321–2: 8 Oct. 1818, 25 Feb., 14 Apr. 1819].

Mayner, Samuel [**5–6**], held in Tothill Fields bridewell,1781, no evidence of prosecution in Bank records or OBSP.

Mazagora, Mary [*205*] sell, Birmingham, Feb. 1815, cap. ch., unsuccessful not guilty plea, Warws. spring ass. 1815, cap. conv., resp. to life trspn, £5 to sail on *Mary Ann*, July 1815 [M5/315: 24 Feb., 24 Apr., 13 July 1815].

Miares, Clementina Rebecca [**532**] utter, Lambeth, PB Surr. spring ass.1821, 14 yrs trspn, £5 to sail on *Mary Ann,* Dec. 1821 [M5/325: 9 May, 5 Dec. 1821].

Middleton, William [**98, 102**] utter, Suss., refused PB Suss. summer ass. 1812, unsuccessful not guilty plea, cap. conv., resp. to life trspn, on *Retribution* hulk, Woolwich 1812–13 [M5/311–12: 29 June, 5 Aug. 1812, 17 Feb.1813].

Miller, Elizabeth [**394**] 1 child, possess Lambeth, guilty, Surr. summer ass. 1818, 14 yrs trspn, paid 5*s*. a week from Nov. 1818 to May 1819, £5 to sail on *Lord Wellington,* May 1819 [M5/320–1: 2 July, 10 Sept., 19 Nov. 1818, 19 May 1819].

Montagu, Elizabeth [**532**] utter, Oxford, PB Oxon. spring ass. 1821, 14 yrs trspn, £5 to sail on *Mary Ann*, Dec. 1821 [M5/325: 28 Feb., 9 May, 5 Dec. 1821, HO17/34/EH38].

Moore, James [**361**] 30, utter, London, PB OB Dec. 1819, 14 yrs trspn [M5/323: 11 Nov., 9 Dec. 1819; OBSP: Dec. 1819, cases 34/5].

Moore, John [**727**] possess, Borough, Surr. summer ass. 1819, 14 yrs trspn, *Bellerophon* hulk, winter 1819 [M5/322–3: 30 Sept., 29 Dec. 1819].

Morris, Elizabeth [**99, 231,** *627*] no-one of this name prosecuted by Bank around this date; presumably wife of Thomas Slater (see below) and convicted of another offence; Slater about to sail June 1813 asked Bank to give 'allowance' to Elizabeth Morris; refused.

Morris, George [**668–9**, *674*] sell, Birmingham, cap. ch. Warws. summer ass. 1816, cap. conv., resp. to life trspn, on *Bellerophon* hulk giving information, Sheerness Oct./Nov. 1816 [M5/317: 6 June, 19 Sept. 1816].

Morris, John [**306–7**] 33, utter, London, PB OB Dec. 1818, 14 yrs trspn [M5/321: 12 Nov., 24 Dec. 1818; OBSP: Dec. 1818, case 12].

Morris (*alias* **Tongue**)**, William** [**527**] utter, Manchester, PB Lancs. spring ass. 1821, 14 yrs trspn, on hulk *Justitia* May 1821 [M5/325: 14 Mar., 9 May 1821].

Outridge, John [**708**] utter Bedford, PB Beds. spring ass. 1818, 14 yrs trspn [M5/320: 19 Feb., 8 Apr. 1818].

Owen, Thomas [**357–8**] 37, said to have been in Newgate before, utter, London, PB OB Sept. 1819, 14 yrs trspn [M5/322: 8 Sept., 30 Sept. 1819: OBSP: Sept. 1819, cases 1125/6].

Owens, John [**312**] 35, sell, London, PB OB June 1818, 14 yrs trspn, sailed on *Mallow* Aug. 1818 [M5/320: 14 May, 26 June 1818; OBSP: June 1818, cases 91/2].

Paley, Sarah [**475–7, 506,** *533*] 25, utter, London, with husband, George (executed), PB OB Jan. 1820, 14 yrs trspn, granted £5 to sail Apr. 1820, but too ill to go; 5*s*. a week from July 1820 until at least Jan. 1822; employed as wardswoman; keeper of Newgate reported she had worked and behaved well; granted conditional pardon May 1824 to reduce 14 yr trspn sentence to 7 yrs in prison (of which 5 already served) [M5/323–5: 9 Dec.1819, 26 Jan., 1 Mar., 8 Mar., 12 Apr., 5 July, 13 July 1820, 9 Jan. 1822; OBSP: Jan.1820, cases 248/9; HO17/44/1/Gk22].

Pascoe, Elizabeth [**533**] 33, utter, London, PB OB June 1821, 14 yrs trspn, £5 to sail on *Mary Ann*, Dec. 1821 [M5/325: 20 June, 5 Dec. 1821; OBSP: June 1821, case 731].

Paul, Ann [**188**] utter, Lancaster, PB, Lancs. summer ass. 1814, 14 yrs trspn, held Lancaster castle until moved to Deptford Nov. 1814; £5 to sail on *Northampton,* Jan. 1815 [M5/314/15: 23 Mar., 23 Sept., 22 Nov. 1814].

Pearson (*alias* **Wright**), **Elizabeth** [*159,* **165, 183–4, 187**] utter, London (with husband John), PB OB May 1814, 14 yrs trspn, granted 5*s*. a week from May 1814, £5 to sail on *Northampton*, Jan. 1815 although likely to have continued selling notes in Newgate [M5/314: 16 Mar., 29 Apr., 24 May 1814; OBSP: May 1814, cases 314/5].

Pearson, John [**159**] 37, utter, London (with wife Elizabeth) PB OB May 1814, 14 yrs trspn, on *Retribution* hulk, Woolwich during 1814, sailed on *Marquis of Wellington,* Sept. 1814 [M5/314: 16 Mar., 29 Apr., 24 May 1814; OBSP: May 1814, cases 314/5].

Pedley, Martha [**628, 636–7**] utter, Birmingham, PB Warws. spring ass. 1813, 14 yrs trspn, £5 to sail on *Wanstead,* July 1813 [M5/313: 28 Apr., 7 July 1813].

Pendleton, Mary (or **Martha**) [*317,* **320, 377, 460**] 18, utter, London, PB OB Sept. 1818, 14 yrs trspn, refused money in prison until end Jan. 1819 when £2 for her sent to keeper of Newgate [M5/320–22: 26 June, 24 Sept., 8 Oct., 3 Dec. 1818, 28 Jan. 1819; OBSP: Sept. 1818, case 1107].

Pendray, William [349] man's mercer of Bodmin, utter, Plymouth, PB Devon summer ass. 1817, 14 yrs trspn; on *Justitia* Hulk, Woolwich, in 1817 [M5/319: 26 June, 11 Sept. 1817].

Peters (*alias* **Walker**), **William [586]** possess, Gloucester, sentenced 14 yrs trspn Glos. spring ass. 1809; wife, Martha, petitioned Bank for help to return with her 5 children to their parish in Gloucester and was paid £5, June 1810. [M5/308: 2 Feb., 5 Apr. 1809, 13 June 1810].

Philips, William [575–6, *591,* **596]** jailed Warwick castle 1808, no record of prosecution in BECLS; likely not prosecuted but used as informer, since set free from gaol by Mar. 1809.

Pierce, Hugh [600] utter, Birmingham, cap. ch. cap. conv. Warws. spring ass. 1811, resp. to life trspn, on *Portland* hulk, Langstone harbour 1811 [M5/310: 29 Jan., 24 Apr. 1811].

Pilcher (or **Pitcher**), **Sarah**, **[55]** 32, widow, 2 children, utter, London, jointly indicted with Judith Kelly (*alias* Jane Smith, see below); PB OB Sept. 1806, 14 yrs trspn; £5 to sail on *Sydney Cove*, Jan. 1807 [M5/307: 20 Aug., 24 Sept., 23 Oct. 1806; OBSP: Sept. 1806, cases 455/6].

Pilkington, Anne [326] 25, 2 children, utter, London, PB OB Jan. 1818, 14 yrs trspn, 7*s.* 6*d.* a week from 5 Feb. 1818, £5 to sail on *Maria*, May 1818 [M5/ 320: 1 Jan., 22 Jan., 5 Feb., 25 Mar. 1818; OBSP: Jan. 1818, cases 202 & 263].

Pimblott (*alias* **Collins**), **Mary [532]** sell, Lancs., PB Lancs. spring ass. 1821, £5 to sail on *Mary Ann,* Dec. 1821 [M5/324–5: 7 Mar., 9 May, 5 Dec. 1821].

Platt, Mary Ann [536] utter, London, PB OB Dec. 1820, 14 yrs trspn, £5 to sail on *Providence*, June 1821 [M5/324–5: 8 Nov.1820, 3 Jan., 2 June 1821; OBSP: Dec. 1820, cases 29/30].

Polley, Hannah [369, 413, 430–1] 51, said to have been in Newgate before, sell London, cap. ch., persuaded by Bank to plead guilty on guarantee of life trspn, OB June 1818, judge refused to accede to this, cap. conv.; resp. to life trspn Feb. 1819. Sec./state & Prince Regent objected to Bank strategies and reprimanded them. This appears to have been held against her; appeals for relief refused until Feb. 1819 when in great distress and keeper was paid £2 for her. [M5/320–1: 15 June, 26 June, 2 July, 15 Oct. 1818, 2 Feb., 9 June 1819; OBSP: June 1818, case 915].

Porter, Thomas [**166,** *402,* **445, 740**] 40, said to have been in Newgate before, possess, London, OB May 1819, unsuccessful not guilty plea, 14 yrs trspn, on *Retribution* hulk July 1819, where paid £5 for assisting Bank with information [M5/322: 19 May, 2 June 1819; OBSP: May 1819, case 829].

Price, George [**446**] 20, utter (2 x £20), London, cap. ch., cap. conv. OB Apr. 1819, executed [M5/321–2: 24 Mar. 1819, 5 May 1819; OBSP: Apr. 1819, case 567].

Prichard, Benjamin [**233**] possess, Surr., PB Surr. spring ass. 1817, 14 yrs trspn [M5/318: 17 Oct. 1816, 1 May 1817].

Prince, Ann [**542,** *543*] 22, 1 child (aged 4 weeks) utter, London, PB OB Nov. 1820, 14 yrs trspn, 5*s.* a week in Newgate, £5 to sail on *Providence*, June 1821 [M5/324–5: 20 Sept., 8 & 22 Nov. 1820, 2 June 1821; OBSP: Nov. 1821, case 1253].

Prince, Mary [**46, 52**] 50 (she says 60), single, utter, London, PB OB Feb. 1807, 14 yrs trspn, from Nov.1807, Bank paid 10*s.* 6*d* a week until18 Feb. 1801, £5 to sail on *Speke*, May 1808 [M5/307–8: 6 Feb., 5 Mar., 1 Oct. 1807, 9 Feb. 1808; OBSP: Feb.1807, cases 210–212].

Prince, Sarah [**532**] utter, Odiham, PB Hants summer ass. 1821, 14 yrs trspn, £5 to sail on *Mary Ann,* Dec. 1821 [BECLS: M5/325: 9 May, 26 Sept. 1821].

Pullen, Mary [**54**] 50, 'old offender', widow with children, utter, London, PB OB Jan. 1806, 14 yrs trspn, paid 10*s.* 6*d* a week from Oct. 1806 until sailed on *Sydney Cove*, Jan. 1807 [M5/307: 15 Jan., 1 Oct. 1806; OBSP: Jan. 1806, cases 121–2].

Quin, James [**663**] utter, Liverpool, PB Lancs. spring ass. 1816, 14 yrs trspn, sailed on *Elizabeth*, May 1816 [M5/316–7: 10 Nov. 1815, 3 May 1816].

Quinn, Catherine [**532**] sell, Manchester, PB Lancs. spring ass. 1821, 14 yrs trspn, £5 to sail on *Mary Ann,* Dec. 1821 [M5/324–5: 18 Oct. 1820, 9 May, 5 Dec. 1821].

Radford, Richard [**301, 373**] utter, London, PB OB Apr. 1818, 14 yrs trspn, sailed on *Mallow,* Aug. 1818 [M5/320: 13 Mar., 8 Apr. 1818; OBSP: Apr. 1818, cases 578, 611, 626].

Radford, William [**592**] utter, Monmouth, PB Mon. spring ass. 1807, 14 yrs trspn, *Captivity* hulk, Portsmouth, Nov. 1808 [M5/307–8: 5 Mar. 1807, 23 June 1808].

Redding (or **Reading** or **Reeding**), **Sarah** [**511, 533**] 18, utter, London, PB OB June 1821, 14 yrs trspn, relief refused in Newgate, £5 to sail on *Mary Ann*, Dec. 1821 [M5/325: 18 Apr., 20 June, 11 July, 5 Dec. 1821; OBSP: June 1821, case 731].

Redgrave, Elizabeth [**391**] utter, Borough, PB, Surr. spring ass. 1820, 14 yrs trspn, £5 to sail on *Morley*, Apr. 1820 [M5/323–4: 17 Dec. 1819, 19 Apr. 1820].

Reed, Mary Ann [**311, 412, 438,** *453*] 32, 1 child, utter, London, PB OB June 1818, 14 yrs trspn, paid 7*s*. 6*d*. a week from 16 July 1818, £5 to sail on *Lord Wellington*, May 1819 [M5/320–2: 11 June, 26 June, 16 July 1818, 5 May 1819; OBSP: June 1818, cases 914 & 927].

Rhodes, Elizabeth [**360, 432**] 22, utter, London, PB OB Apr. 1819, 14 yrs trspn, was refused relief, Sept. 1819 found in great distress and very ill, given £5 (or £2), also £5 to sail on *Janus*, Oct. 1819 [M5/321–3: 18 Feb., 5 May, 29 July, 15 Sept., 14 Oct. 1819; OBSP: Apr. 1819, case 530/1].

Riley, John [**321, 373**], utter, London, PB OB Jan. 1818; no trace of sailing with those in prison with him, but asked relief with others May 1818 [M5/319–20: 18 Dec. 1817, 22 Jan. 1818; OBSP: Jan 1818, cases 203 & 264].

Rimes, John [**579**], no trace of this name in BECLS records; sailed on *Fortune* early 1806.

Roberts, Thomas [**653**] sell, Preston, cap. ch. Lancs. summer ass. 1814, unsuccessful not guilty plea, cap. conv., resp. to life trspn, sailed on *Baring*, Mar. 1815 [M5/314–15: 18 Aug., 23 Sept. 1814, 30 Mar. 1815].

Robinson, George [**243**] no trace of this name in BECLS; no record in OBSP of trial for Bank note crime.

Robinson (*alias* **Singleton**), **Mary** [*465, 467, 469,* **470**] 19, utter, London, PB OB Apr. 1820, 14 yrs trspn, £5 to sail on *Providence*, June 1821 [M5/323–5: 1 Feb., 10 May, 1 Nov. 1820, 2 June 1821; OBSP: Apr. 1820, cases 436/7].

Rodgers (or **Rogers**), **Henry** [**626,** *627*] utter, London, PB OB Dec. 1812, 14 yrs trspn, sailed on *Earl Spencer*, June 1813 [M5/312–13: 9 Dec. 1812, 28 Apr. 1813; OBSP: Dec.1812, case 45].

Roe, Mrs. H. [**26**] may have been held as witness in Bank case, or may have been prosecuted, prior to BECLS records. No trace as defendant in OBSP. Bank gave her payment of 10*s*. 6*d*.

INDEX

Names in **bold** are those of prisoner letter-writers involved in forged note activities; more details on these individuals are to be found in the index of prisoner/writers.

The designation 'utterer', 'seller', 'possessor', 'forger' is to be understood as 'person accused or convicted of uttering, selling etc. forged Bank notes'.

Arabic numbers refer to letters; references to the introduction are in roman numerals.

LONDON RECORD SOCIETY

President: The Rt. Hon. the Lord Mayor of London

Chairman: Professor Caroline M. Barron, MA, PhD, FRHistS
Hon. Secretary: Dr Helen Bradley
Hon. Treasurer: Dr David Lewis
Hon. General Editors: Dr Robin Eagles, Dr Stephen O'Connor,
Dr Hannes Kleineke

The London Record Society was founded in December 1964 to publish transcripts, abstracts and lists of the primary sources for the history of London, and generally to stimulate interest in archives relating to London. Membership is open to any individual or institution; the annual subscription is £12 (US $22) for individuals and £18 (US $35) for institutions. Prospective members should apply to the Hon. Secretary, Dr Helen Bradley, c/o Institute of Historical Research, Senate House, London WC1E 7HU (email londonrecord.society@ntlworld.com).

The following volumes have already been published:

1. *London Possessory Assizes: a calendar*, edited by Helena M. Chew (1965)
2. *London Inhabitants within the Walls, 1695*, with an introduction by D.V.Glass (1966)
3. *London Consistory Court Wills, 1492–1547*, edited by Ida Darlington (1967)
4. *Scriveners' Company Common Paper, 1357–1628, with a continuation to 1678*, edited by Francis W. Steer (1968)
5. *London Radicalism, 1830–1843: a selection from the papers of Francis Place*, edited by D. J. Rowe (1970)
6. *The London Eyre of 1244*, edited by Helena M. Chew and Martin Weinbaum (1970)
7. *The Cartulary of Holy Trinity Aldgate*, edited by Gerald A. J. Hodgett (1971)
8. *The Port and Trade of early Elizabethan London: Documents*, edited by Brian Dietz (1972)
9. *The Spanish Company*, edited by Pauline Croft (1973)
10. *London Assize of Nuisance, 1301–1431: a calendar*, edited by Helena M. Chew and William Kellaway (1973)
11. *Two Calvinistic Methodist Chapels, 1748–1811: the London Tabernacle and Spa Fields Chapel*, edited by Edwin Welch (1975)
12. *The London Eyre of 1276*, edited by Martin Weinbaum (1976)
13. *The Church in London, 1375–1392*, edited by A. K. McHardy (1977)
14. *Committees for the Repeal of the Test and Corporation Acts: Minutes, 1786–90 and 1827–8*, edited by Thomas W. Davis (1978)
15. *Joshua Johnson's Letterbook, 1771–4: letters from a merchant in London to his partners in Maryland*, edited by Jacob M. Price (1979)
16. *London and Middlesex Chantry Certificate, 1548*, edited by C. J. Kitching (1980)

17. *London Politics, 1713–1717: Minutes of a Whig Club, 1714–17*, edited by H.Horwitz; *London Pollbooks, 1713*, edited by W.A. Speck and W.A. Gray (1981)
18. *Parish Fraternity Register: Fraternity of the Holy Trinity and SS.Fabian and Sebastian in the parish of St. Botolph without Aldersgate*, edited by Patricia Basing (1982)
19. *Trinity House of Deptford: Transactions, 1609–35*, edited by G.G.Harris (1983)
20. *Chamber Accounts of the sixteenth century*, edited by Betty R. Masters (1984)
21. *The Letters of John Paige, London Merchant, 1648–58*, edited by George F. Steckley (1984)
22. *A Survey of Documentary Sources for Property Holding in London before the Great Fire*, by Derek Keene and Vanessa Harding (1985)
23. *The Commissions for Building Fifty New Churches*, edited by M.H.Port (1986)
24. *Richard Hutton's Complaints Book*, edited by Timothy V. Hitchcock (1987)
25. *Westminster Abbey Charters, 1066-c. 1214*, edited by Emma Mason (1988)
26. *London Viewers and their Certificates, 1508–1558*, edited by Janet S. Loengard (1989)
27. *The Overseas Trade of London: Exchequer Customs Accounts, 1480–1*, edited by H.S.Cobb (1990)
28. *Justice in Eighteenth-century Hackney: the Justicing Notebook of Henry Norris and the Hackney Petty Sessions Book*, edited by Ruth Paley (1991)
29. *Two Tudor Subsidy Assessment Rolls for the City of London: 1541 and 1582*, edited by R.G.Lang (1993)
30. *London Debating Societies, 1776–1799*, compiled and introduced by Donna T. Andrew (1994)
31. *London Bridge: selected accounts and rentals, 1381–1538*, edited by Vanessa Harding and Laura Wright (1995)
32. *London Consistory Court Depositions, 1586–1611: list and indexes*, by Loreen L.Giese (1997)
33. *Chelsea settlement and bastardy examinations, 1733–66*, edited by Tim Hitchcock and John Black (1999)
34. *The church records of St Andrew Hubbard Eastcheap, c. 1450-c. 1570*, edited by Clive Burgess (1999)
35. *Calendar of Exchequer Equity pleadings, 1685–6 and 1784–5*, edited by Henry Horwitz and Jessica Cooke (2000)
36. *The Letters of William Freeman, London Merchant, 1678 1685*, edited by David Hancock (2002)
37. *Unpublished London diaries. A checklist of unpublished diaries by Londoners and visitors, with a select bibliography of published diaries*, compiled by Heather Creaton (2003)
38. *The English Fur Trade in the later Middle Ages*, by Elspeth M.Veale (2003; reprinted from 1966 edition)
39. *The Bede Roll of the Fraternity of St Nicholas*, edited by N.W. and V.A. James (2 vols., 2004)
40. *The estate and household accounts of William Worsley, Dean of St Paul's Cathedral, 1479–1497*, edited by Hannes Kleineke and Stephanie R. Hovland (2004)
41. *A woman in wartime London: the diary of Kathleen Tipper 1941–1945*, edited by Patricia and Robert Malcolmson (2006)
42. *Prisoners' Letters to the Bank of England 1783–1827*, edited by Deirdre Palk (2007)

Most volumes are still in print; apply to the Hon. Secretary, who will forward requests to the distributor. Price to individual members £12 ($22) each, to non-members £20 ($38) each.